Pandora Hearts

Jun Mochizuki

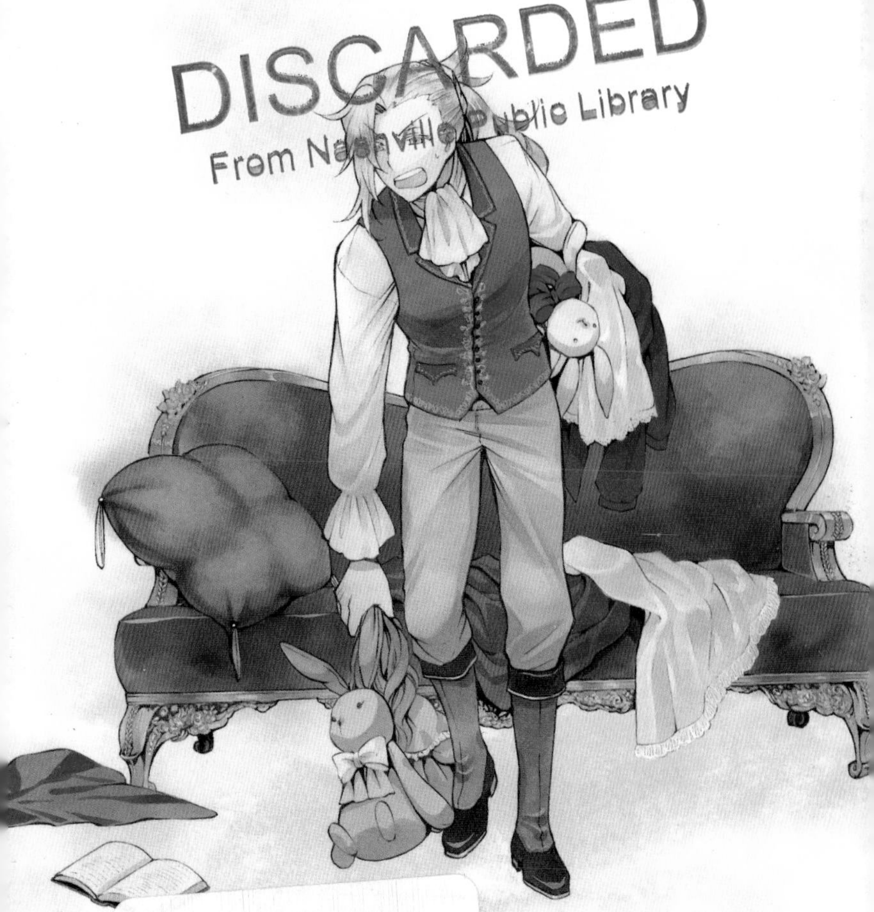

CONTENTS

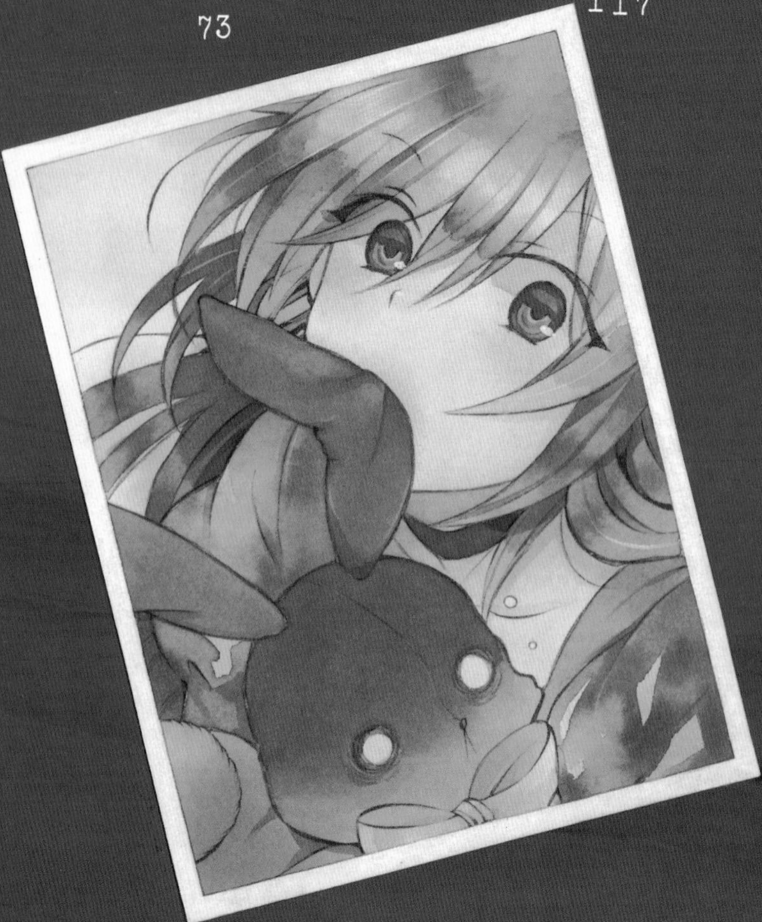

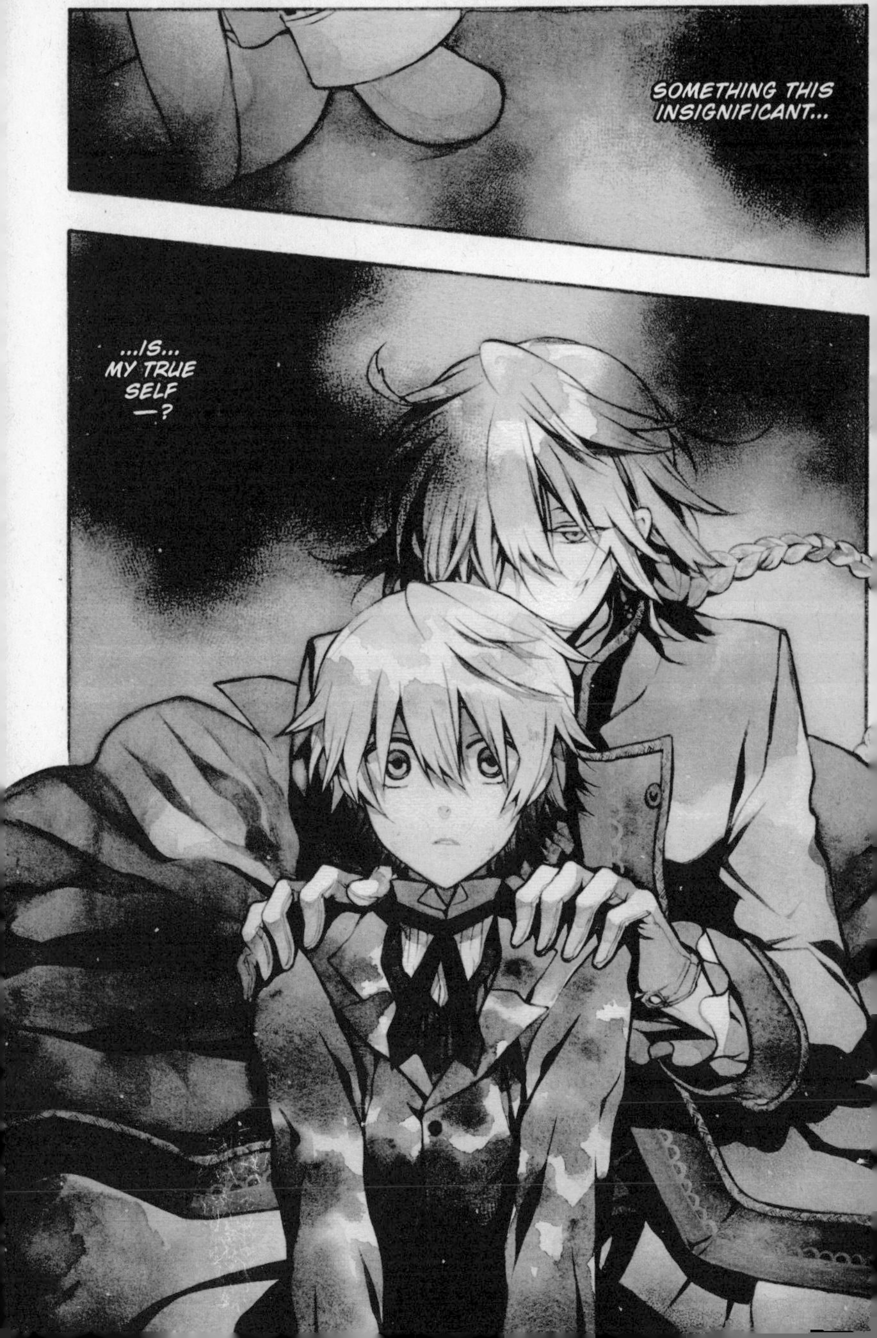
SOMETHING THIS INSIGNIFICANT...
...IS... MY TRUE SELF —?

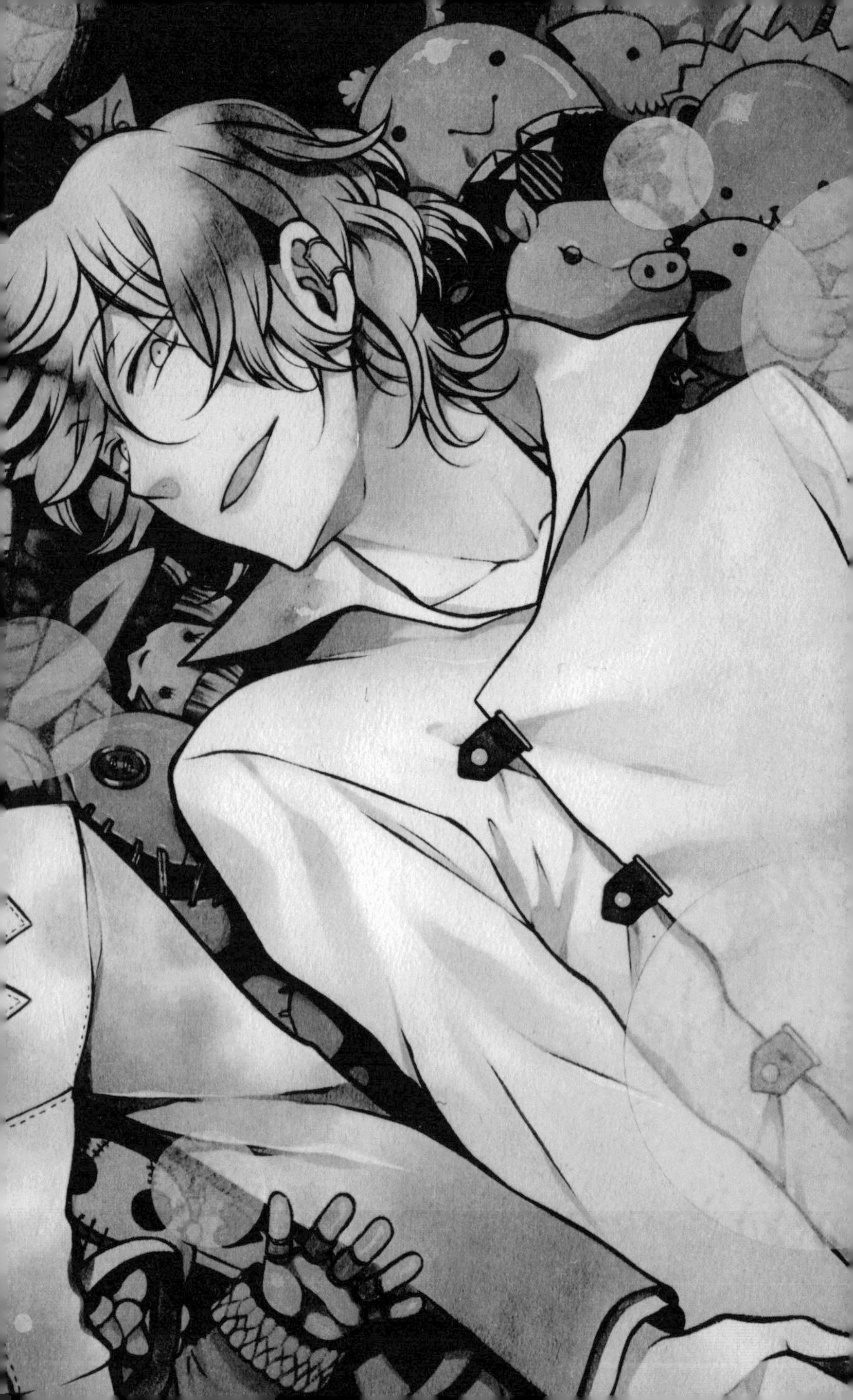

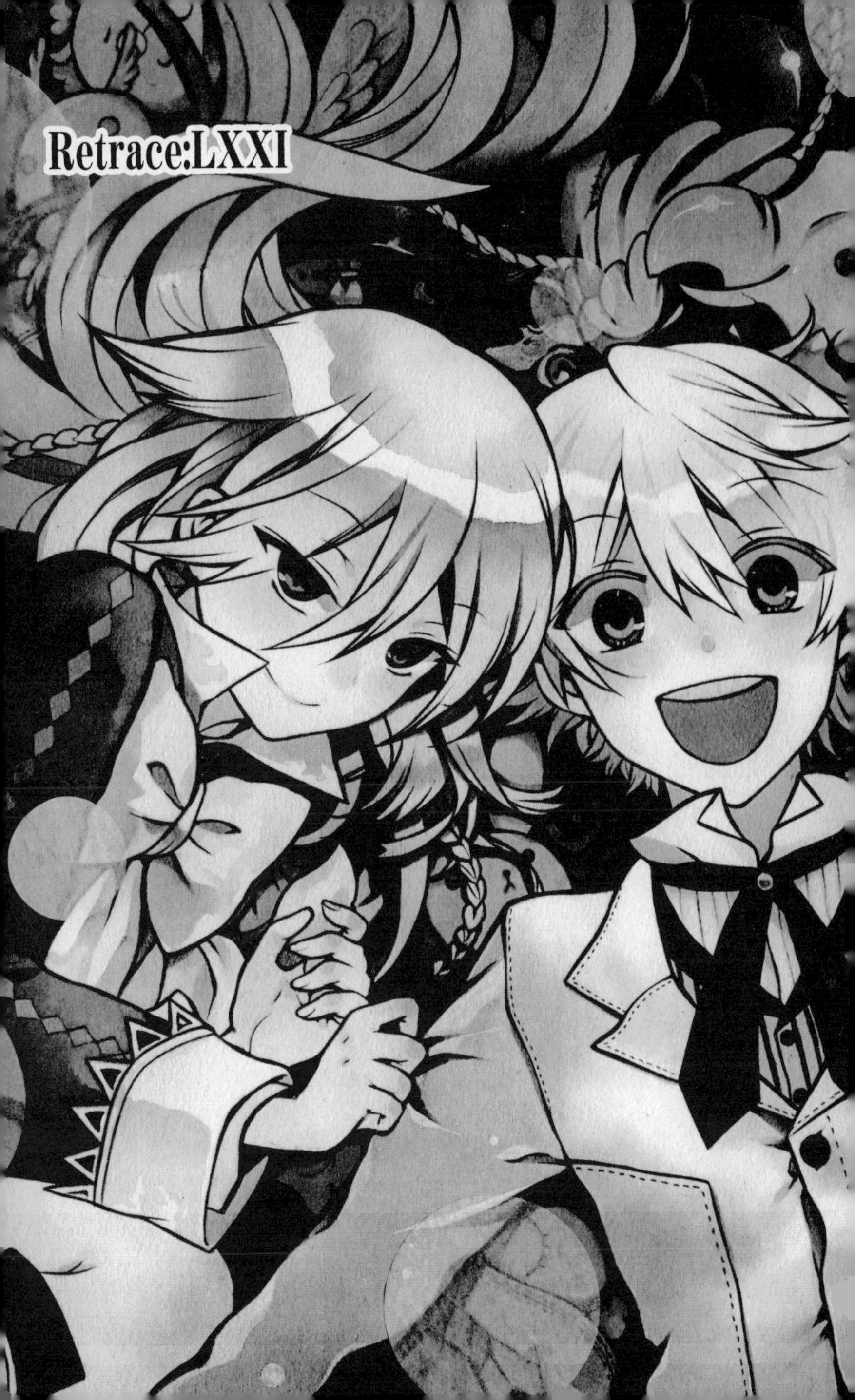
Retrace:LXXI

BONUS: MISS ALICE'S OBSESSION

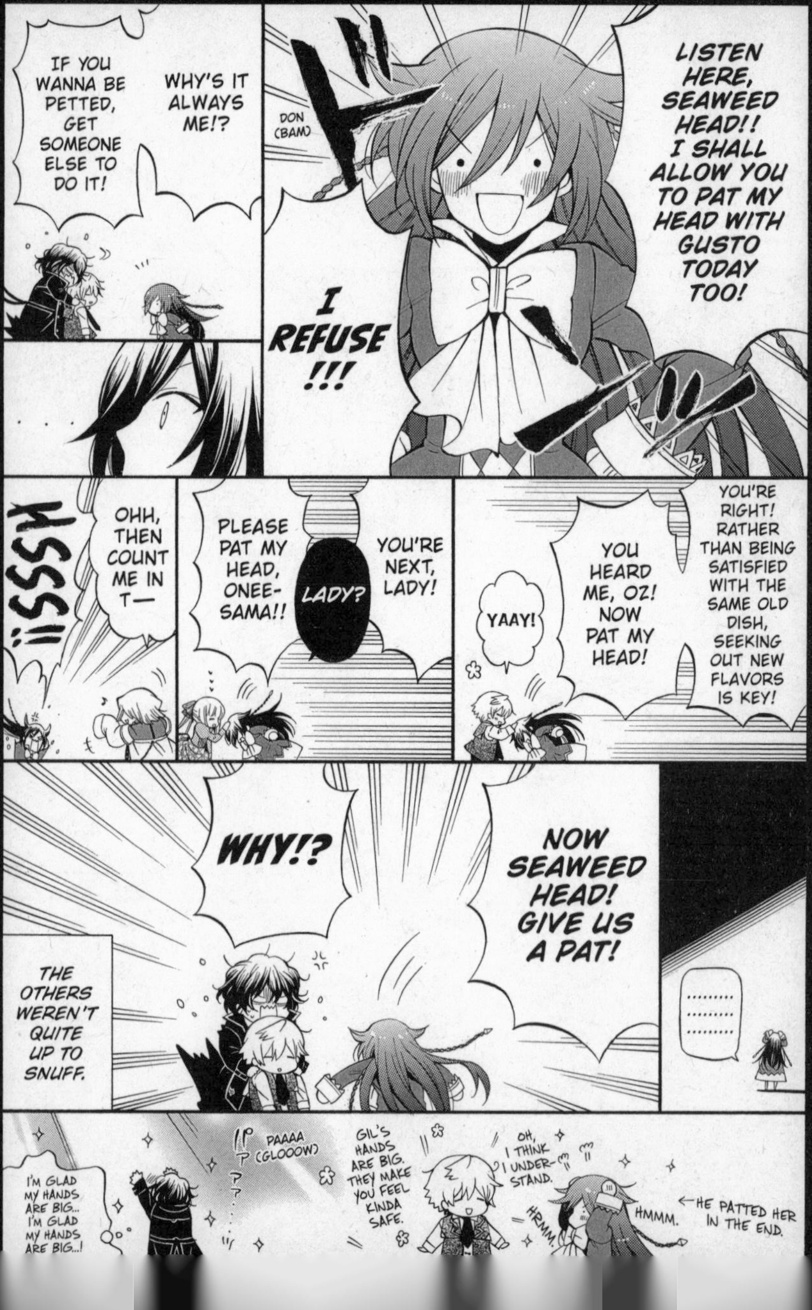
LISTEN HERE, SEAWEED HEAD!! I SHALL ALLOW YOU TO PAT MY HEAD WITH GUSTO TODAY TOO!
DON (BAM)
I REFUSE!!!
WHY'S IT ALWAYS ME!?
IF YOU WANNA BE PETTED, GET SOMEONE ELSE TO DO IT!
. . .
YOU'RE RIGHT! RATHER THAN BEING SATISFIED WITH THE SAME OLD DISH, SEEKING OUT NEW FLAVORS IS KEY!
YOU HEARD ME, OZ! NOW PAT MY HEAD!
YAAY!
YOU'RE NEXT, LADY!
LADY?
PLEASE PAT MY HEAD, ONEE-SAMA!!
OHH, THEN COUNT ME IN T—
HSSSS!!
....
....
....
NOW SEAWEED HEAD! GIVE US A PAT!
WHY!?
THE OTHERS WEREN'T QUITE UP TO SNUFF.
←HE PATTED HER IN THE END.
HMMM.
HRMM.
OH, I THINK I UNDER-STAND.
GIL'S HANDS ARE BIG. THEY MAKE YOU FEEL KINDA SAFE.
PAAAA (GLOOOW)
I'M GLAD MY HANDS ARE BIG... I'M GLAD MY HANDS ARE BIG...!

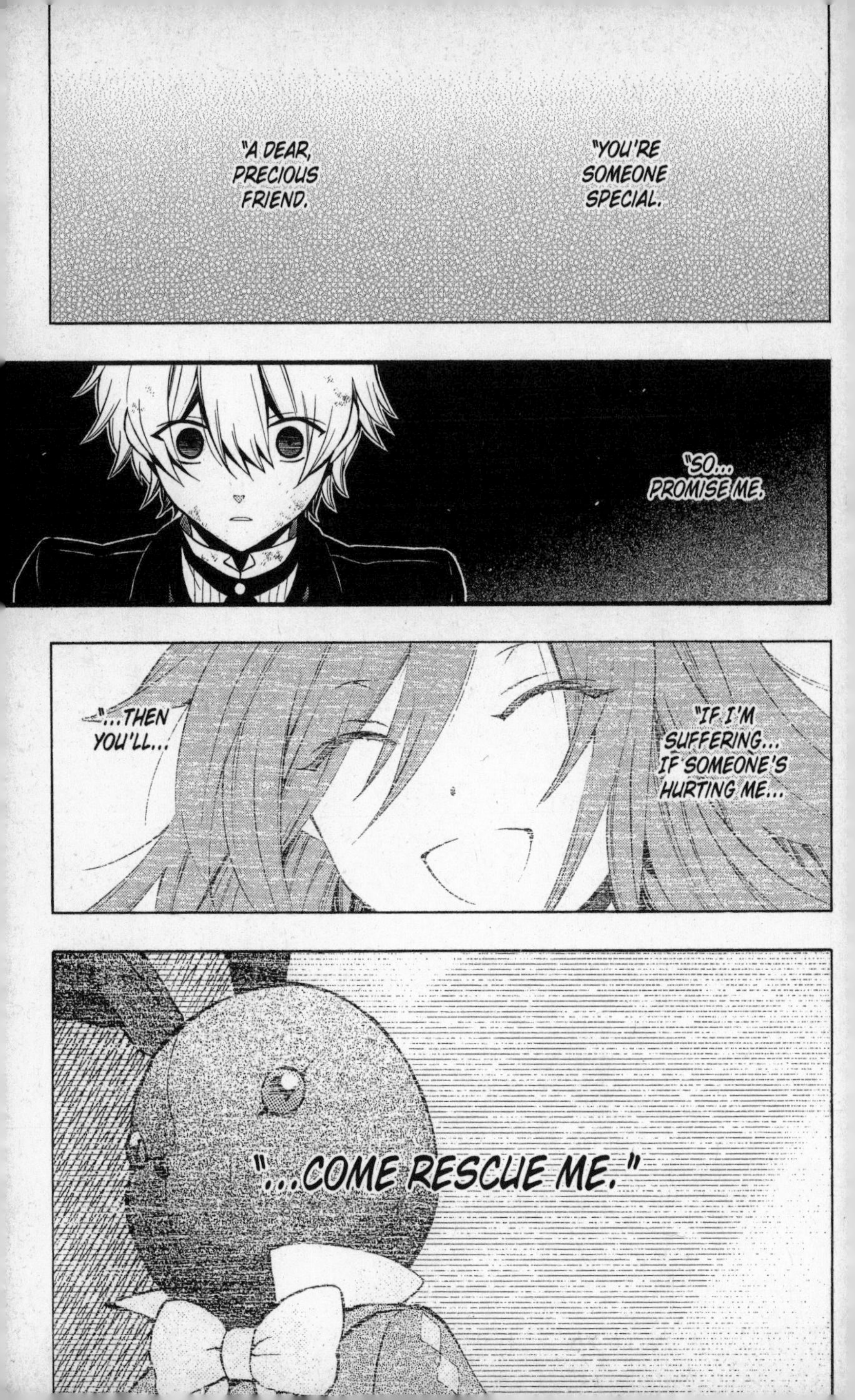
"YOU'RE SOMEONE SPECIAL.
"A DEAR, PRECIOUS FRIEND.
"SO... PROMISE ME.
"IF I'M SUFFERING... IF SOMEONE'S HURTING ME...
"...THEN YOU'LL...
"...COME RESCUE ME."

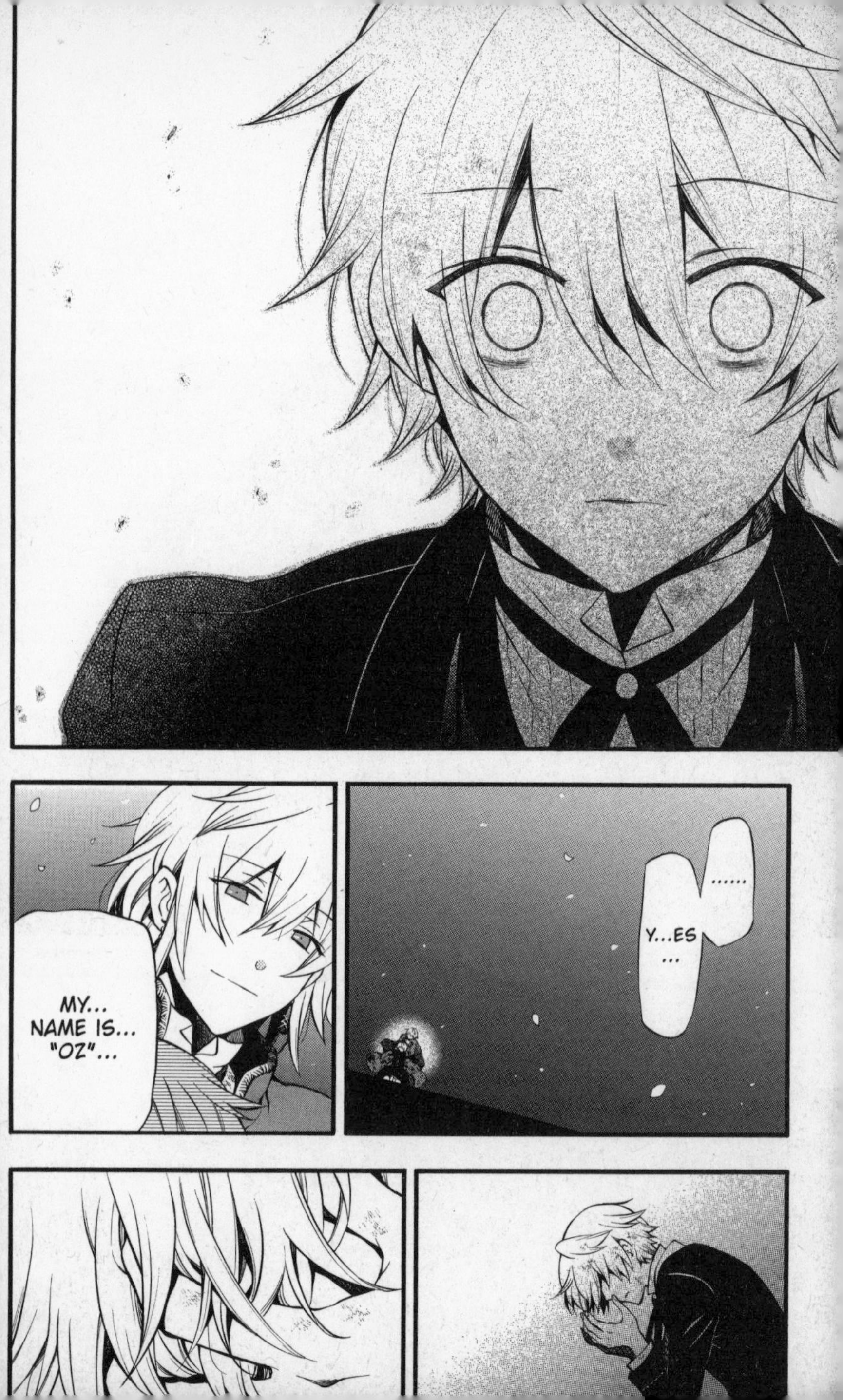
......
Y...ES ...
MY... NAME IS... "OZ"...

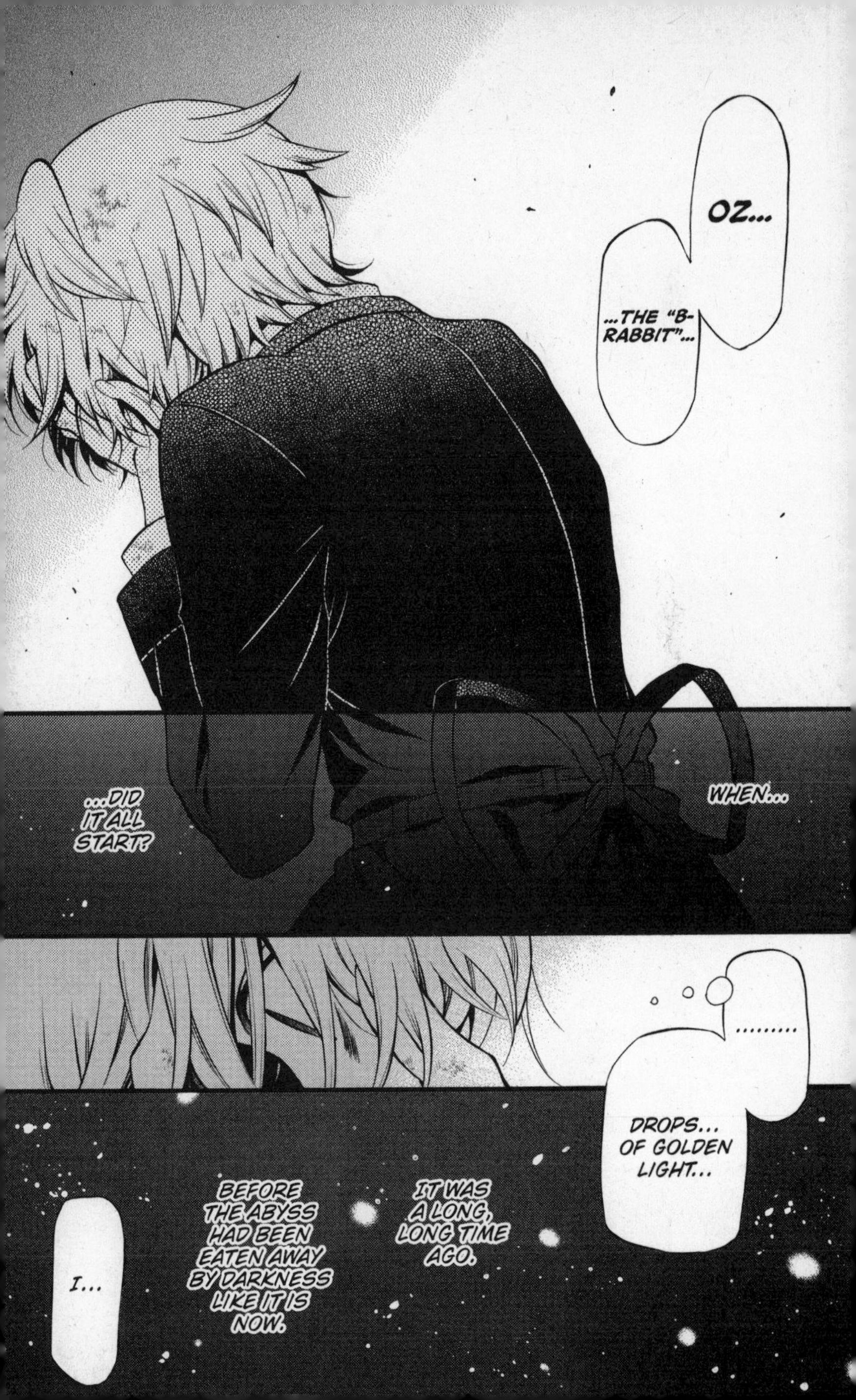
OZ...
...THE "B-RABBIT"...
WHEN...
...DID IT ALL START?
....
DROPS... OF GOLDEN LIGHT...
IT WAS A LONG, LONG TIME AGO.
BEFORE THE ABYSS HAD BEEN EATEN AWAY BY DARKNESS LIKE IT IS NOW.
I...

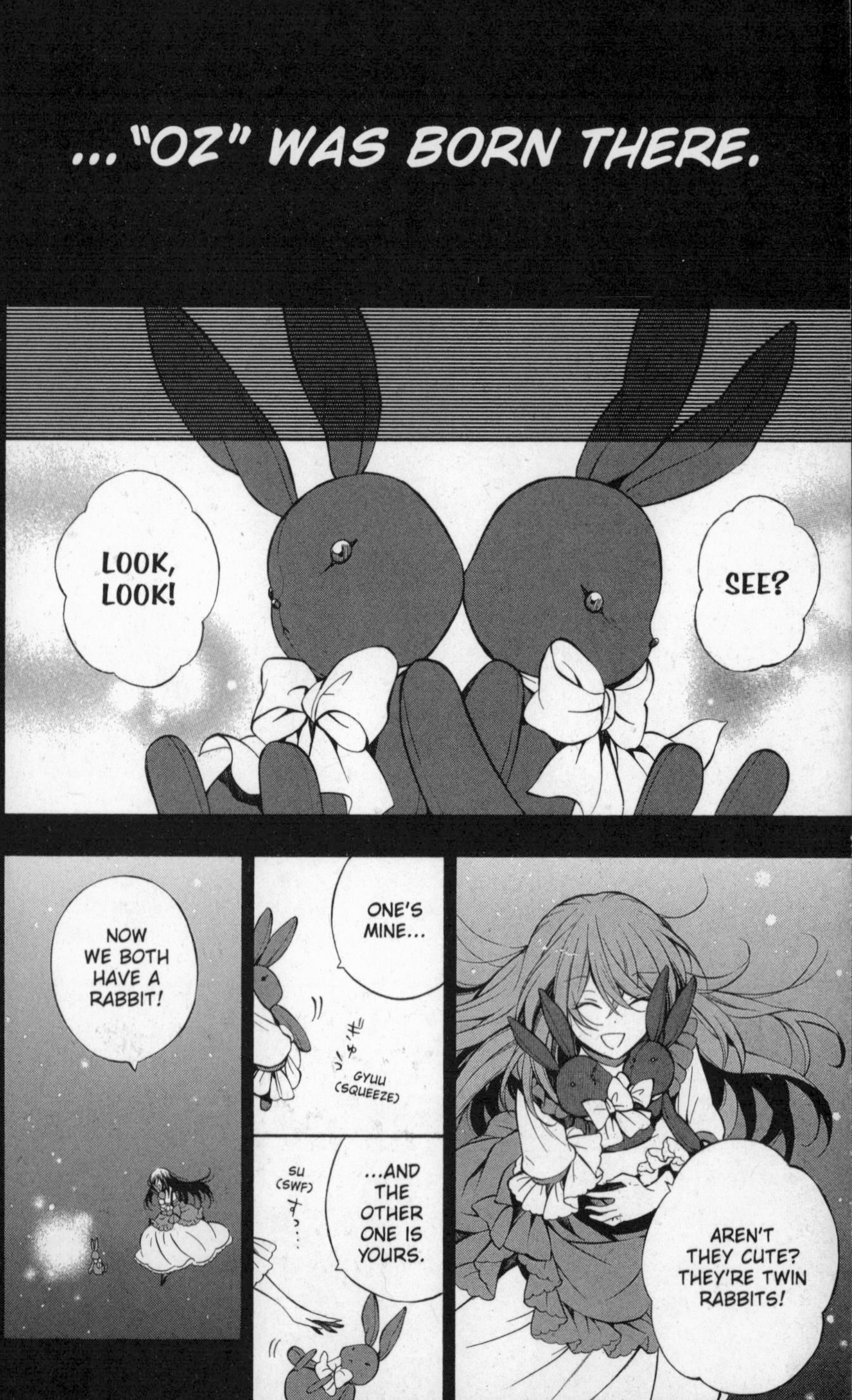
..."OZ" WAS BORN THERE.
SEE?
LOOK, LOOK!
AREN'T THEY CUTE? THEY'RE TWIN RABBITS!
ONE'S MINE...
GYUU (SQUEEZE)
...AND THE OTHER ONE IS YOURS.
SU (SWF)
NOW WE BOTH HAVE A RABBIT!

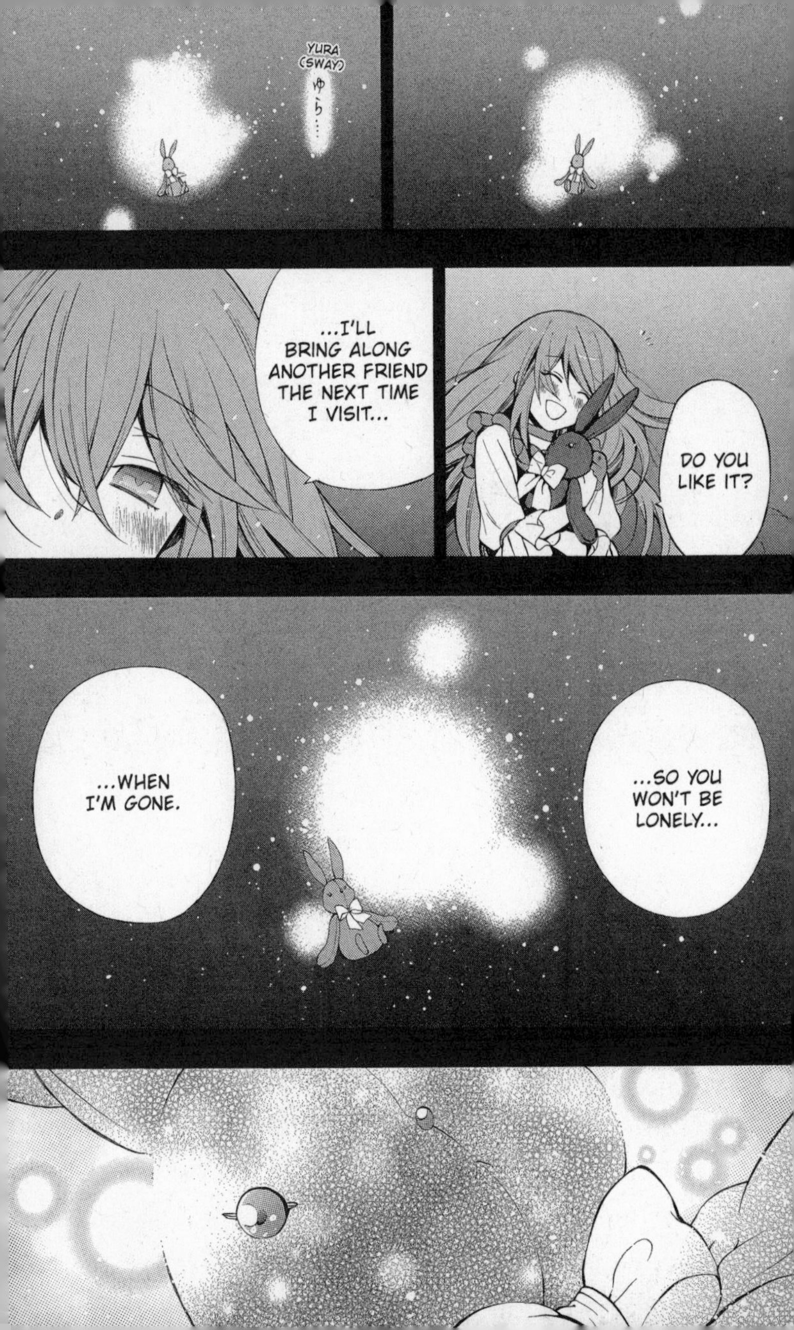
YURA (SWAY)
ゆら…
DO YOU LIKE IT?
...I'LL BRING ALONG ANOTHER FRIEND THE NEXT TIME I VISIT...
...SO YOU WON'T BE LONELY...
...WHEN I'M GONE.

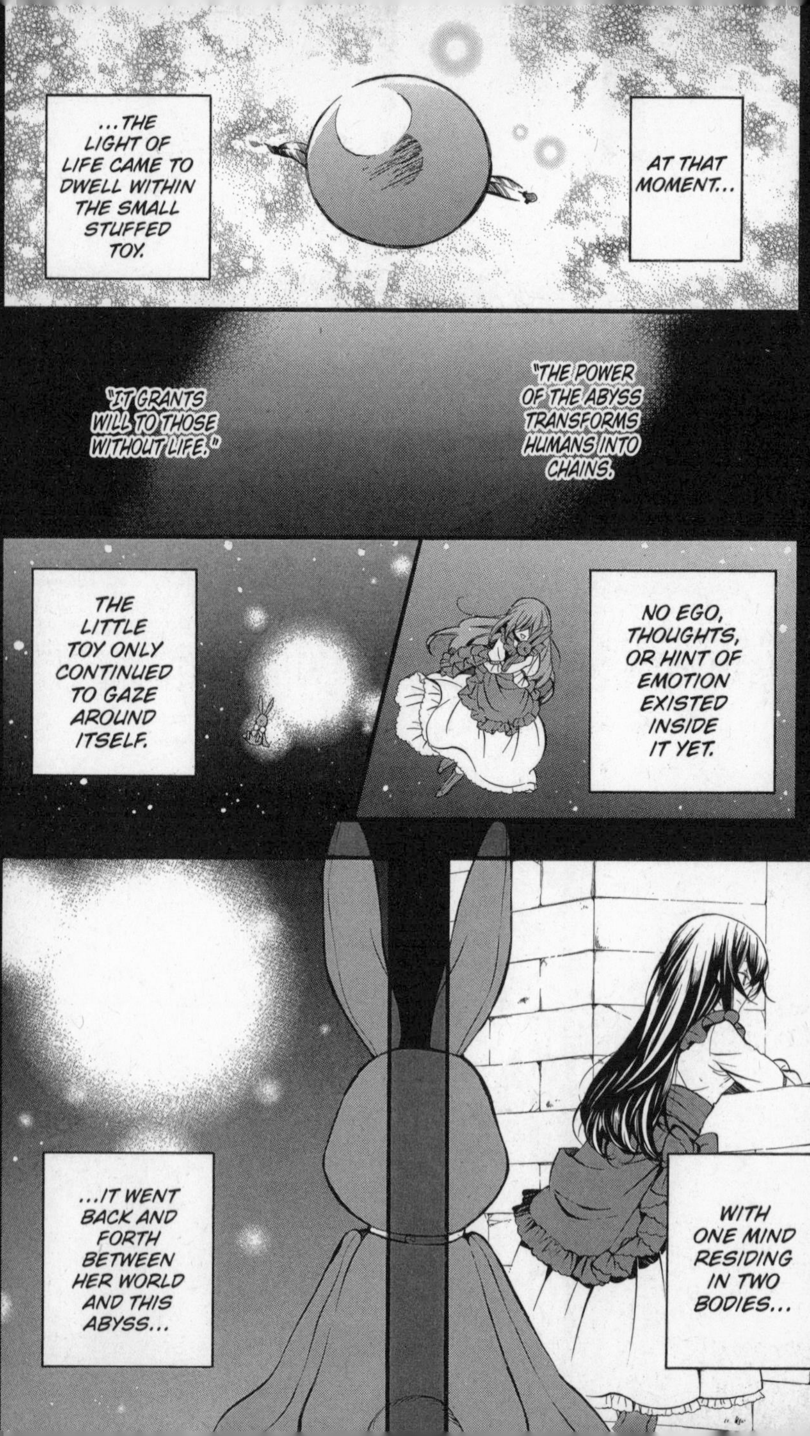
AT THAT MOMENT...
...THE LIGHT OF LIFE CAME TO DWELL WITHIN THE SMALL STUFFED TOY.
"THE POWER OF THE ABYSS TRANSFORMS HUMANS INTO CHAINS.
"IT GRANTS WILL TO THOSE WITHOUT LIFE."
NO EGO, THOUGHTS, OR HINT OF EMOTION EXISTED INSIDE IT YET.
THE LITTLE TOY ONLY CONTINUED TO GAZE AROUND ITSELF.
WITH ONE MIND RESIDING IN TWO BODIES...
...IT WENT BACK AND FORTH BETWEEN HER WORLD AND THIS ABYSS...

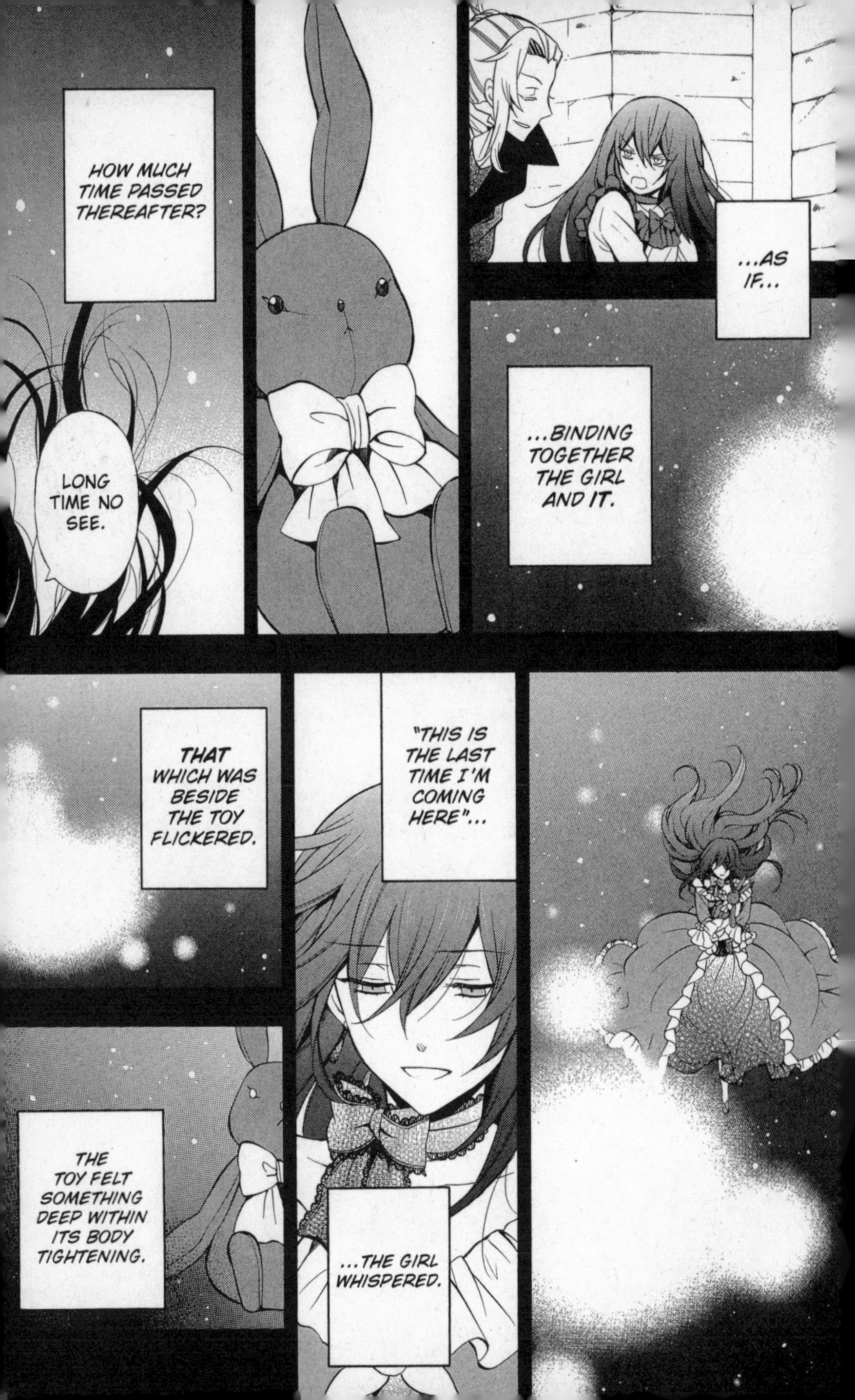
...AS IF...
...BINDING TOGETHER THE GIRL AND IT.
HOW MUCH TIME PASSED THEREAFTER?
LONG TIME NO SEE.
"THIS IS THE LAST TIME I'M COMING HERE"...
...THE GIRL WHISPERED.
THAT WHICH WAS BESIDE THE TOY FLICKERED.
THE TOY FELT SOMETHING DEEP WITHIN ITS BODY TIGHTENING.

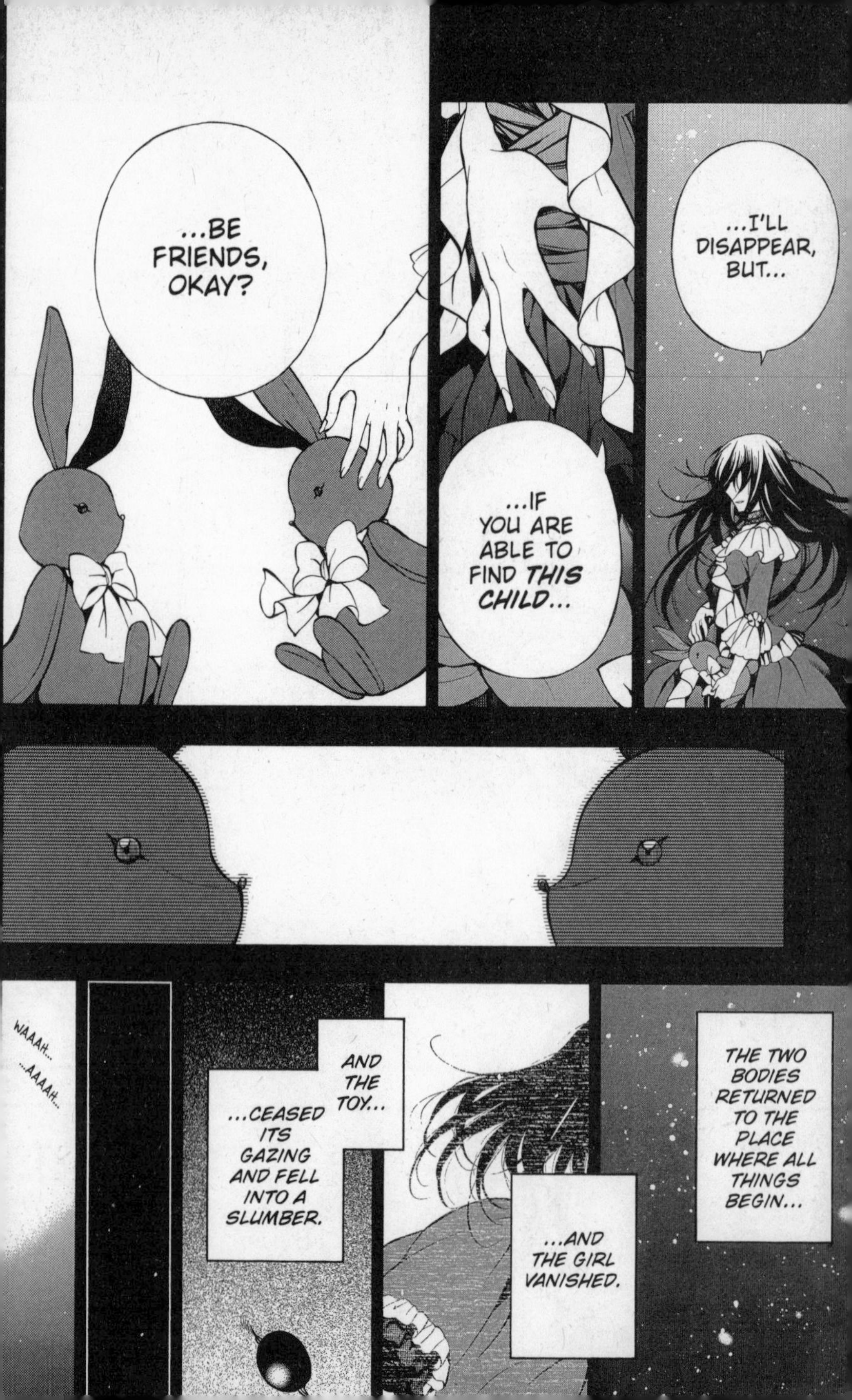
...I'LL DISAPPEAR, BUT...
...IF YOU ARE ABLE TO FIND THIS CHILD...
...BE FRIENDS, OKAY?
THE TWO BODIES RETURNED TO THE PLACE WHERE ALL THINGS BEGIN...
...AND THE GIRL VANISHED.
AND THE TOY...
...CEASED ITS GAZING AND FELL INTO A SLUMBER.
WAAAH...
...AAAAH...

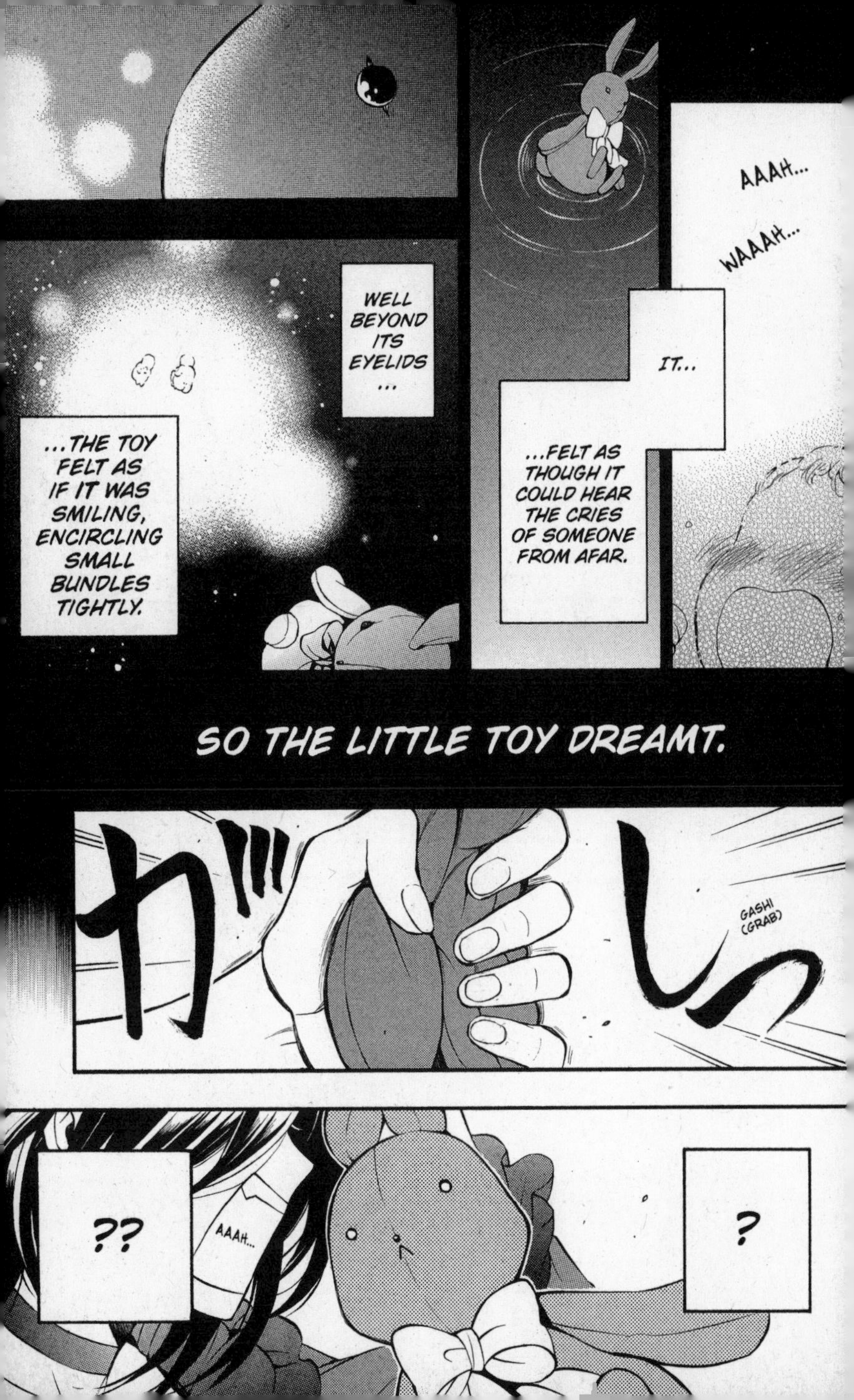

AAAH...
WAAAH...
IT...
...FELT AS THOUGH IT COULD HEAR THE CRIES OF SOMEONE FROM AFAR.
WELL BEYOND ITS EYELIDS...
...THE TOY FELT AS IF IT WAS SMILING, ENCIRCLING SMALL BUNDLES TIGHTLY.
SO THE LITTLE TOY DREAMT.
ガシ
GASHI (GRAB)
?
AAAH...
??

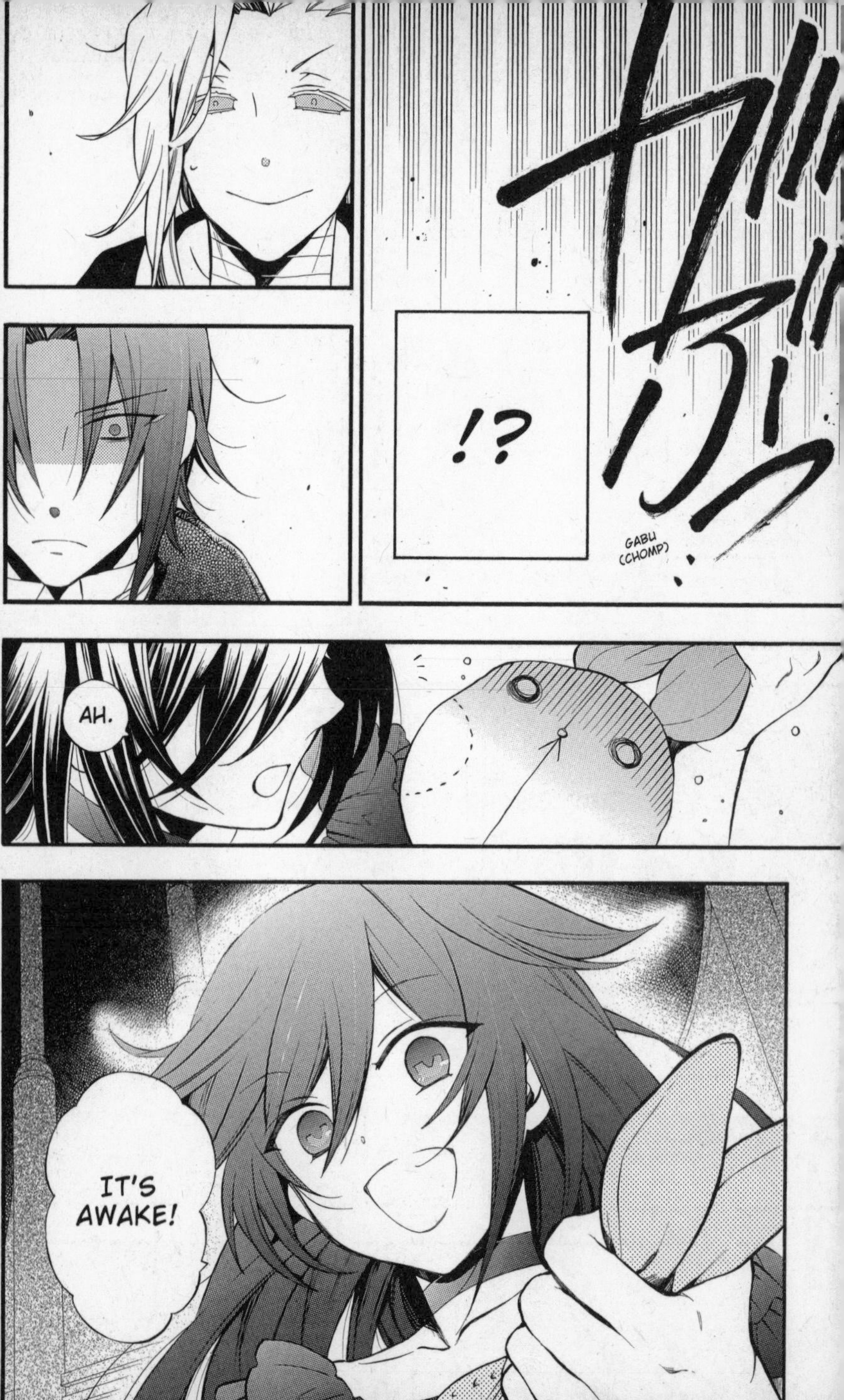
GABU
(CHOMP)
!?
AH.
IT'S AWAKE!

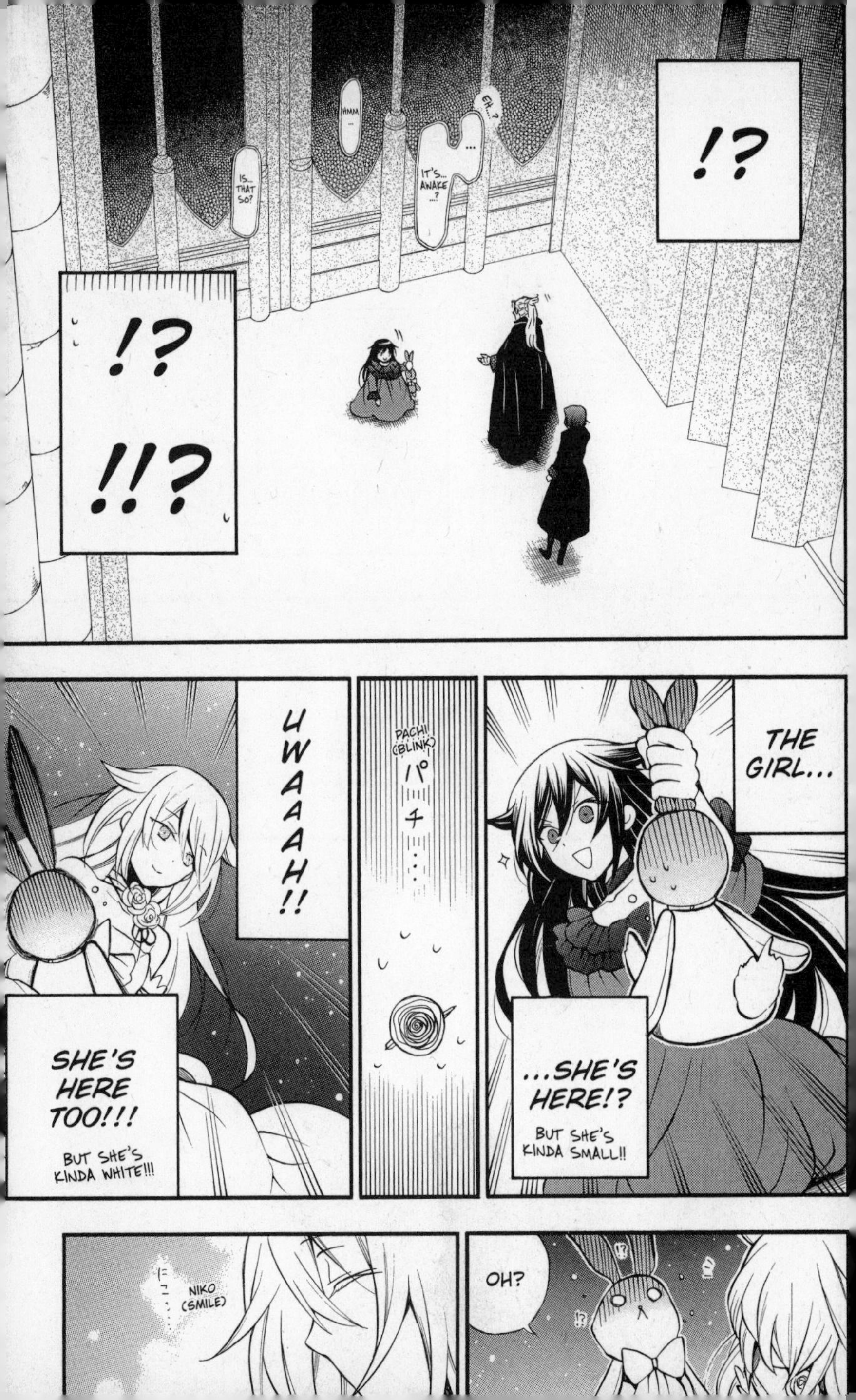
!?
EH...?
...
IT'S... AWAKE ...?
HMM...
IS... THAT SO?
!?
!!?
THE GIRL...
...SHE'S HERE!?
BUT SHE'S KINDA SMALL!!
PACHI (BLINK)
パチ...
UWAAAAH!!
SHE'S HERE TOO!!!
BUT SHE'S KINDA WHITE!!!
OH?
!?
!?
NIKO (SMILE)
ニコ...

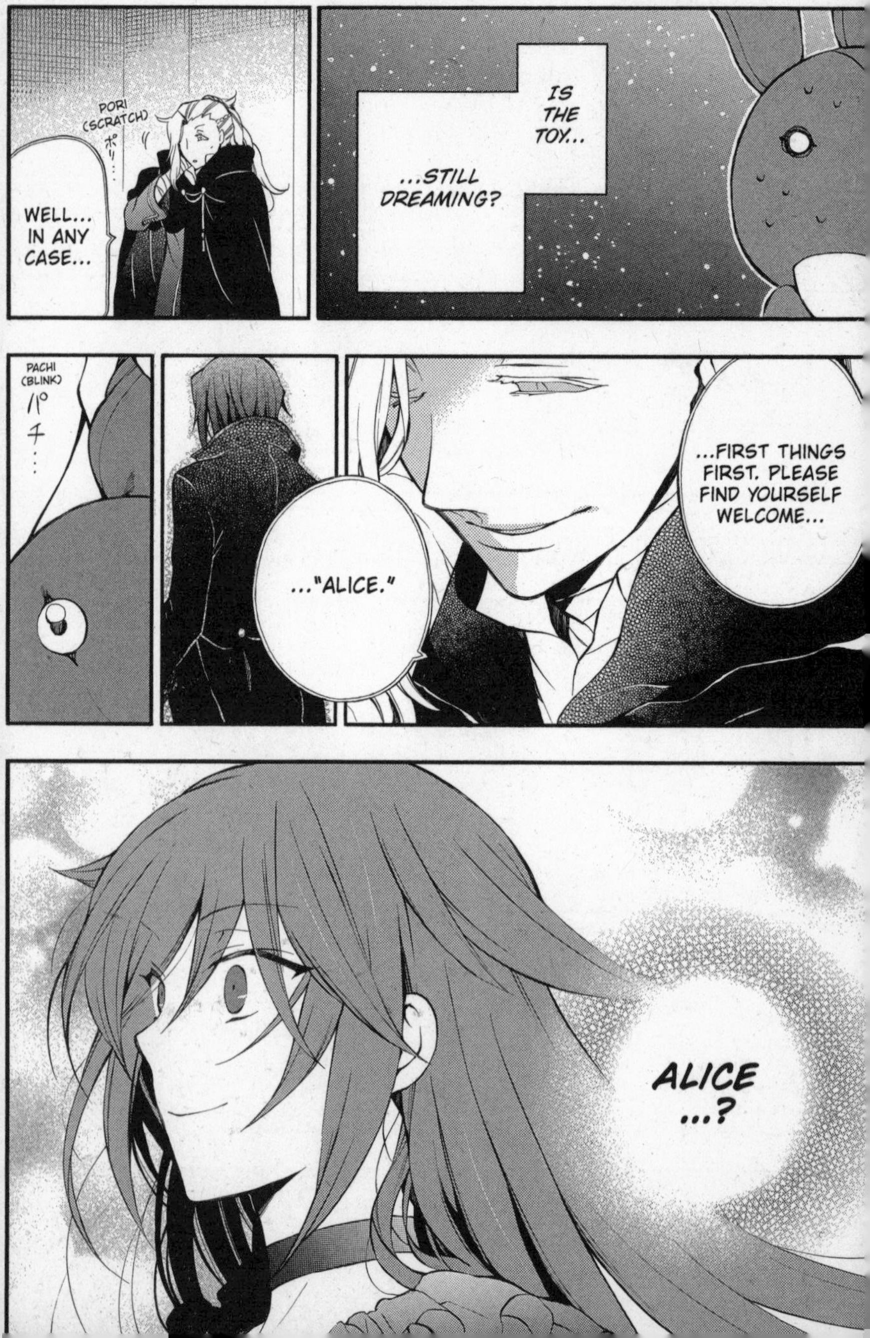
IS THE TOY...
...STILL DREAMING?
PORI (SCRATCH)
ポリ…
WELL... IN ANY CASE...
...FIRST THINGS FIRST. PLEASE FIND YOURSELF WELCOME...
..."ALICE."
PACHI (BLINK)
パチ…
ALICE ...?

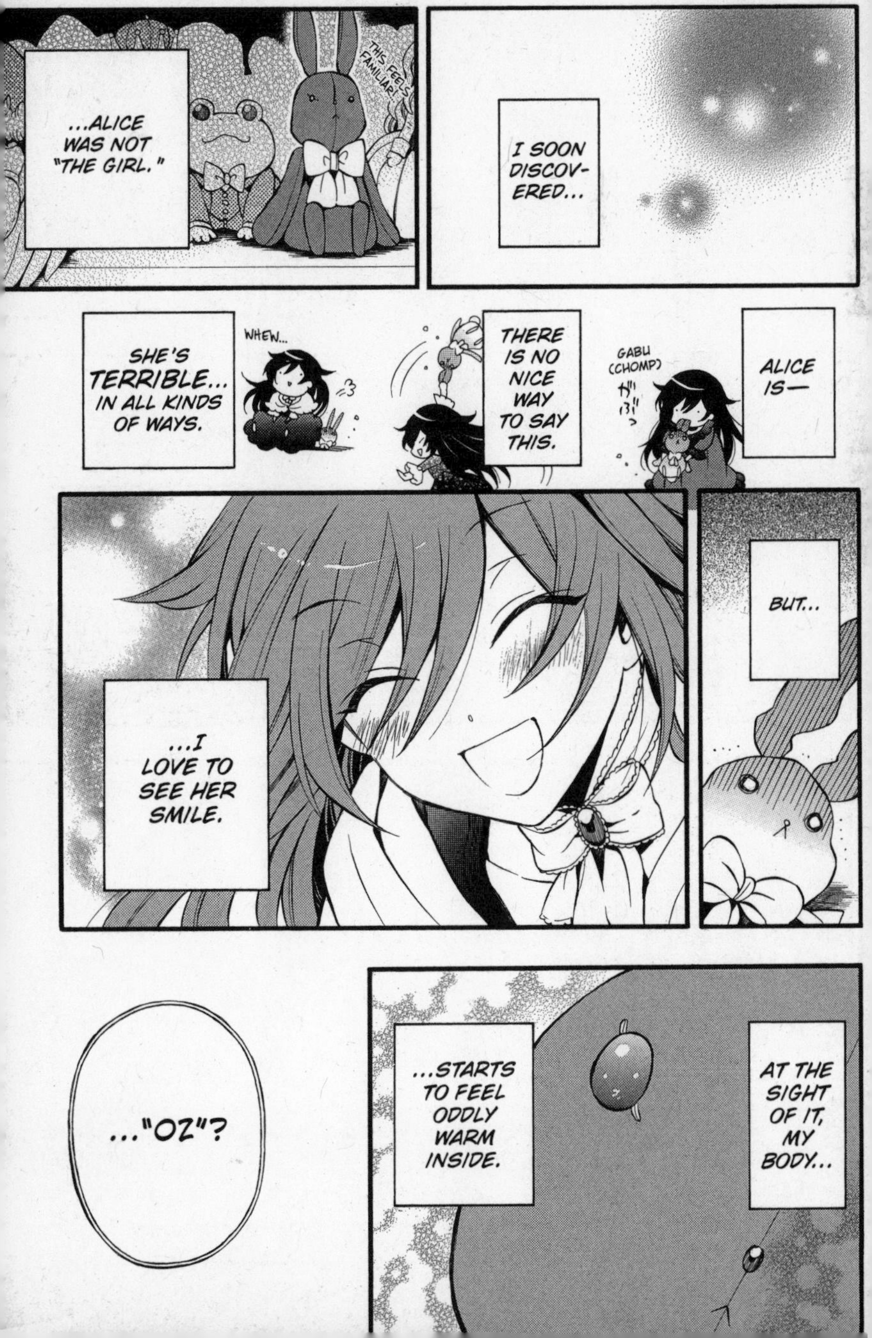
I SOON DISCOVERED...
...ALICE WAS NOT "THE GIRL."
THIS FEELS FAMILIAR!
ALICE IS—
GABU (CHOMP)
THERE IS NO NICE WAY TO SAY THIS.
WHEW...
SHE'S TERRIBLE... IN ALL KINDS OF WAYS.
BUT...
...I LOVE TO SEE HER SMILE.
AT THE SIGHT OF IT, MY BODY...
...STARTS TO FEEL ODDLY WARM INSIDE.
..."OZ"?

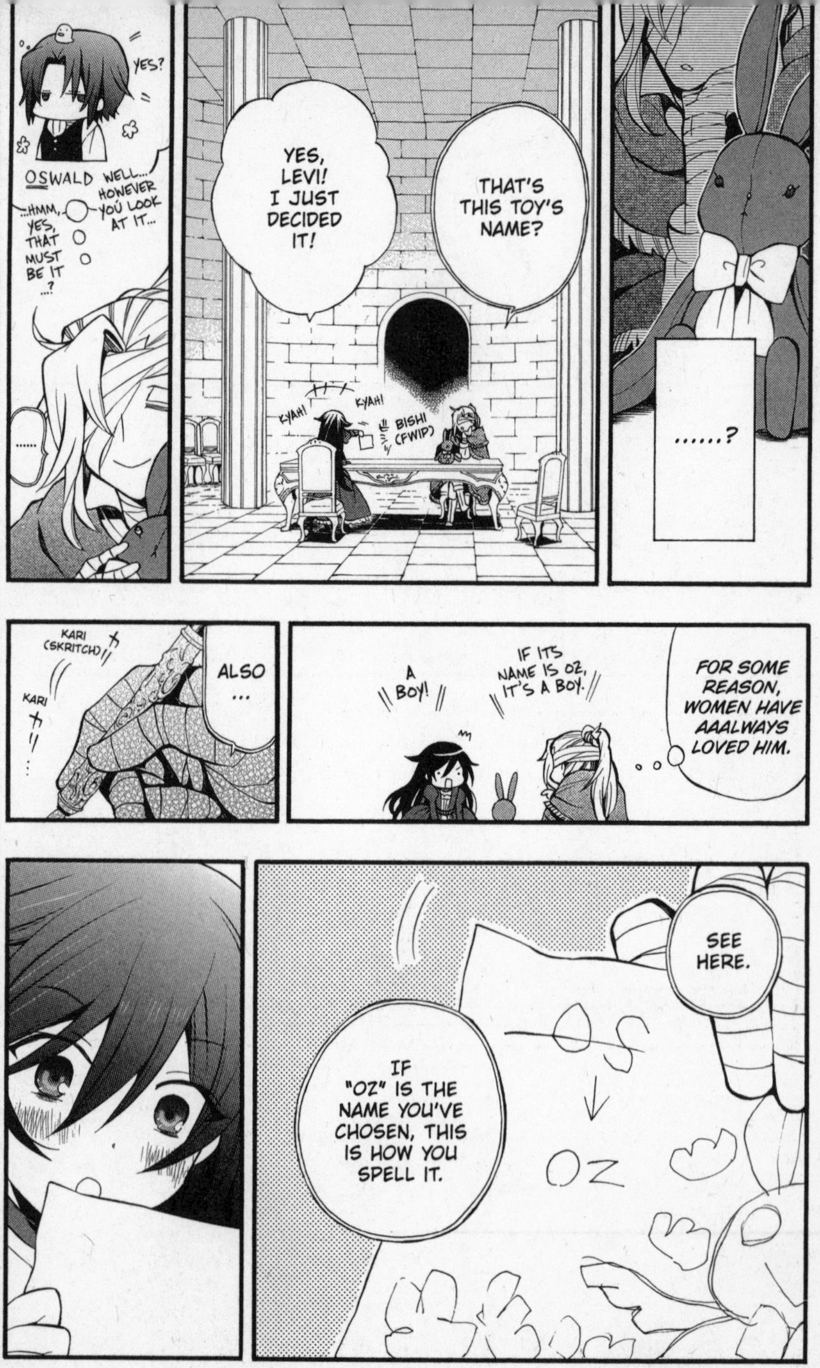
......?
THAT'S THIS TOY'S NAME?
YES, LEVI! I JUST DECIDED IT!
KYAH!
KYAH!
BISHI (FWIP)
YES?
OSWALD WELL... HOWEVER YOU LOOK AT IT...
...HMM, YES, THAT MUST BE IT ...?
......
FOR SOME REASON, WOMEN HAVE AAALWAYS LOVED HIM.
IF ITS NAME IS OZ, IT'S A BOY.
A BOY!
ALSO ...
KARI (SKRITCH)
KARI
SEE HERE.
IF "OZ" IS THE NAME YOU'VE CHOSEN, THIS IS HOW YOU SPELL IT.
OS
OZ

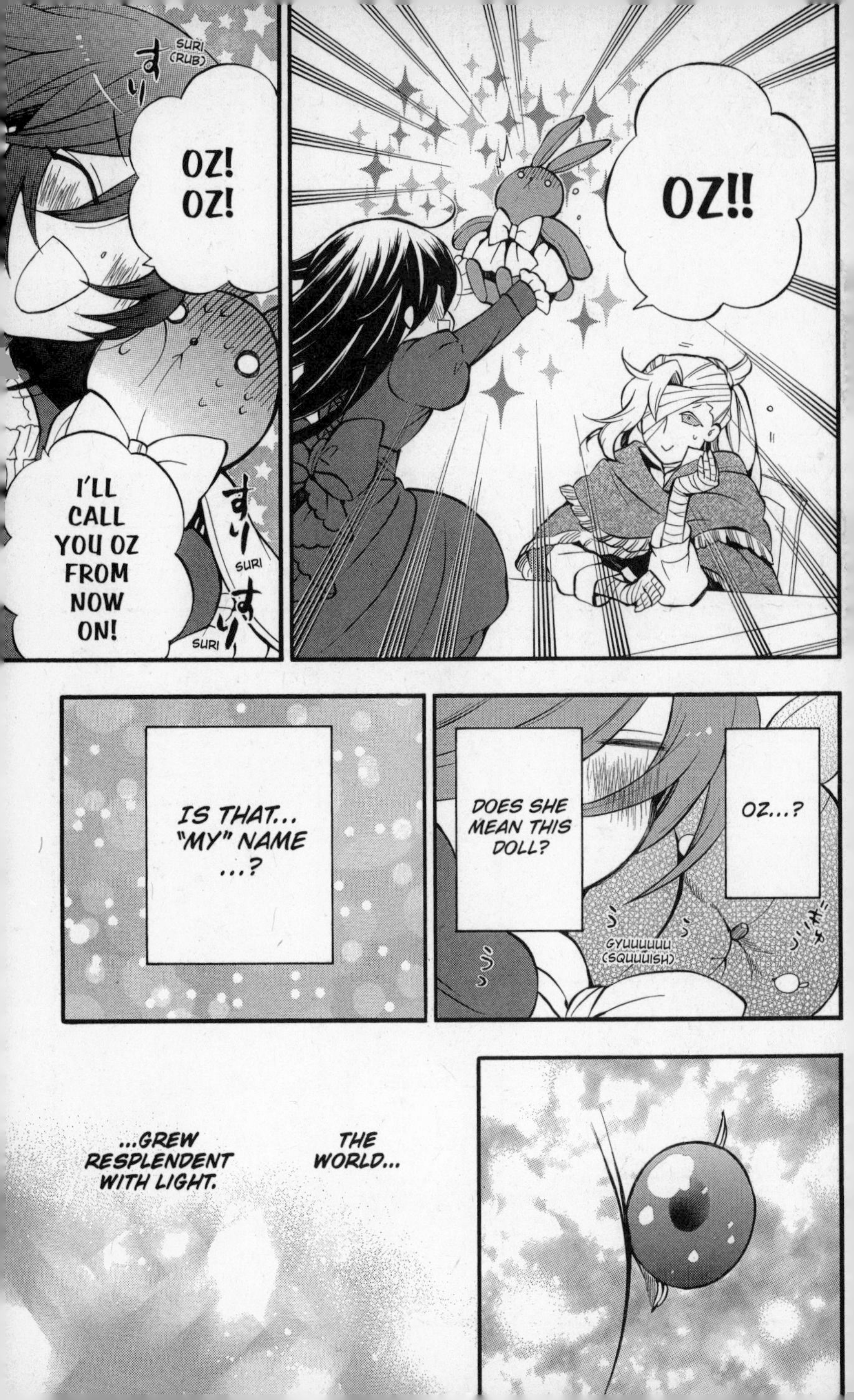
OZ!!
SURI (RUB)
OZ! OZ!
I'LL CALL YOU OZ FROM NOW ON!
SURI
SURI
OZ...?
DOES SHE MEAN THIS DOLL?
GYUUUUUU (SQUUUISH)
IS THAT... "MY" NAME ...?
THE WORLD...
...GREW RESPLENDENT WITH LIGHT.

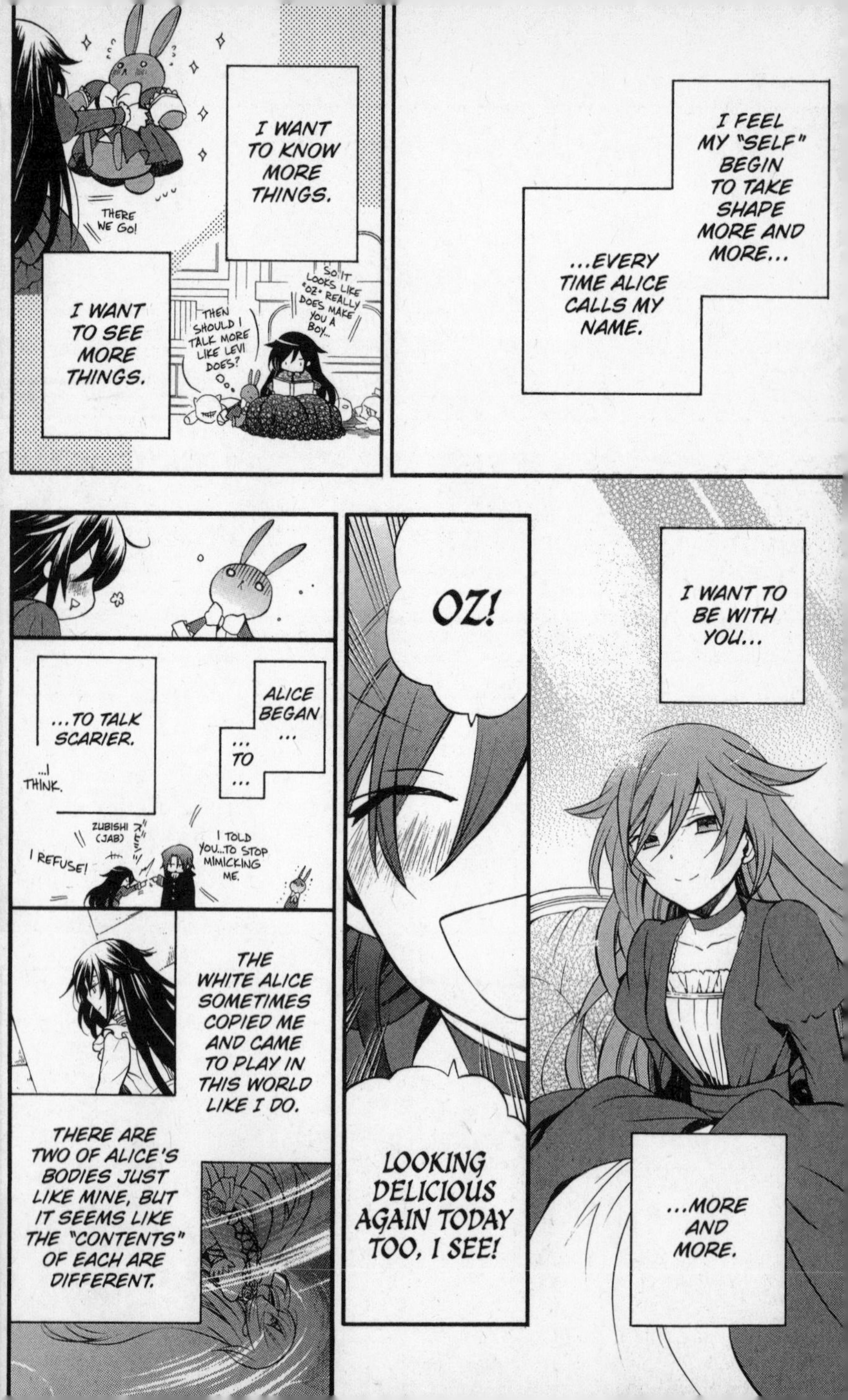
I FEEL MY "SELF" BEGIN TO TAKE SHAPE MORE AND MORE...
...EVERY TIME ALICE CALLS MY NAME.
I WANT TO KNOW MORE THINGS.
THERE WE GO!
I WANT TO SEE MORE THINGS.
SO IT LOOKS LIKE "OZ" REALLY DOES MAKE YOU A BOY...
THEN SHOULD I TALK MORE LIKE LEVI DOES?
I WANT TO BE WITH YOU...
...MORE AND MORE.
OZ!
LOOKING DELICIOUS AGAIN TODAY TOO, I SEE!
ALICE BEGAN...
...TO...
...TO TALK SCARIER.
...I THINK.
I TOLD YOU...TO STOP MIMICKING ME.
ZUBISHI (JAB)
I REFUSE!
THE WHITE ALICE SOMETIMES COPIED ME AND CAME TO PLAY IN THIS WORLD LIKE I DO.
THERE ARE TWO OF ALICE'S BODIES JUST LIKE MINE, BUT IT SEEMS LIKE THE "CONTENTS" OF EACH ARE DIFFERENT.

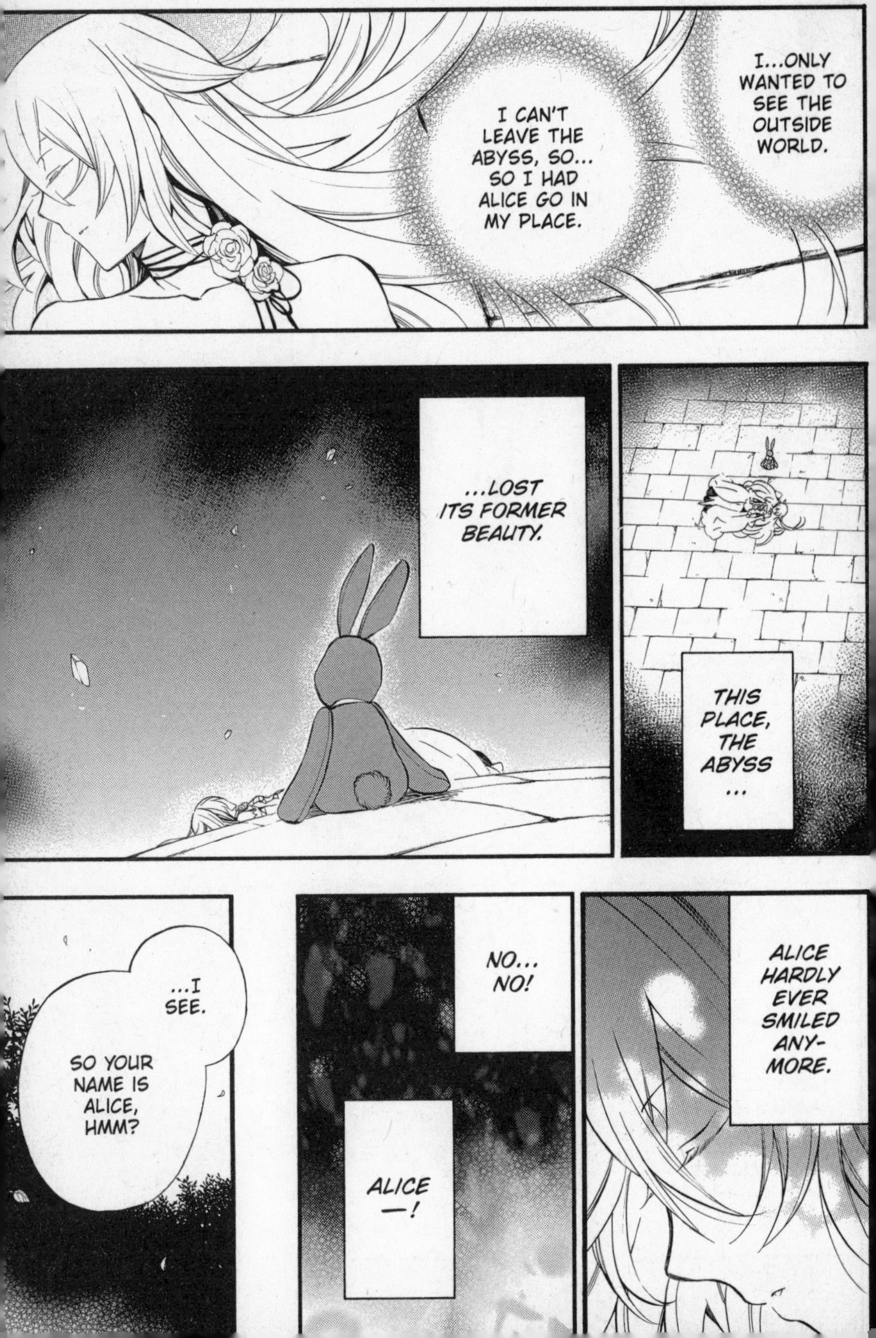
I...ONLY WANTED TO SEE THE OUTSIDE WORLD.
I CAN'T LEAVE THE ABYSS, SO... SO I HAD ALICE GO IN MY PLACE.
THIS PLACE, THE ABYSS ...
...LOST ITS FORMER BEAUTY.
ALICE HARDLY EVER SMILED ANY-MORE.
NO... NO!
ALICE —!
...I SEE.
SO YOUR NAME IS ALICE, HMM?

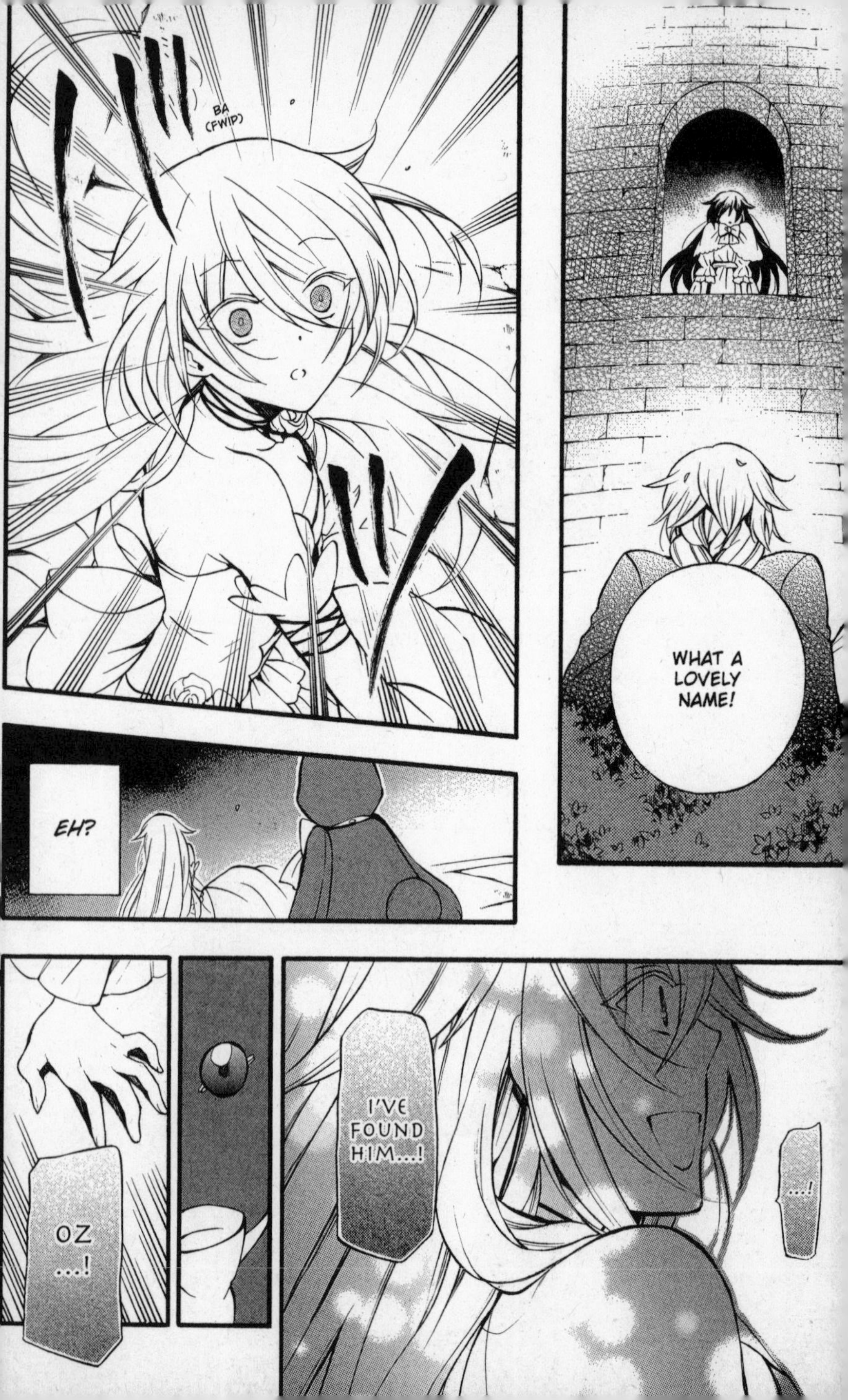
WHAT A LOVELY NAME!
BA (FWIP)
EH?
...!
I'VE FOUND HIM...!
OZ ...!

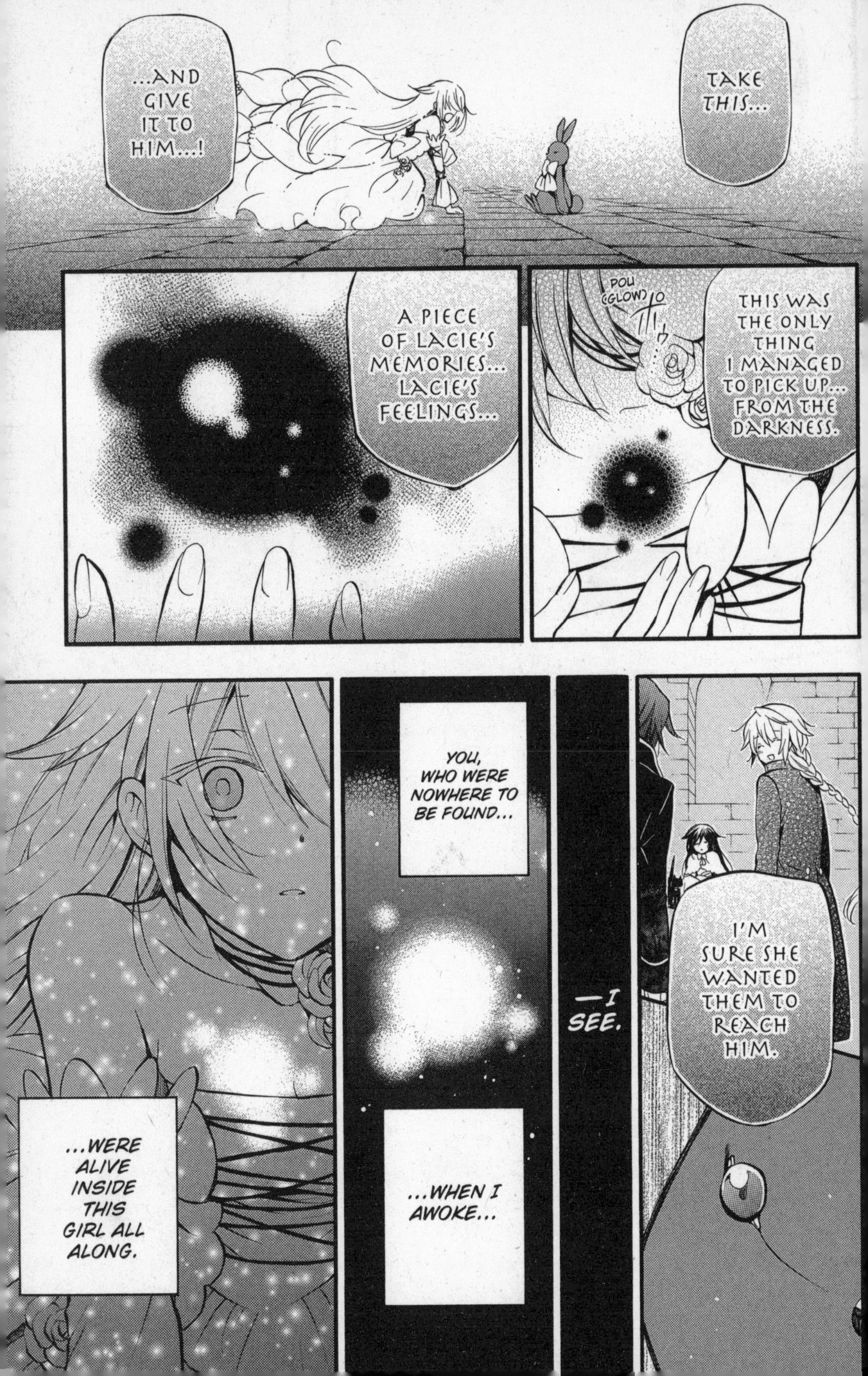
TAKE THIS...
...AND GIVE IT TO HIM...!
POU (GLOW)
THIS WAS THE ONLY THING I MANAGED TO PICK UP... FROM THE DARKNESS.
A PIECE OF LACIE'S MEMORIES... LACIE'S FEELINGS...
I'M SURE SHE WANTED THEM TO REACH HIM.
—I SEE.
YOU, WHO WERE NOWHERE TO BE FOUND...
...WHEN I AWOKE...
...WERE ALIVE INSIDE THIS GIRL ALL ALONG.

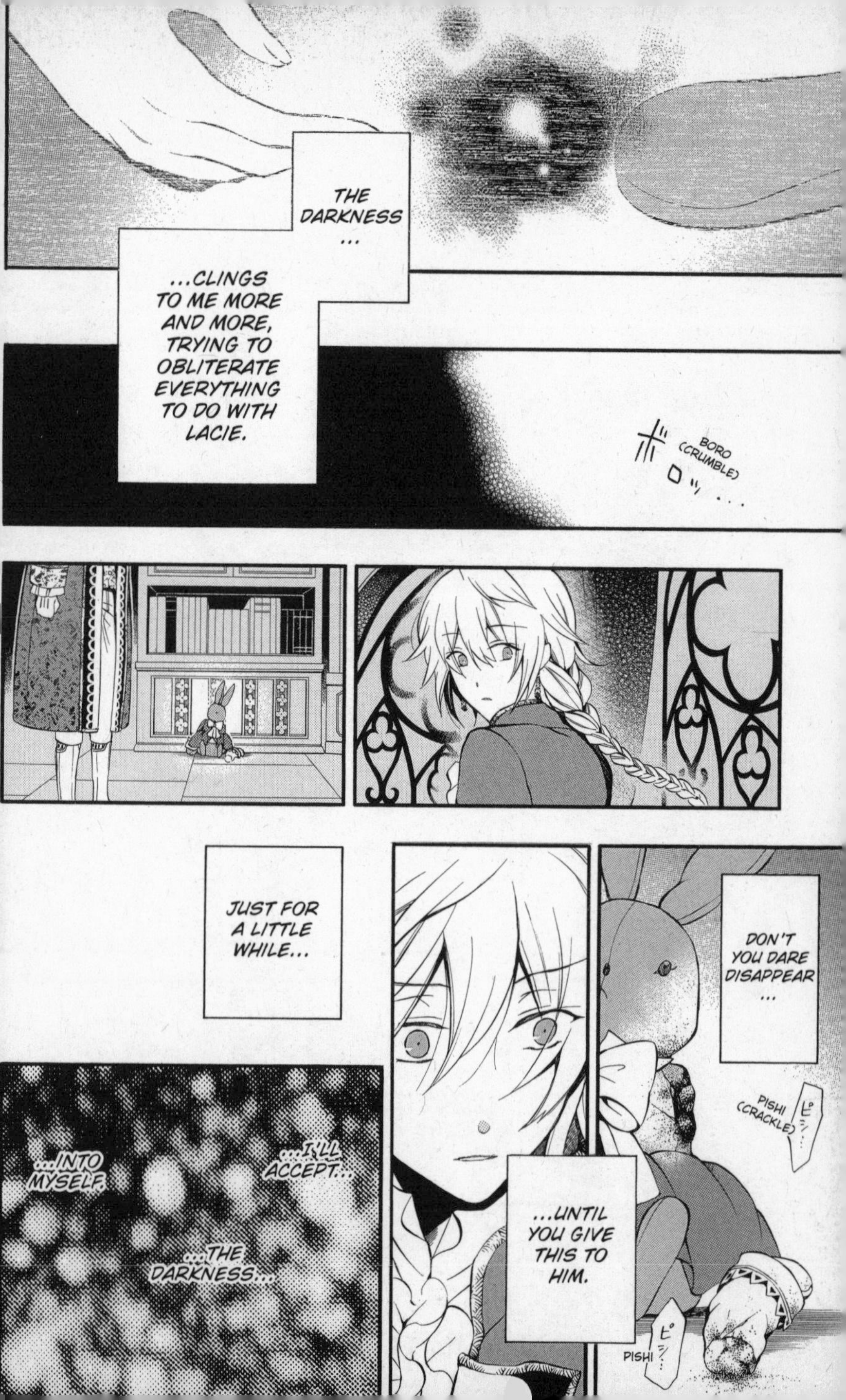
THE DARKNESS ...
...CLINGS TO ME MORE AND MORE, TRYING TO OBLITERATE EVERYTHING TO DO WITH LACIE.
BORO (CRUMBLE)
DON'T YOU DARE DISAPPEAR ...
PISHI (CRACKLE)
...UNTIL YOU GIVE THIS TO HIM.
PISHI
JUST FOR A LITTLE WHILE...
...I'LL ACCEPT...
...INTO MYSELF.
...THE DARKNESS...

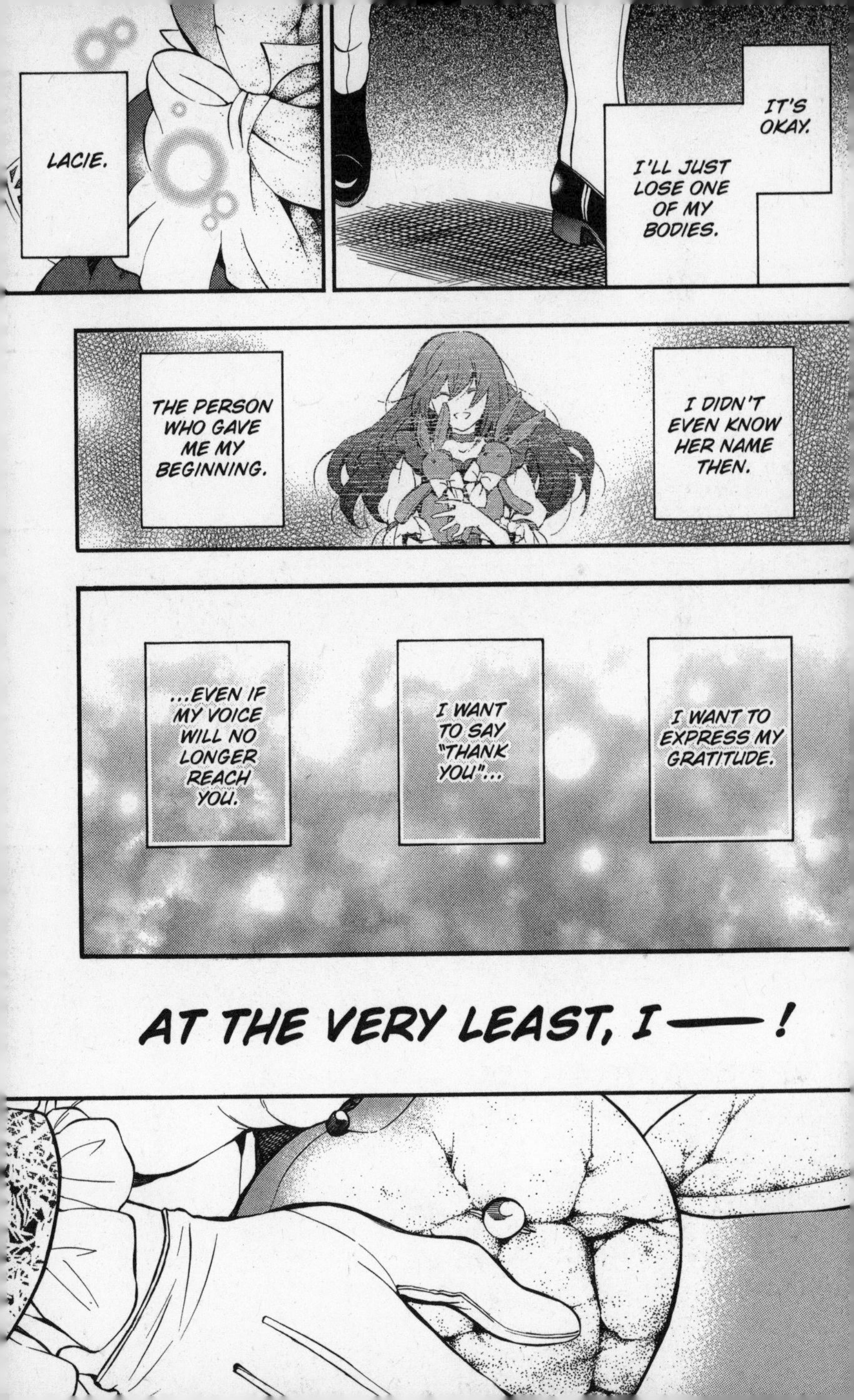
IT'S OKAY.
I'LL JUST LOSE ONE OF MY BODIES.
LACIE.
I DIDN'T EVEN KNOW HER NAME THEN.
THE PERSON WHO GAVE ME MY BEGINNING.
I WANT TO EXPRESS MY GRATITUDE.
I WANT TO SAY "THANK YOU"...
...EVEN IF MY VOICE WILL NO LONGER REACH YOU.
AT THE VERY LEAST, I—!

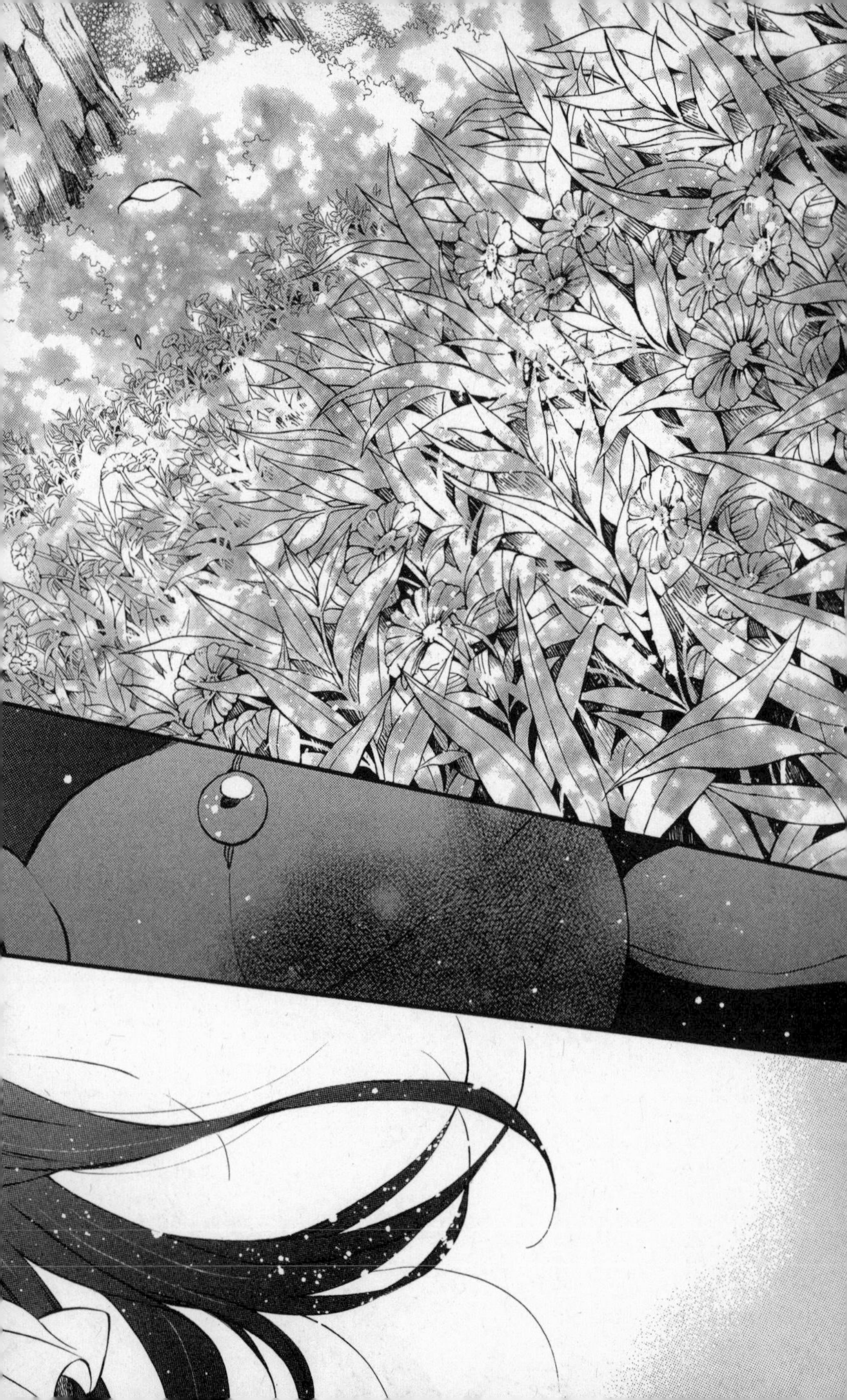

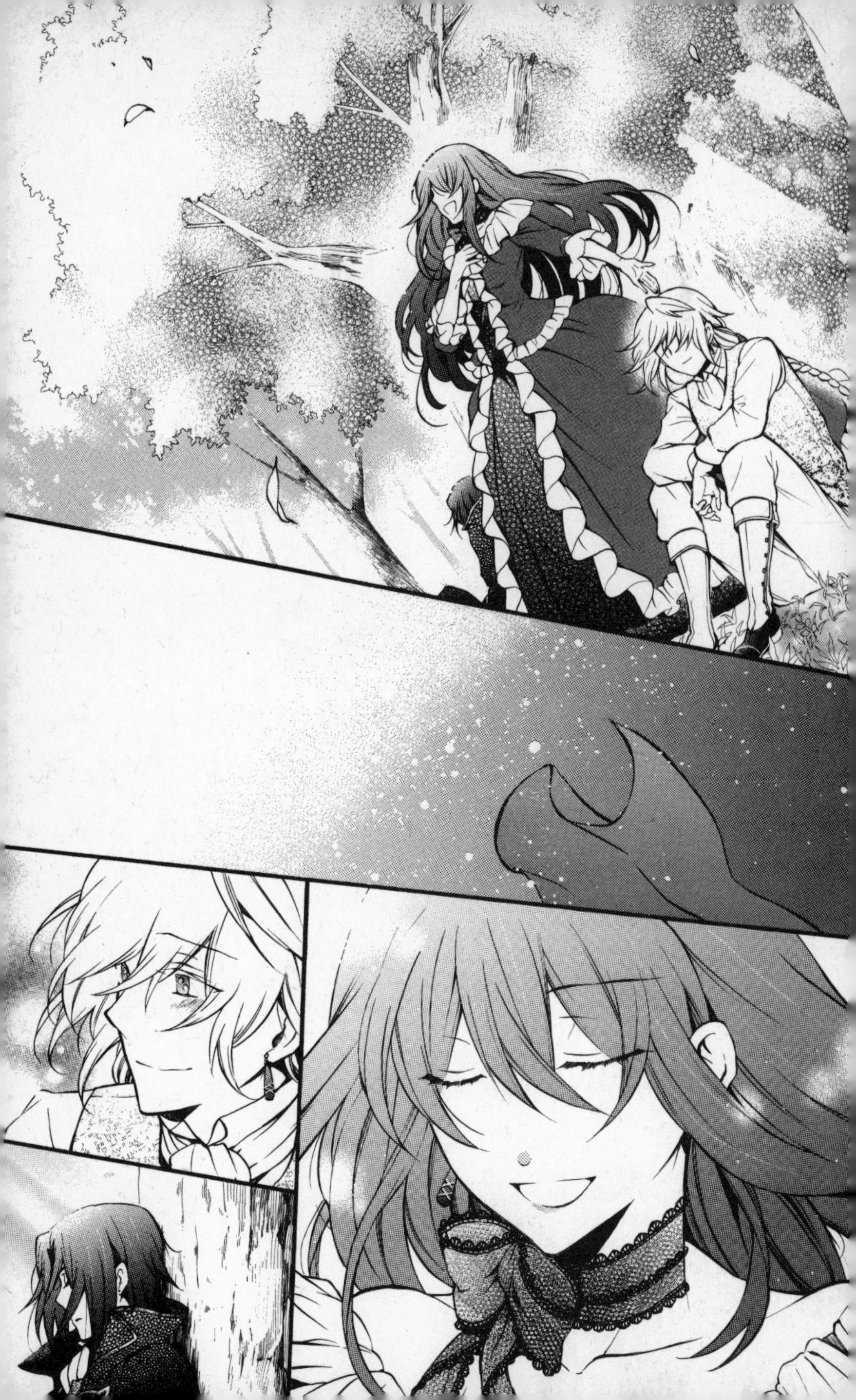

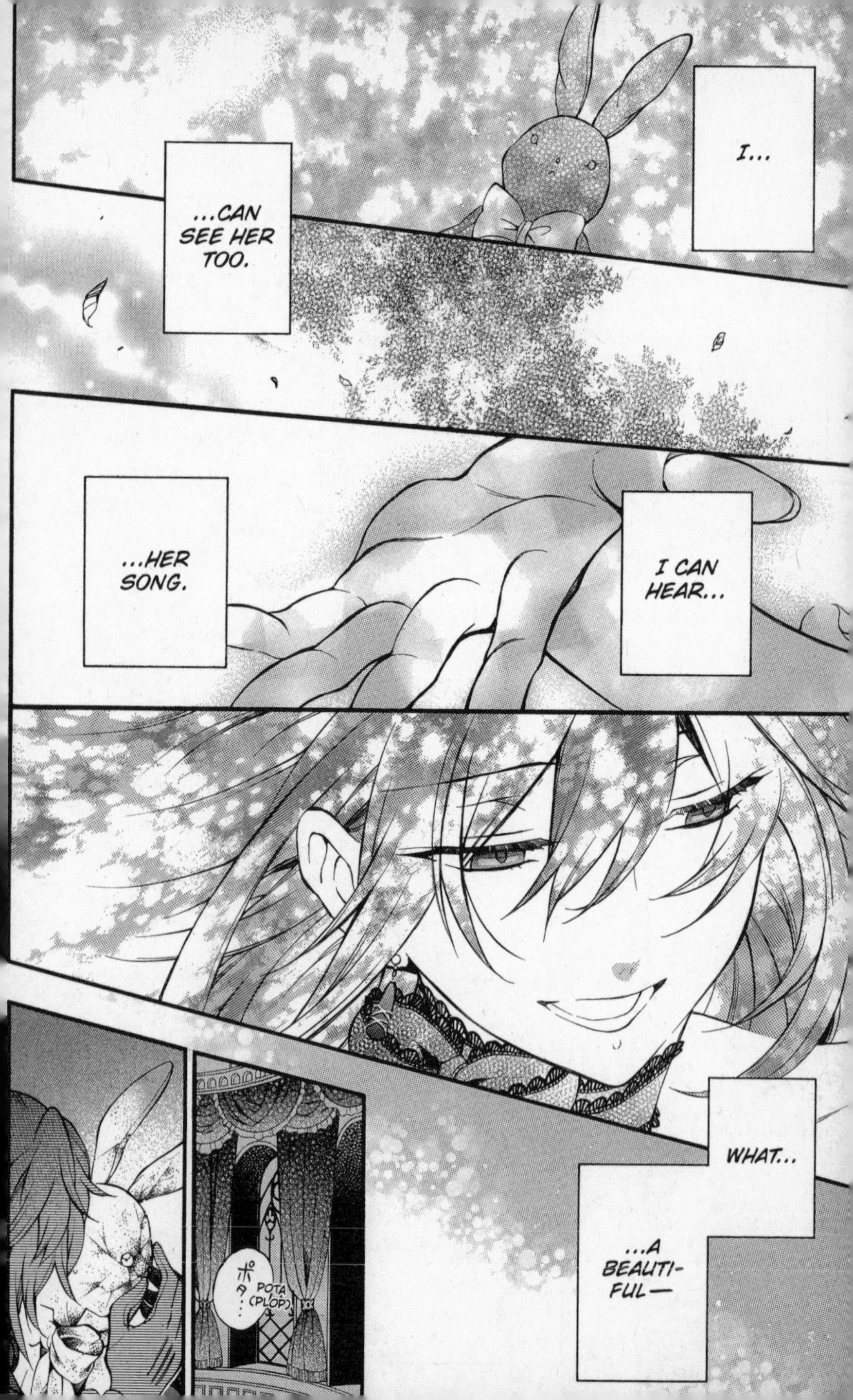
I...
...CAN SEE HER TOO.
I CAN HEAR...
...HER SONG.
WHAT...
...A BEAUTIFUL—
ポタ...
POTA (PLOP)

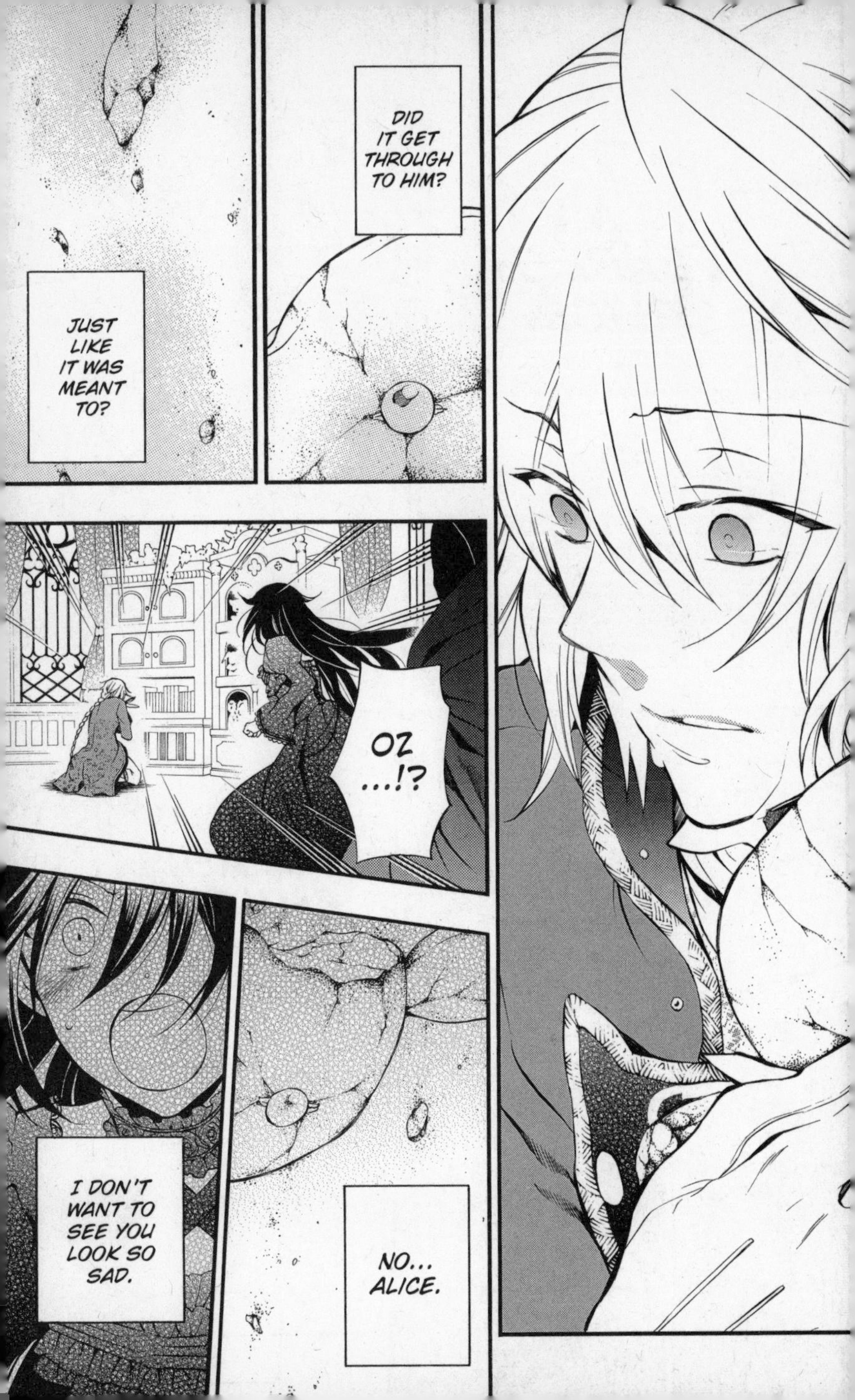
DID IT GET THROUGH TO HIM?
JUST LIKE IT WAS MEANT TO?
OZ ...!?
NO... ALICE.
I DON'T WANT TO SEE YOU LOOK SO SAD.

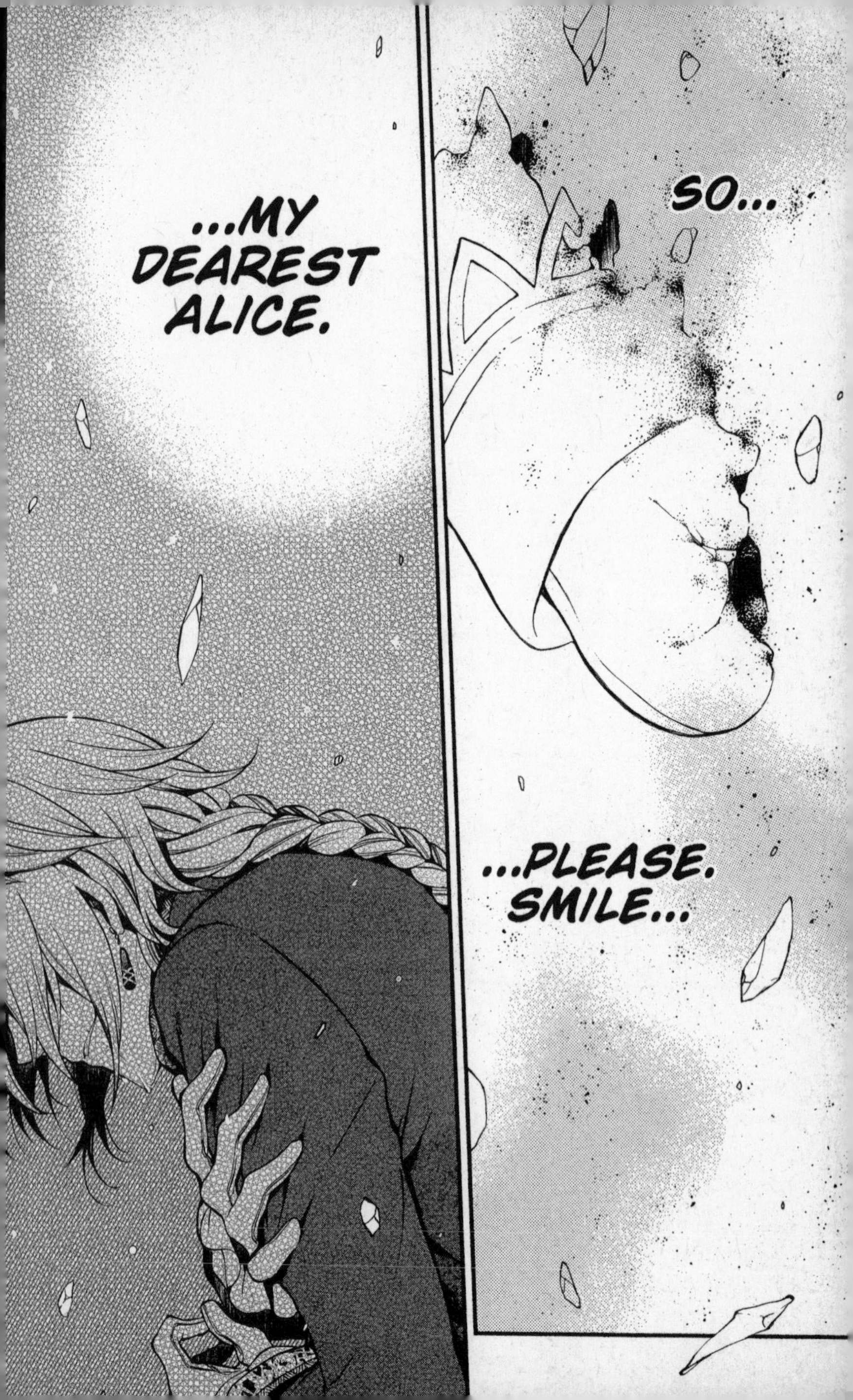
SO...
...PLEASE. SMILE...
...MY DEAREST ALICE.

Retrace:LXXI Black Rabbit

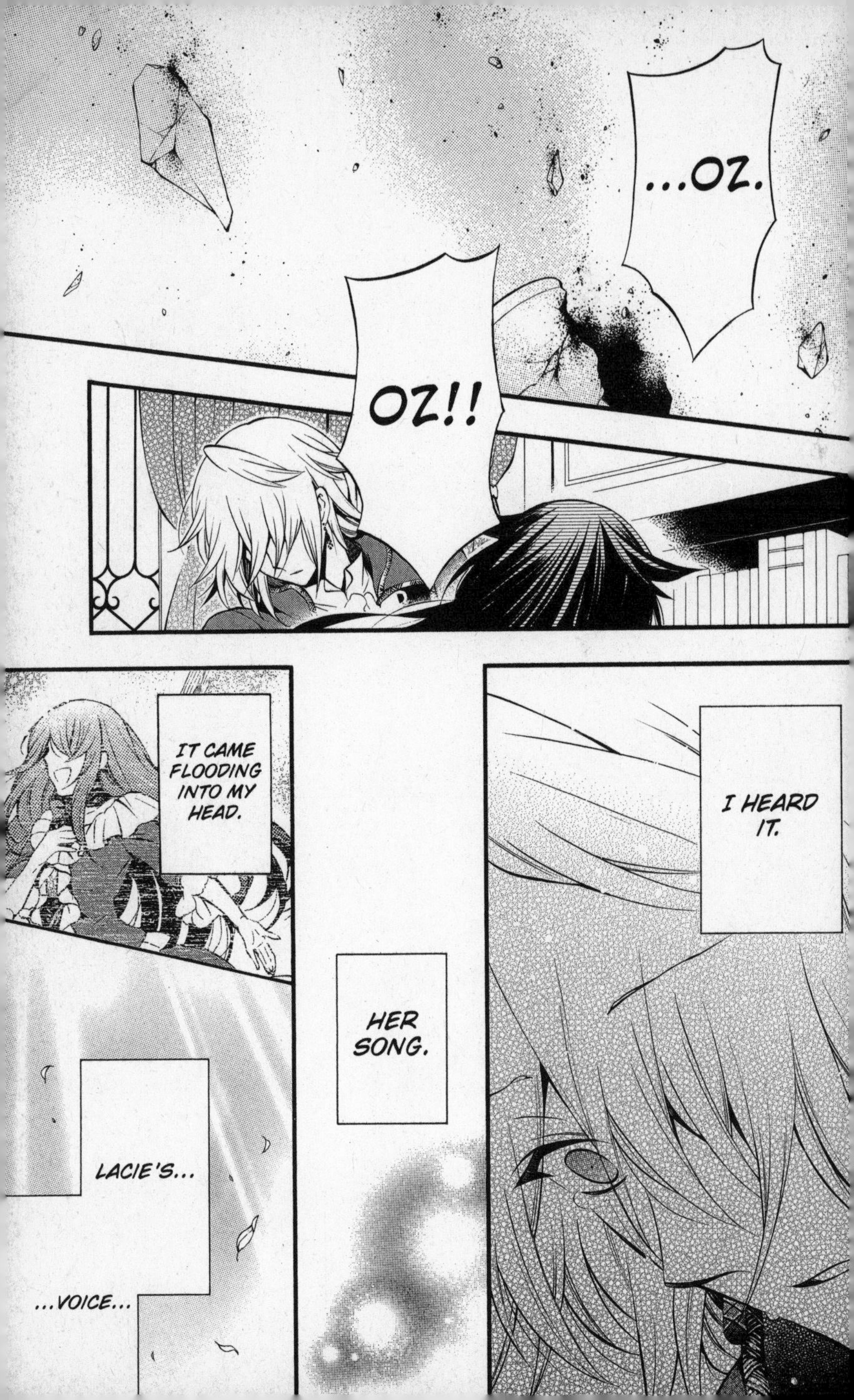
...OZ.
OZ!!
I HEARD IT.
HER SONG.
IT CAME FLOODING INTO MY HEAD.
LACIE'S...
...VOICE...

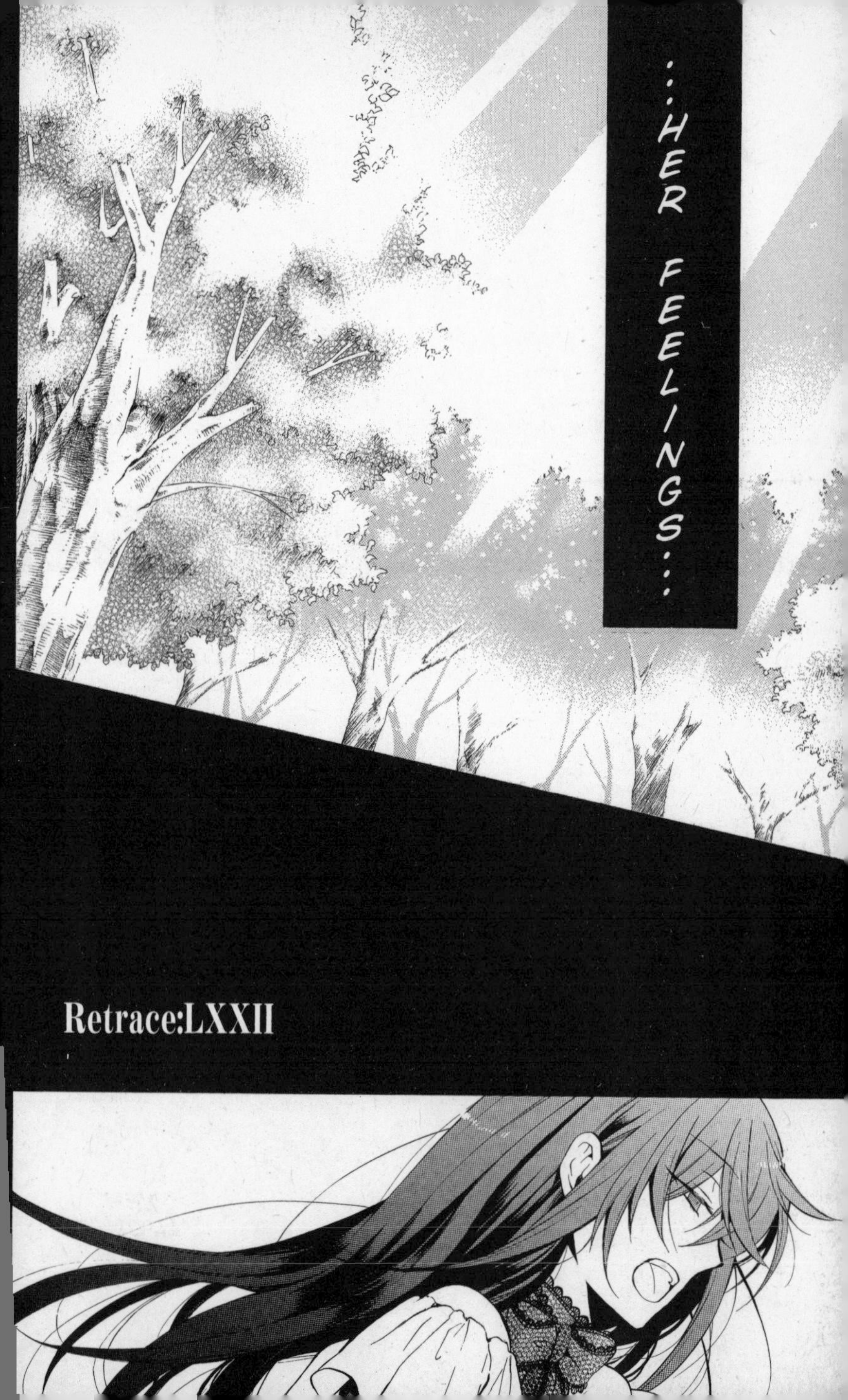
...HER FEELINGS...
Retrace:LXXII

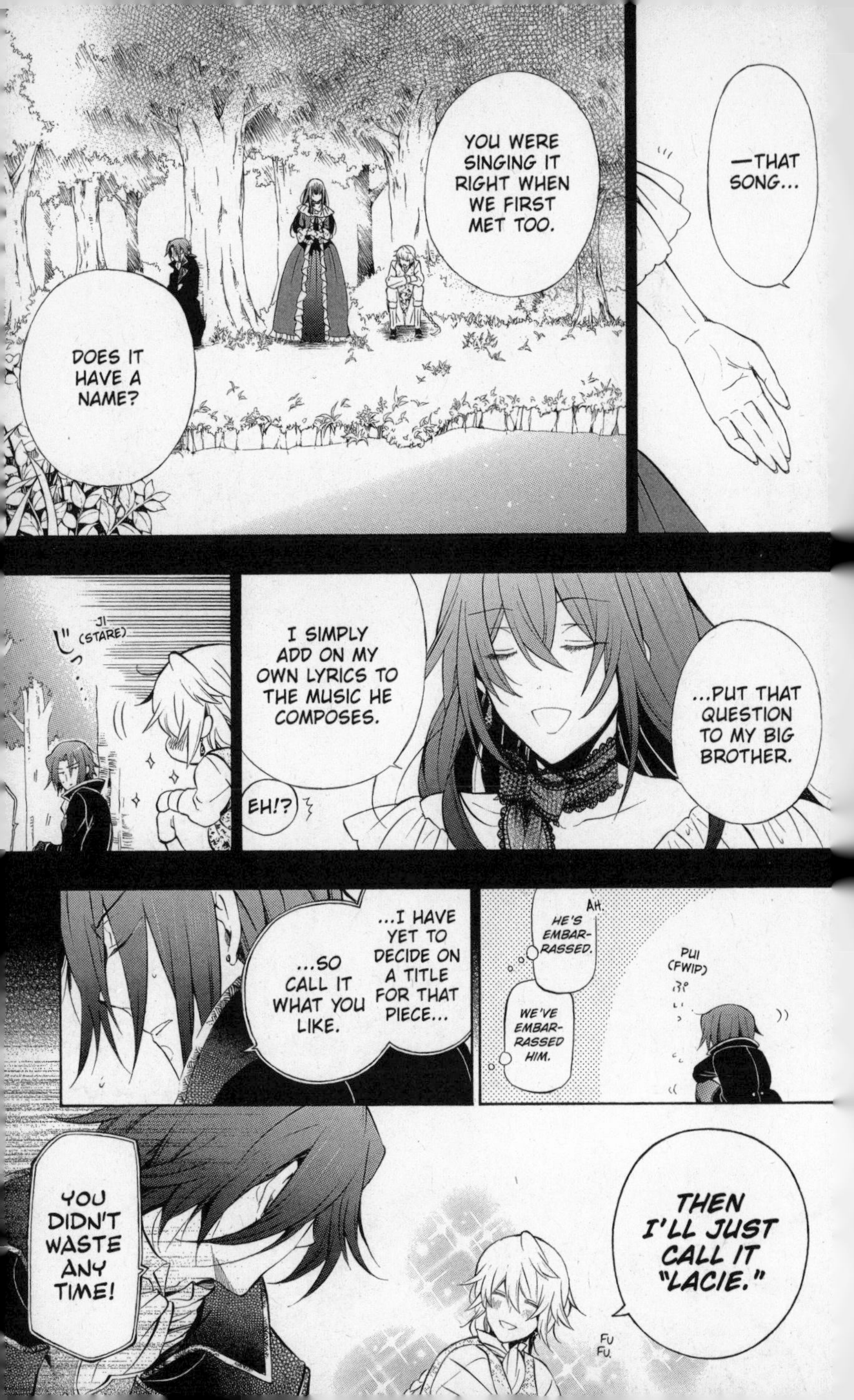
—THAT SONG...
YOU WERE SINGING IT RIGHT WHEN WE FIRST MET TOO.
DOES IT HAVE A NAME?
...PUT THAT QUESTION TO MY BIG BROTHER.
I SIMPLY ADD ON MY OWN LYRICS TO THE MUSIC HE COMPOSES.
EH!?
JI (STARE)
AH.
HE'S EMBARRASSED.
WE'VE EMBARRASSED HIM.
PUI (FWIP)
...I HAVE YET TO DECIDE ON A TITLE FOR THAT PIECE...
...SO CALL IT WHAT YOU LIKE.
THEN I'LL JUST CALL IT "LACIE."
FU FU.
YOU DIDN'T WASTE ANY TIME!

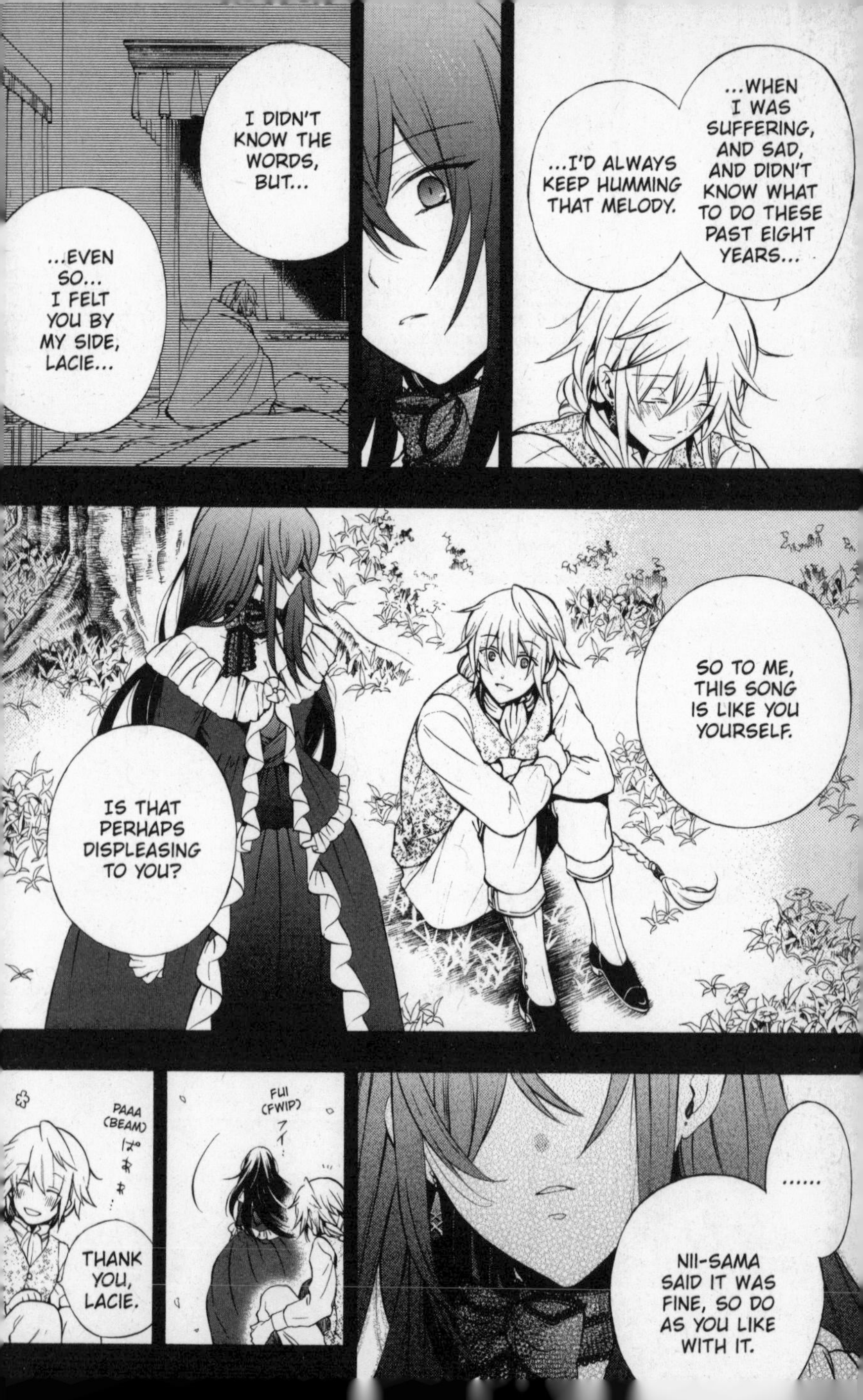
...WHEN I WAS SUFFERING, AND SAD, AND DIDN'T KNOW WHAT TO DO THESE PAST EIGHT YEARS...
...I'D ALWAYS KEEP HUMMING THAT MELODY.
I DIDN'T KNOW THE WORDS, BUT...
...EVEN SO... I FELT YOU BY MY SIDE, LACIE...
SO TO ME, THIS SONG IS LIKE YOU YOURSELF.
IS THAT PERHAPS DISPLEASING TO YOU?
......
NII-SAMA SAID IT WAS FINE, SO DO AS YOU LIKE WITH IT.
FUI (FWIP)
PAAA (BEAM)
THANK YOU, LACIE.

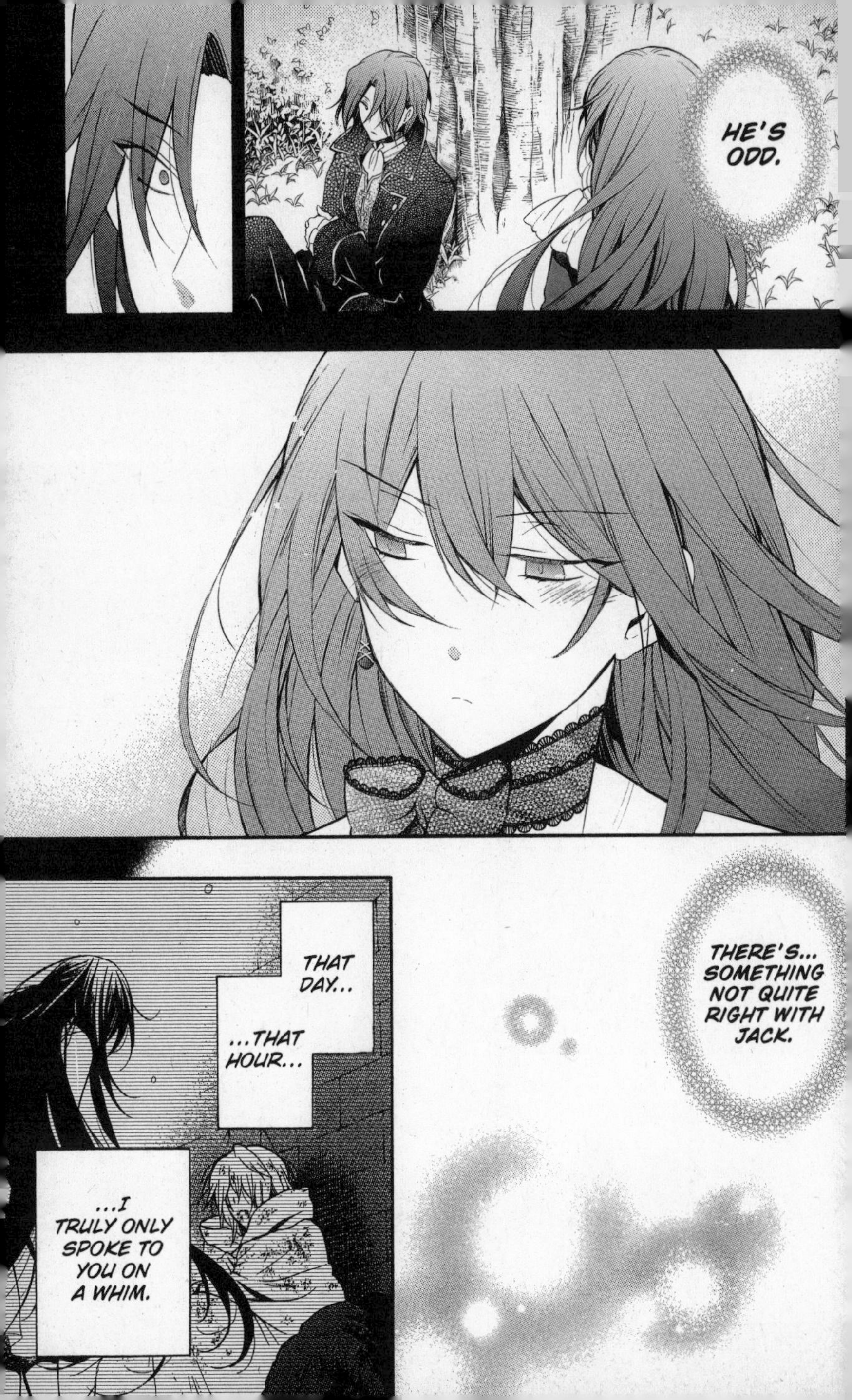
HE'S ODD.
THERE'S... SOMETHING NOT QUITE RIGHT WITH JACK.
THAT DAY...
...THAT HOUR...
...I TRULY ONLY SPOKE TO YOU ON A WHIM.

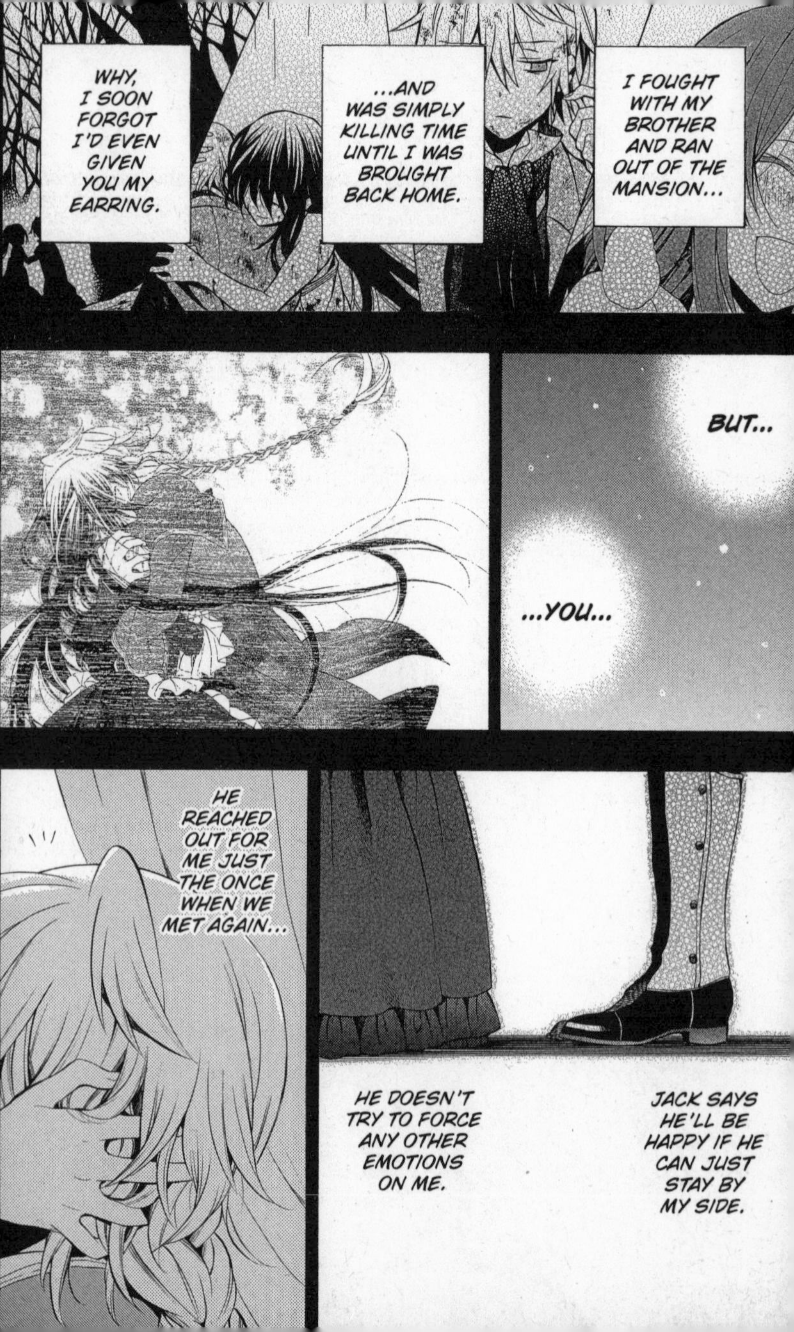
I FOUGHT WITH MY BROTHER AND RAN OUT OF THE MANSION...
...AND WAS SIMPLY KILLING TIME UNTIL I WAS BROUGHT BACK HOME.
WHY, I SOON FORGOT I'D EVEN GIVEN YOU MY EARRING.
BUT...
...YOU...
JACK SAYS HE'LL BE HAPPY IF HE CAN JUST STAY BY MY SIDE.
HE DOESN'T TRY TO FORCE ANY OTHER EMOTIONS ON ME.
HE REACHED OUT FOR ME JUST THE ONCE WHEN WE MET AGAIN...

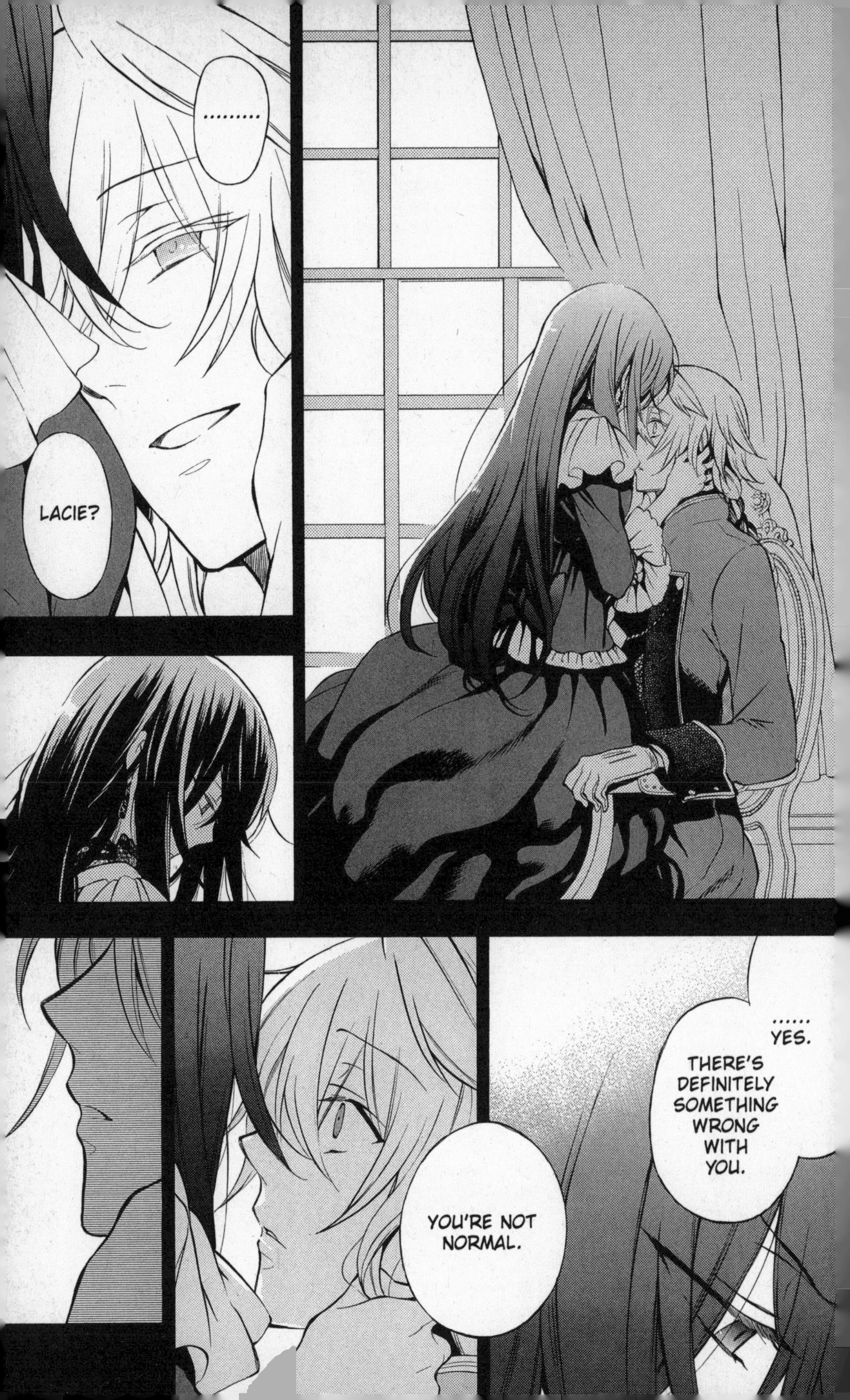
....
LACIE?
......
YES.
THERE'S DEFINITELY SOMETHING WRONG WITH YOU.
YOU'RE NOT NORMAL.

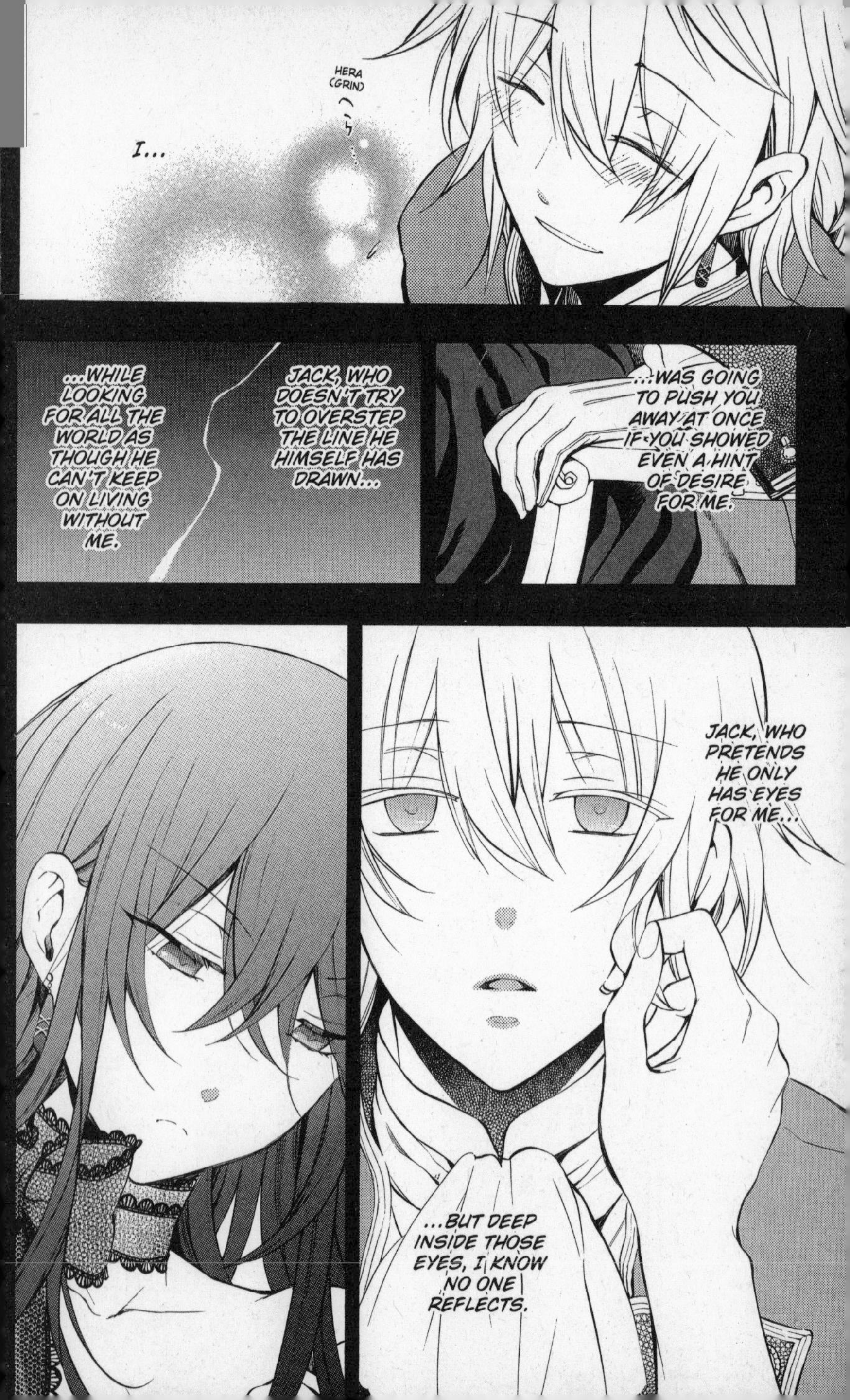
HERA (GRIN)
I...
...WAS GOING TO PUSH YOU AWAY AT ONCE IF YOU SHOWED EVEN A HINT OF DESIRE FOR ME.
JACK, WHO DOESN'T TRY TO OVERSTEP THE LINE HE HIMSELF HAS DRAWN...
...WHILE LOOKING FOR ALL THE WORLD AS THOUGH HE CAN'T KEEP ON LIVING WITHOUT ME.
JACK, WHO PRETENDS HE ONLY HAS EYES FOR ME...
...BUT DEEP INSIDE THOSE EYES, I KNOW NO ONE REFLECTS.

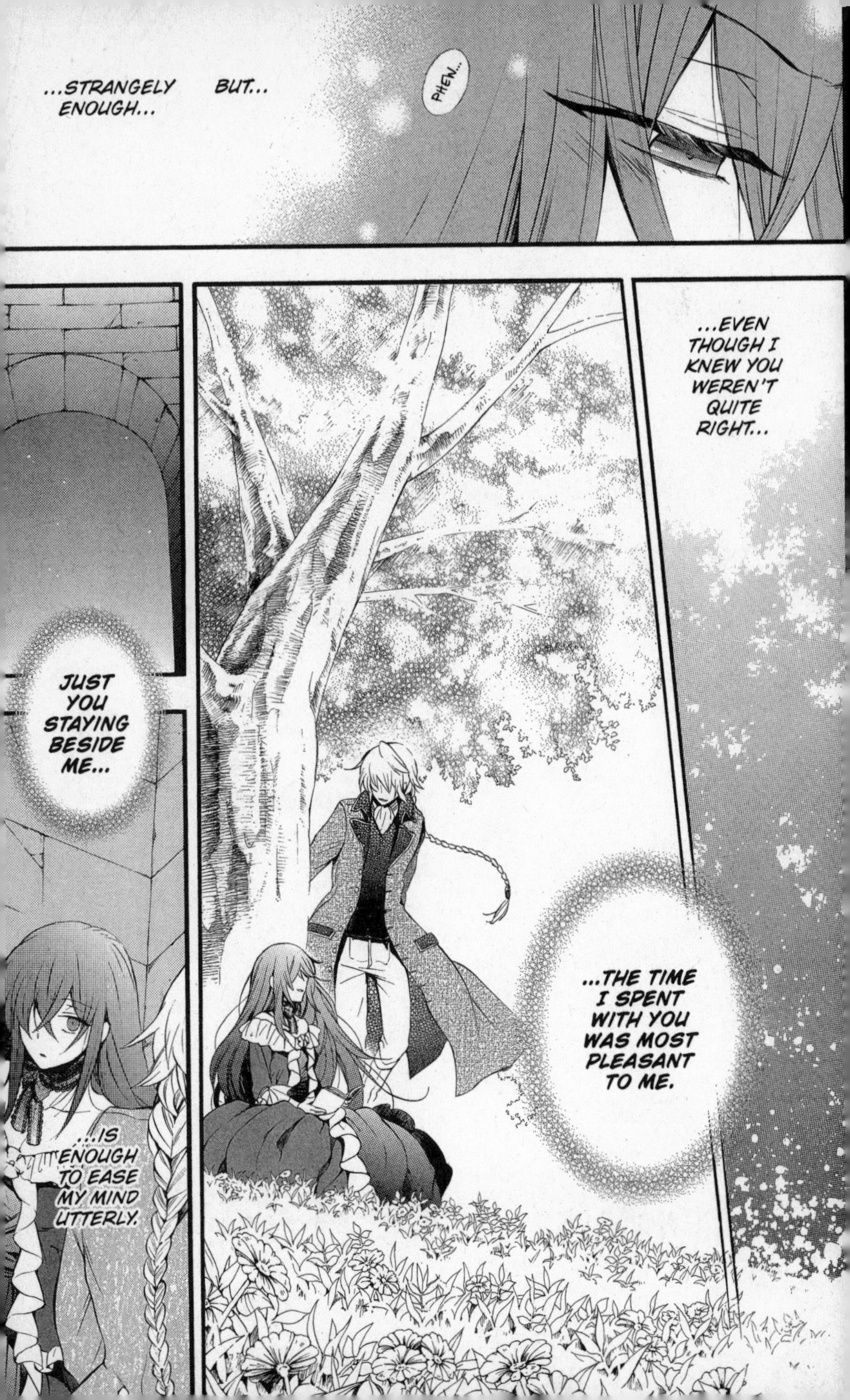
PHEW...
BUT...
...STRANGELY ENOUGH...
...EVEN THOUGH I KNEW YOU WEREN'T QUITE RIGHT...
...THE TIME I SPENT WITH YOU WAS MOST PLEASANT TO ME.
JUST YOU STAYING BESIDE ME...
...IS ENOUGH TO EASE MY MIND UTTERLY.

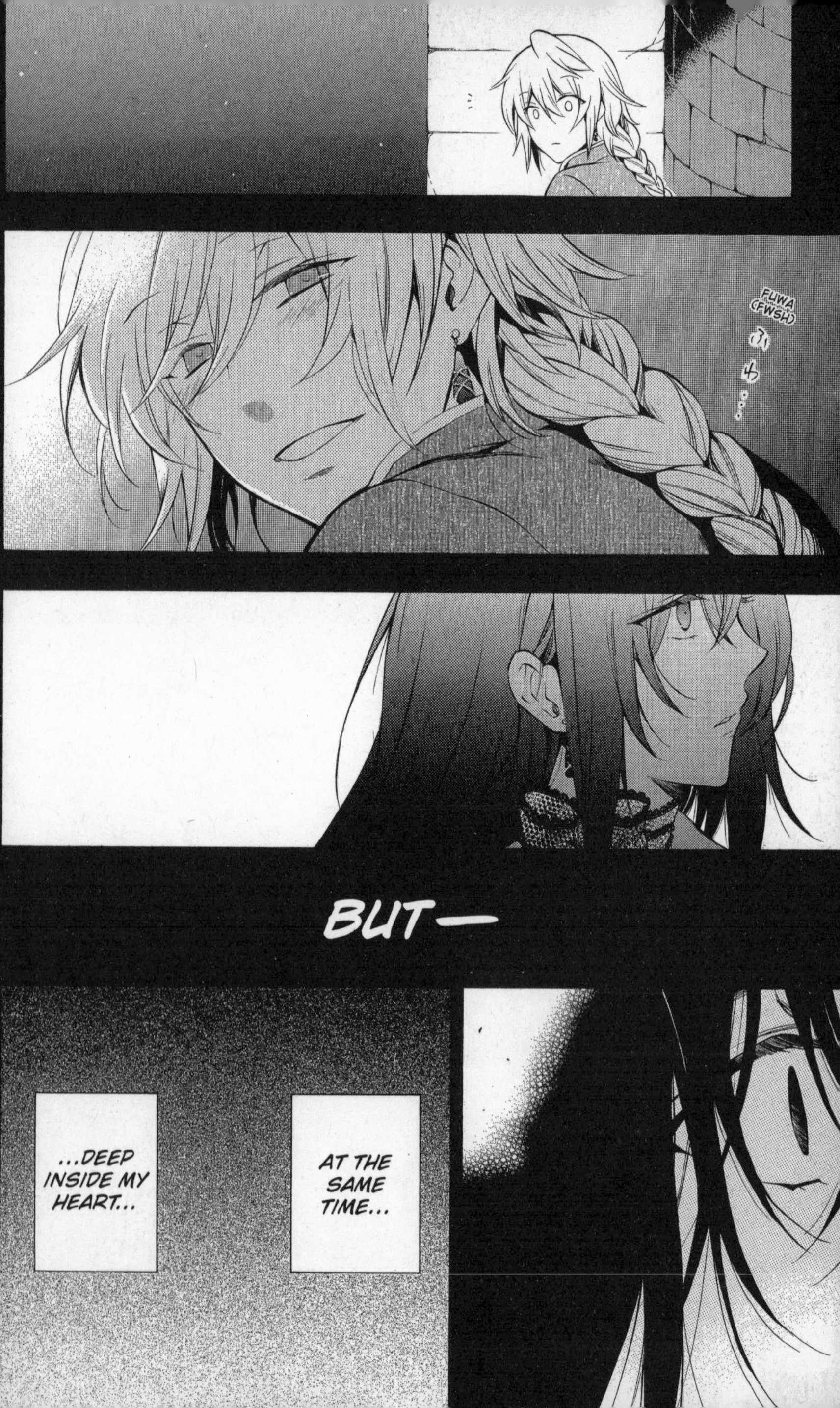
FUWA (FWSH)
ふわ…
BUT—
AT THE SAME TIME...
...DEEP INSIDE MY HEART...

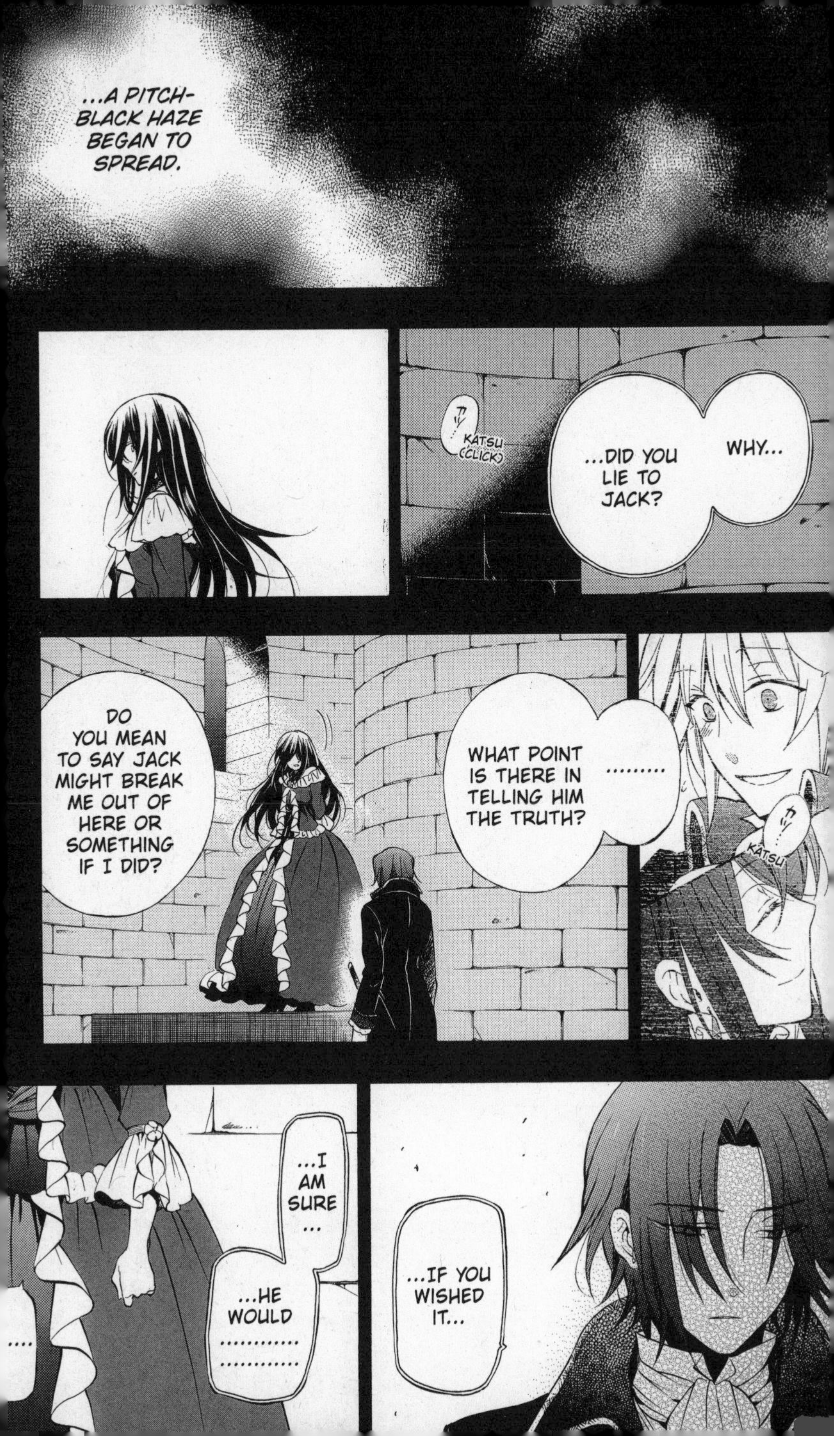
...A PITCH-BLACK HAZE BEGAN TO SPREAD.
WHY...
...DID YOU LIE TO JACK?
KATSU (CLICK)
KATSU
....
WHAT POINT IS THERE IN TELLING HIM THE TRUTH?
DO YOU MEAN TO SAY JACK MIGHT BREAK ME OUT OF HERE OR SOMETHING IF I DID?
...IF YOU WISHED IT...
...I AM SURE...
...HE WOULD ....
....

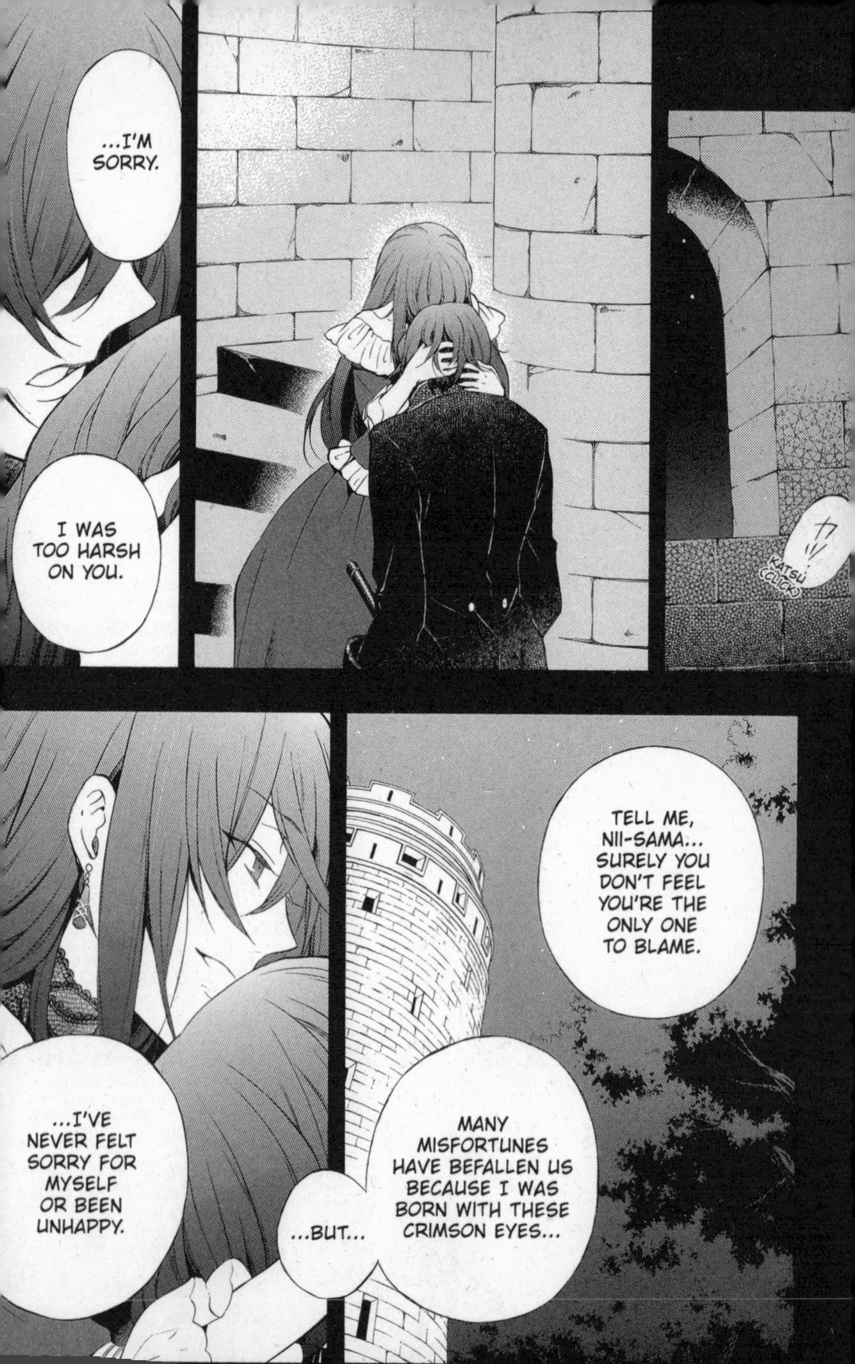
カッ!!
KATSU (CLICK)
...I'M SORRY.
I WAS TOO HARSH ON YOU.
TELL ME, NII-SAMA... SURELY YOU DON'T FEEL YOU'RE THE ONLY ONE TO BLAME.
MANY MISFORTUNES HAVE BEFALLEN US BECAUSE I WAS BORN WITH THESE CRIMSON EYES...
...BUT...
...I'VE NEVER FELT SORRY FOR MYSELF OR BEEN UNHAPPY.

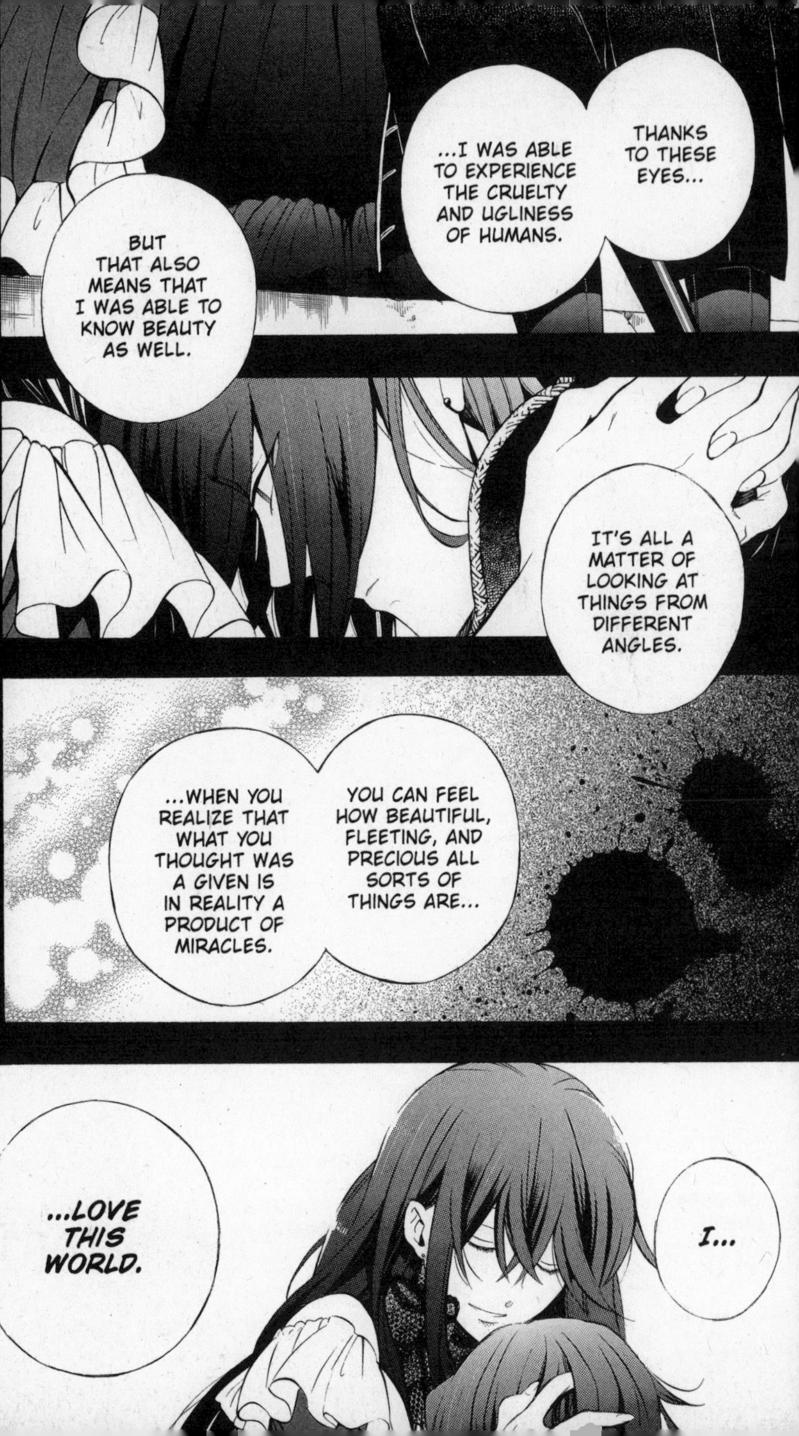
THANKS TO THESE EYES...
...I WAS ABLE TO EXPERIENCE THE CRUELTY AND UGLINESS OF HUMANS.
BUT THAT ALSO MEANS THAT I WAS ABLE TO KNOW BEAUTY AS WELL.
IT'S ALL A MATTER OF LOOKING AT THINGS FROM DIFFERENT ANGLES.
YOU CAN FEEL HOW BEAUTIFUL, FLEETING, AND PRECIOUS ALL SORTS OF THINGS ARE...
...WHEN YOU REALIZE THAT WHAT YOU THOUGHT WAS A GIVEN IS IN REALITY A PRODUCT OF MIRACLES.
I...
...LOVE THIS WORLD.

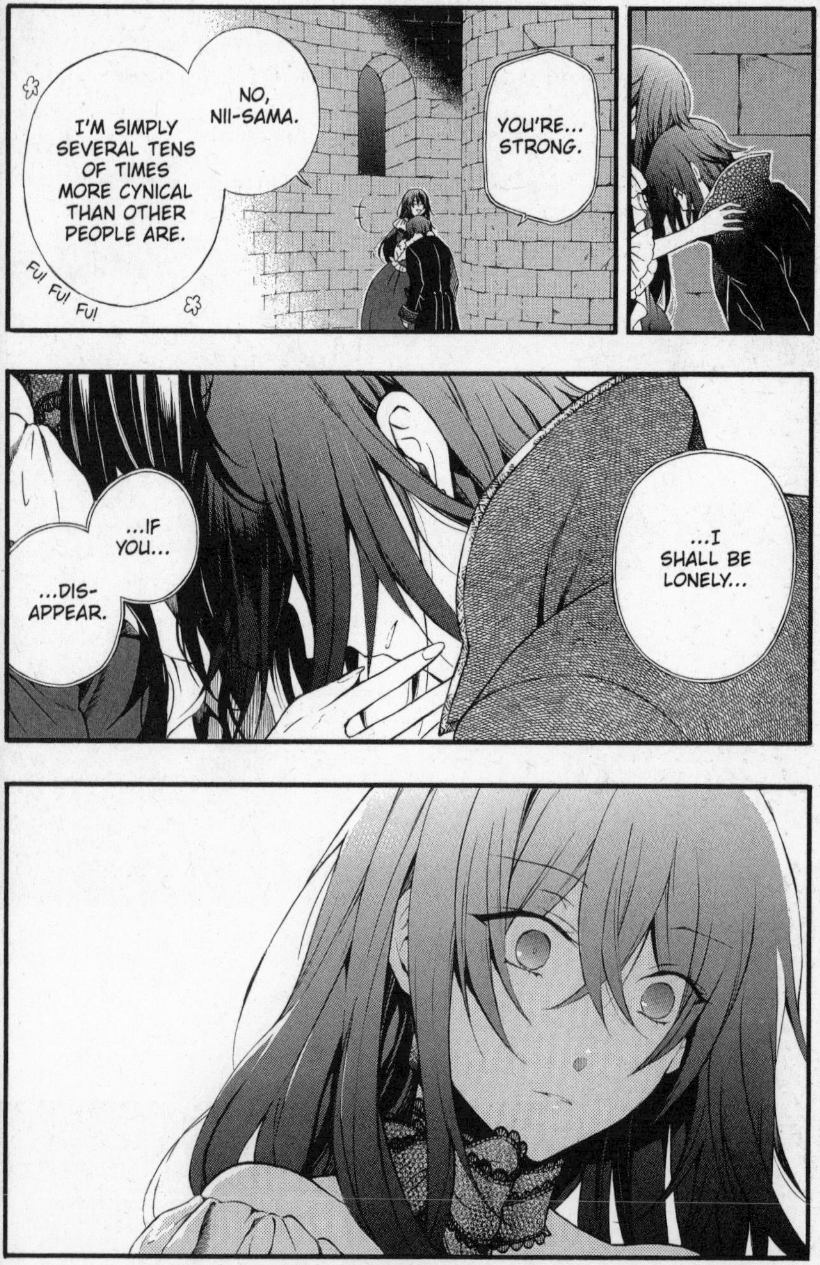
YOU'RE... STRONG.
NO, NII-SAMA.
I'M SIMPLY SEVERAL TENS OF TIMES MORE CYNICAL THAN OTHER PEOPLE ARE.
FU! FU! FU!
...I SHALL BE LONELY...
...IF YOU...
...DIS-APPEAR.

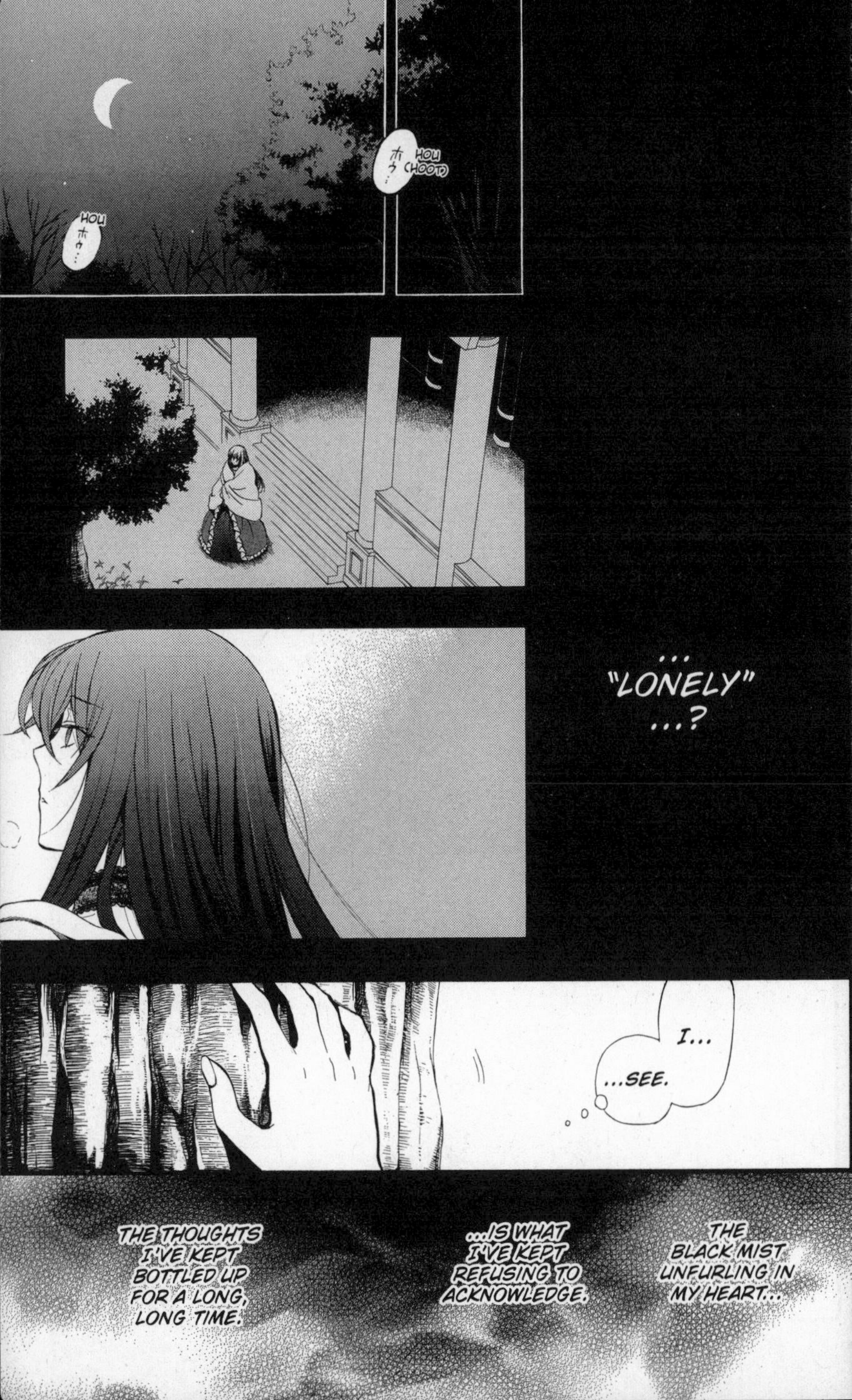
HOU (HOOT)
ホウ…
HOU
ホウ…
... "LONELY" ...?
I... ...SEE.
THE BLACK MIST UNFURLING IN MY HEART...
...IS WHAT I'VE KEPT REFUSING TO ACKNOWLEDGE.
THE THOUGHTS I'VE KEPT BOTTLED UP FOR A LONG, LONG TIME.

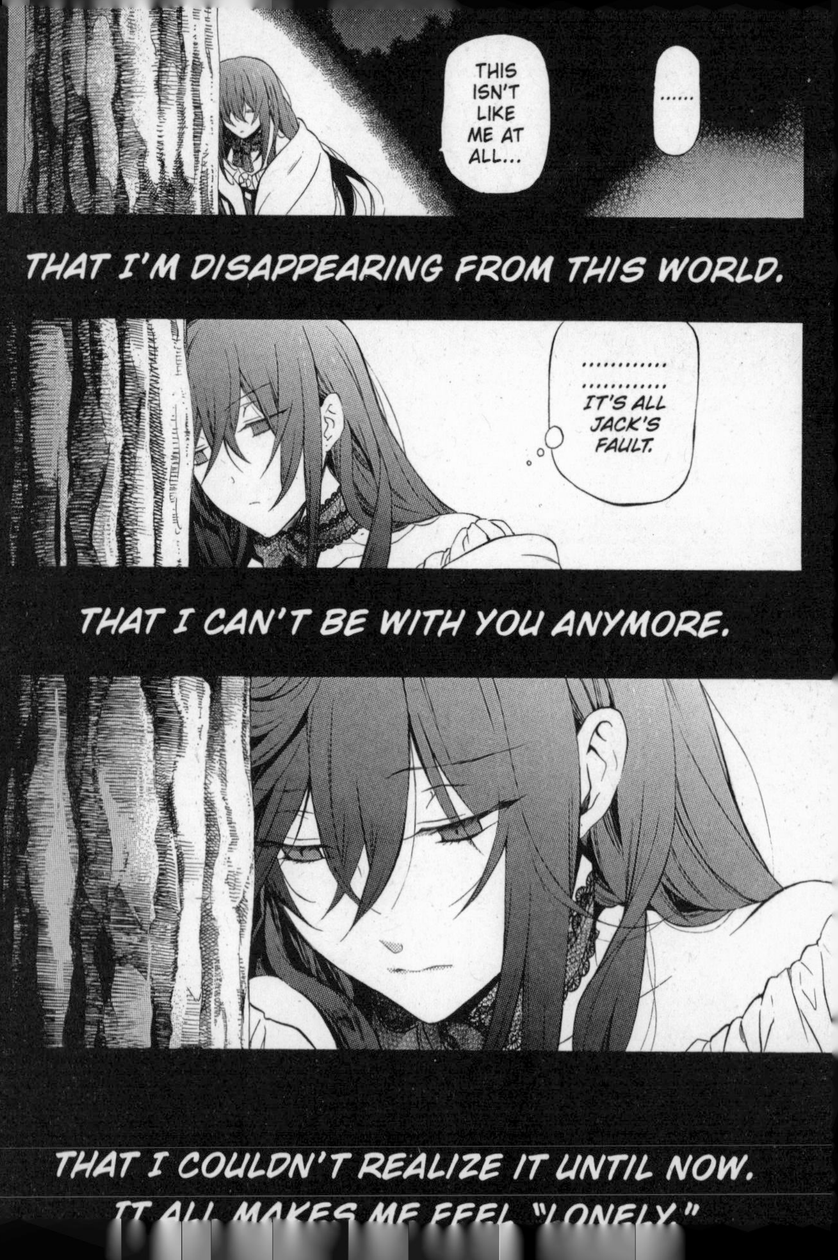
......
THIS ISN'T LIKE ME AT ALL...
THAT I'M DISAPPEARING FROM THIS WORLD.
.... IT'S ALL JACK'S FAULT.
THAT I CAN'T BE WITH YOU ANYMORE.
THAT I COULDN'T REALIZE IT UNTIL NOW.
IT ALL MAKES ME FEEL "LONELY."

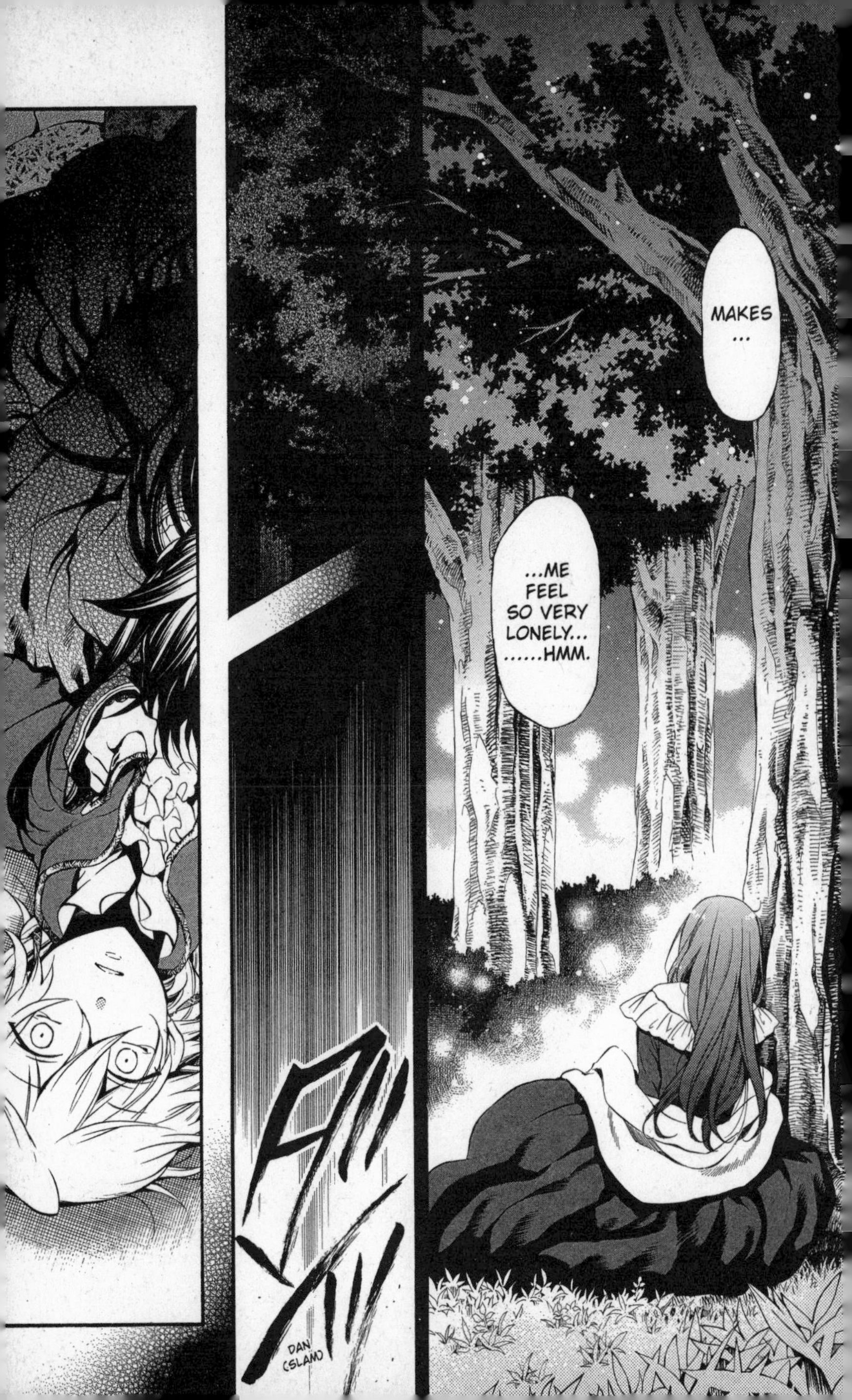
MAKES
...
...ME FEEL SO VERY LONELY... ......HMM.
DAN (SLAM)

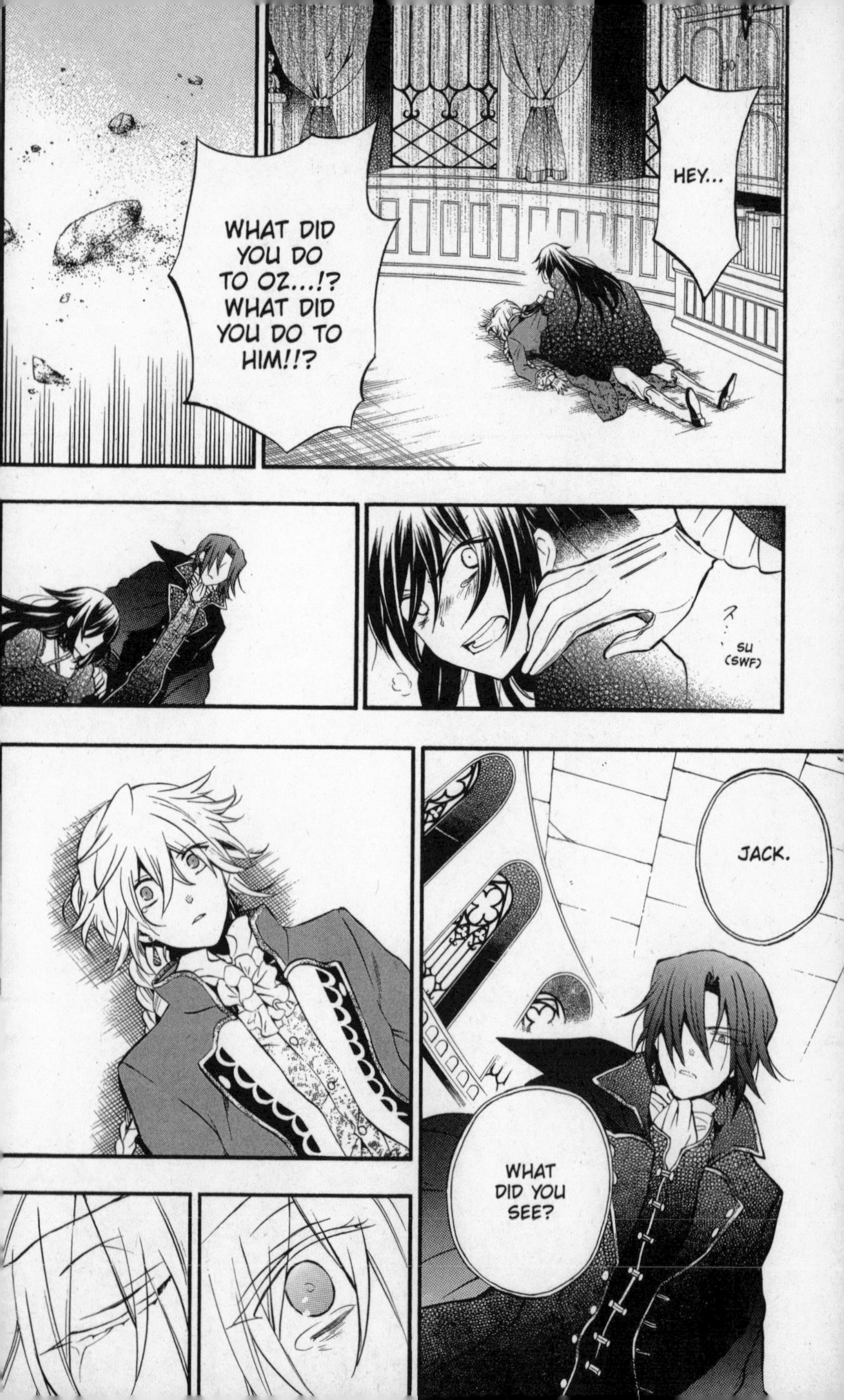
HEY...
WHAT DID YOU DO TO OZ...!? WHAT DID YOU DO TO HIM!!?
ス
SU (SWF)
JACK.
WHAT DID YOU SEE?

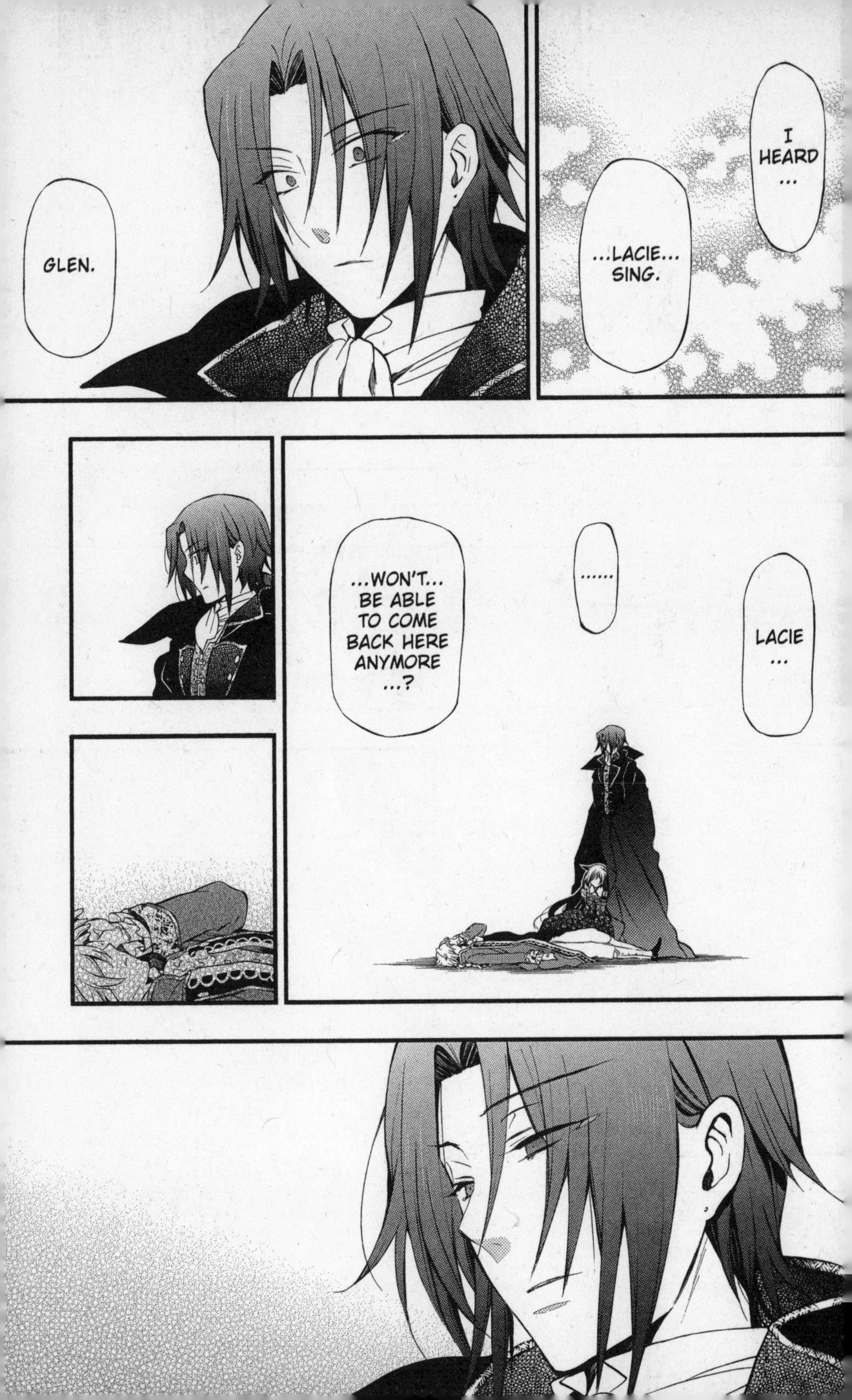
I HEARD...
...LACIE... SING.
GLEN.
LACIE...
......
...WON'T... BE ABLE TO COME BACK HERE ANYMORE...?

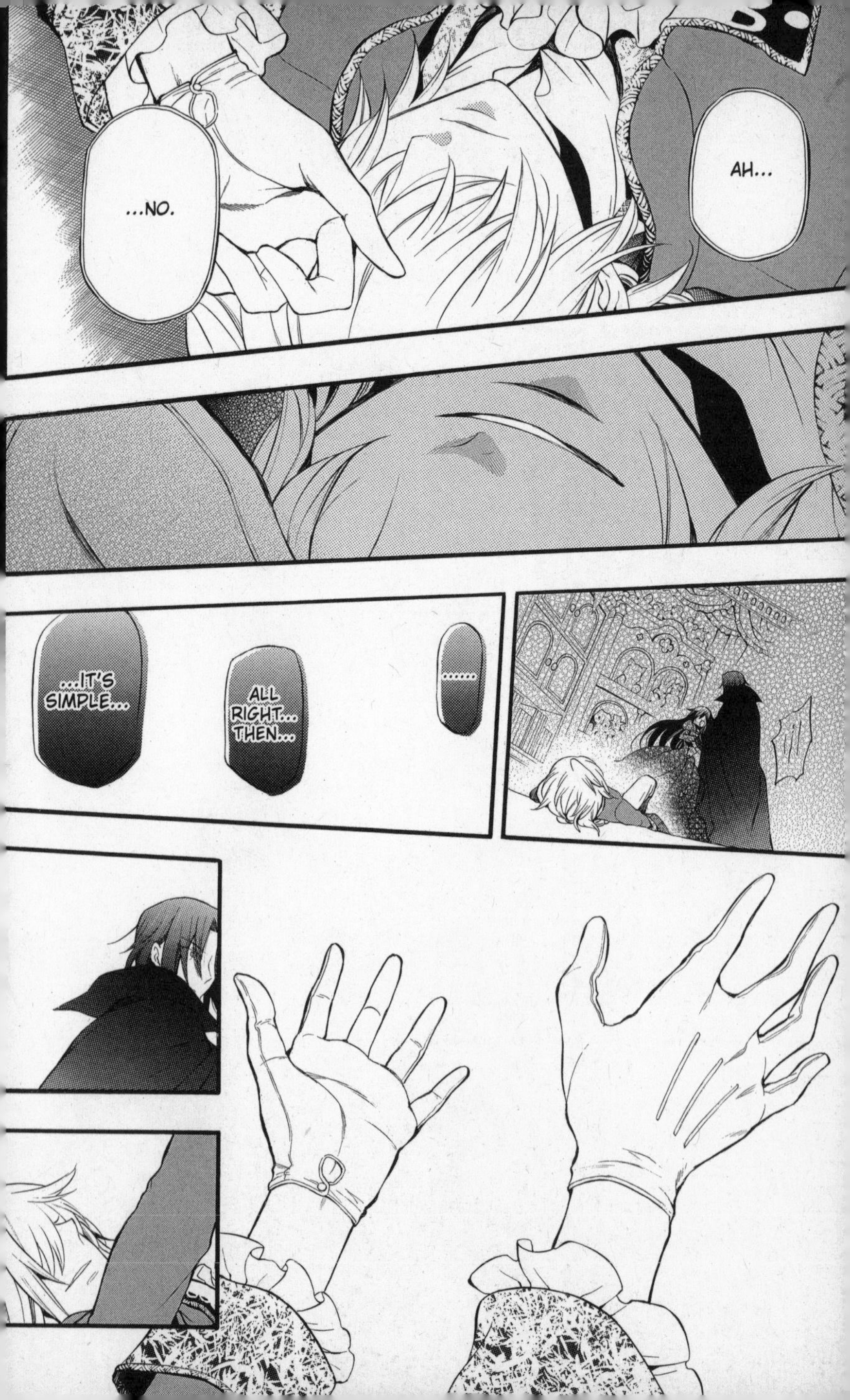
AH...
...NO.
......
ALL RIGHT... THEN...
...IT'S SIMPLE...

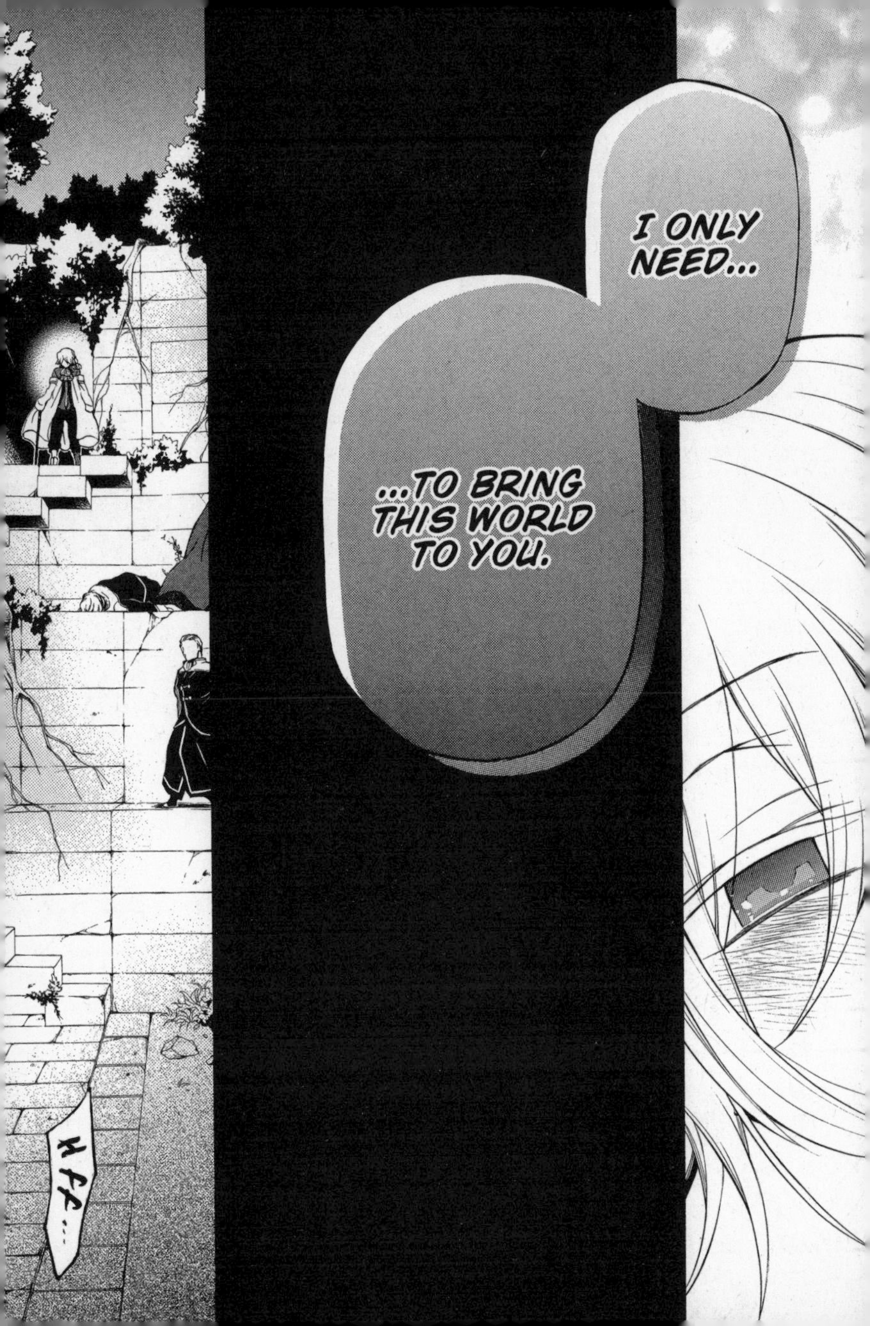
I ONLY NEED...
...TO BRING THIS WORLD TO YOU.
HFF...

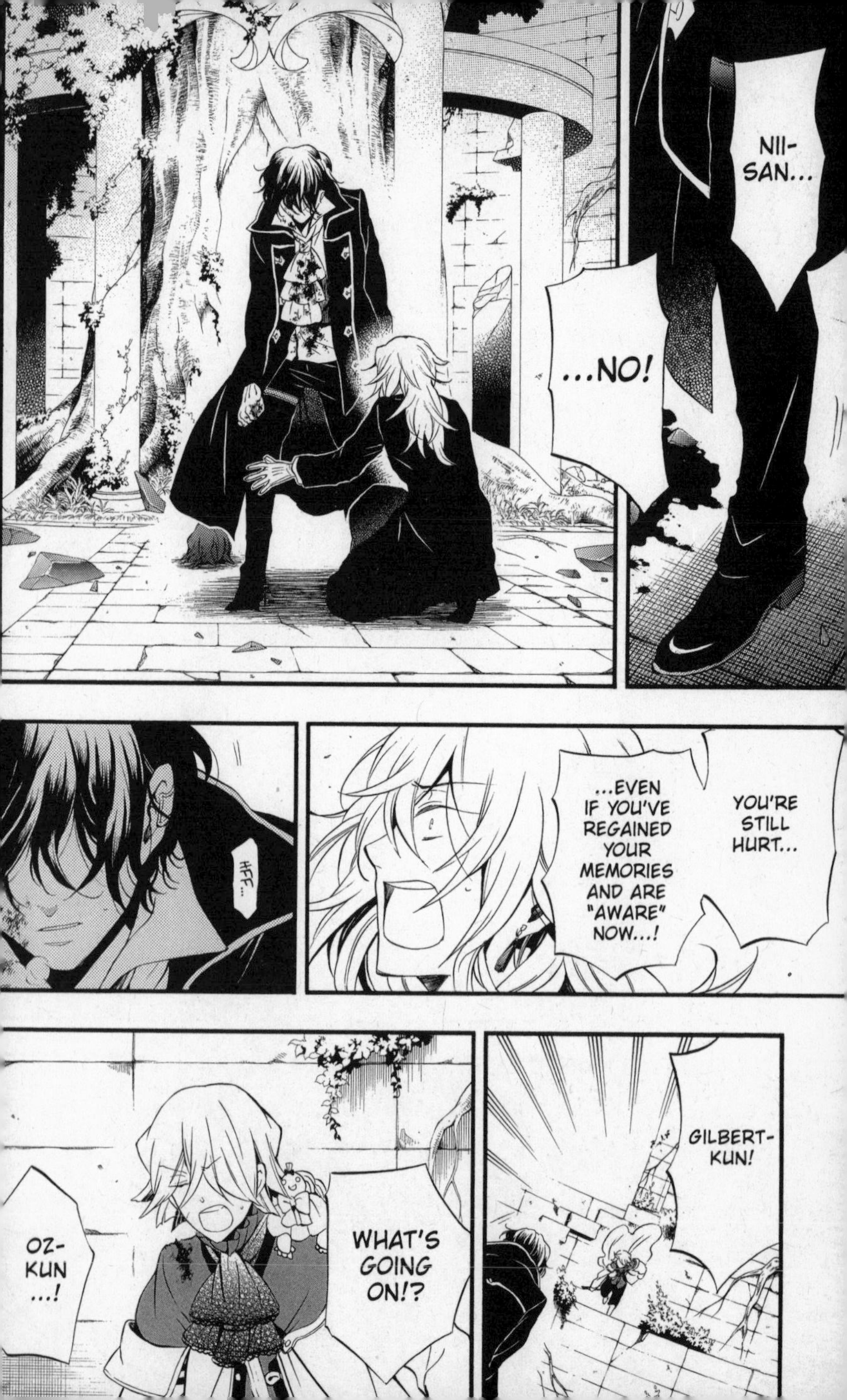
NII-SAN...
...NO!
YOU'RE STILL HURT...
...EVEN IF YOU'VE REGAINED YOUR MEMORIES AND ARE "AWARE" NOW...!
HFF...
GILBERT-KUN!
WHAT'S GOING ON!?
OZ-KUN...!

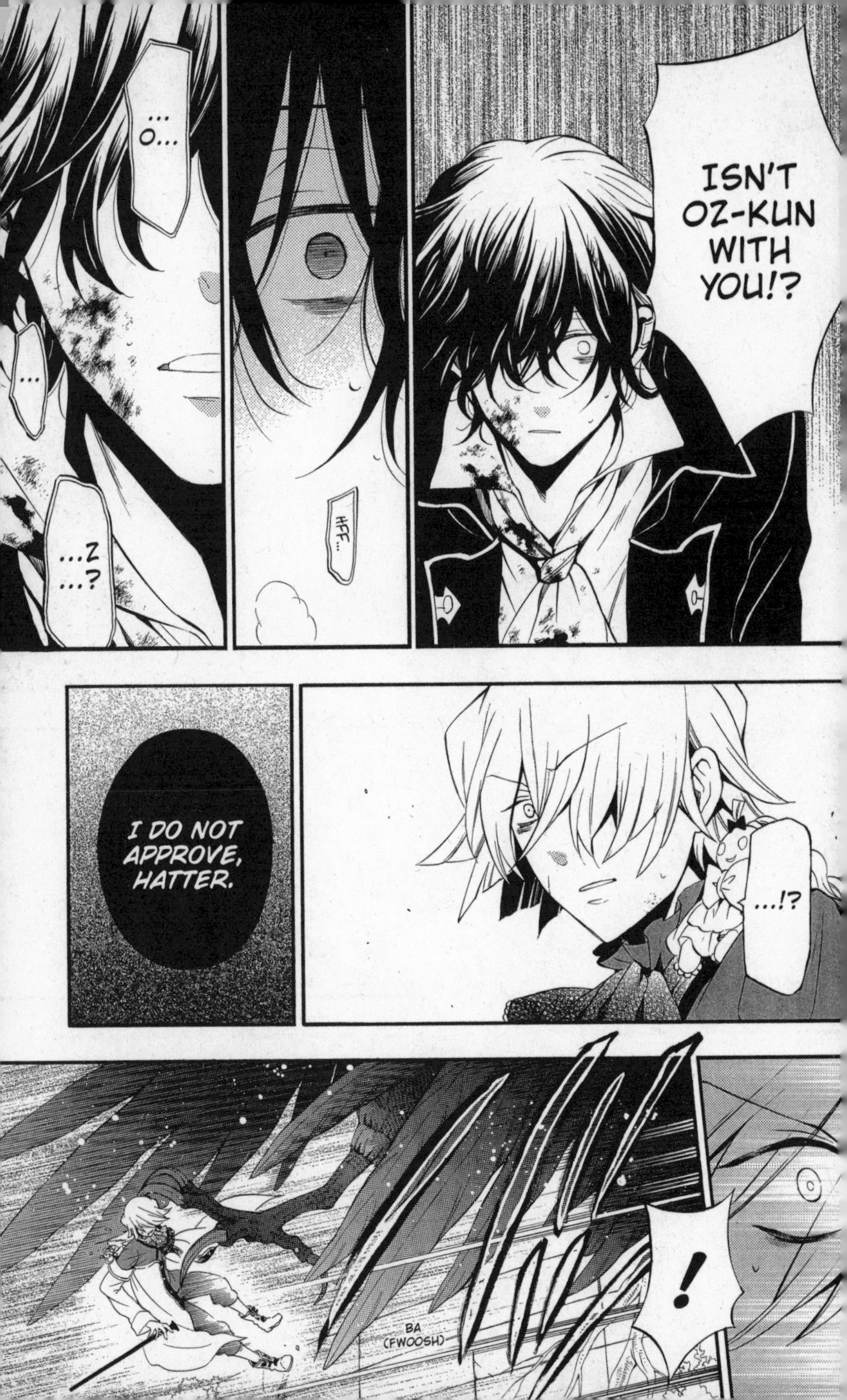
ISN'T OZ-KUN WITH YOU!?
HFF...
...O...
...
...Z ...?
...!?
I DO NOT APPROVE, HATTER.
!
BA (FWOOSH)

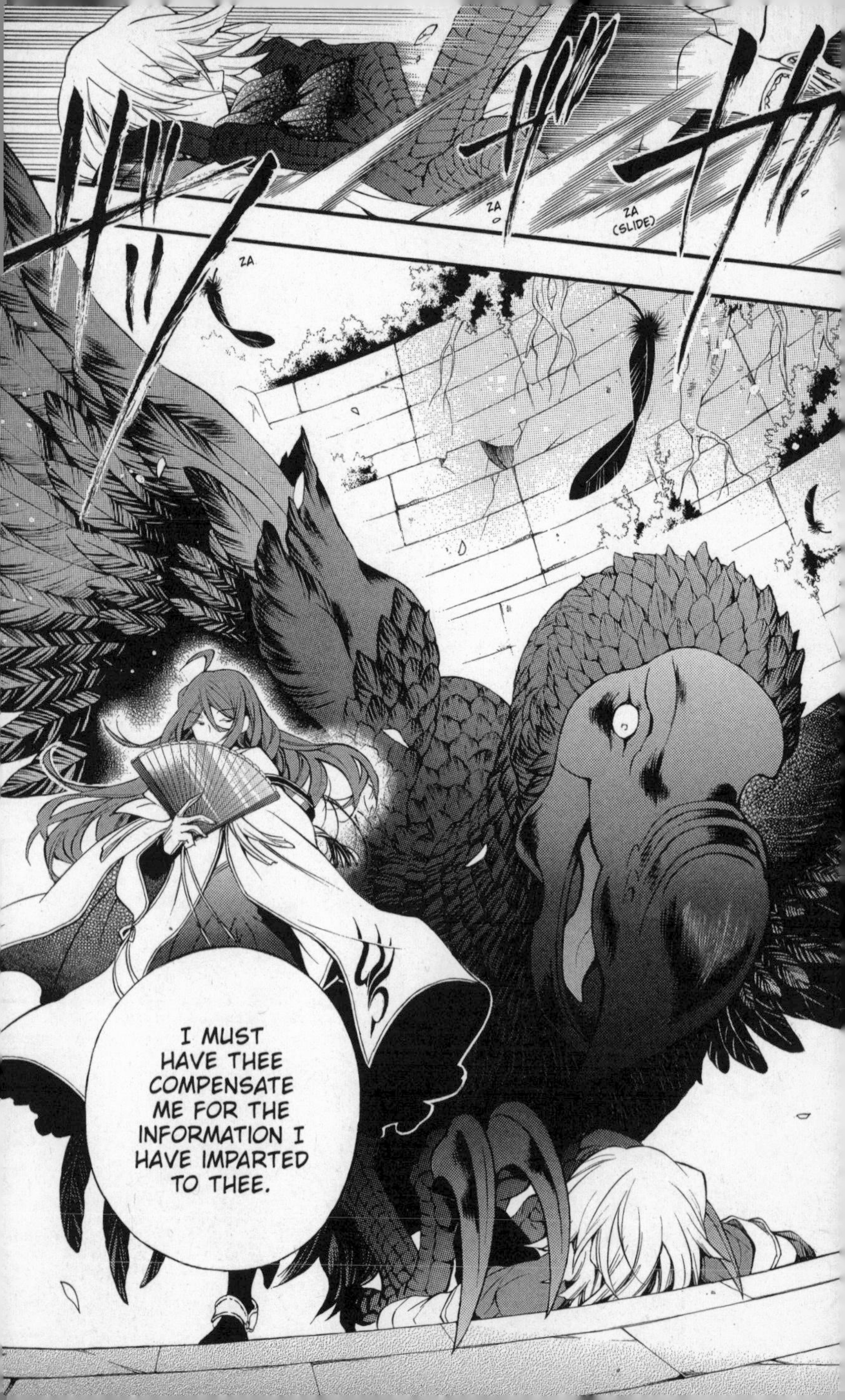
ZA (SLIDE)
ZA
ZA
I MUST HAVE THEE COMPENSATE ME FOR THE INFORMATION I HAVE IMPARTED TO THEE.

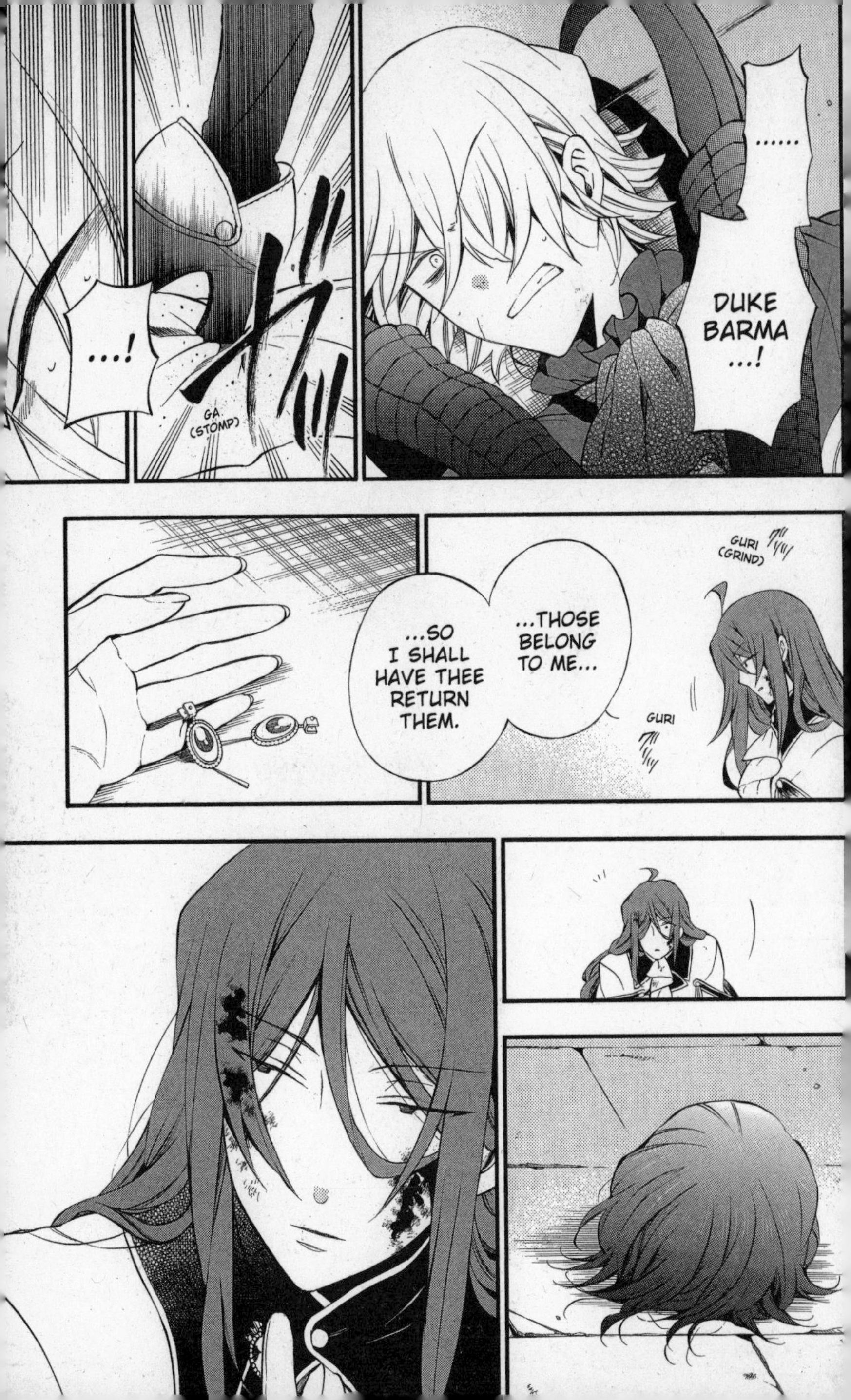
......
DUKE BARMA ...!
GA. (STOMP)
...!
GURI (GRIND)
...THOSE BELONG TO ME...
...SO I SHALL HAVE THEE RETURN THEM.
GURI

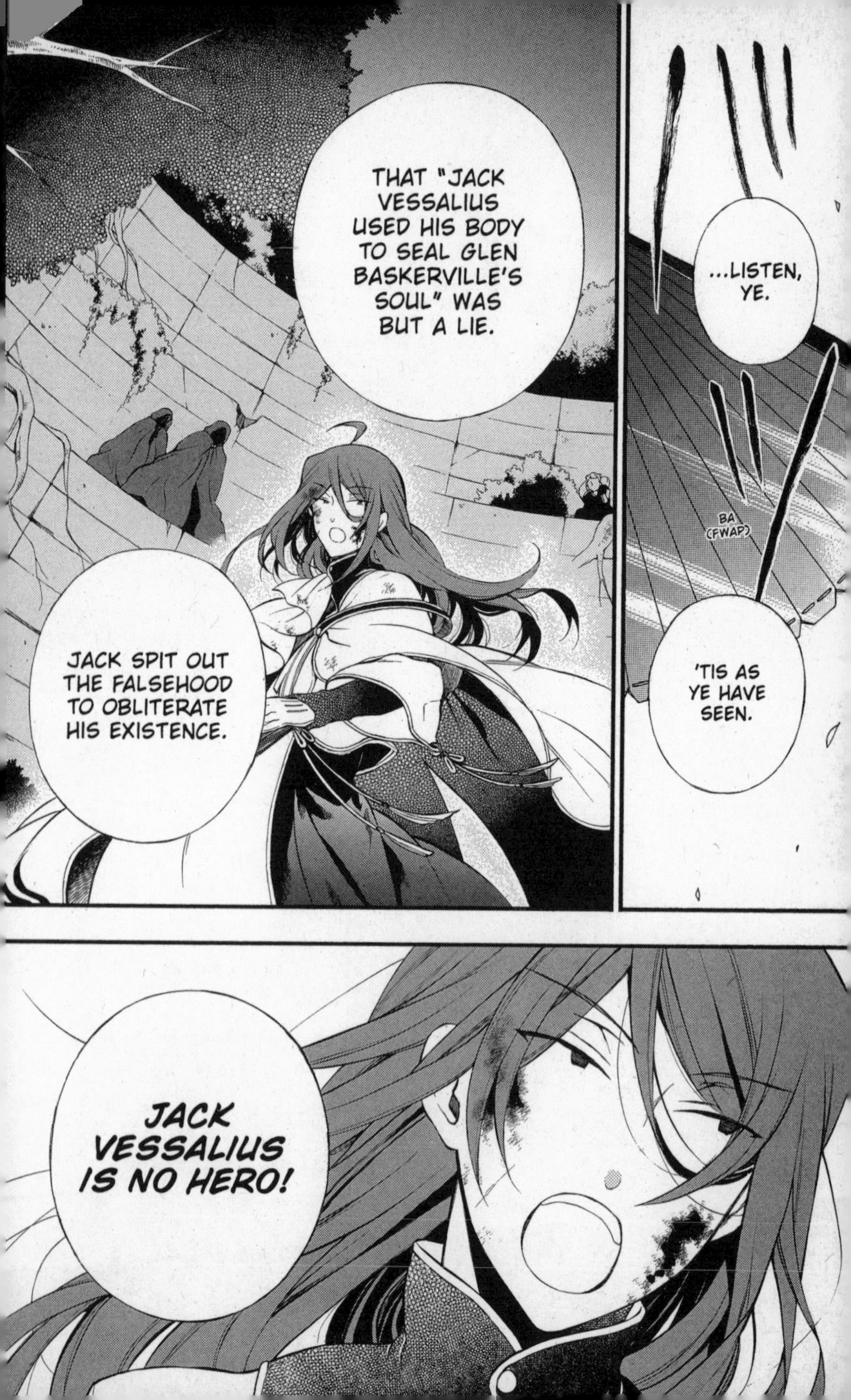
...LISTEN, YE.
BA (FWAP)
'TIS AS YE HAVE SEEN.
THAT "JACK VESSALIUS USED HIS BODY TO SEAL GLEN BASKERVILLE'S SOUL" WAS BUT A LIE.
JACK SPIT OUT THE FALSEHOOD TO OBLITERATE HIS EXISTENCE.
JACK VESSALIUS IS NO HERO!

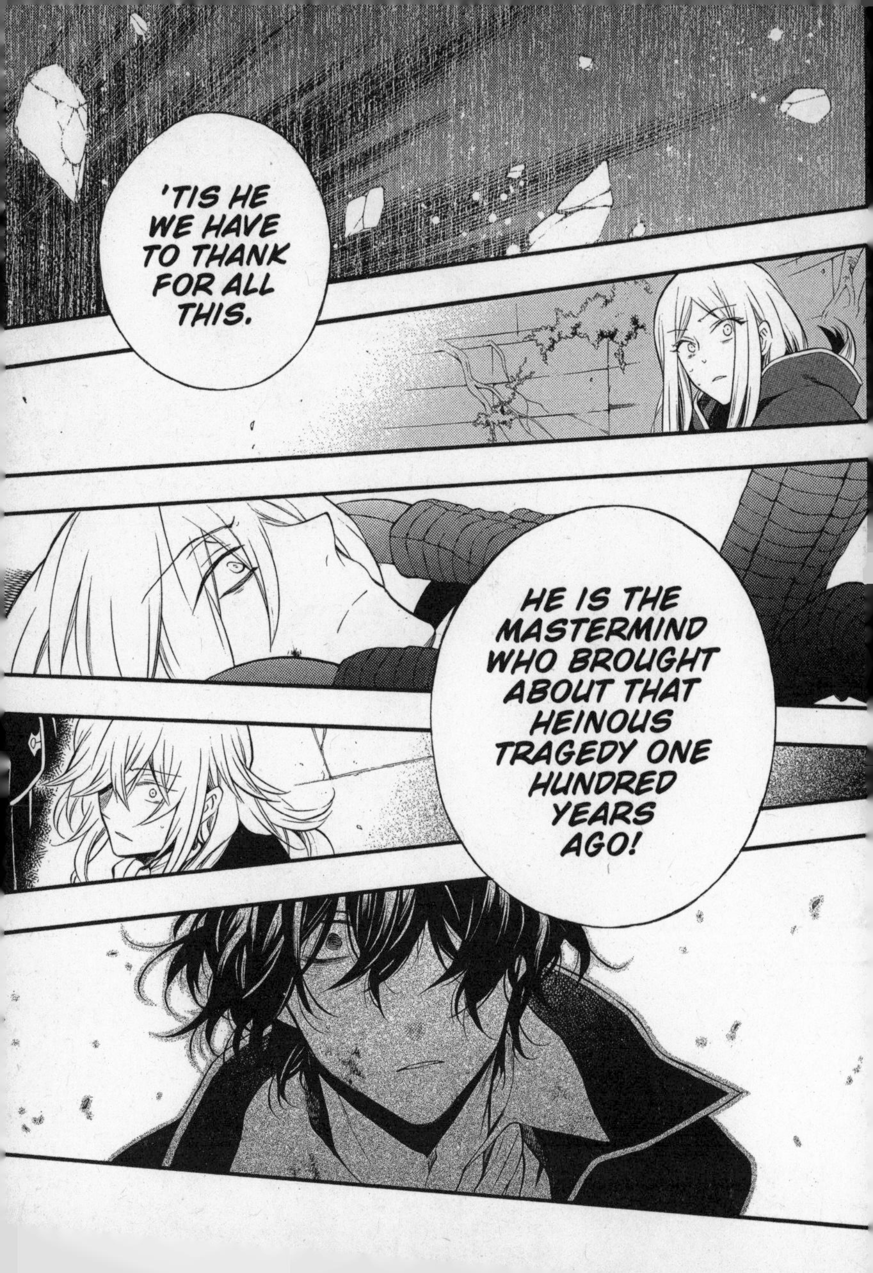
'TIS HE WE HAVE TO THANK FOR ALL THIS.
HE IS THE MASTERMIND WHO BROUGHT ABOUT THAT HEINOUS TRAGEDY ONE HUNDRED YEARS AGO!

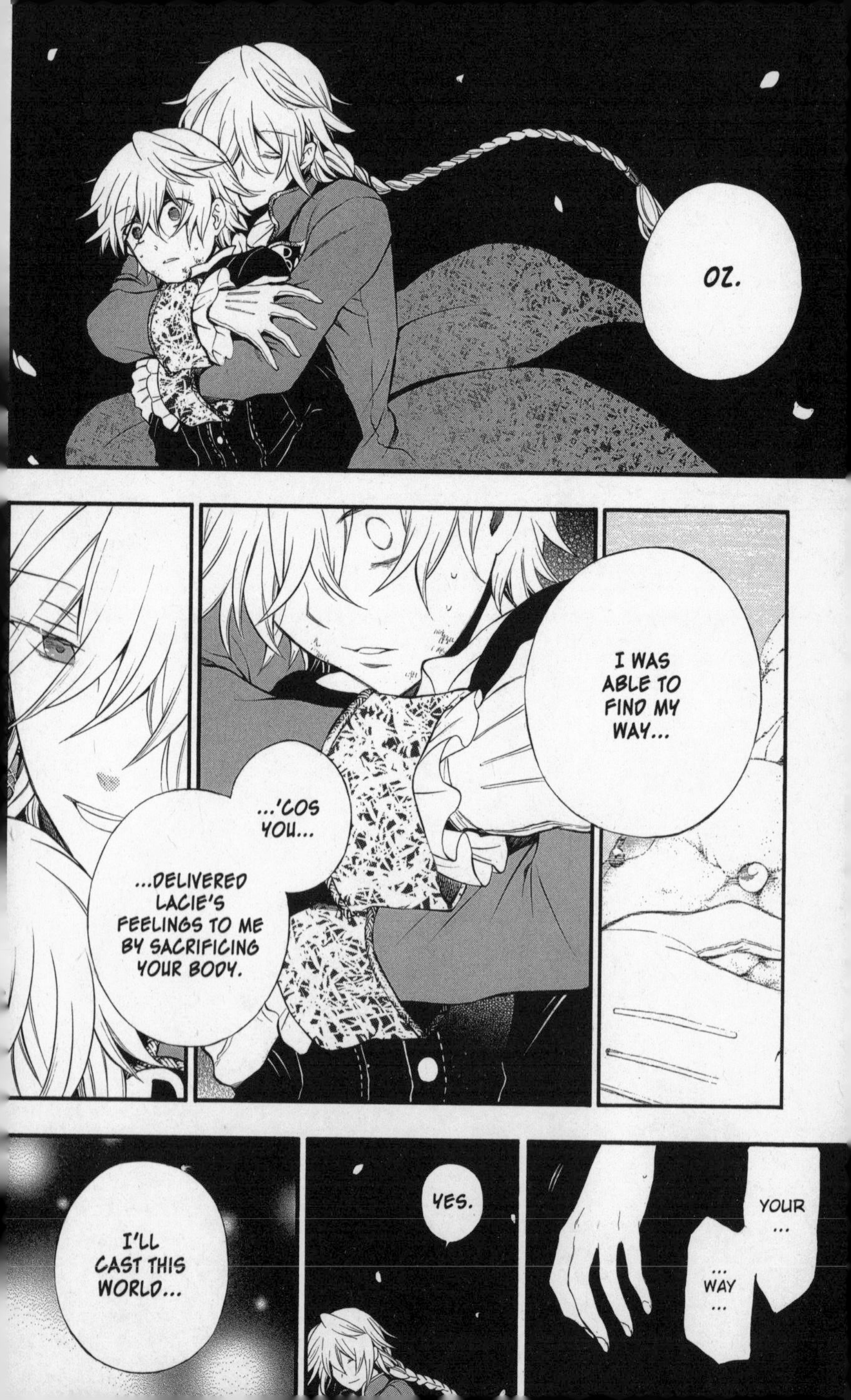
OZ.
I WAS ABLE TO FIND MY WAY...
...'COS YOU...
...DELIVERED LACIE'S FEELINGS TO ME BY SACRIFICING YOUR BODY.
YOUR...
...WAY...
YES.
I'LL CAST THIS WORLD...

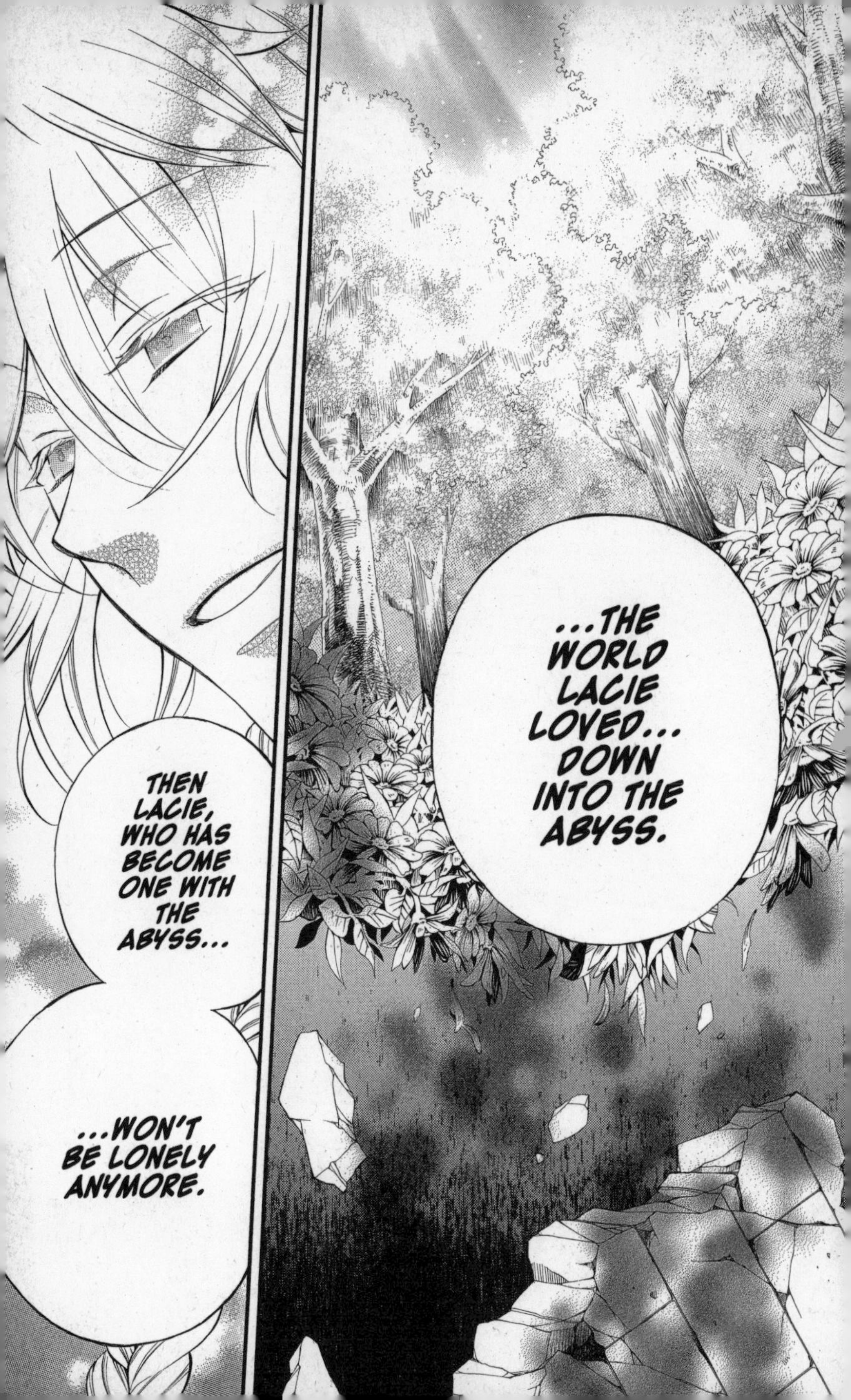
...THE WORLD LACIE LOVED... DOWN INTO THE ABYSS.
THEN LACIE, WHO HAS BECOME ONE WITH THE ABYSS...
...WON'T BE LONELY ANYMORE.

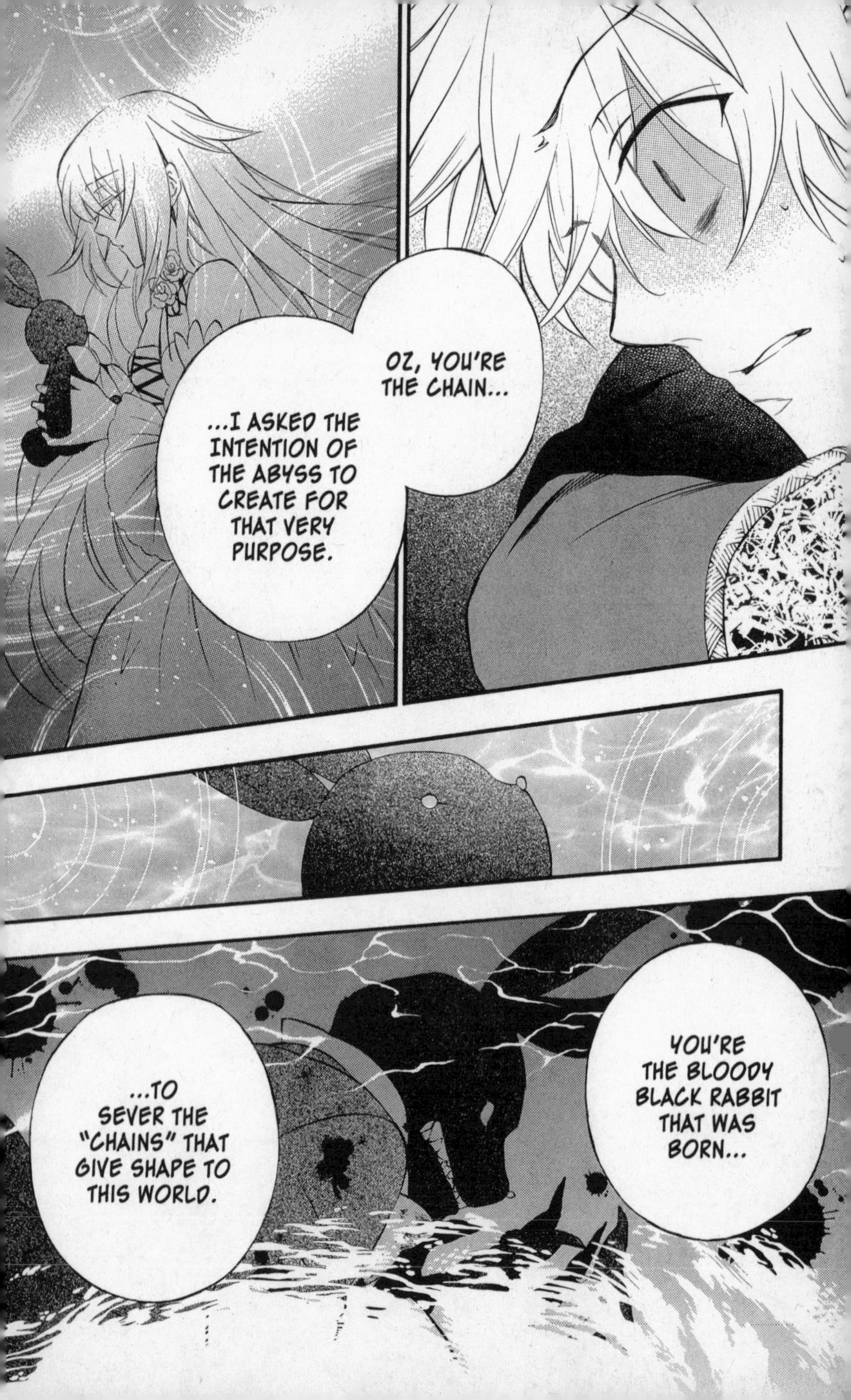
OZ, YOU'RE THE CHAIN...
...I ASKED THE INTENTION OF THE ABYSS TO CREATE FOR THAT VERY PURPOSE.
YOU'RE THE BLOODY BLACK RABBIT THAT WAS BORN...
...TO SEVER THE "CHAINS" THAT GIVE SHAPE TO THIS WORLD.

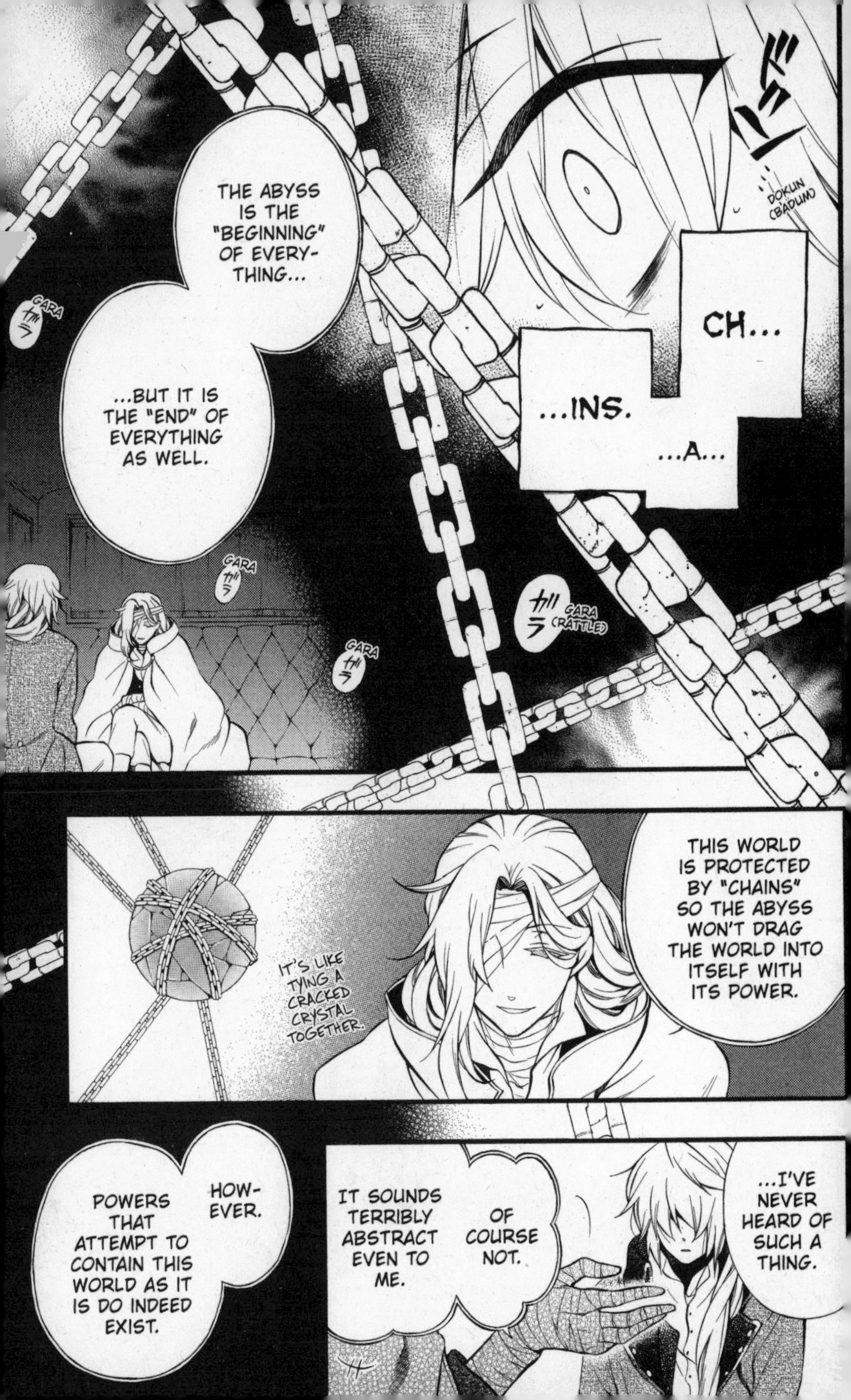
DOKUN (BADUM)
CH...
...A...
...INS.
GARA (RATTLE)
THE ABYSS IS THE "BEGINNING" OF EVERY-THING...
...BUT IT IS THE "END" OF EVERYTHING AS WELL.
GARA
GARA
GARA
THIS WORLD IS PROTECTED BY "CHAINS" SO THE ABYSS WON'T DRAG THE WORLD INTO ITSELF WITH ITS POWER.
IT'S LIKE TYING A CRACKED CRYSTAL TOGETHER.
...I'VE NEVER HEARD OF SUCH A THING.
OF COURSE NOT.
IT SOUNDS TERRIBLY ABSTRACT EVEN TO ME.
HOW-EVER.
POWERS THAT ATTEMPT TO CONTAIN THIS WORLD AS IT IS DO INDEED EXIST.

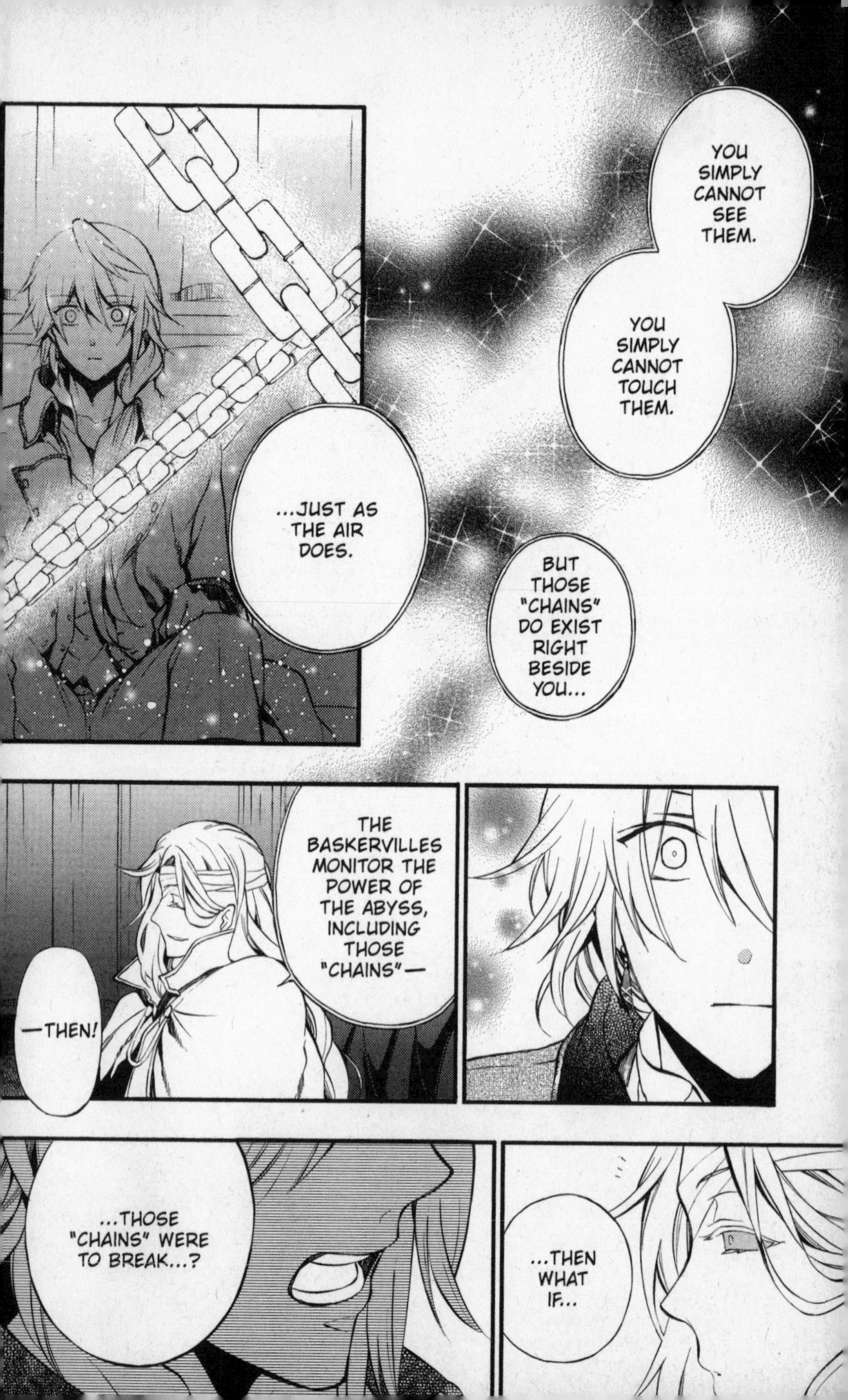
YOU SIMPLY CANNOT SEE THEM.
YOU SIMPLY CANNOT TOUCH THEM.
...JUST AS THE AIR DOES.
BUT THOSE "CHAINS" DO EXIST RIGHT BESIDE YOU...
THE BASKERVILLES MONITOR THE POWER OF THE ABYSS, INCLUDING THOSE "CHAINS"—
—THEN!
...THEN WHAT IF...
...THOSE "CHAINS" WERE TO BREAK...?

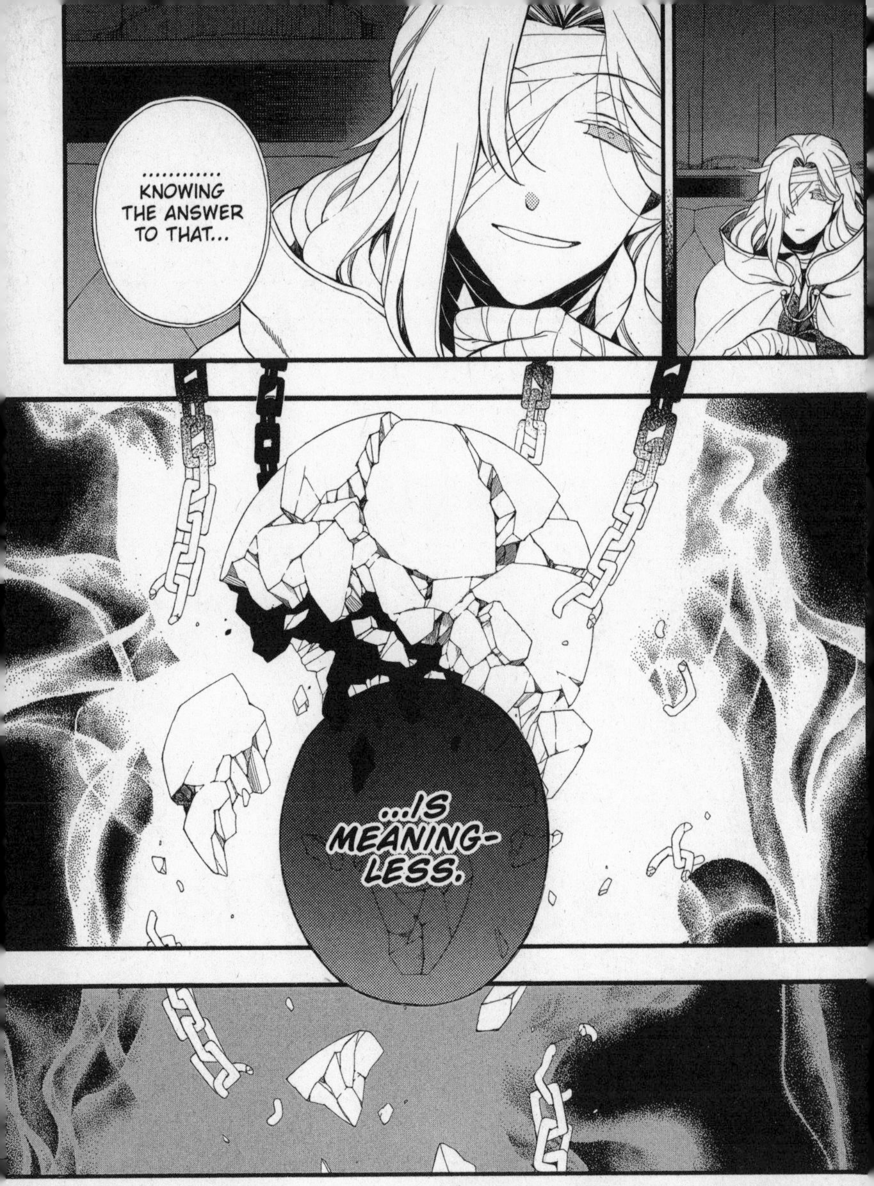
.... KNOWING THE ANSWER TO THAT...
...IS MEANING-LESS.

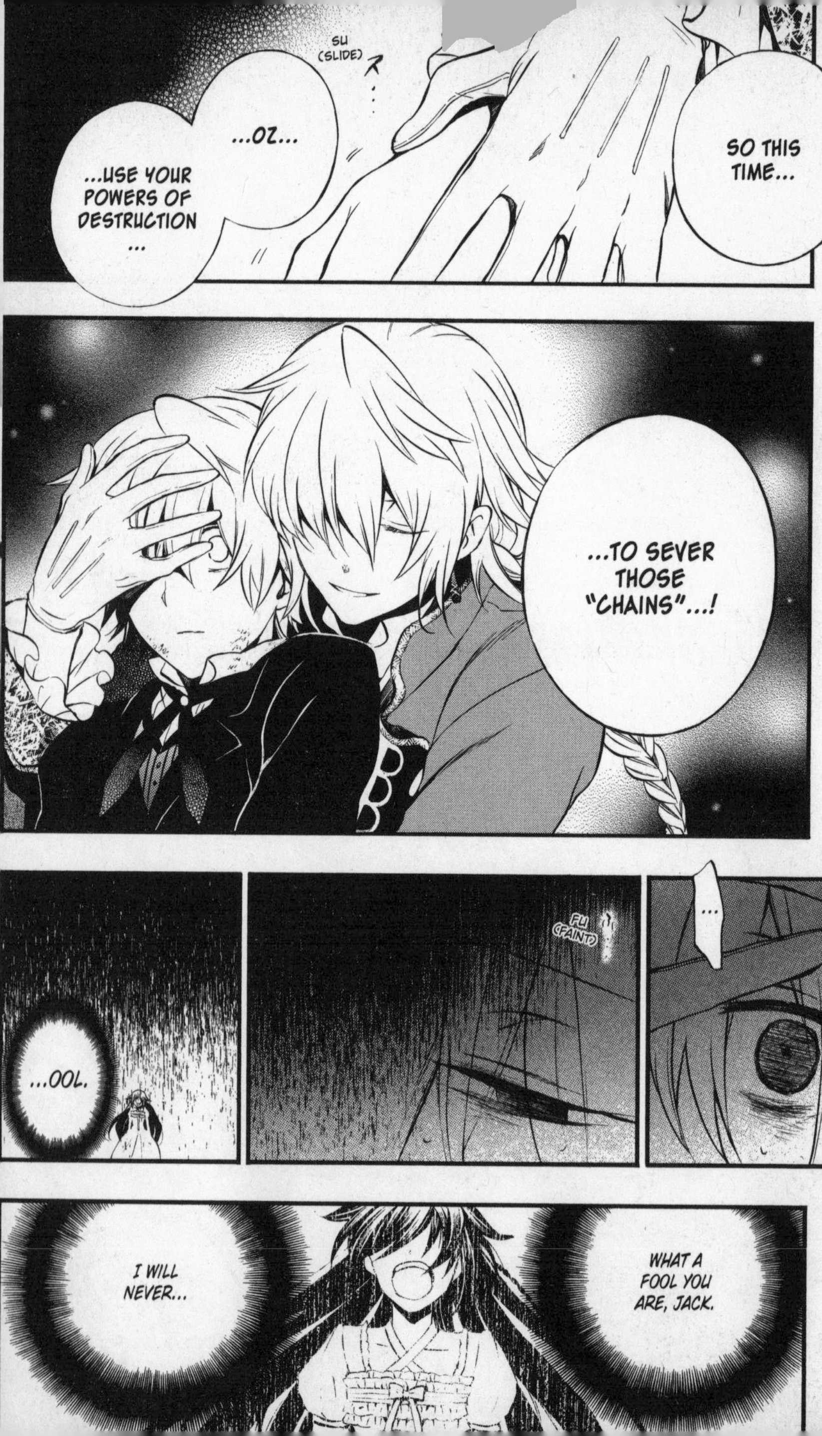
SO THIS TIME...
SU (SLIDE)
...OZ...
...USE YOUR POWERS OF DESTRUCTION ...
...TO SEVER THOSE "CHAINS"...!
...
FU (FAINT)
...OOL.
WHAT A FOOL YOU ARE, JACK.
I WILL NEVER...

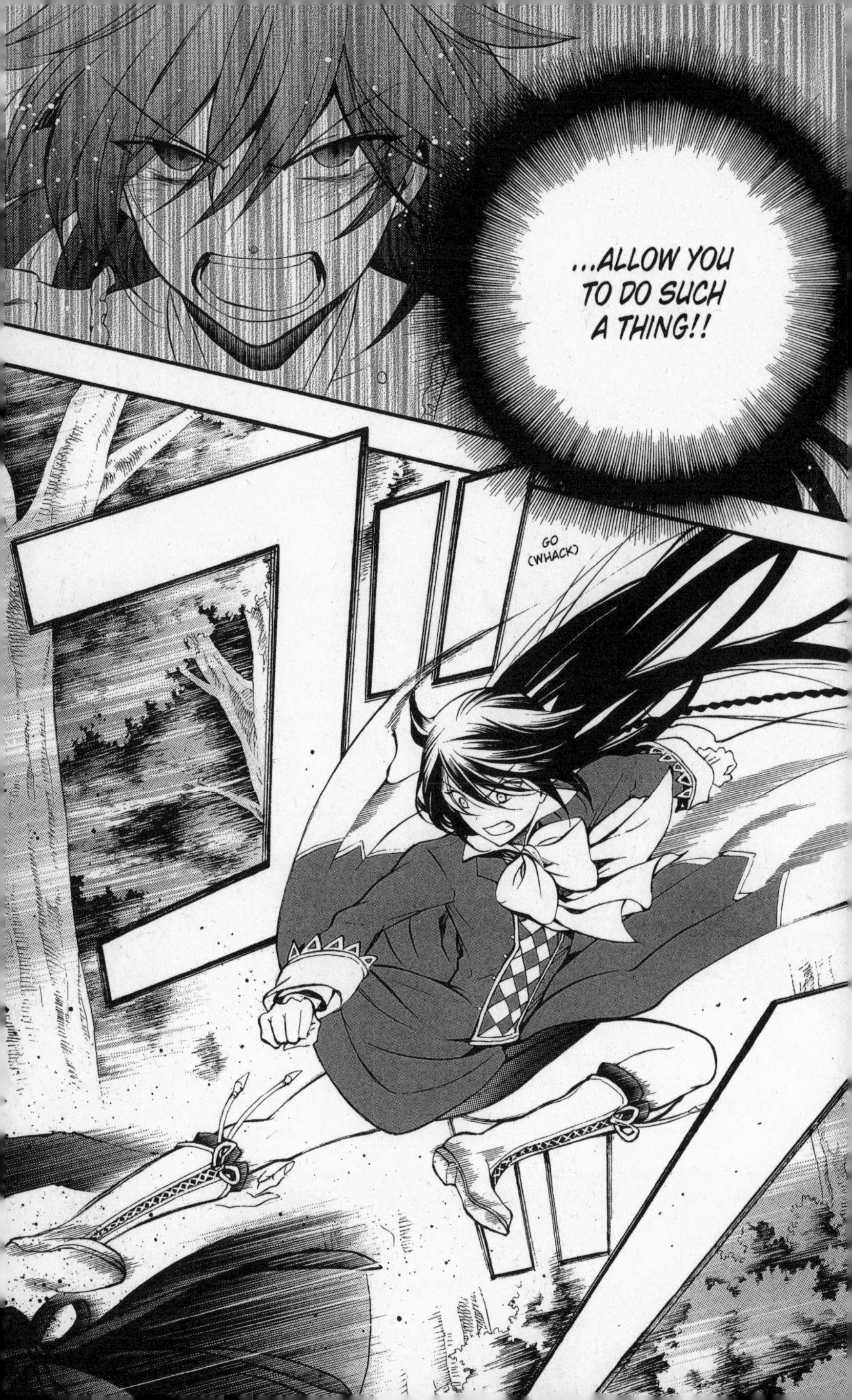
...ALLOW YOU TO DO SUCH A THING!!
GO (WHACK)

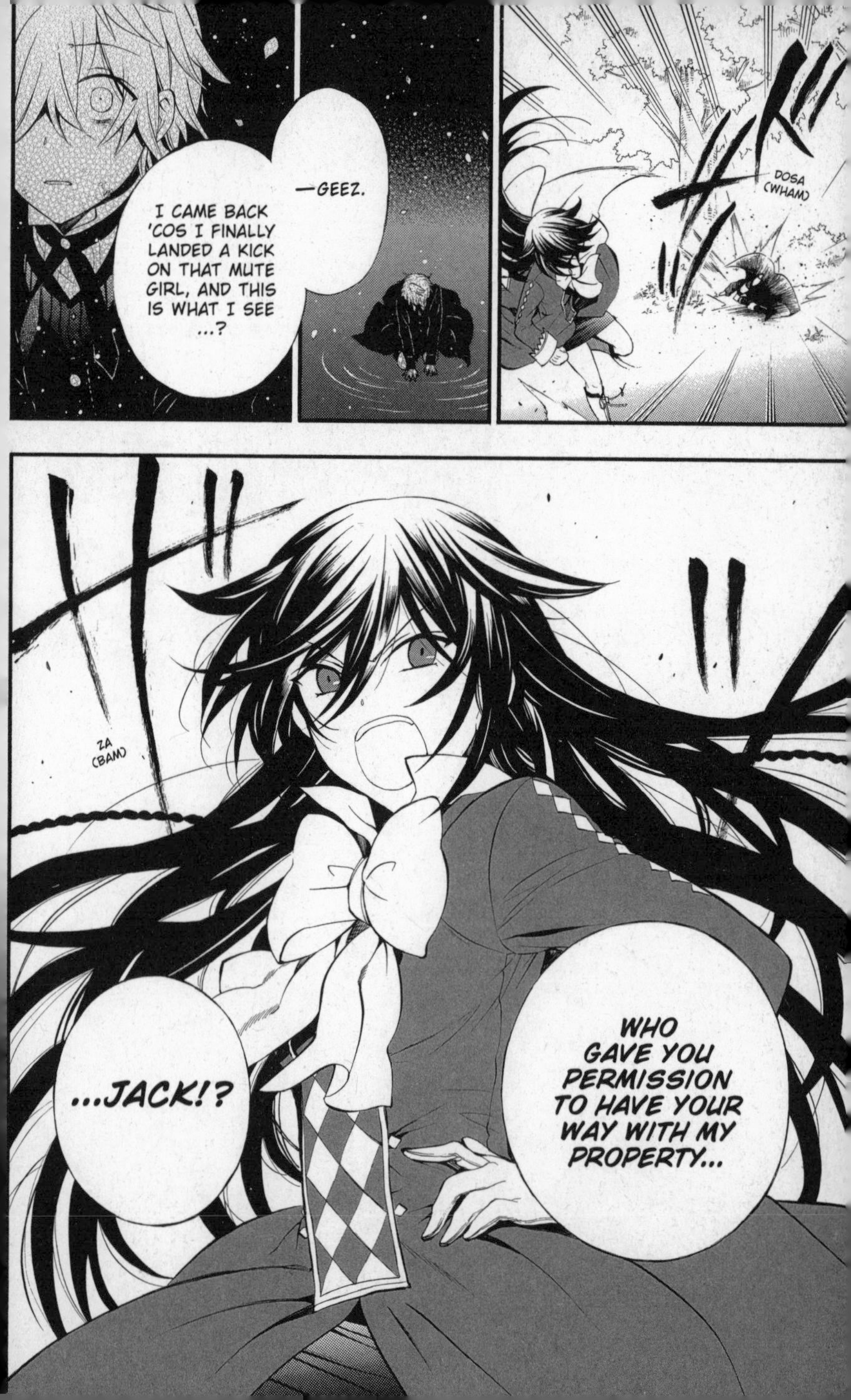
DOSA (WHAM)
—GEEZ.
I CAME BACK 'COS I FINALLY LANDED A KICK ON THAT MUTE GIRL, AND THIS IS WHAT I SEE ...?
ZA (BAM)
WHO GAVE YOU PERMISSION TO HAVE YOUR WAY WITH MY PROPERTY...
...JACK!?

Retrace:LXXII Bloody Rabbit

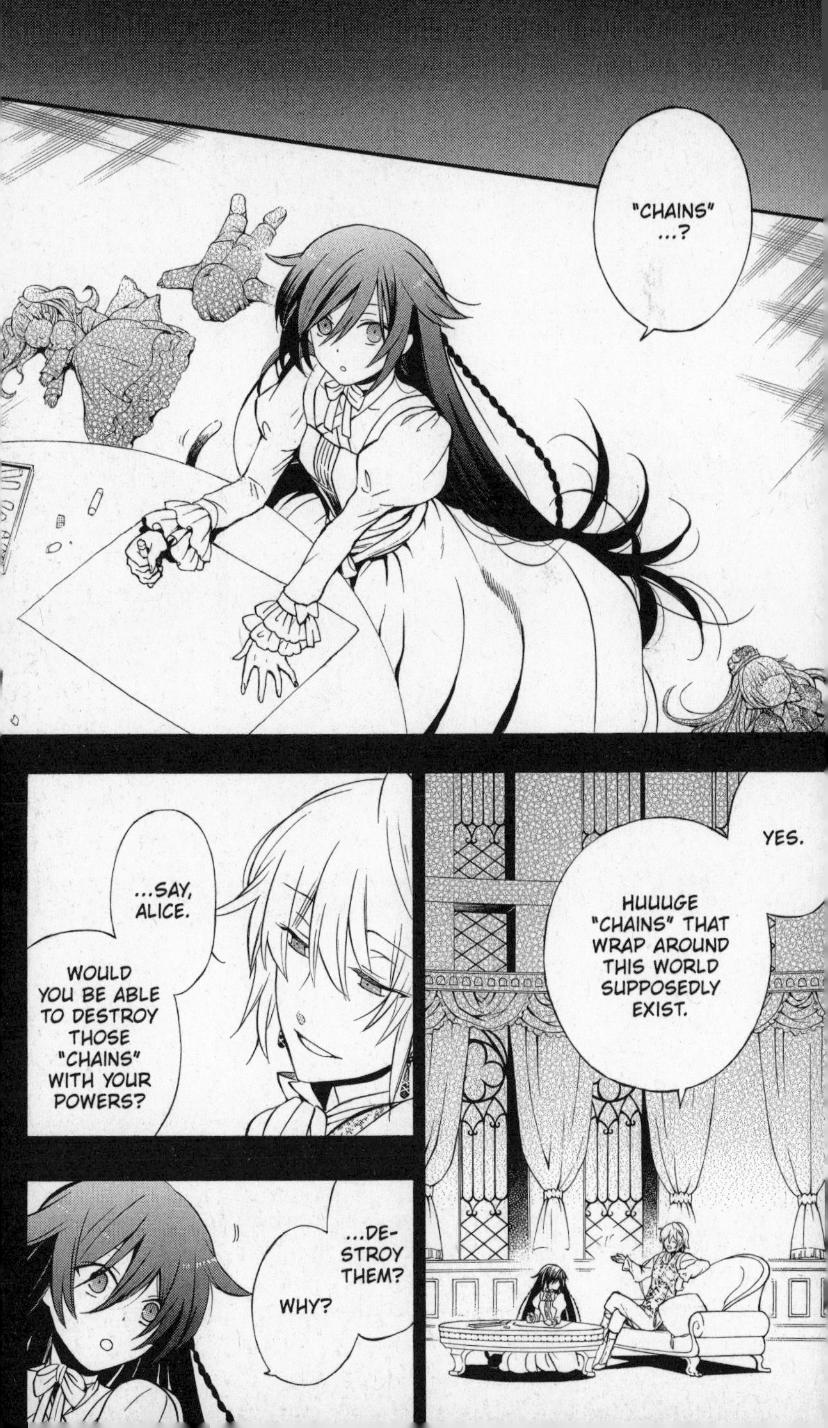
"CHAINS" ...?
YES.
HUUUGE "CHAINS" THAT WRAP AROUND THIS WORLD SUPPOSEDLY EXIST.
...SAY, ALICE.
WOULD YOU BE ABLE TO DESTROY THOSE "CHAINS" WITH YOUR POWERS?
...DE-STROY THEM?
WHY?

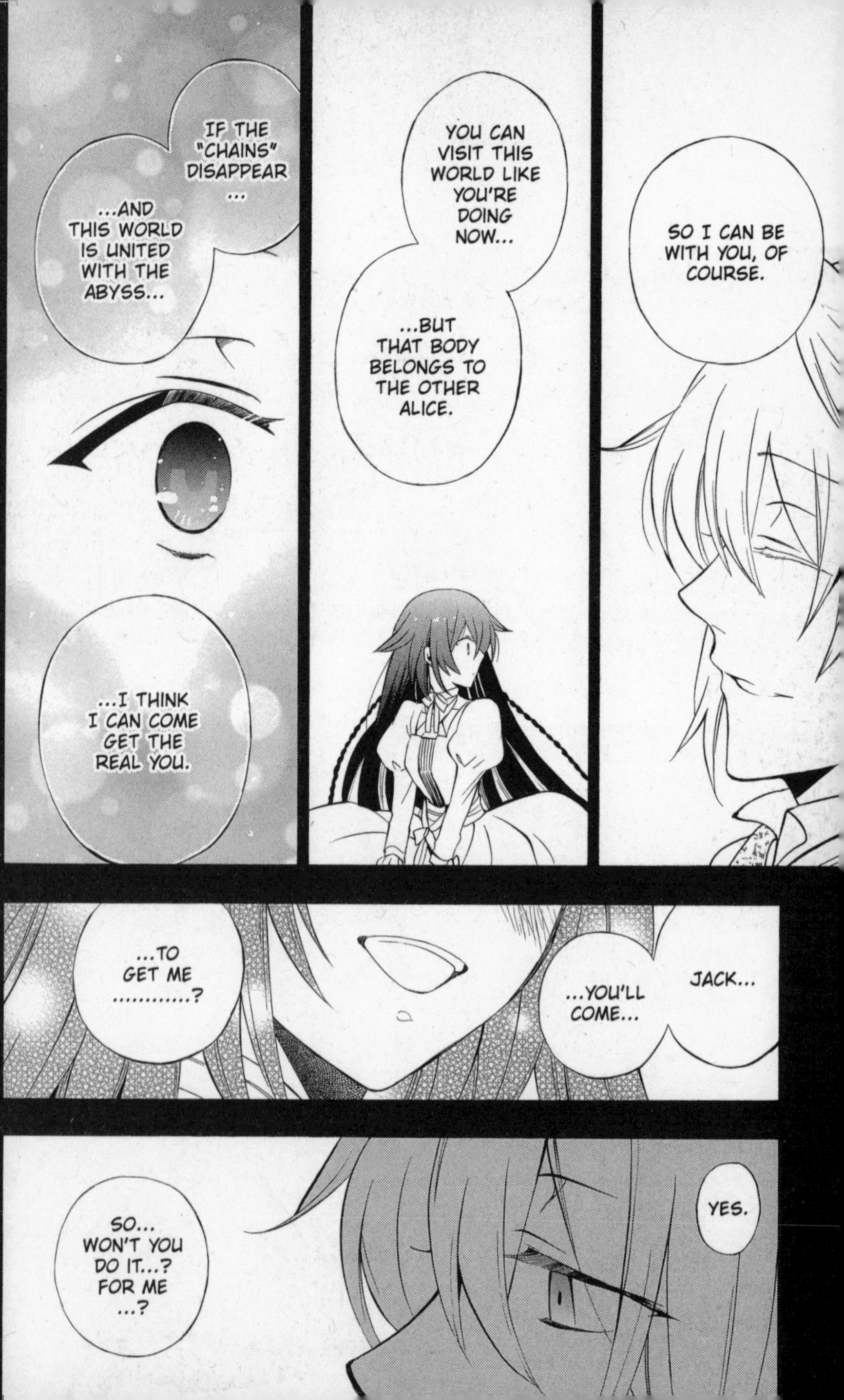
SO I CAN BE WITH YOU, OF COURSE.
YOU CAN VISIT THIS WORLD LIKE YOU'RE DOING NOW...
...BUT THAT BODY BELONGS TO THE OTHER ALICE.
IF THE "CHAINS" DISAPPEAR...
...AND THIS WORLD IS UNITED WITH THE ABYSS...
...I THINK I CAN COME GET THE REAL YOU.
JACK...
...YOU'LL COME...
...TO GET ME ....?
YES.
SO... WON'T YOU DO IT...? FOR ME ...?

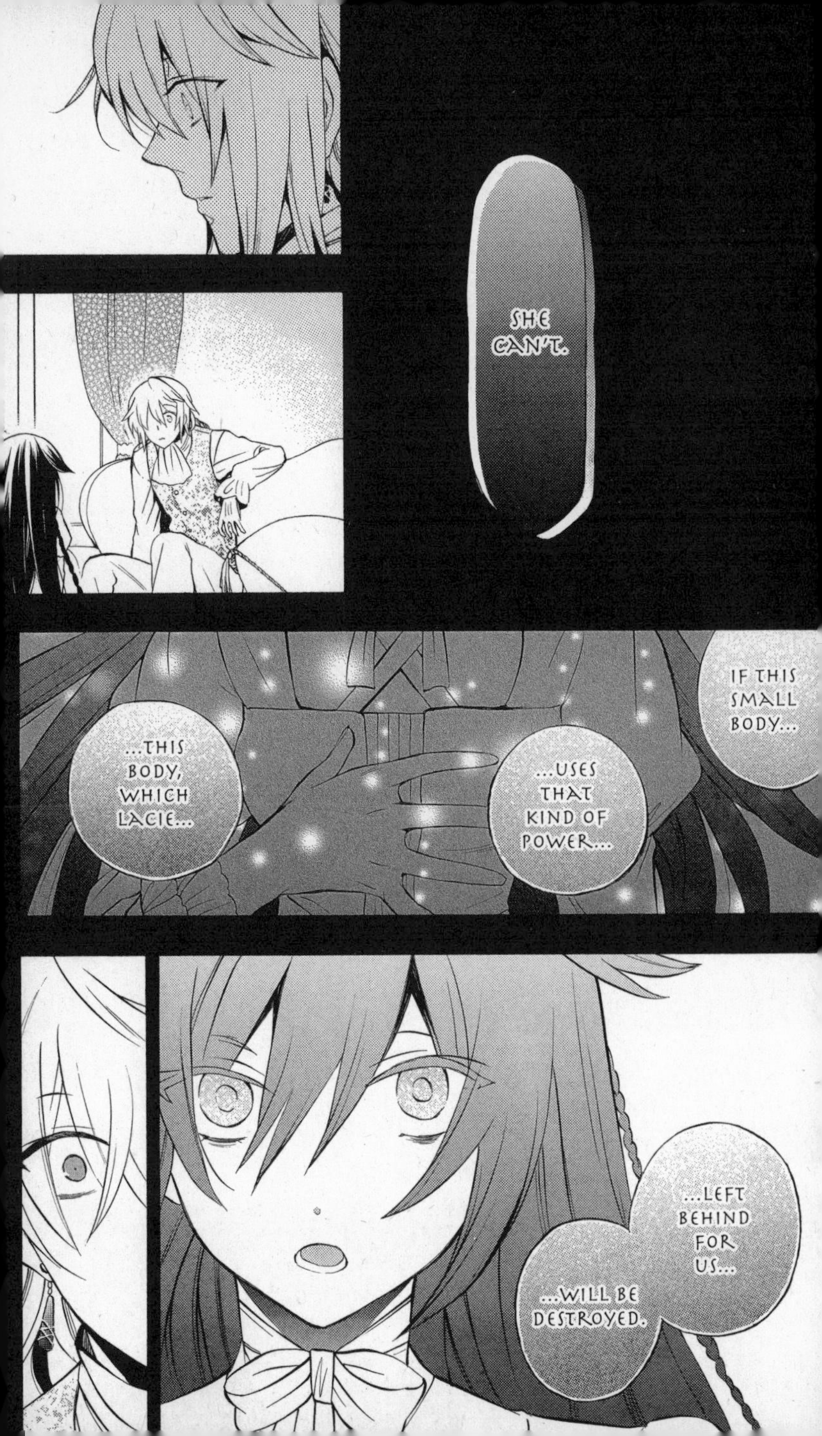
SHE CAN'T.
IF THIS SMALL BODY...
...USES THAT KIND OF POWER...
...THIS BODY, WHICH LACIE...
...LEFT BEHIND FOR US...
...WILL BE DESTROYED.

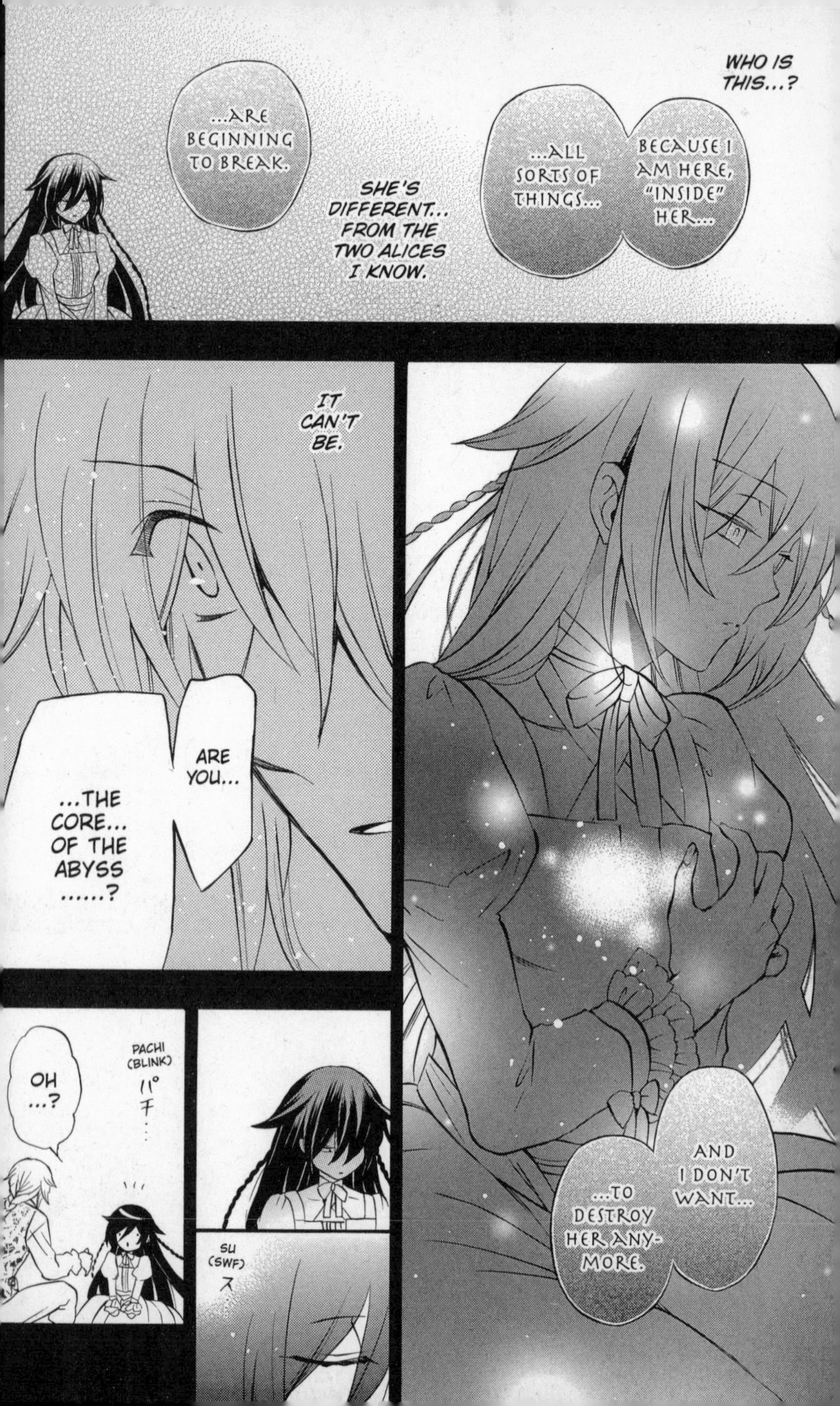
WHO IS THIS...?
BECAUSE I AM HERE, "INSIDE" HER...
...ALL SORTS OF THINGS...
SHE'S DIFFERENT... FROM THE TWO ALICES I KNOW.
...ARE BEGINNING TO BREAK.
AND I DON'T WANT...
...TO DESTROY HER ANY-MORE.
IT CAN'T BE.
ARE YOU...
...THE CORE... OF THE ABYSS ......?
SU (SWF)
ス
PACHI (BLINK)
パチ…
OH ...?

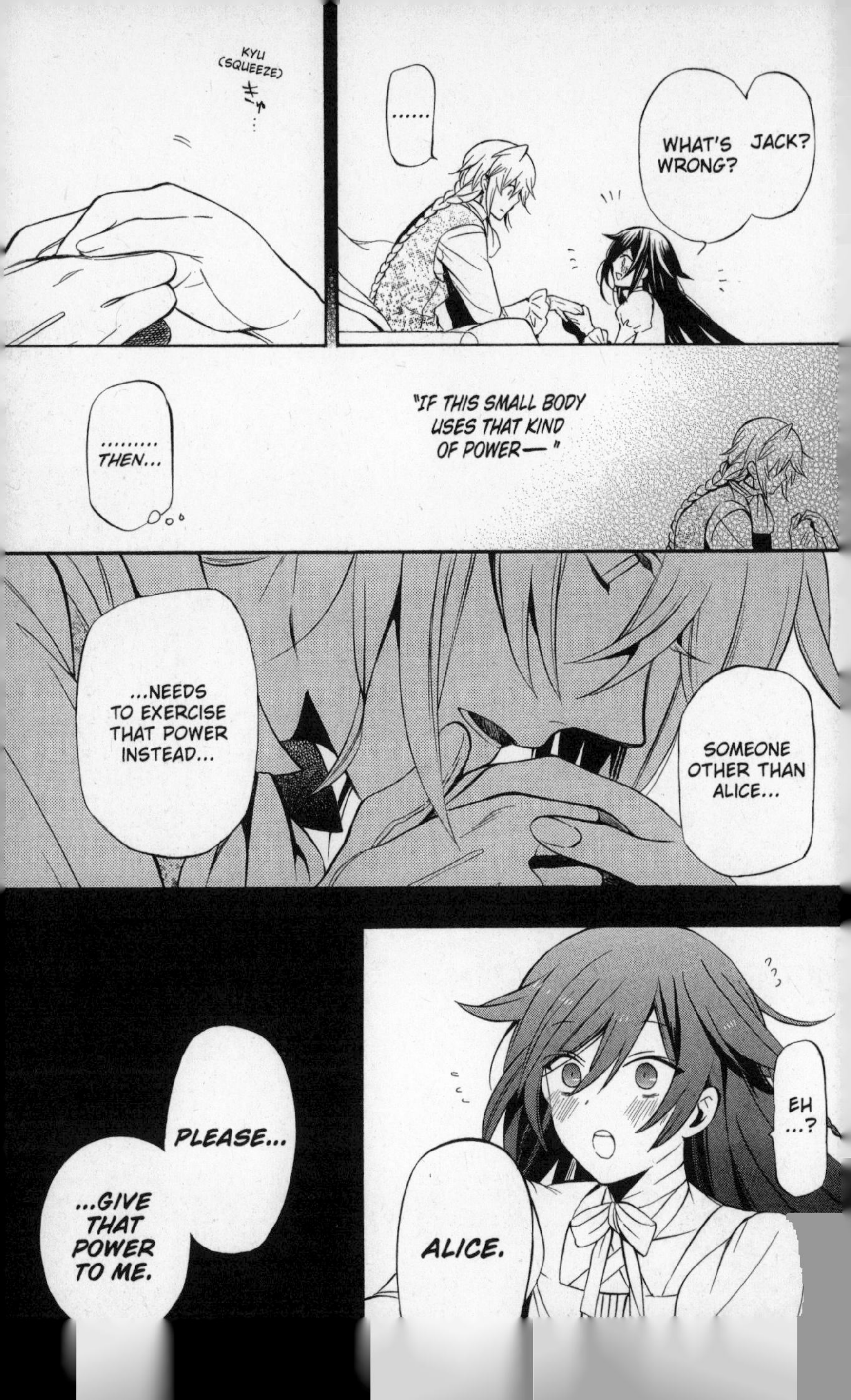
JACK? WHAT'S WRONG?
......
KYU (SQUEEZE)
"IF THIS SMALL BODY USES THAT KIND OF POWER—"
.... THEN...
SOMEONE OTHER THAN ALICE...
...NEEDS TO EXERCISE THAT POWER INSTEAD...
EH ...?
ALICE.
PLEASE...
...GIVE THAT POWER TO ME.

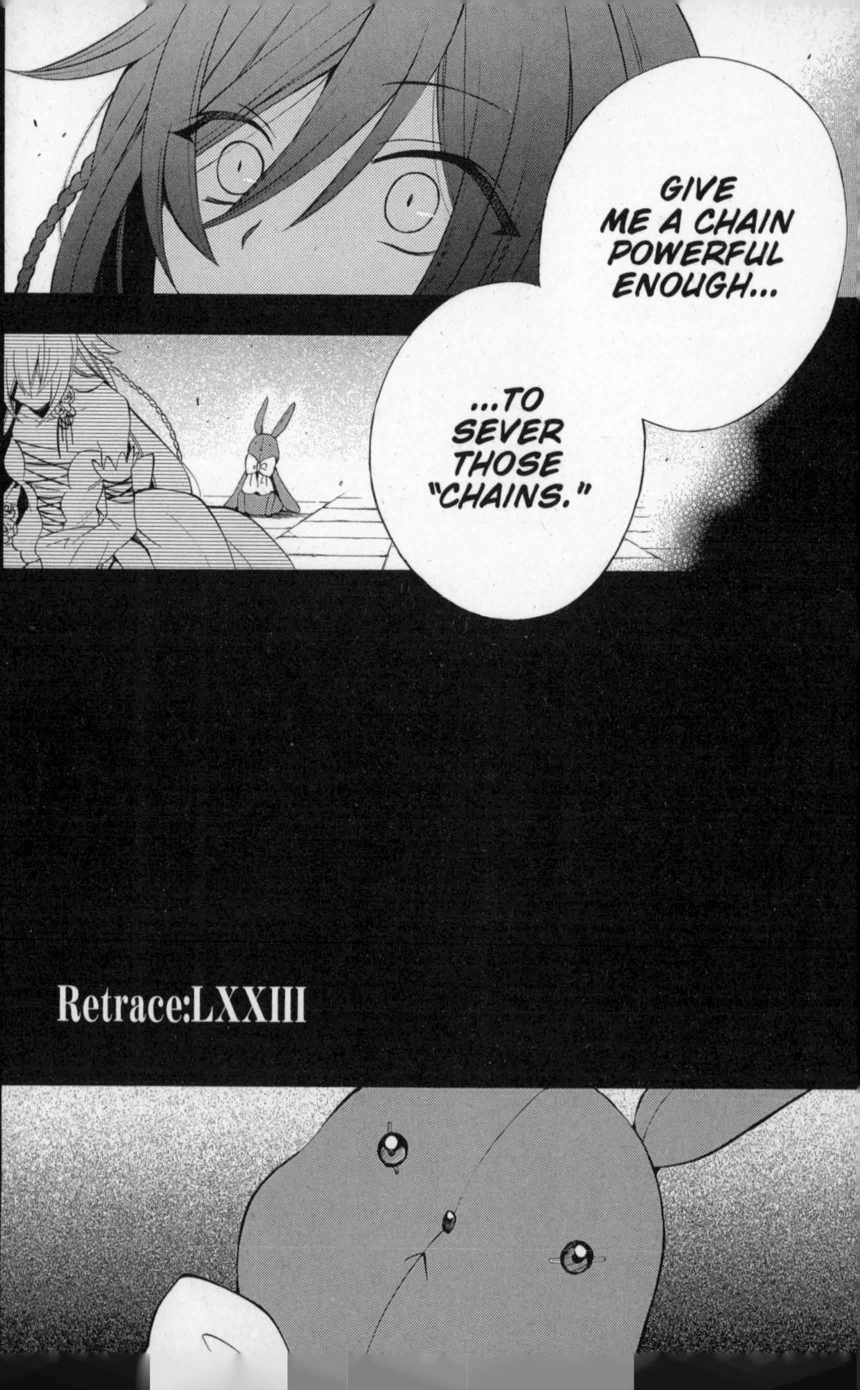
GIVE ME A CHAIN POWERFUL ENOUGH...
...TO SEVER THOSE "CHAINS."
Retrace:LXXIII

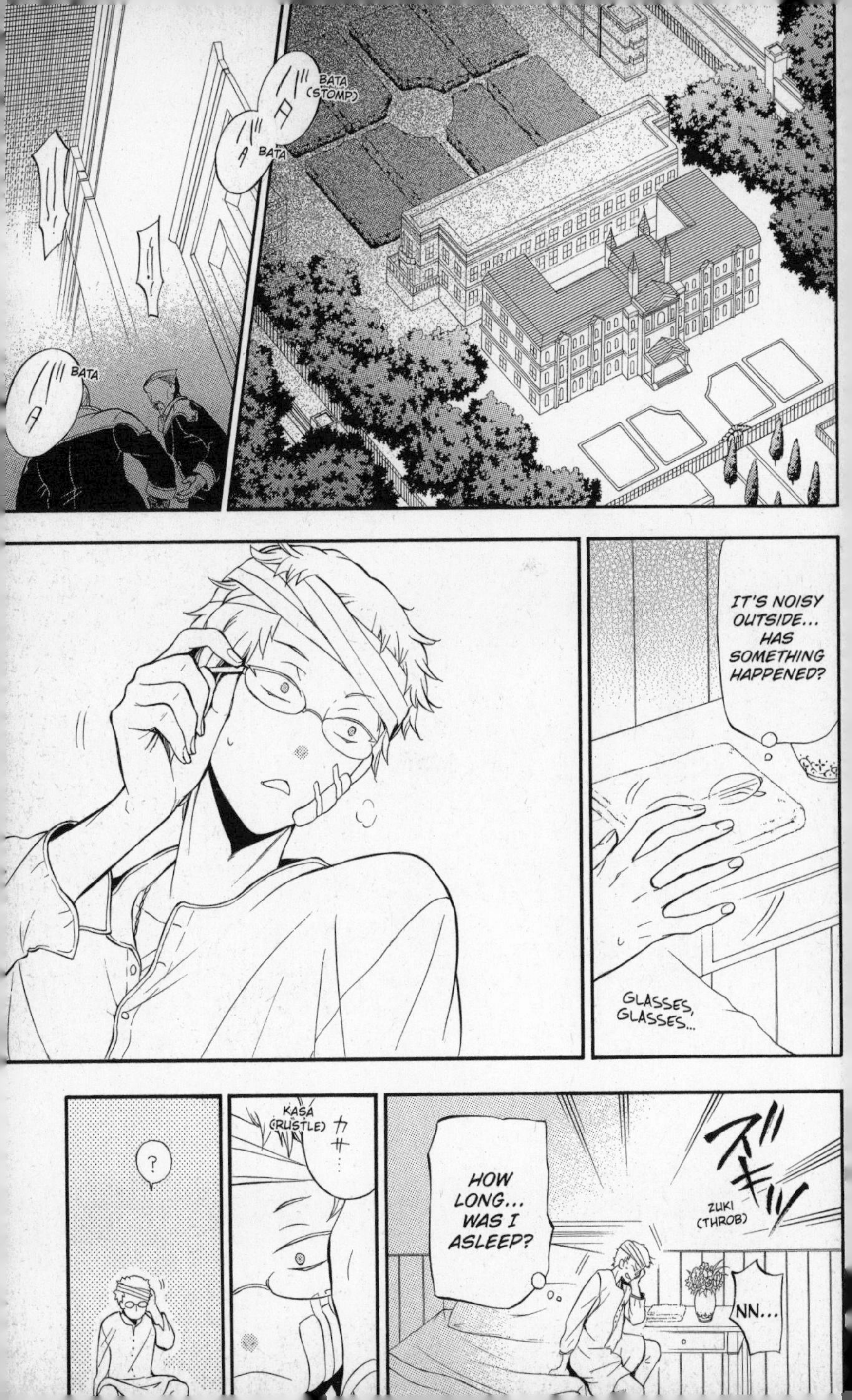
BATA (STOMP)
BATA
BATA
IT'S NOISY OUTSIDE... HAS SOMETHING HAPPENED?
GLASSES, GLASSES...
ZUKI (THROB)
NN...
HOW LONG... WAS I ASLEEP?
KASA (RUSTLE)
?

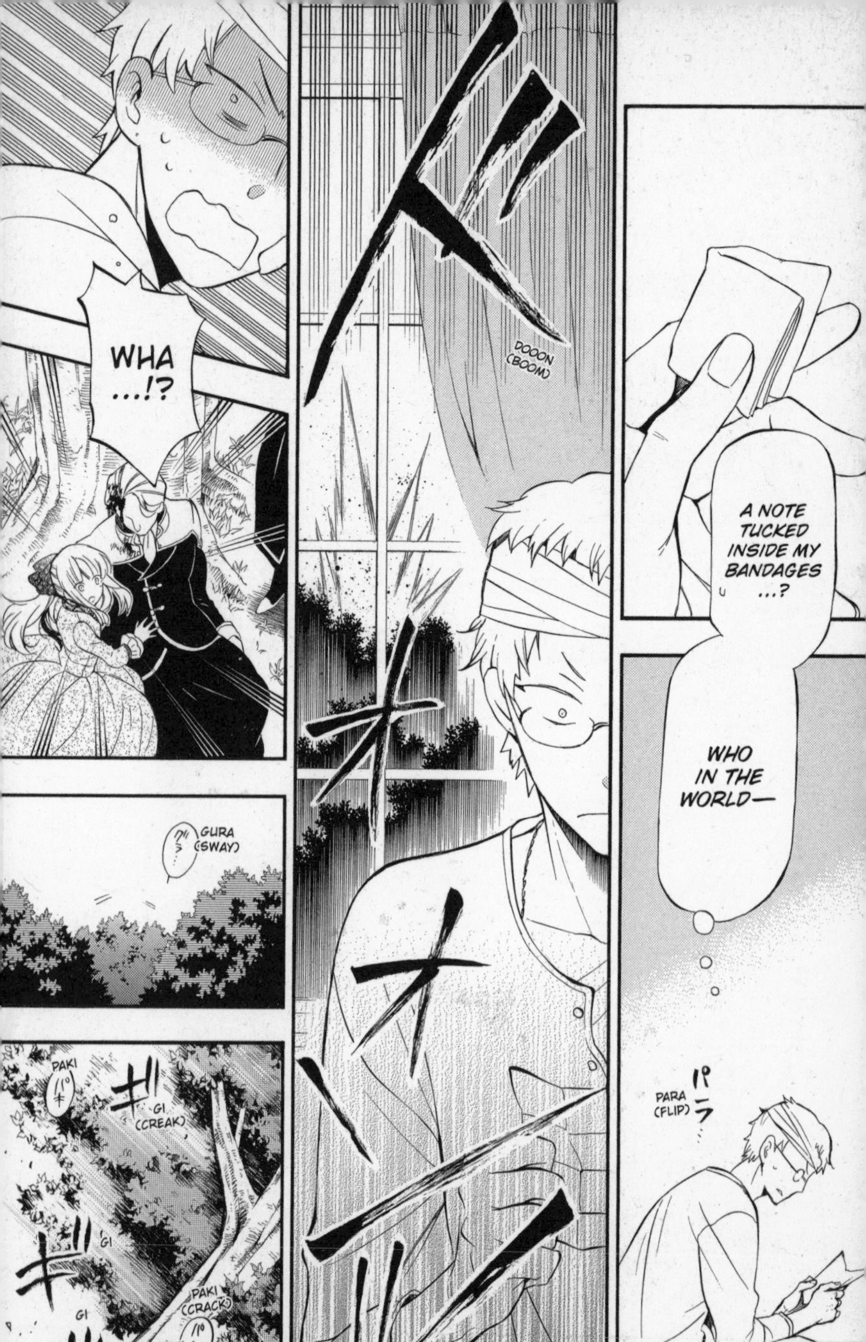
A NOTE TUCKED INSIDE MY BANDAGES ...?
WHO IN THE WORLD—
PARA (FLIP)
DOOON (BOOM)
WHA ...!?
GURA (SWAY)
PAKI
GI (CREAK)
GI
PAKI (CRACK)
GI
PAKI

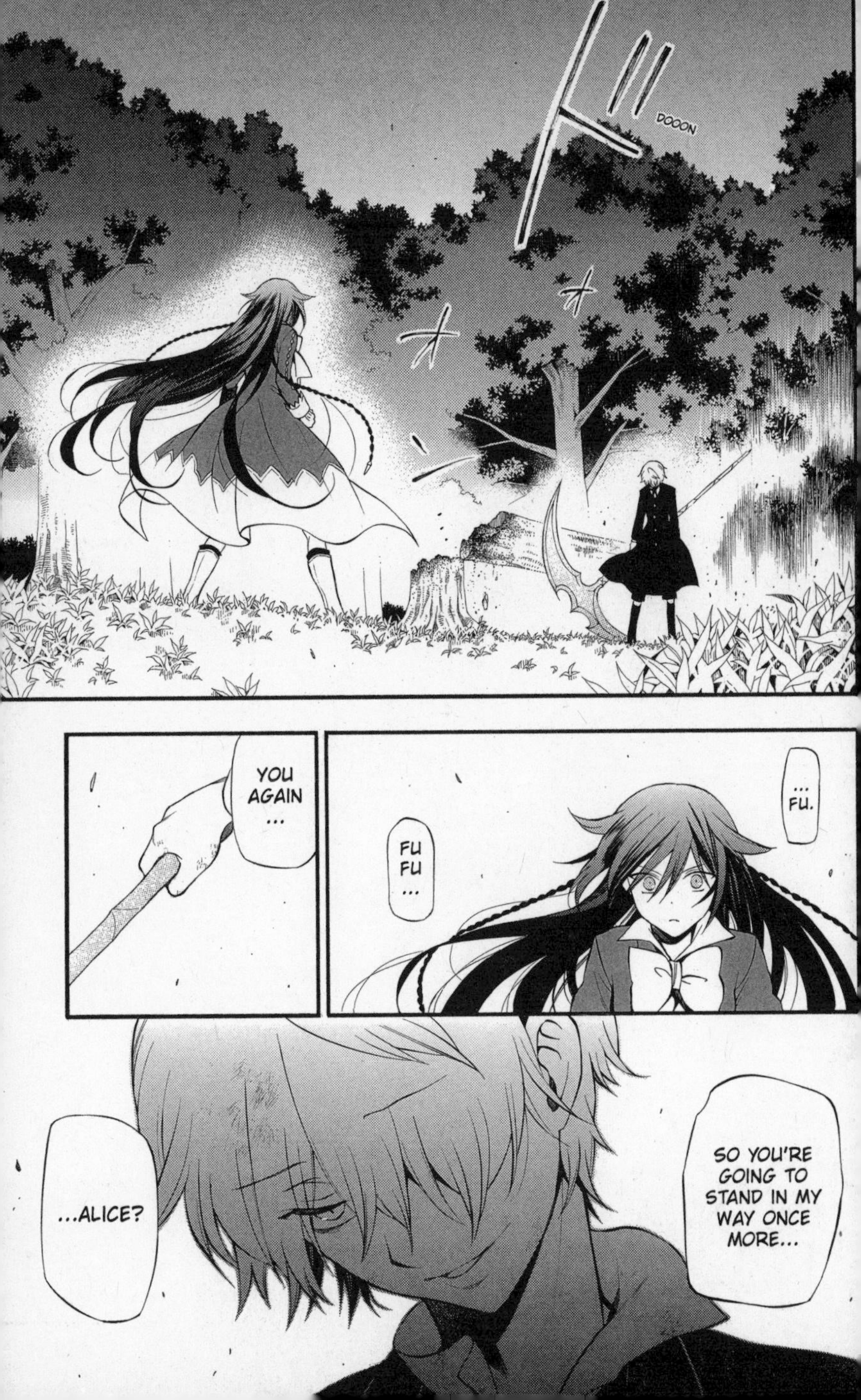
DOOON
...FU.
FU FU ...
YOU AGAIN ...
SO YOU'RE GOING TO STAND IN MY WAY ONCE MORE...
...ALICE?

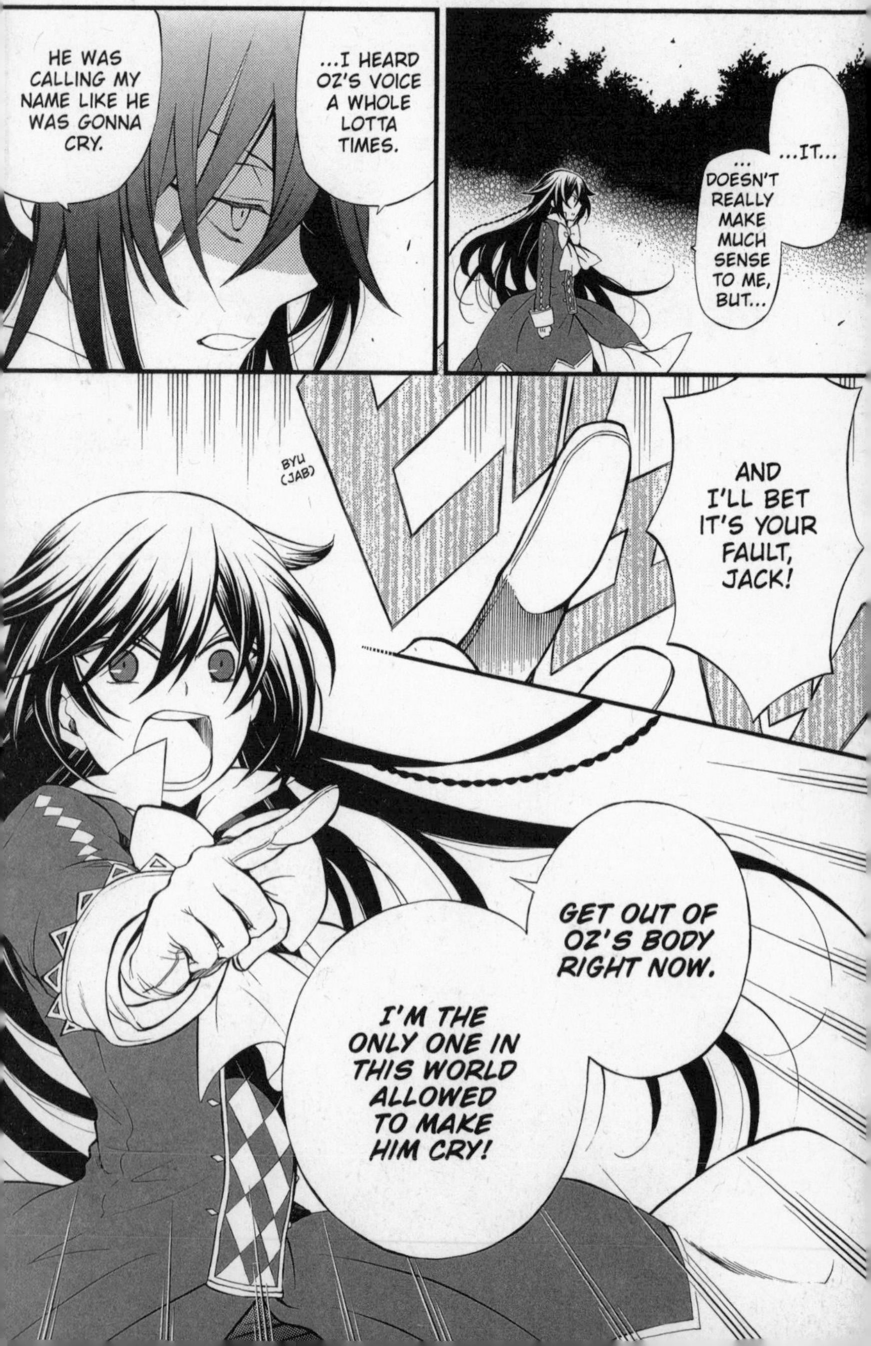

...IT...
... DOESN'T REALLY MAKE MUCH SENSE TO ME, BUT...
...I HEARD OZ'S VOICE A WHOLE LOTTA TIMES.
HE WAS CALLING MY NAME LIKE HE WAS GONNA CRY.
AND I'LL BET IT'S YOUR FAULT, JACK!
BYU (JAB)
GET OUT OF OZ'S BODY RIGHT NOW.
I'M THE ONLY ONE IN THIS WORLD ALLOWED TO MAKE HIM CRY!

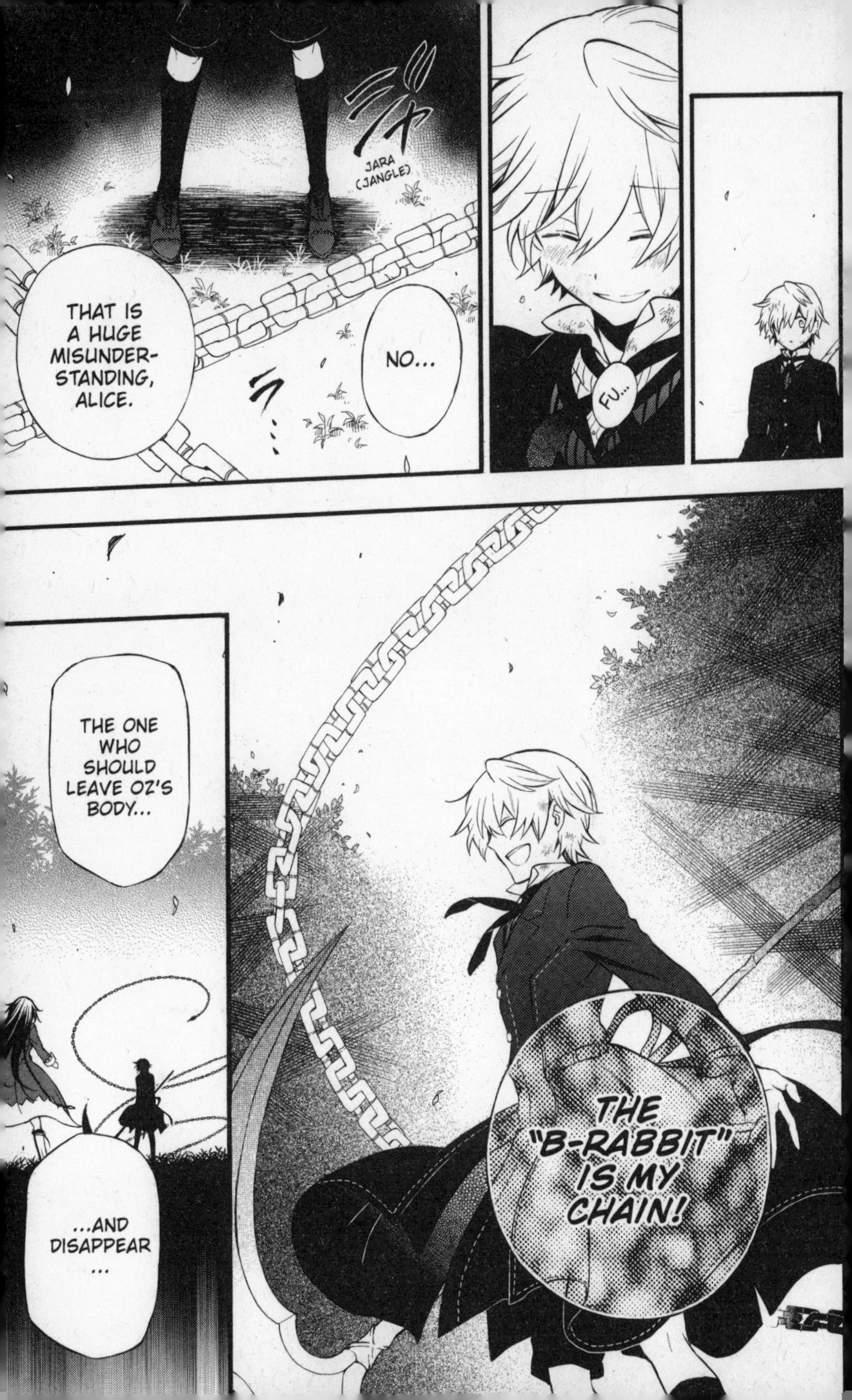
FU...
JARA (JANGLE)
NO...
THAT IS A HUGE MISUNDERSTANDING, ALICE.
THE "B-RABBIT" IS MY CHAIN!
THE ONE WHO SHOULD LEAVE OZ'S BODY...
...AND DISAPPEAR ...

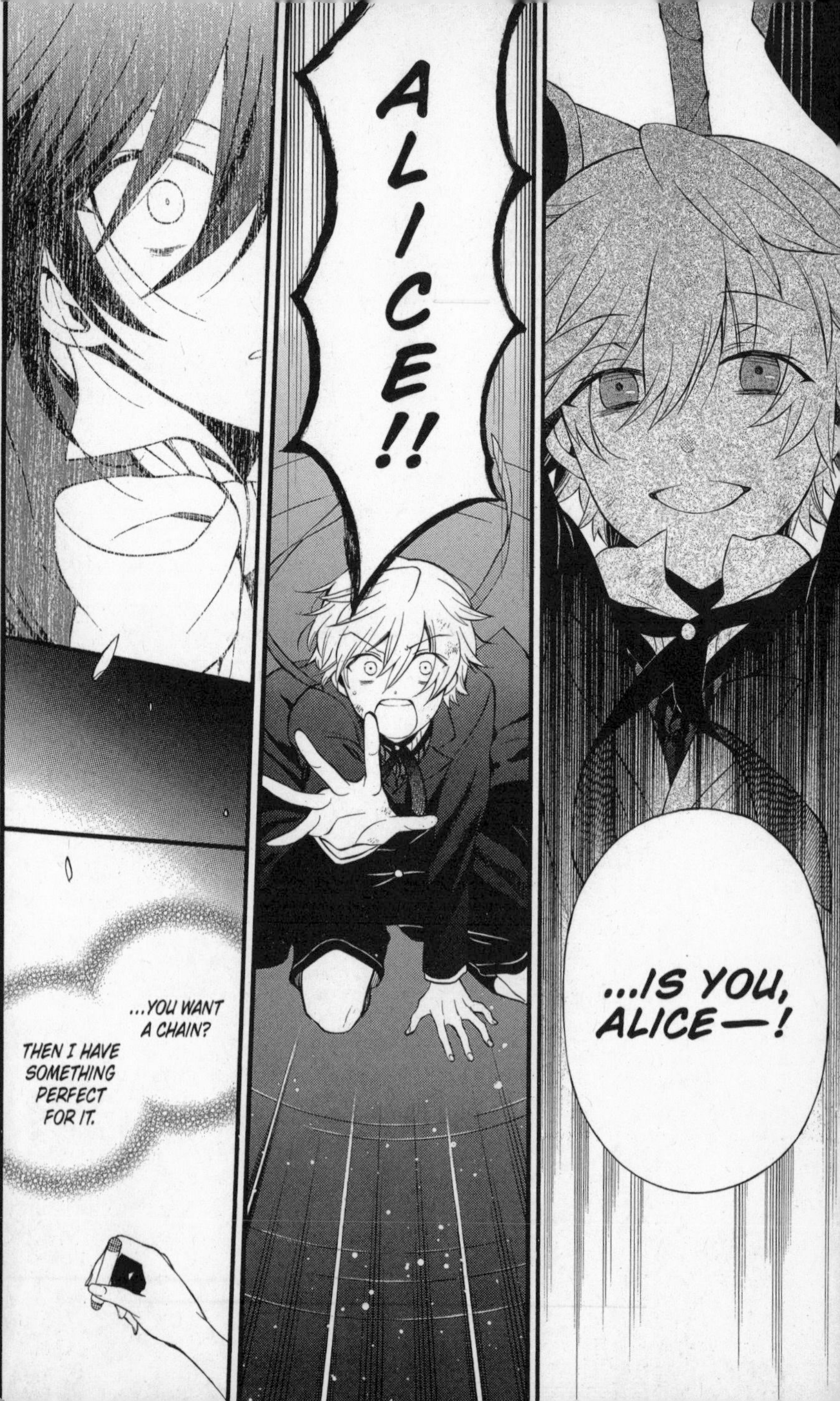
...IS YOU, ALICE—!
ALICE!!
...YOU WANT A CHAIN?
THEN I HAVE SOMETHING PERFECT FOR IT.

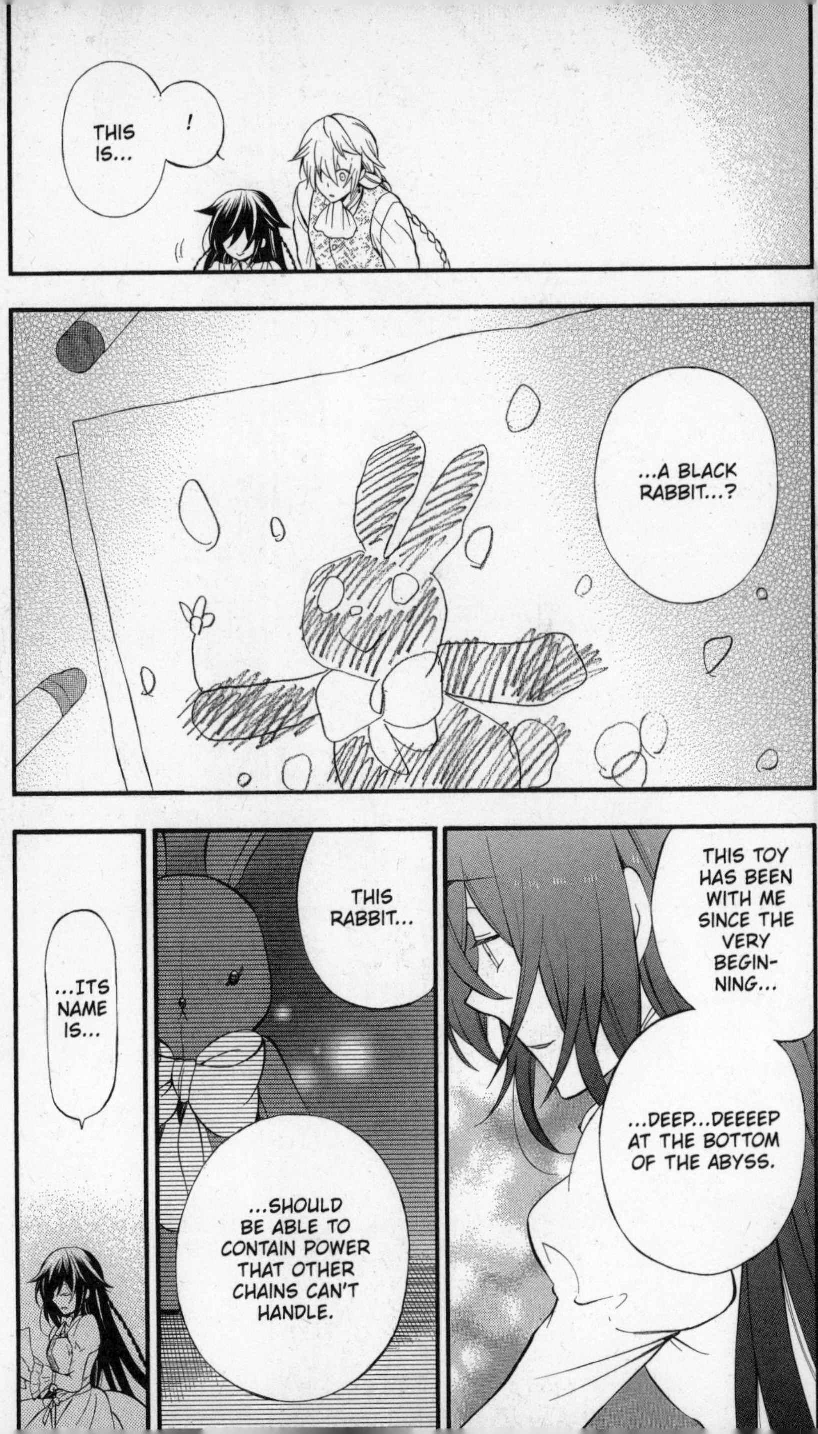
THIS IS... !
...A BLACK RABBIT...?
THIS TOY HAS BEEN WITH ME SINCE THE VERY BEGIN-NING...
...DEEP...DEEEEP AT THE BOTTOM OF THE ABYSS.
THIS RABBIT...
...SHOULD BE ABLE TO CONTAIN POWER THAT OTHER CHAINS CAN'T HANDLE.
...ITS NAME IS...

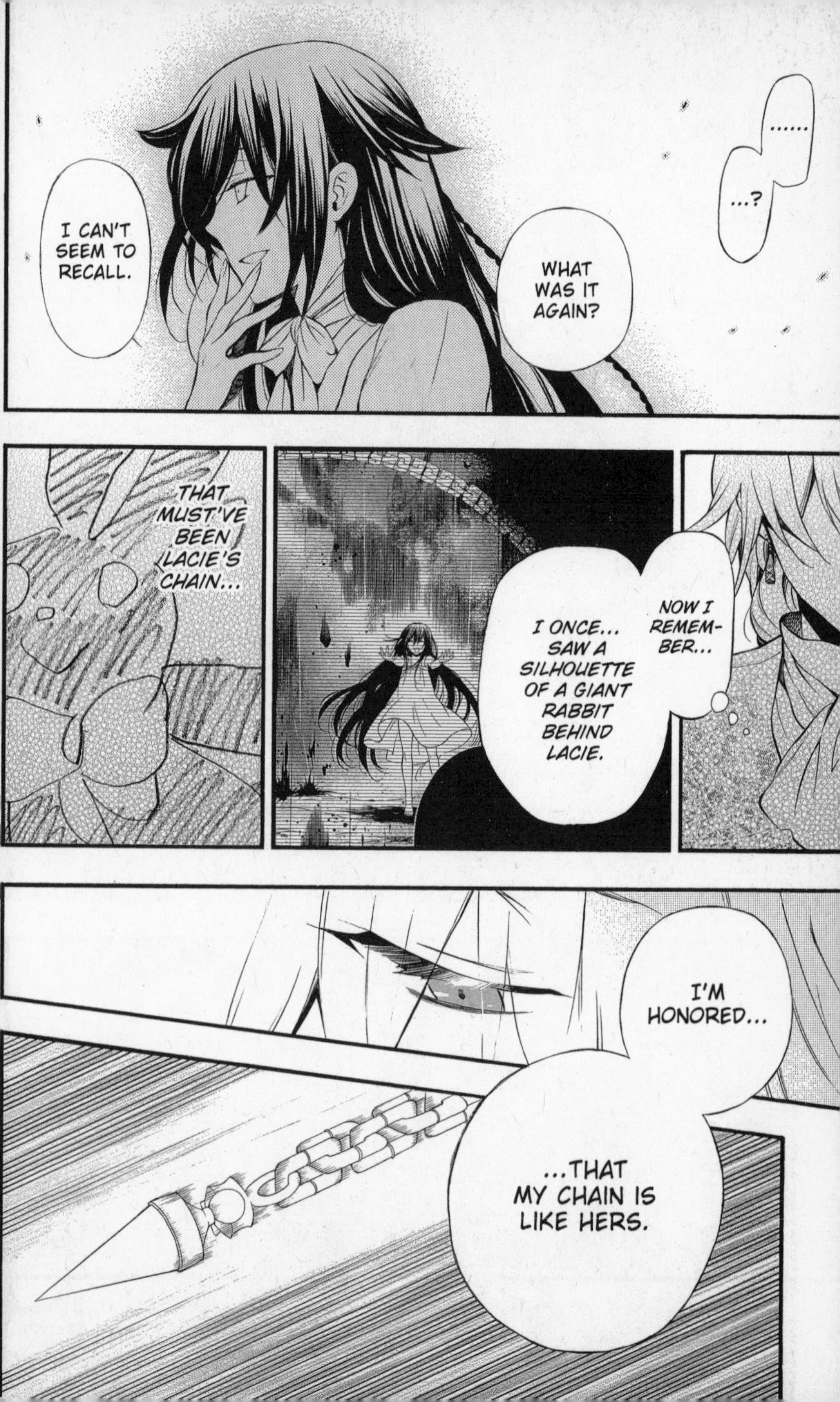
......
...?
WHAT WAS IT AGAIN?
I CAN'T SEEM TO RECALL.
NOW I REMEMBER...
I ONCE... SAW A SILHOUETTE OF A GIANT RABBIT BEHIND LACIE.
THAT MUST'VE BEEN LACIE'S CHAIN...
I'M HONORED...
...THAT MY CHAIN IS LIKE HERS.

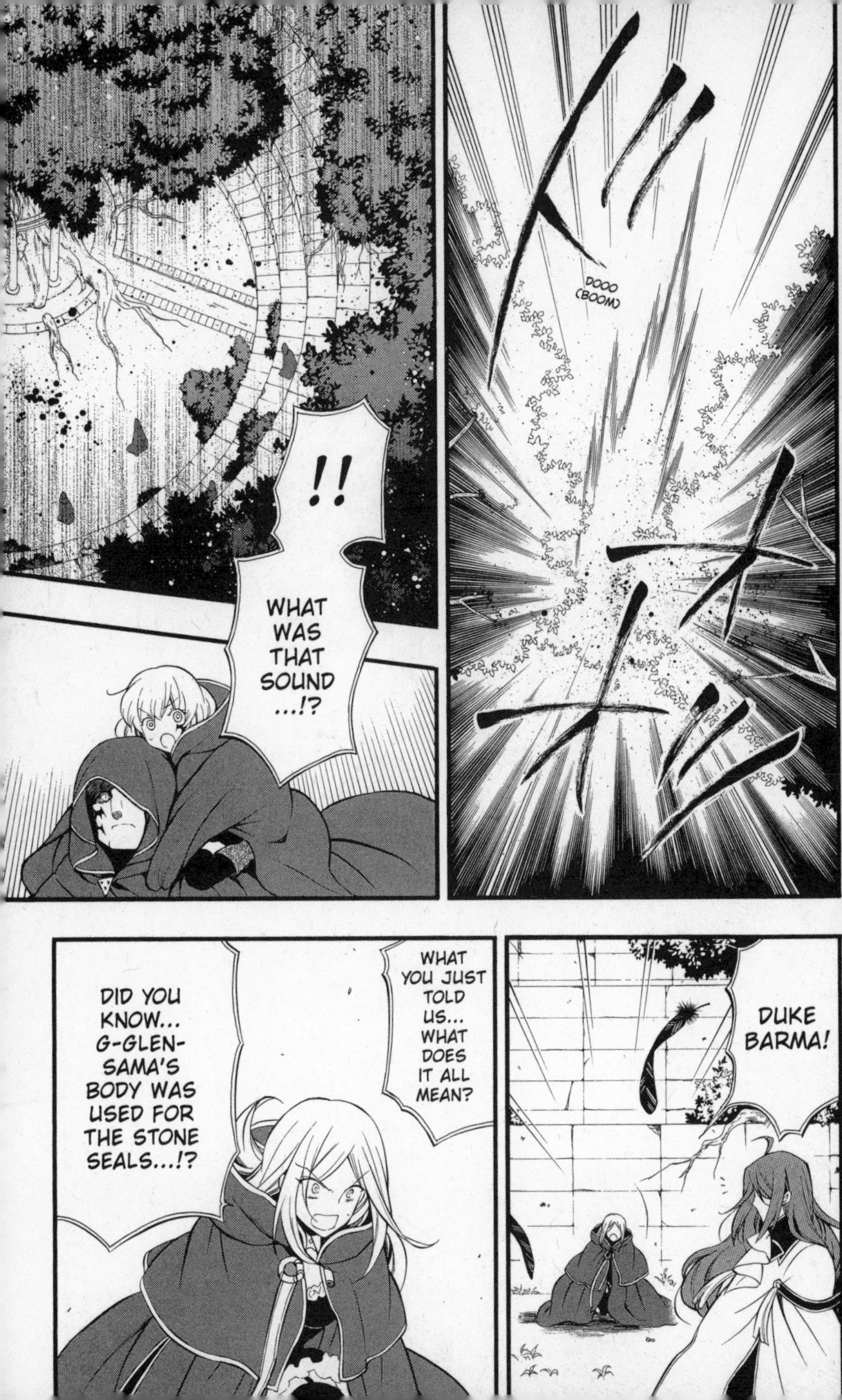
DOOO (BOOM)
!!
WHAT WAS THAT SOUND ...!?
DUKE BARMA!
WHAT YOU JUST TOLD US... WHAT DOES IT ALL MEAN?
DID YOU KNOW... G-GLEN-SAMA'S BODY WAS USED FOR THE STONE SEALS...!?

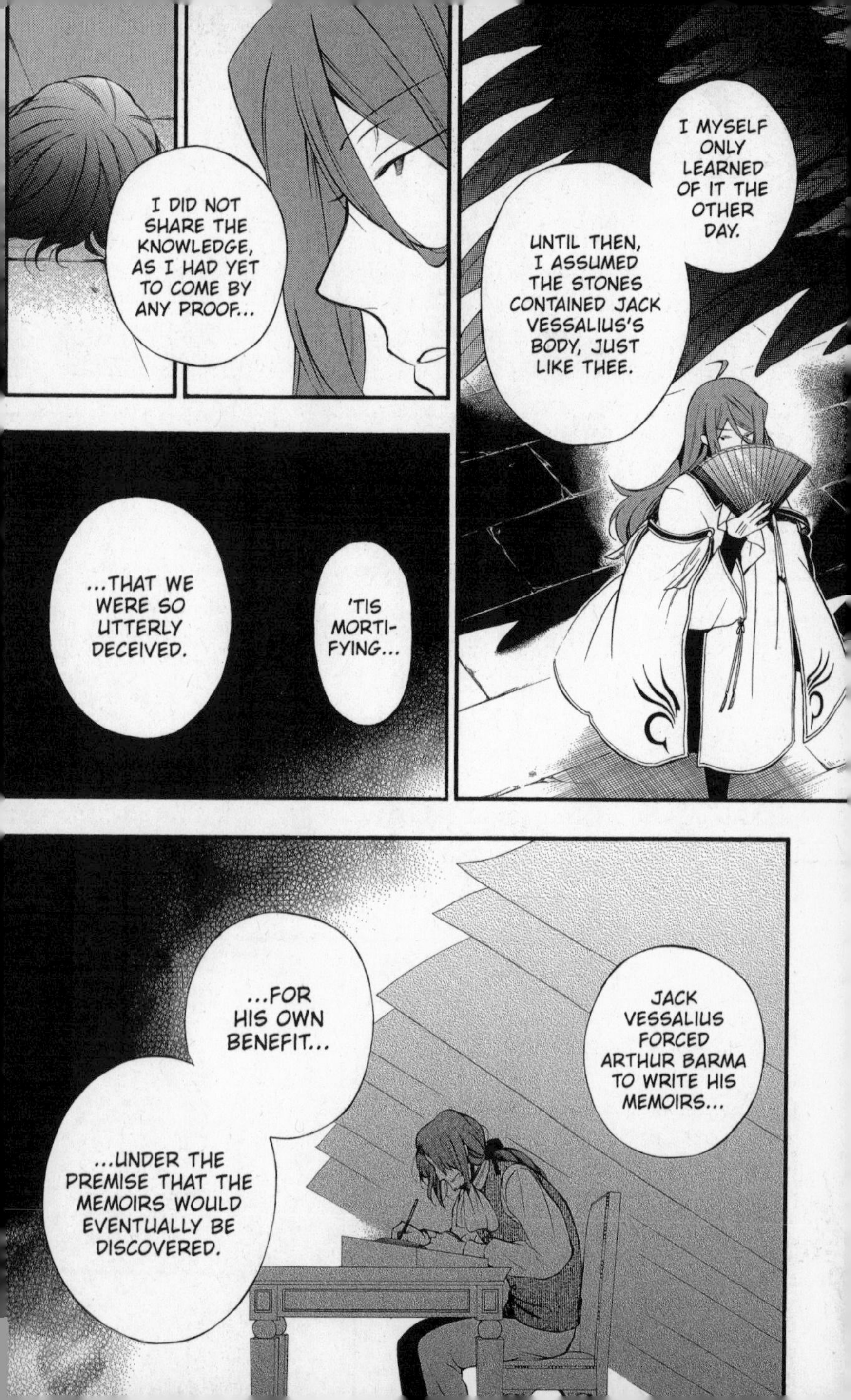
I MYSELF ONLY LEARNED OF IT THE OTHER DAY.
UNTIL THEN, I ASSUMED THE STONES CONTAINED JACK VESSALIUS'S BODY, JUST LIKE THEE.
I DID NOT SHARE THE KNOWLEDGE, AS I HAD YET TO COME BY ANY PROOF...
'TIS MORTI-FYING...
...THAT WE WERE SO UTTERLY DECEIVED.
JACK VESSALIUS FORCED ARTHUR BARMA TO WRITE HIS MEMOIRS...
...FOR HIS OWN BENEFIT...
...UNDER THE PREMISE THAT THE MEMOIRS WOULD EVENTUALLY BE DISCOVERED.

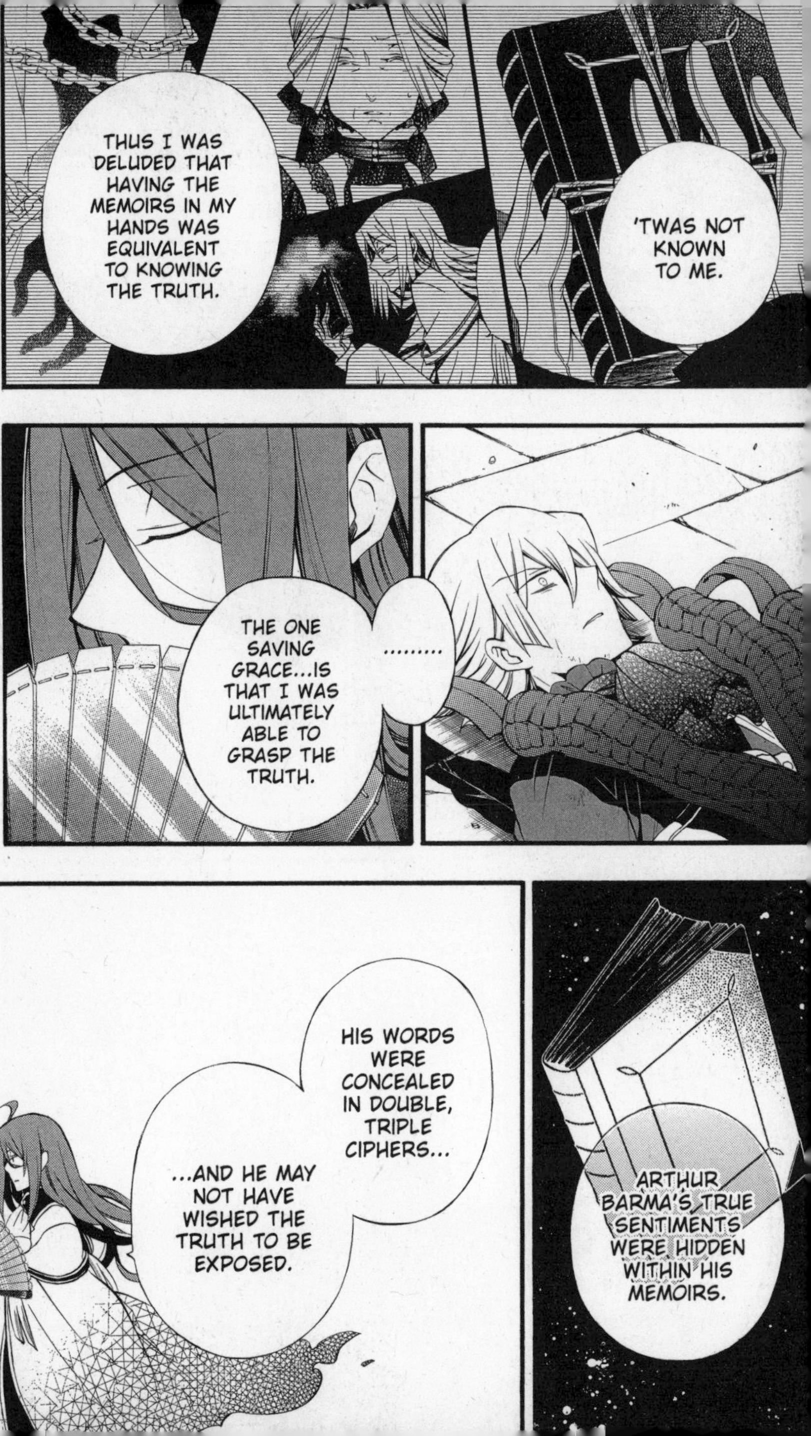
'TWAS NOT KNOWN TO ME.
THUS I WAS DELUDED THAT HAVING THE MEMOIRS IN MY HANDS WAS EQUIVALENT TO KNOWING THE TRUTH.
....
THE ONE SAVING GRACE...IS THAT I WAS ULTIMATELY ABLE TO GRASP THE TRUTH.
ARTHUR BARMA'S TRUE SENTIMENTS WERE HIDDEN WITHIN HIS MEMOIRS.
HIS WORDS WERE CONCEALED IN DOUBLE, TRIPLE CIPHERS...
...AND HE MAY NOT HAVE WISHED THE TRUTH TO BE EXPOSED.

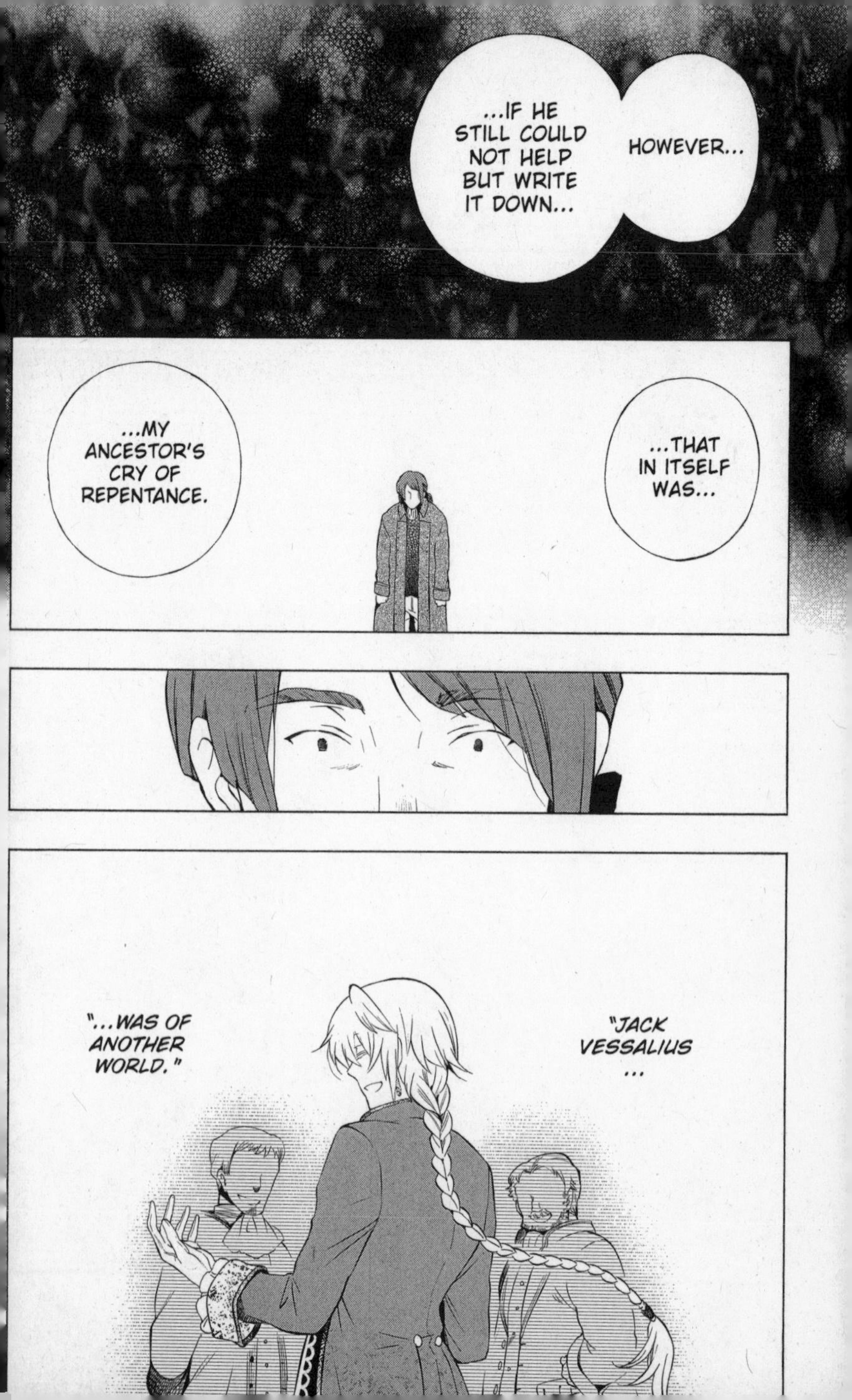
HOWEVER...
...IF HE STILL COULD NOT HELP BUT WRITE IT DOWN...
...THAT IN ITSELF WAS...
...MY ANCESTOR'S CRY OF REPENTANCE.
"JACK VESSALIUS ...
"...WAS OF ANOTHER WORLD."

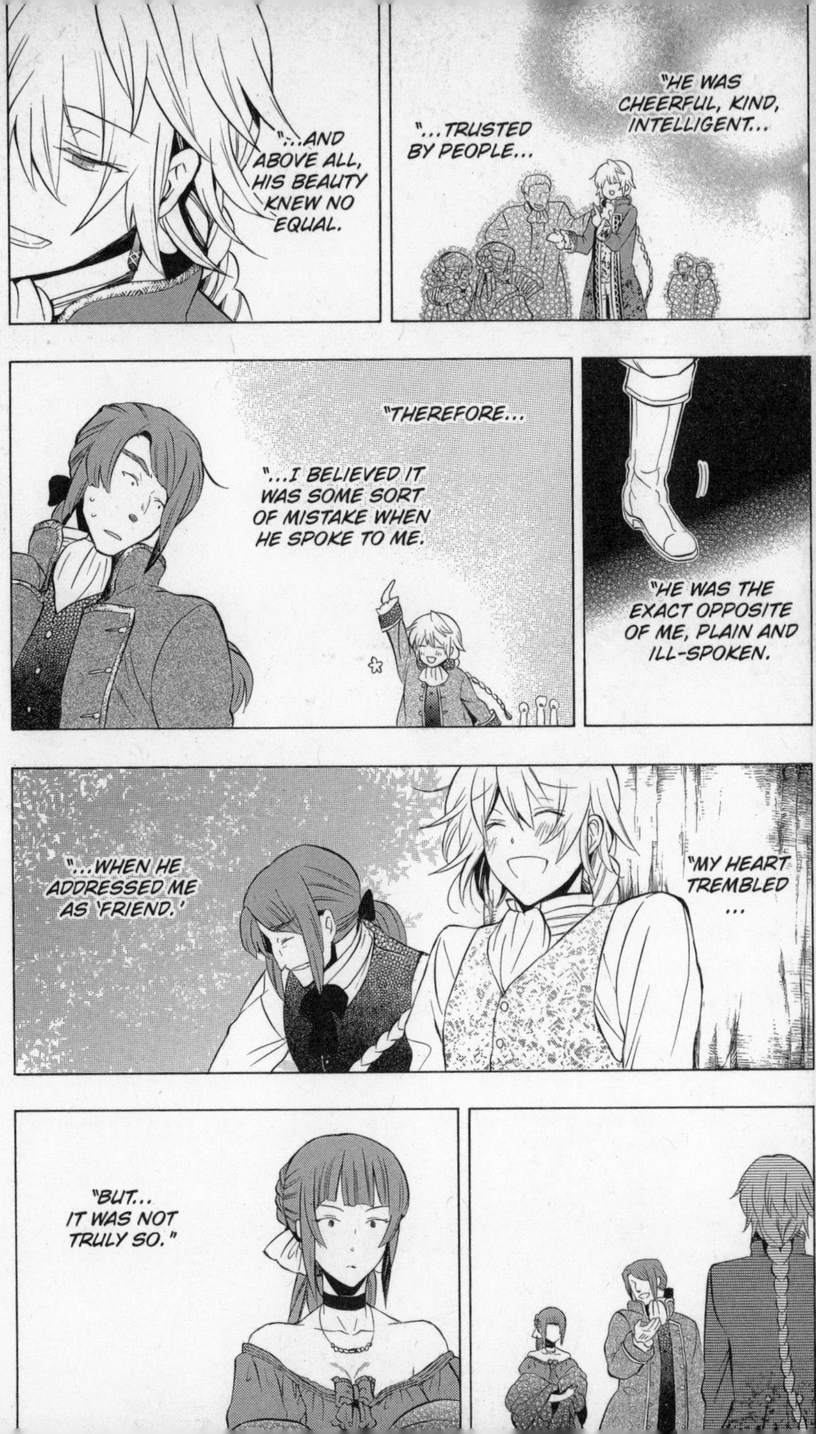
"HE WAS CHEERFUL, KIND, INTELLIGENT...
"...TRUSTED BY PEOPLE...
"...AND ABOVE ALL, HIS BEAUTY KNEW NO EQUAL.
"HE WAS THE EXACT OPPOSITE OF ME, PLAIN AND ILL-SPOKEN.
"THEREFORE...
"...I BELIEVED IT WAS SOME SORT OF MISTAKE WHEN HE SPOKE TO ME.
"MY HEART TREMBLED ...
"...WHEN HE ADDRESSED ME AS 'FRIEND.'
"BUT... IT WAS NOT TRULY SO."

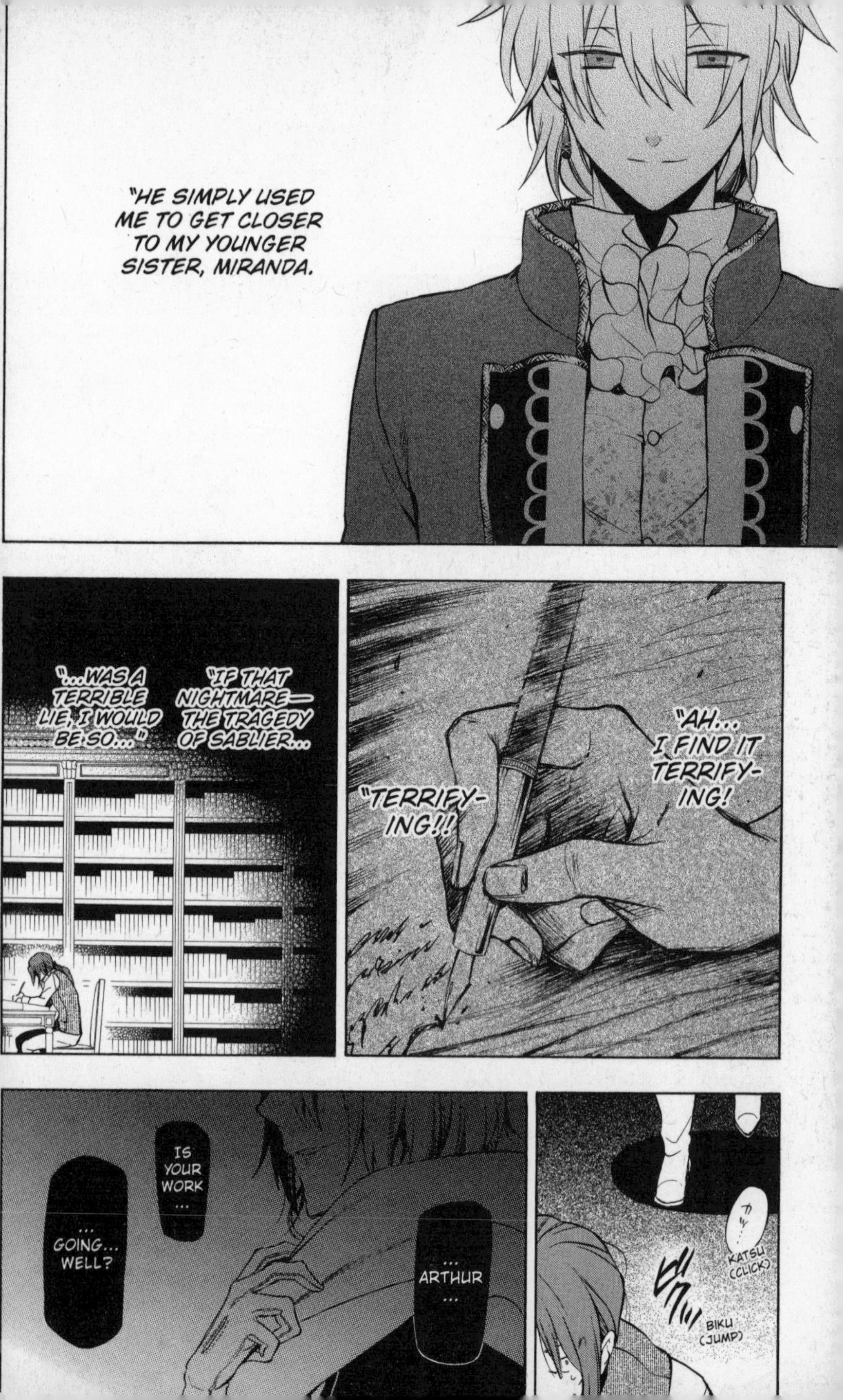
"HE SIMPLY USED ME TO GET CLOSER TO MY YOUNGER SISTER, MIRANDA.
"AH... I FIND IT TERRIFY-ING!
"TERRIFY-ING!!
"IF THAT NIGHTMARE— THE TRAGEDY OF SABLIER...
"...WAS A TERRIBLE LIE, I WOULD BE SO..."
カッ
KATSU (CLICK)
BIKU (JUMP)
... ARTHUR ...
IS YOUR WORK ...
... GOING... WELL?

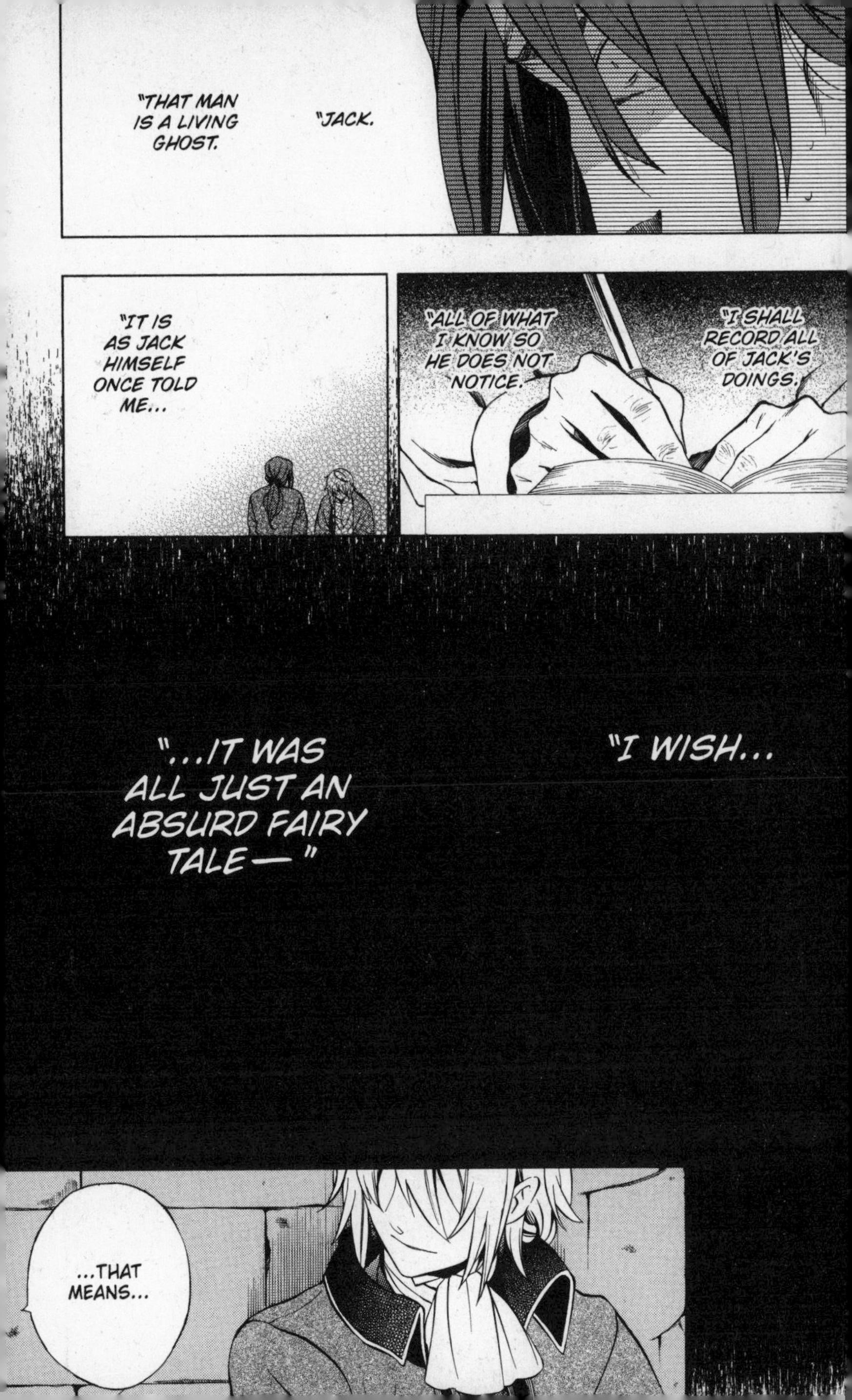
"JACK.
"THAT MAN IS A LIVING GHOST.
"I SHALL RECORD ALL OF JACK'S DOINGS.
"ALL OF WHAT I KNOW SO HE DOES NOT NOTICE.
"IT IS AS JACK HIMSELF ONCE TOLD ME...
"I WISH...
"...IT WAS ALL JUST AN ABSURD FAIRY TALE—"
...THAT MEANS...

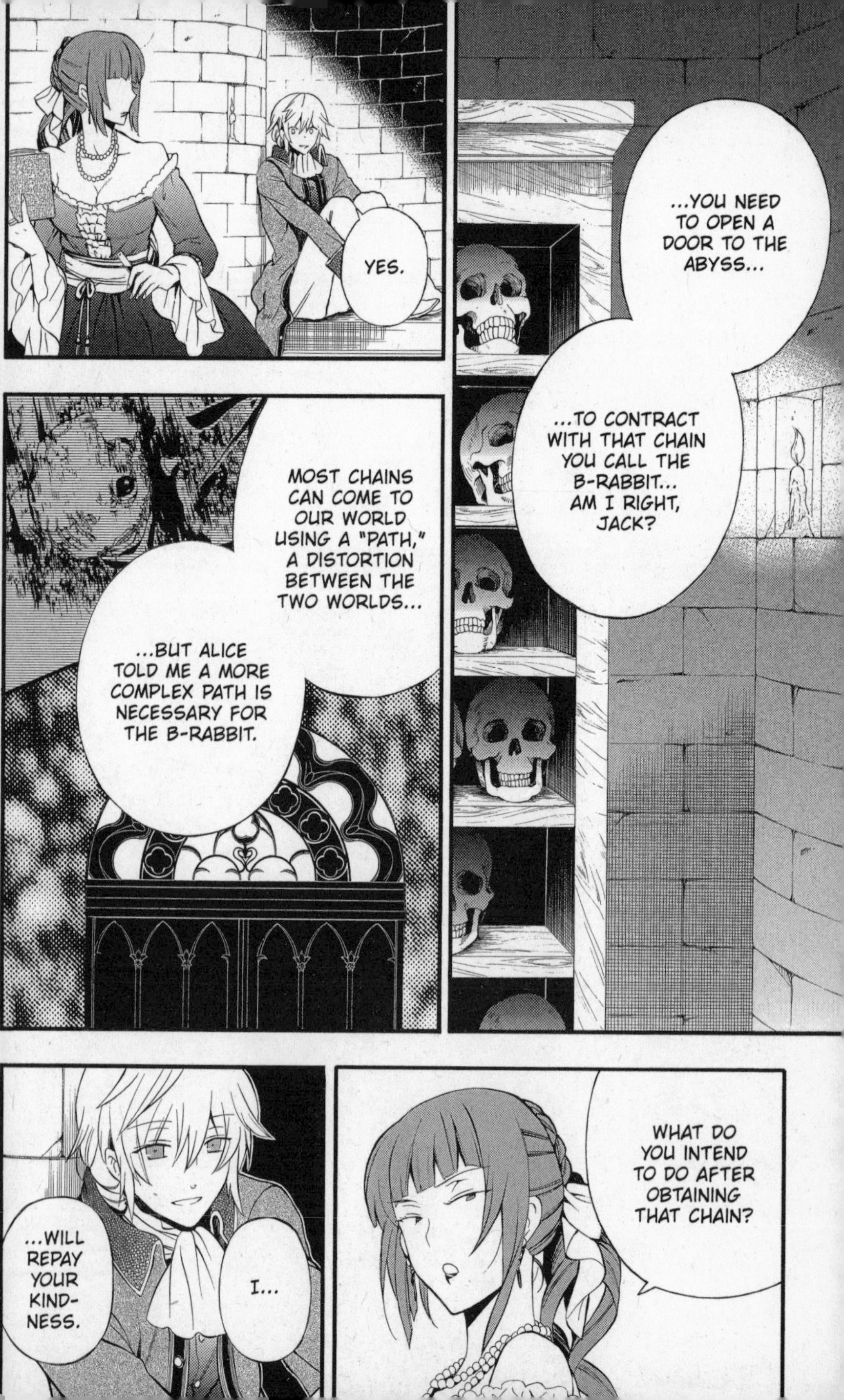
...YOU NEED TO OPEN A DOOR TO THE ABYSS...
...TO CONTRACT WITH THAT CHAIN YOU CALL THE B-RABBIT... AM I RIGHT, JACK?
YES.
MOST CHAINS CAN COME TO OUR WORLD USING A "PATH," A DISTORTION BETWEEN THE TWO WORLDS...
...BUT ALICE TOLD ME A MORE COMPLEX PATH IS NECESSARY FOR THE B-RABBIT.
WHAT DO YOU INTEND TO DO AFTER OBTAINING THAT CHAIN?
I...
...WILL REPAY YOUR KINDNESS.

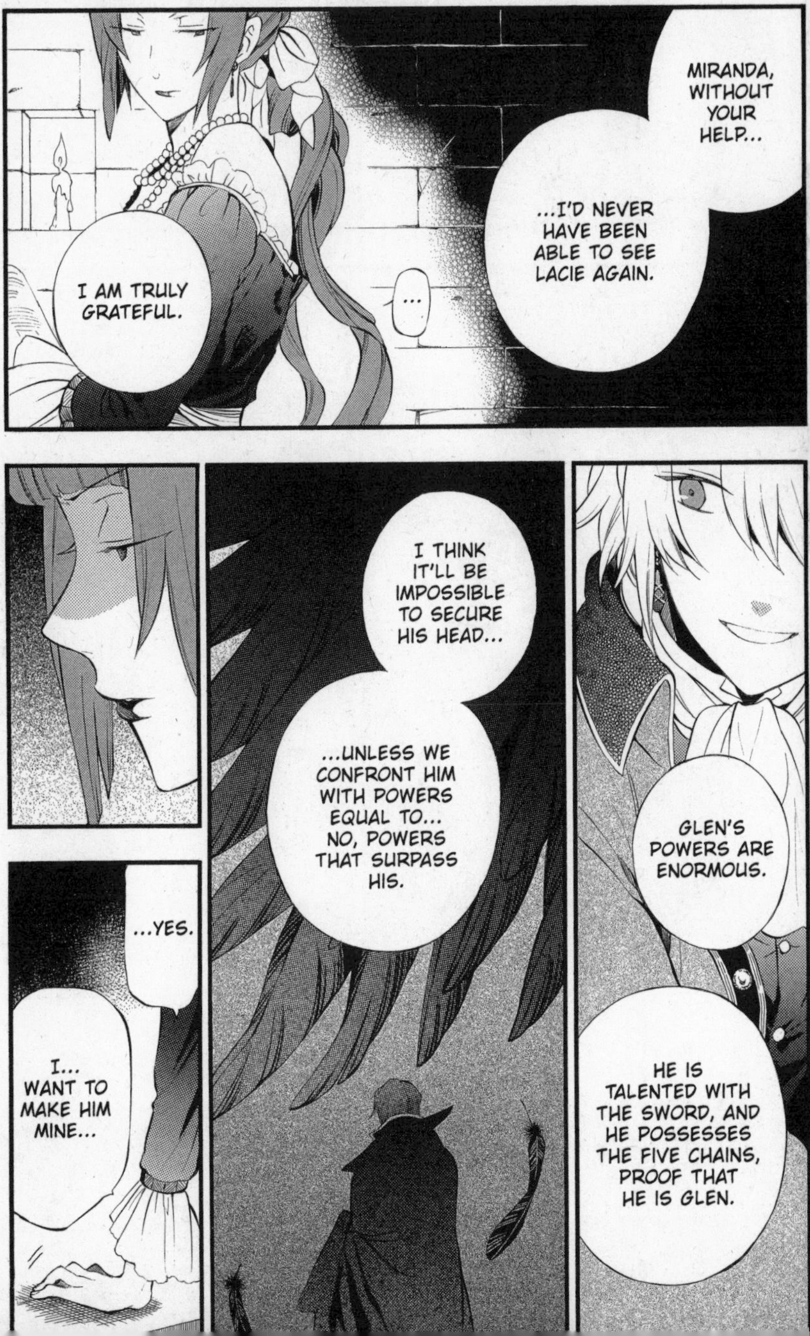
MIRANDA, WITHOUT YOUR HELP...
...I'D NEVER HAVE BEEN ABLE TO SEE LACIE AGAIN.
...
I AM TRULY GRATEFUL.
GLEN'S POWERS ARE ENORMOUS.
HE IS TALENTED WITH THE SWORD, AND HE POSSESSES THE FIVE CHAINS, PROOF THAT HE IS GLEN.
I THINK IT'LL BE IMPOSSIBLE TO SECURE HIS HEAD...
...UNLESS WE CONFRONT HIM WITH POWERS EQUAL TO... NO, POWERS THAT SURPASS HIS.
...YES.
I... WANT TO MAKE HIM MINE...

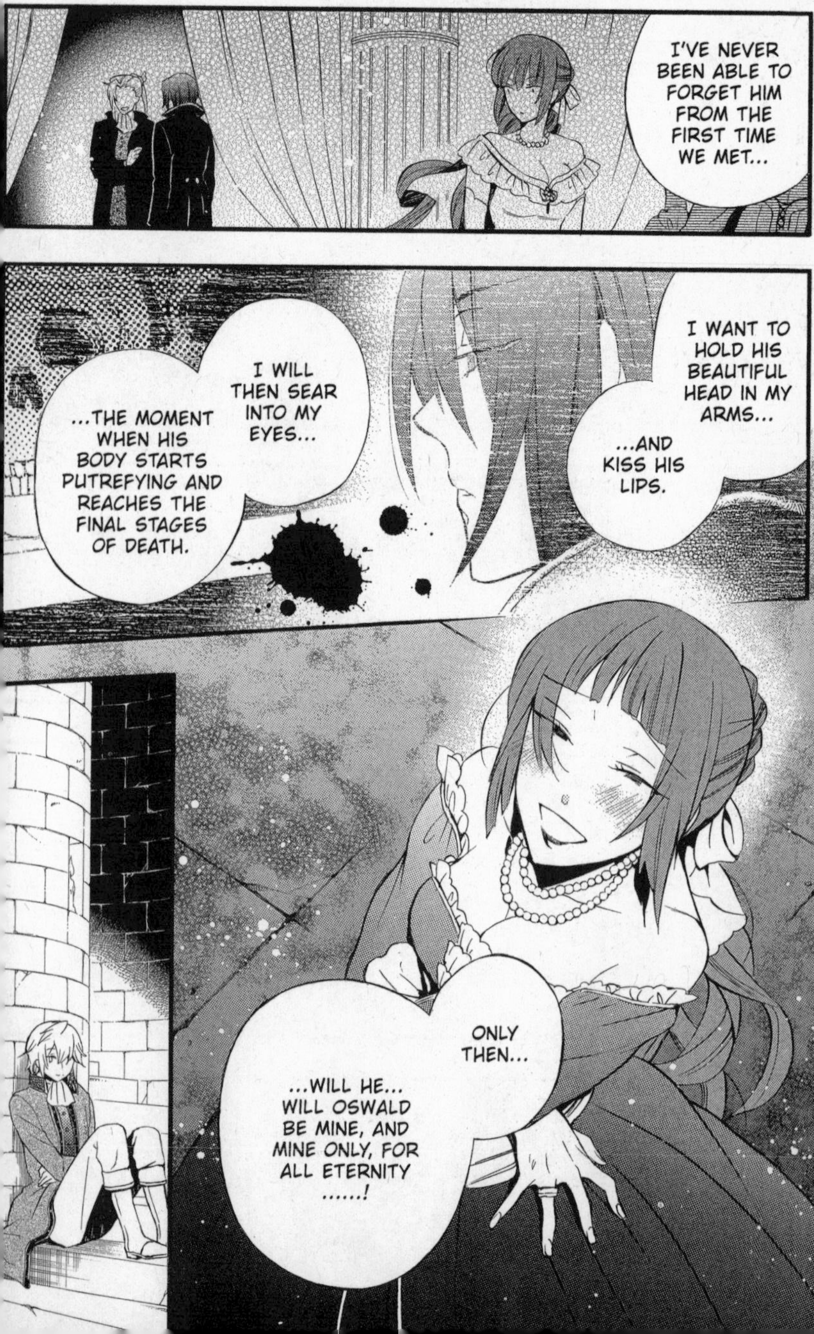
I'VE NEVER BEEN ABLE TO FORGET HIM FROM THE FIRST TIME WE MET...
I WANT TO HOLD HIS BEAUTIFUL HEAD IN MY ARMS...
...AND KISS HIS LIPS.
I WILL THEN SEAR INTO MY EYES...
...THE MOMENT WHEN HIS BODY STARTS PUTREFYING AND REACHES THE FINAL STAGES OF DEATH.
ONLY THEN...
...WILL HE... WILL OSWALD BE MINE, AND MINE ONLY, FOR ALL ETERNITY ......!

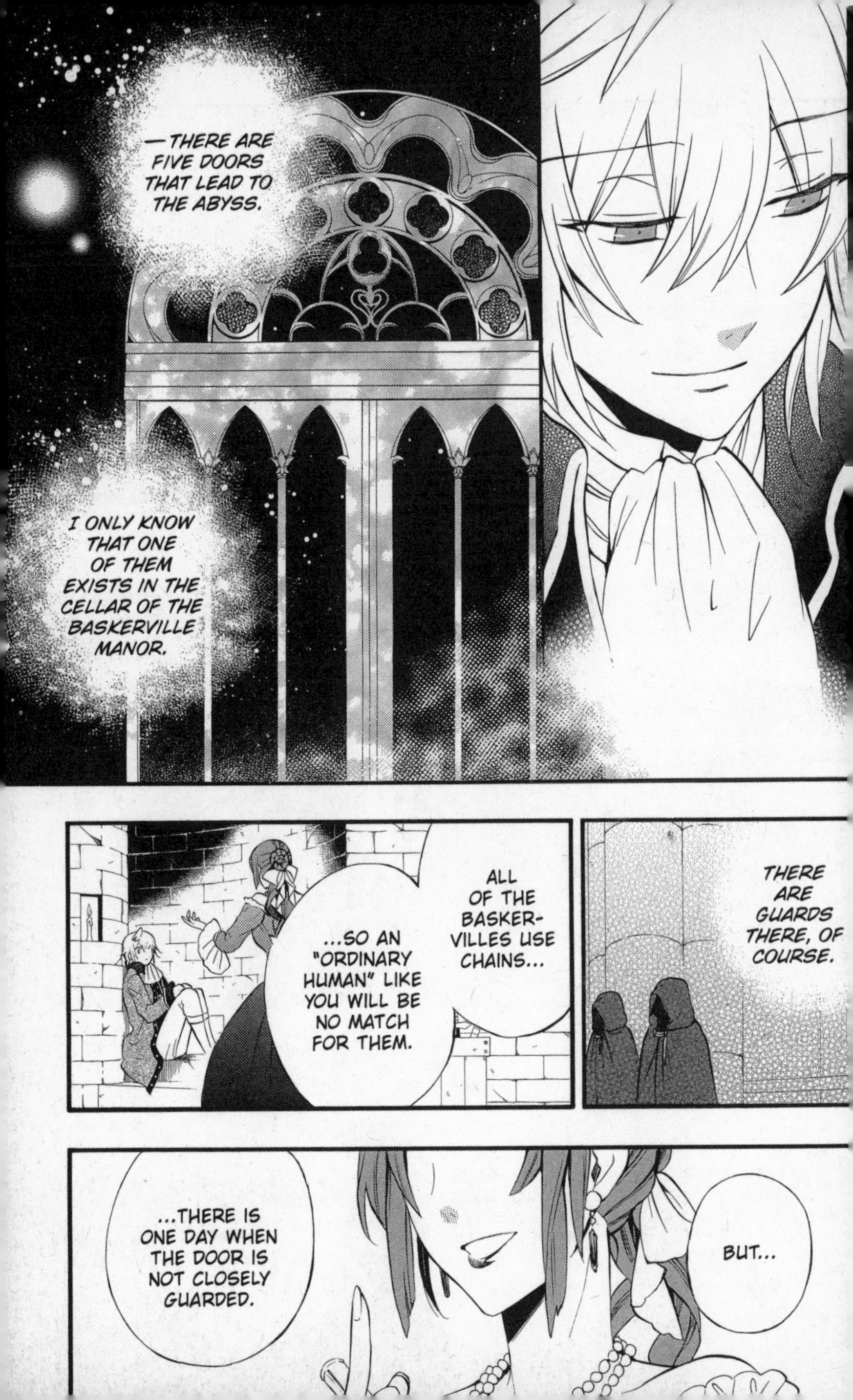
—THERE ARE FIVE DOORS THAT LEAD TO THE ABYSS.
I ONLY KNOW THAT ONE OF THEM EXISTS IN THE CELLAR OF THE BASKERVILLE MANOR.
THERE ARE GUARDS THERE, OF COURSE.
ALL OF THE BASKER-VILLES USE CHAINS...
...SO AN "ORDINARY HUMAN" LIKE YOU WILL BE NO MATCH FOR THEM.
BUT...
...THERE IS ONE DAY WHEN THE DOOR IS NOT CLOSELY GUARDED.

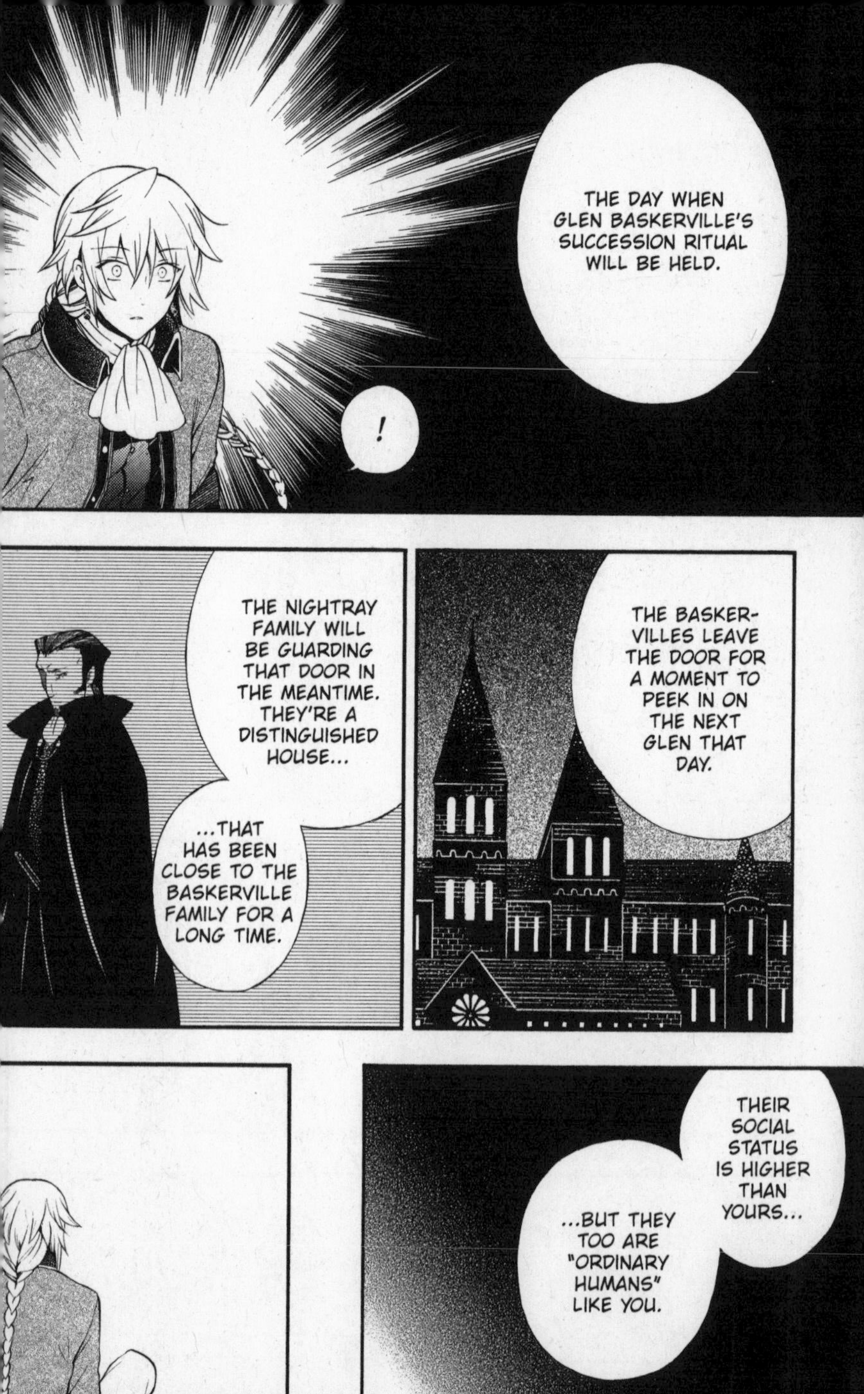
THE DAY WHEN GLEN BASKERVILLE'S SUCCESSION RITUAL WILL BE HELD.
!
THE BASKER-VILLES LEAVE THE DOOR FOR A MOMENT TO PEEK IN ON THE NEXT GLEN THAT DAY.
THE NIGHTRAY FAMILY WILL BE GUARDING THAT DOOR IN THE MEANTIME. THEY'RE A DISTINGUISHED HOUSE...
...THAT HAS BEEN CLOSE TO THE BASKERVILLE FAMILY FOR A LONG TIME.
THEIR SOCIAL STATUS IS HIGHER THAN YOURS...
...BUT THEY TOO ARE "ORDINARY HUMANS" LIKE YOU.

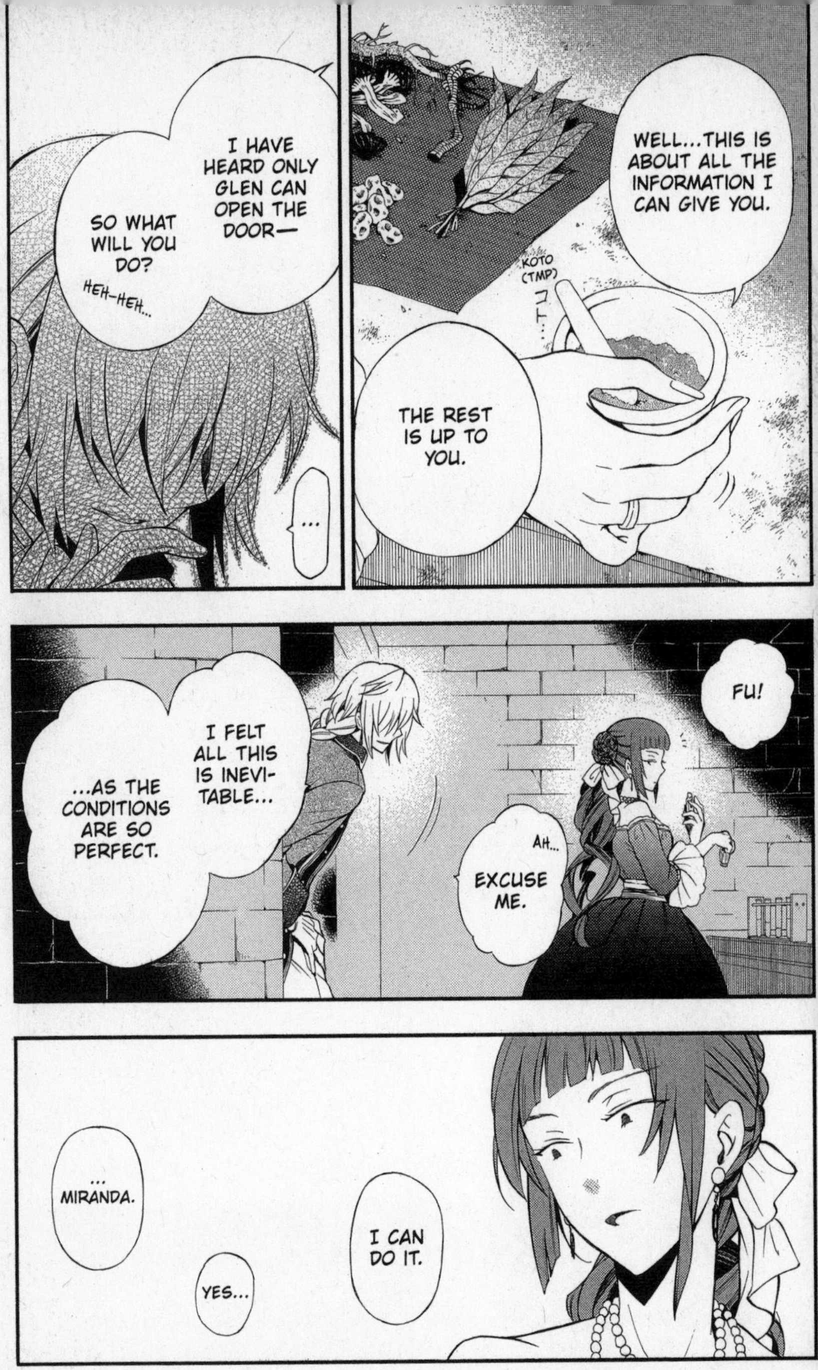
WELL...THIS IS ABOUT ALL THE INFORMATION I CAN GIVE YOU.
KOTO (TMP)
コト...
THE REST IS UP TO YOU.
I HAVE HEARD ONLY GLEN CAN OPEN THE DOOR—
SO WHAT WILL YOU DO?
HEH-HEH...
...
FU!
AH...
EXCUSE ME.
I FELT ALL THIS IS INEVITABLE...
...AS THE CONDITIONS ARE SO PERFECT.
I CAN DO IT.
YES...
...
MIRANDA.

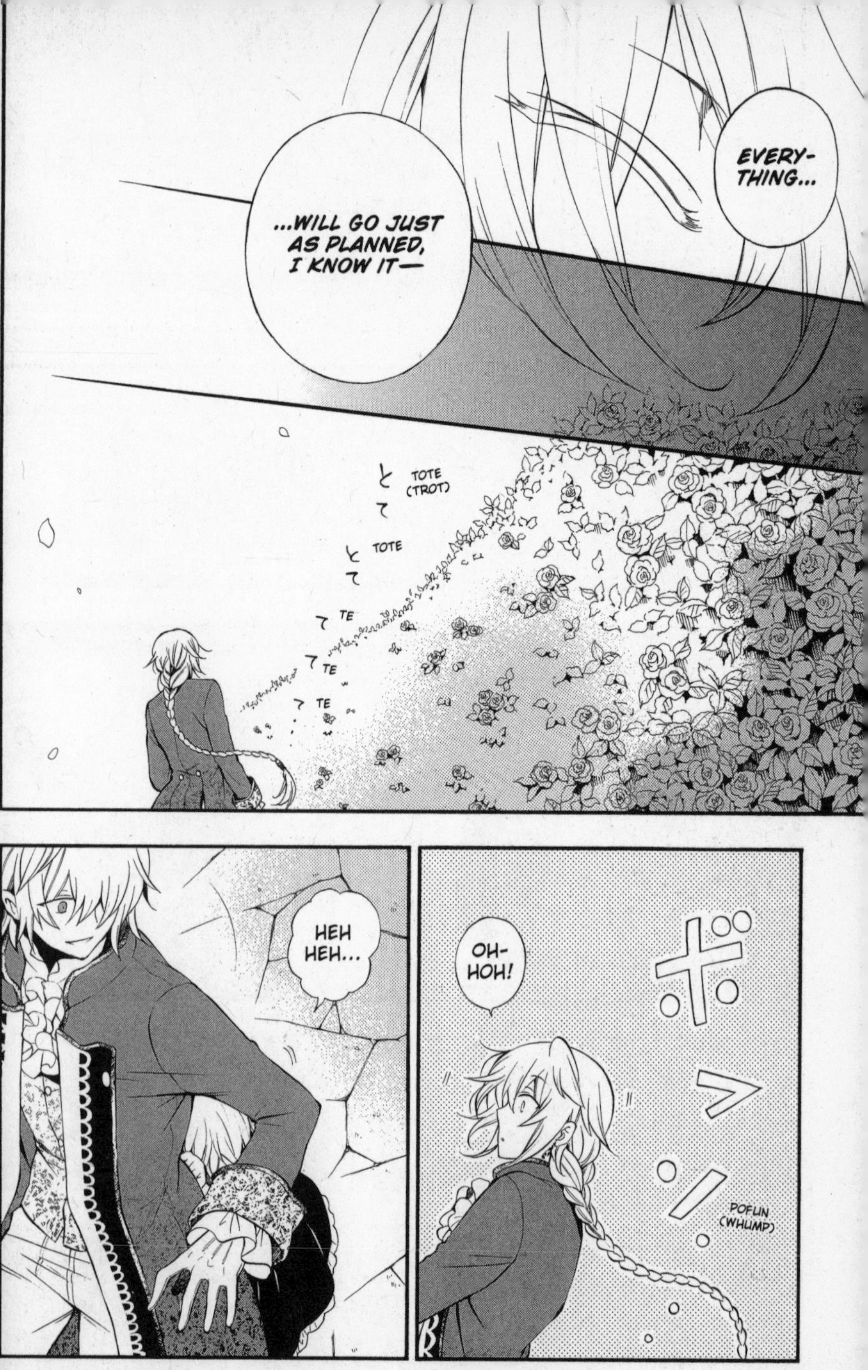
EVERY-THING...
...WILL GO JUST AS PLANNED, I KNOW IT—
TOTE (TROT)
TOTE
TE
TE
TE
OH-HOH!
POFUN (WHUMP)
HEH HEH...

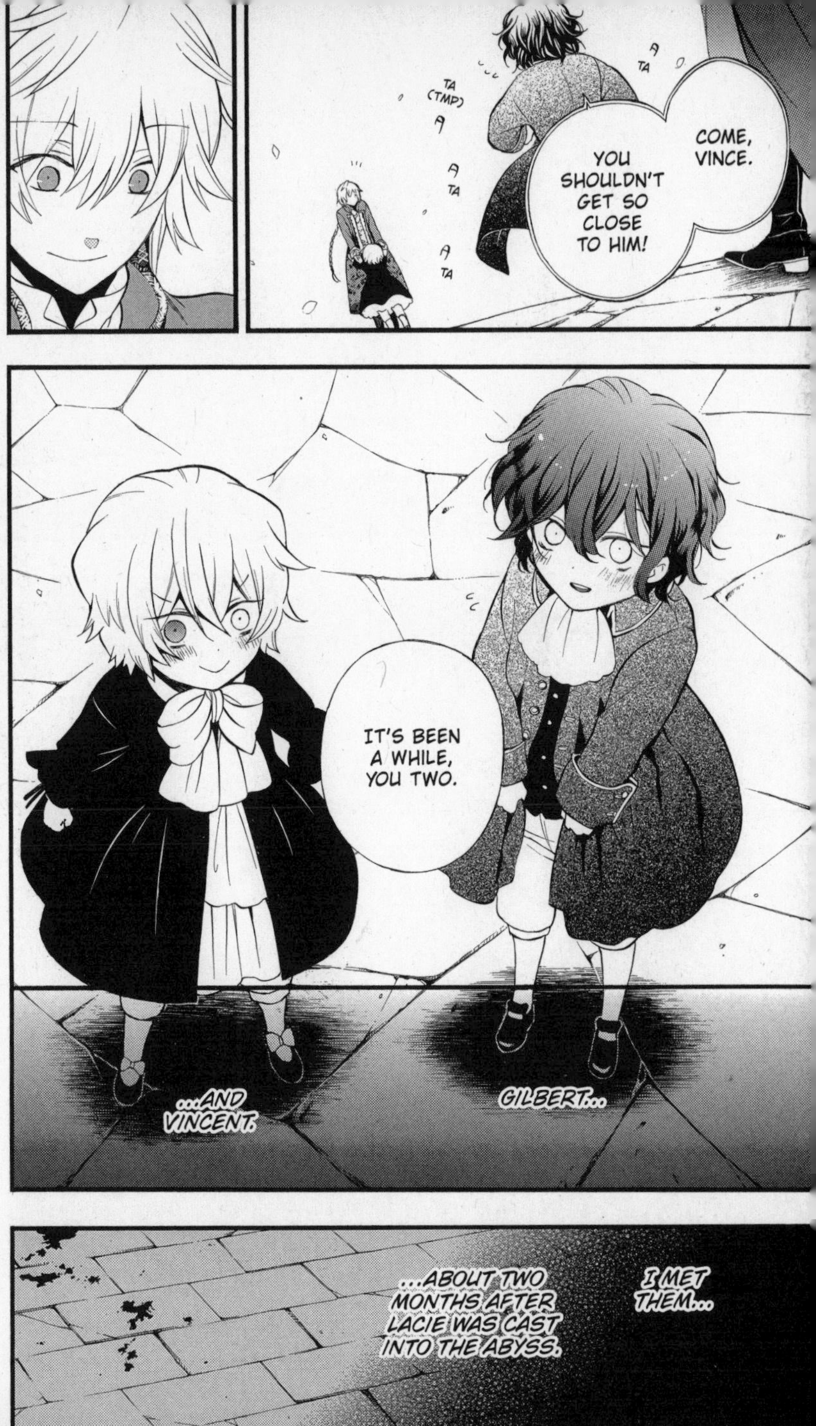
A TA
TA (TMP) A
A TA
A TA
COME, VINCE.
YOU SHOULDN'T GET SO CLOSE TO HIM!
IT'S BEEN A WHILE, YOU TWO.
GILBERT...
...AND VINCENT.
I MET THEM...
...ABOUT TWO MONTHS AFTER LACIE WAS CAST INTO THE ABYSS.

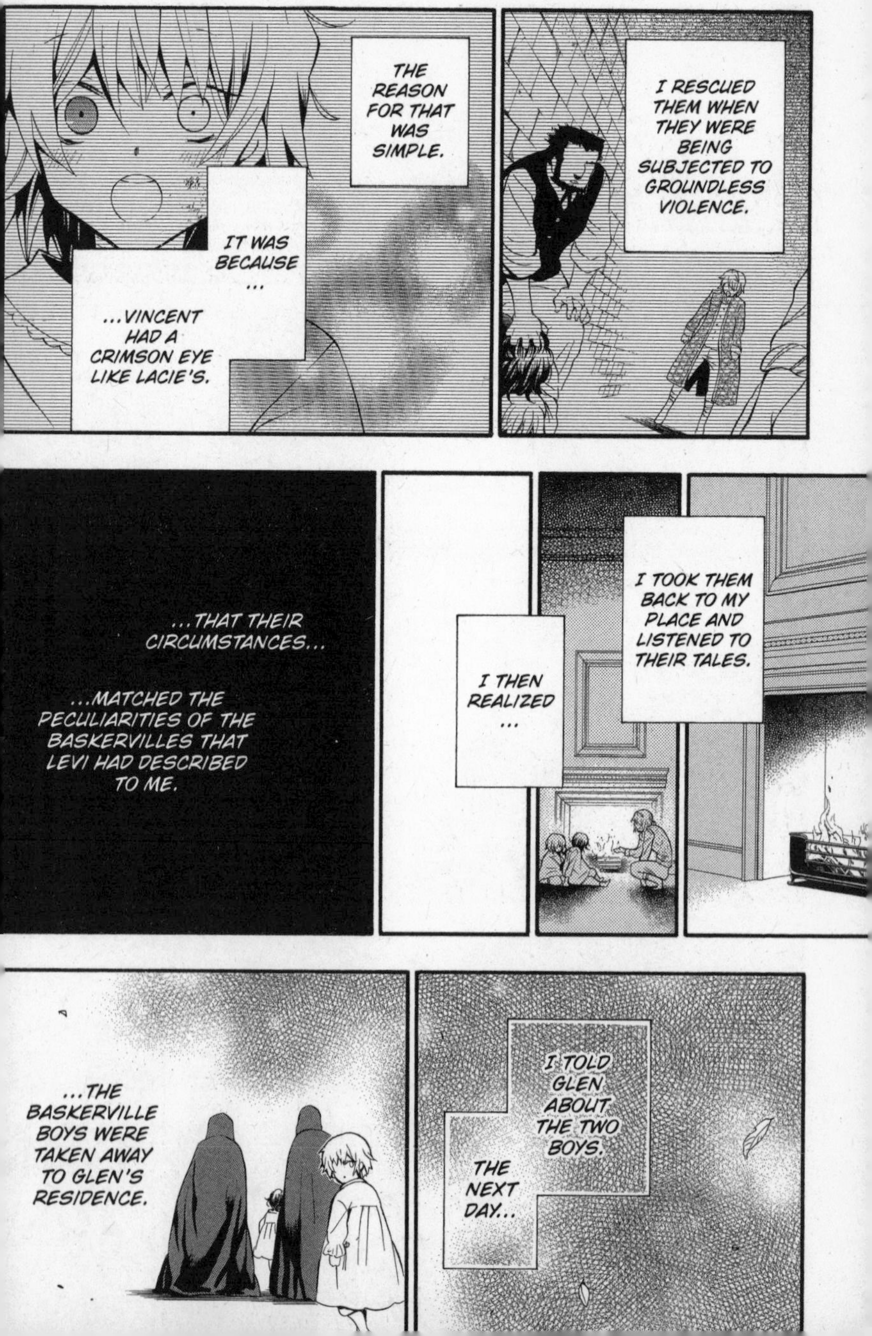
I RESCUED THEM WHEN THEY WERE BEING SUBJECTED TO GROUNDLESS VIOLENCE.
THE REASON FOR THAT WAS SIMPLE.
IT WAS BECAUSE ...
...VINCENT HAD A CRIMSON EYE LIKE LACIE'S.
I TOOK THEM BACK TO MY PLACE AND LISTENED TO THEIR TALES.
I THEN REALIZED ...
...THAT THEIR CIRCUMSTANCES...
...MATCHED THE PECULIARITIES OF THE BASKERVILLES THAT LEVI HAD DESCRIBED TO ME.
I TOLD GLEN ABOUT THE TWO BOYS.
THE NEXT DAY...
...THE BASKERVILLE BOYS WERE TAKEN AWAY TO GLEN'S RESIDENCE.

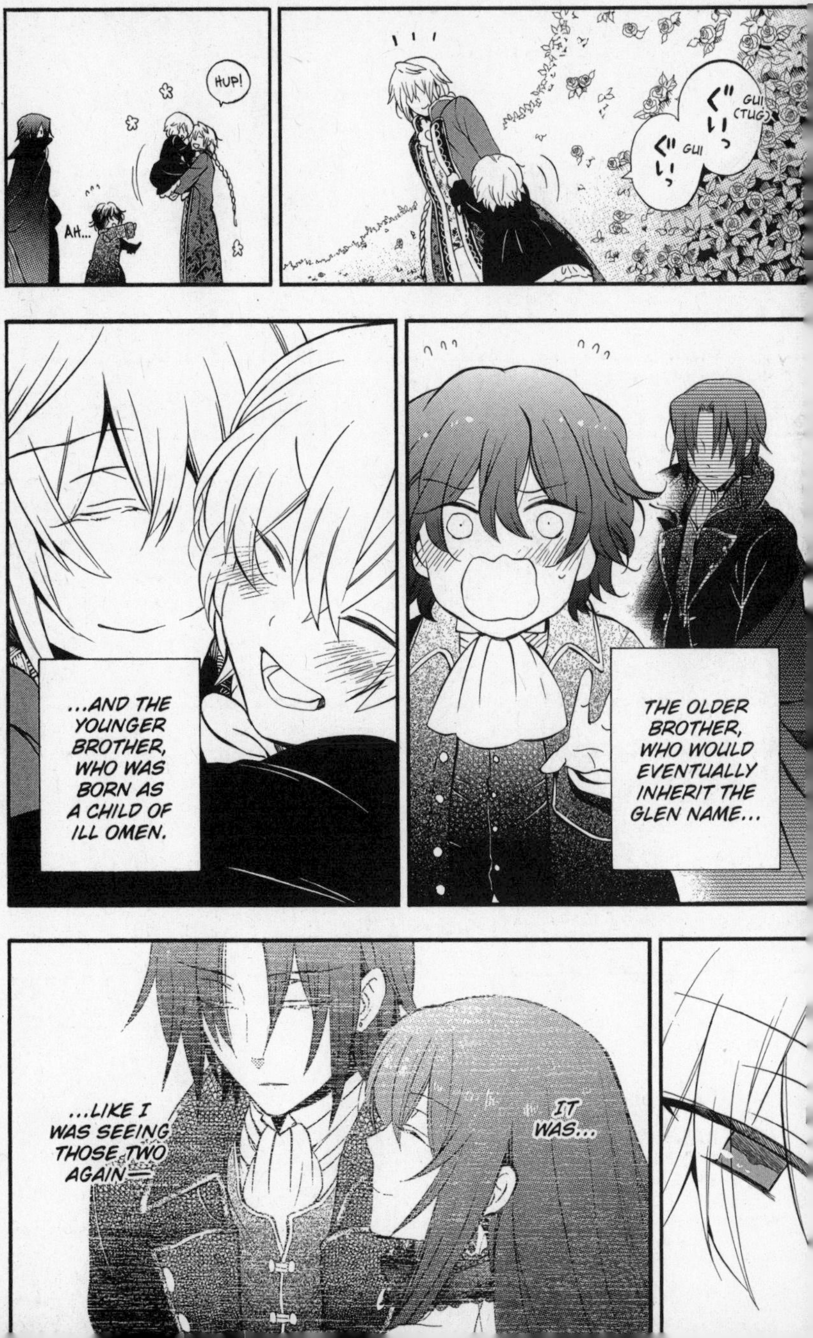
ぐいっ
GUI (TUG)
ぐいっ
GUI
HUP!
AH...
THE OLDER BROTHER, WHO WOULD EVENTUALLY INHERIT THE GLEN NAME...
...AND THE YOUNGER BROTHER, WHO WAS BORN AS A CHILD OF ILL OMEN.
IT WAS...
...LIKE I WAS SEEING THOSE TWO AGAIN—

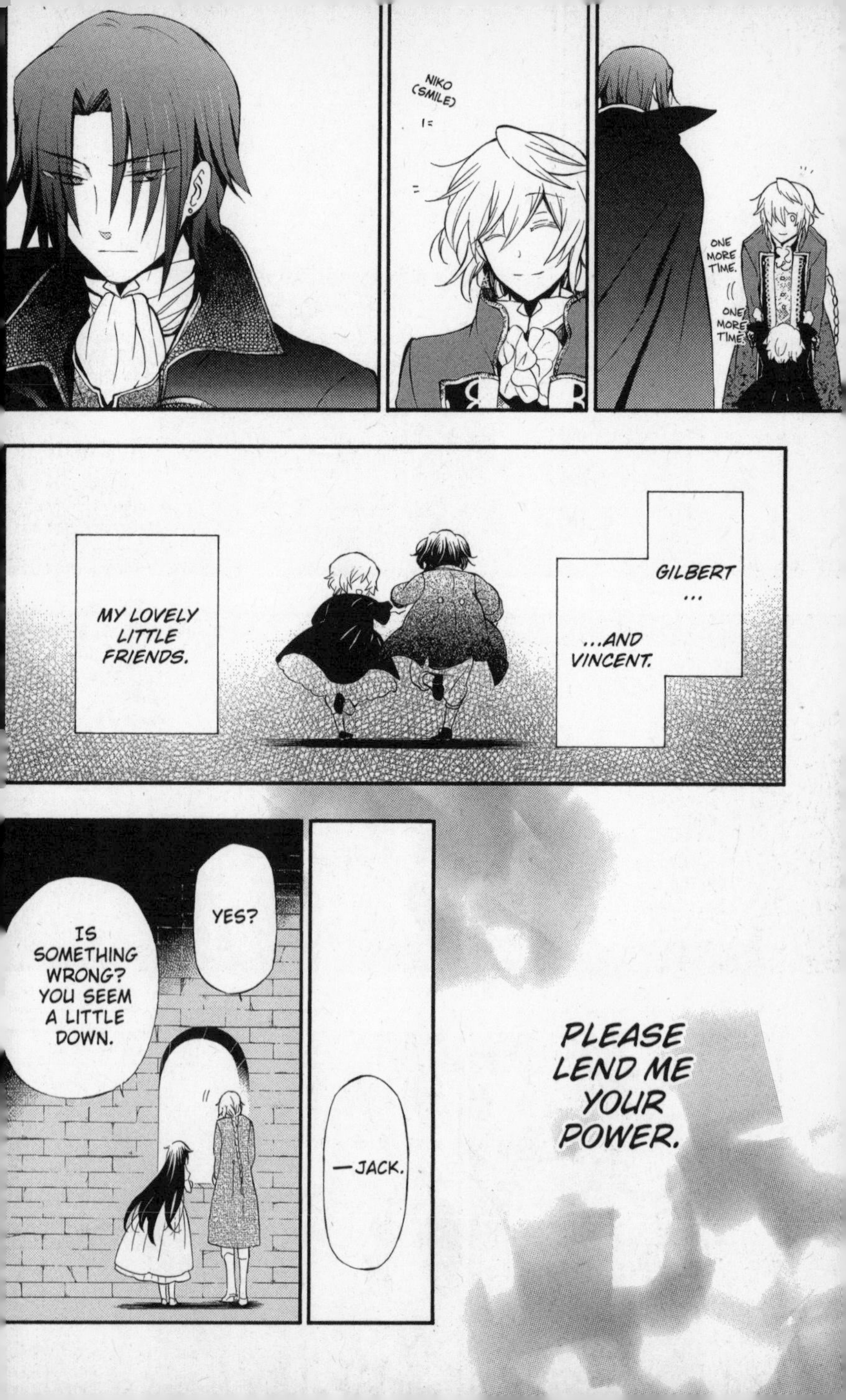
ONE MORE TIME.
ONE MORE TIME.
NIKO (SMILE)
GILBERT...
...AND VINCENT.
MY LOVELY LITTLE FRIENDS.
PLEASE LEND ME YOUR POWER.
—JACK.
YES?
IS SOMETHING WRONG? YOU SEEM A LITTLE DOWN.

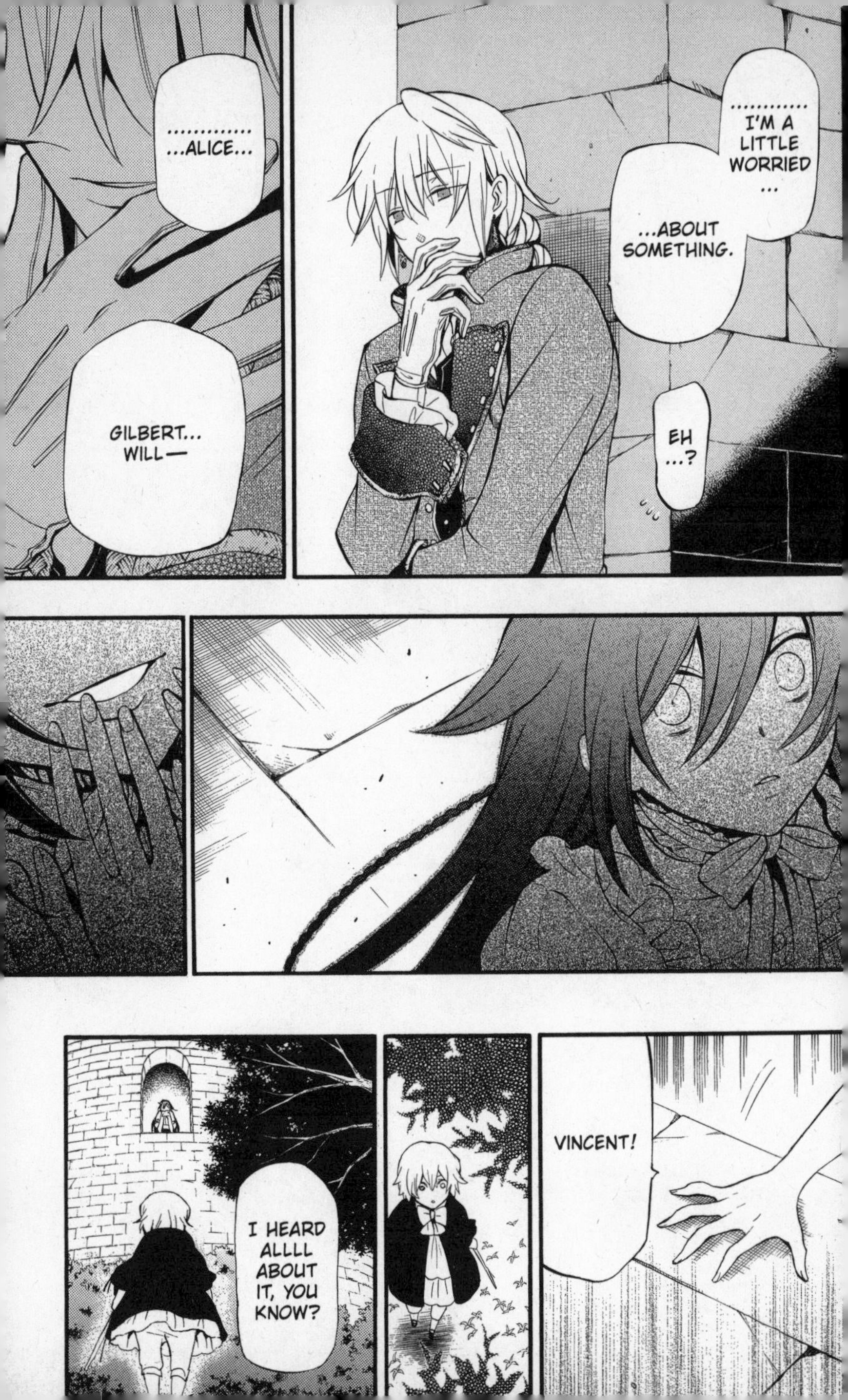
....
I'M A LITTLE WORRIED ...
...ABOUT SOMETHING.
EH ...?
....
...ALICE...
GILBERT... WILL—
VINCENT!
I HEARD ALLLL ABOUT IT, YOU KNOW?

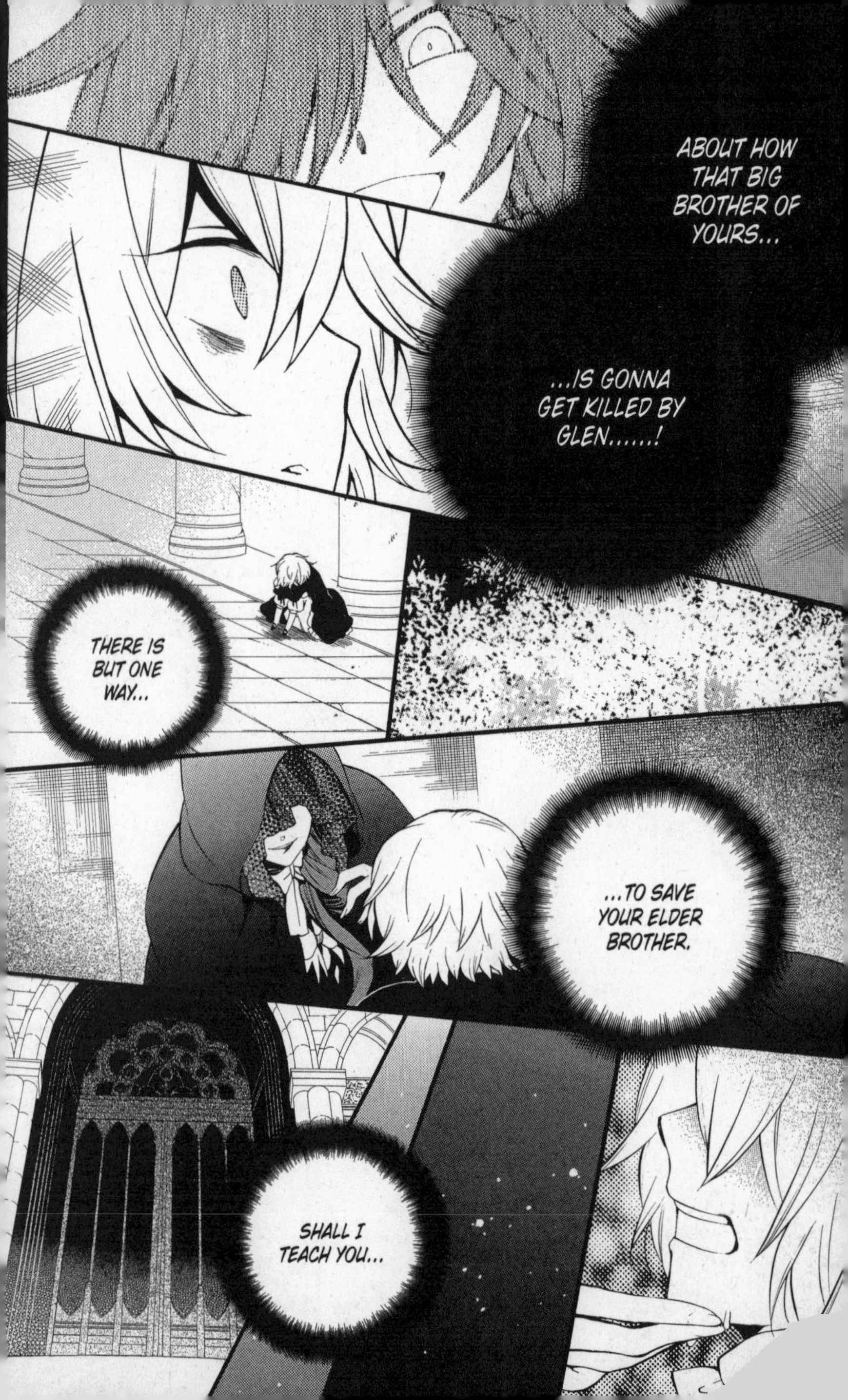
ABOUT HOW THAT BIG BROTHER OF YOURS...
...IS GONNA GET KILLED BY GLEN......!
THERE IS BUT ONE WAY...
...TO SAVE YOUR ELDER BROTHER.
SHALL I TEACH YOU...

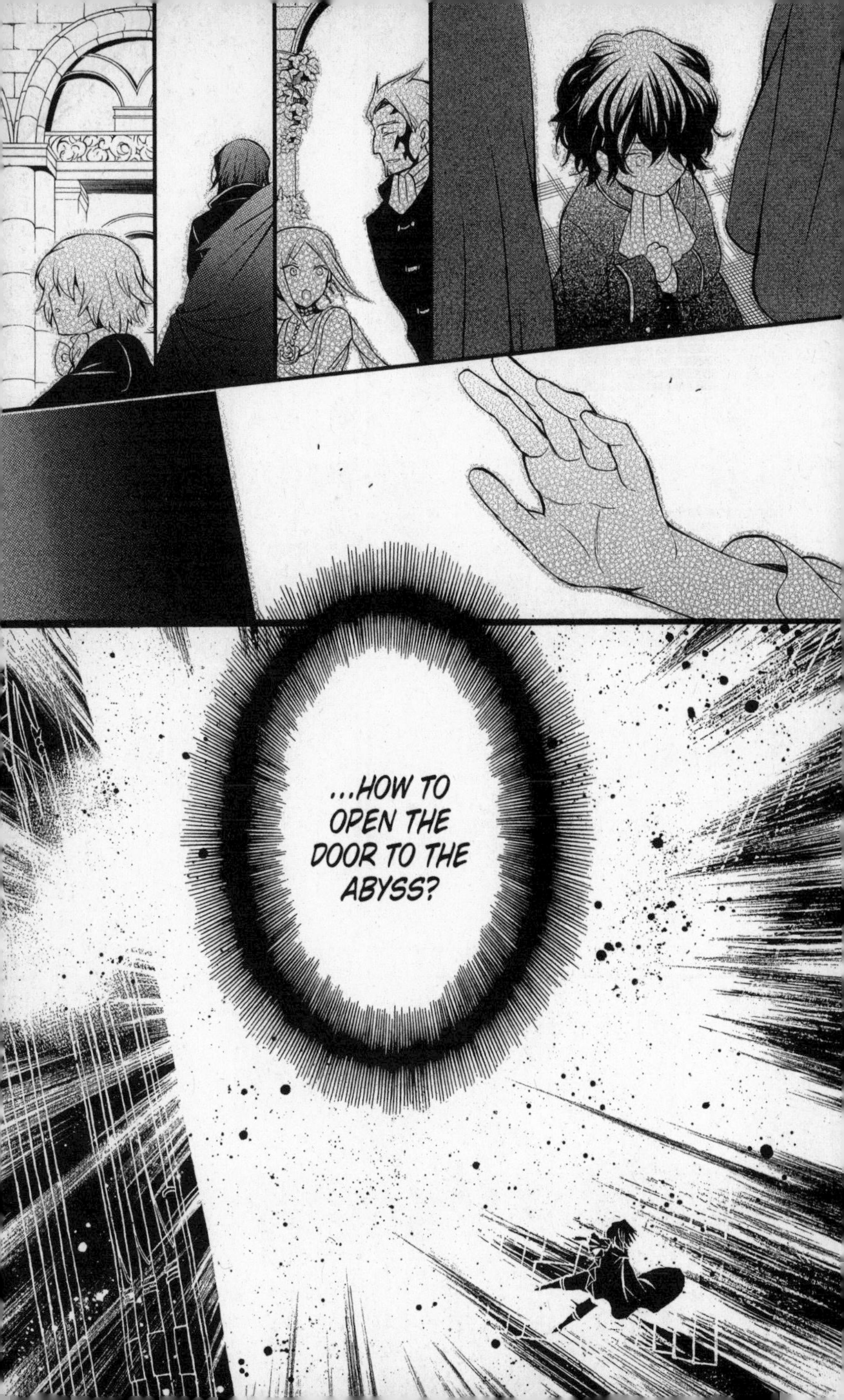
...HOW TO OPEN THE DOOR TO THE ABYSS?

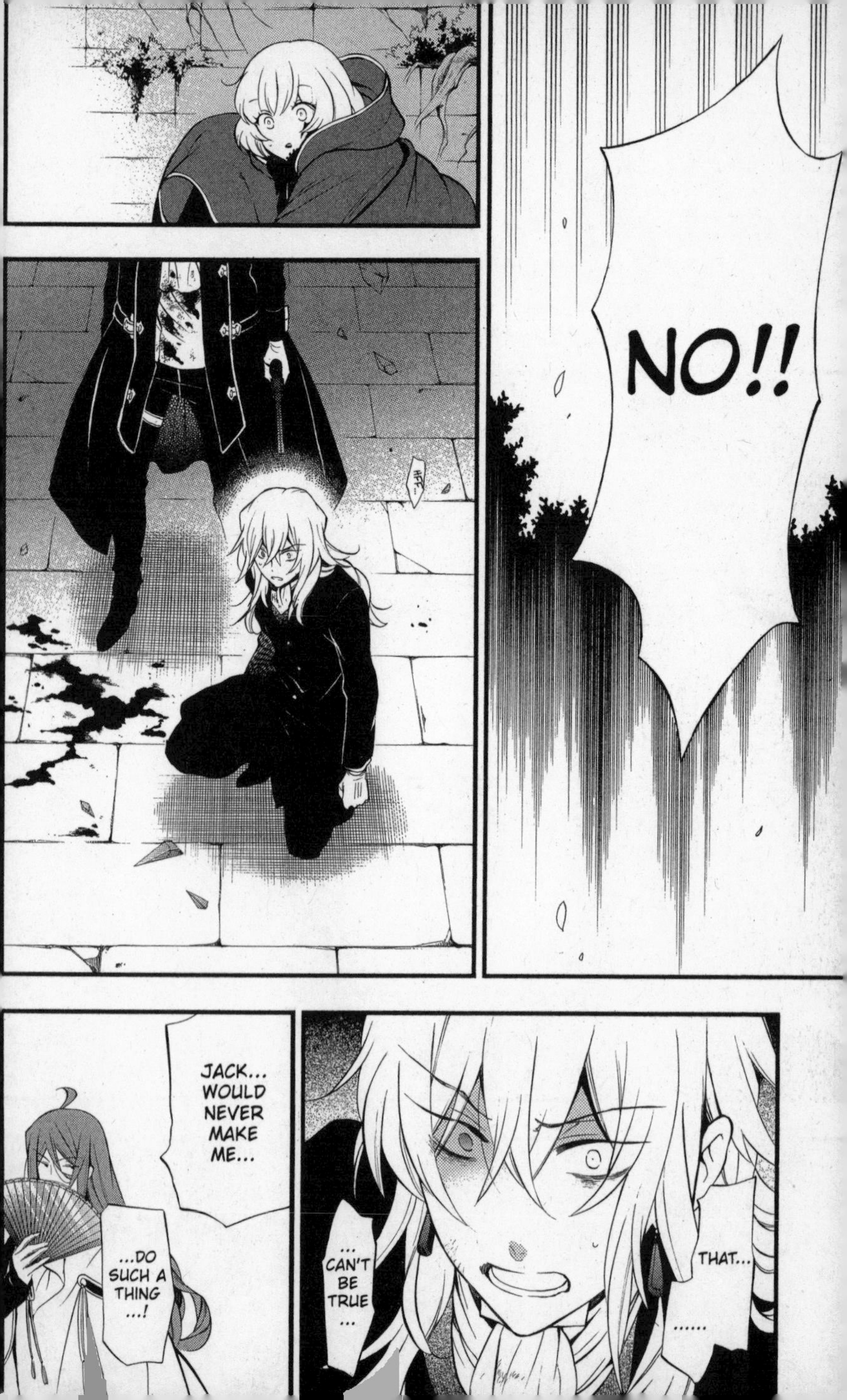
NO!!
HFF...
THAT...
......
...CAN'T BE TRUE...
JACK... WOULD NEVER MAKE ME...
...DO SUCH A THING...!

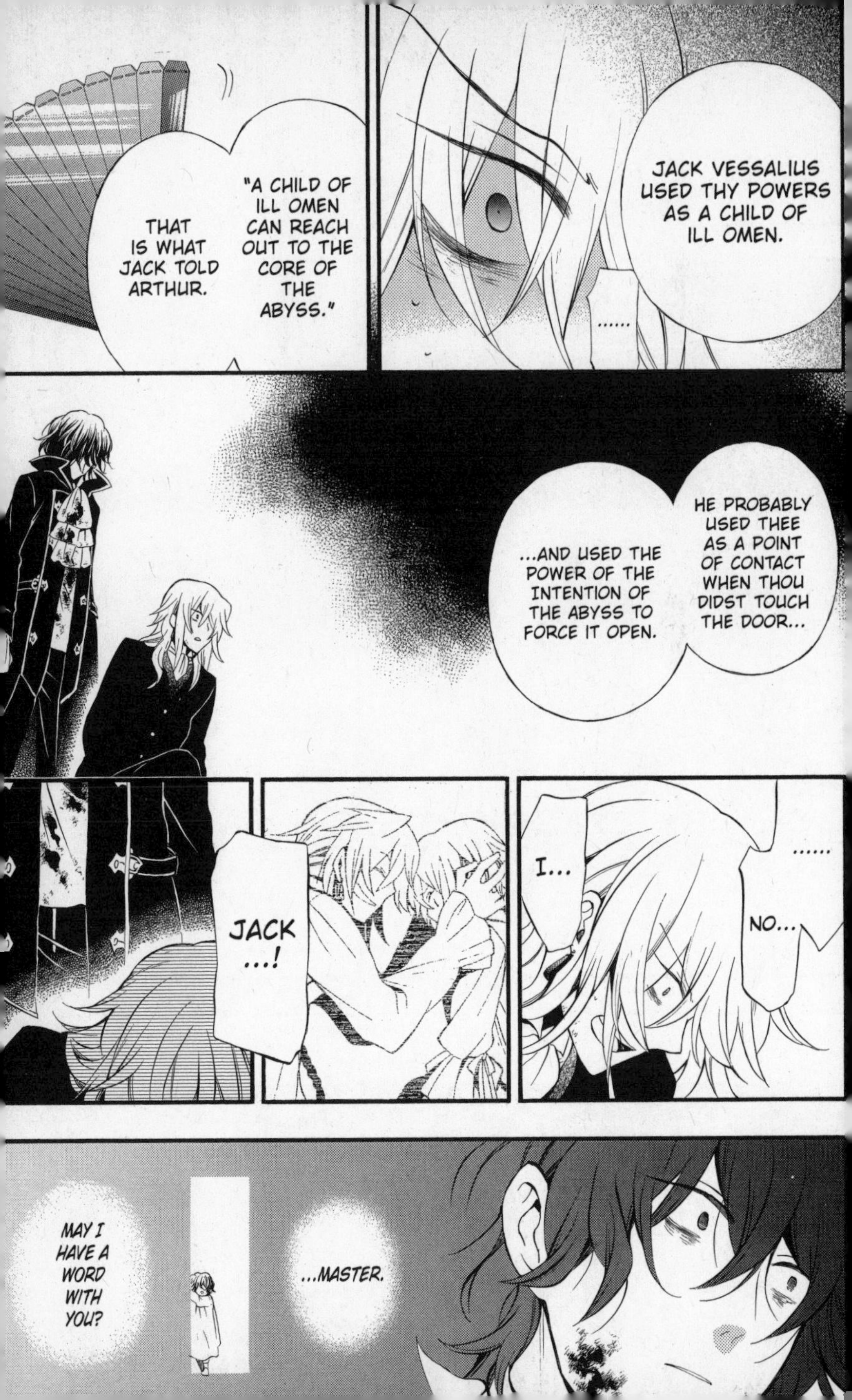
JACK VESSALIUS USED THY POWERS AS A CHILD OF ILL OMEN.
......
"A CHILD OF ILL OMEN CAN REACH OUT TO THE CORE OF THE ABYSS."
THAT IS WHAT JACK TOLD ARTHUR.
HE PROBABLY USED THEE AS A POINT OF CONTACT WHEN THOU DIDST TOUCH THE DOOR...
...AND USED THE POWER OF THE INTENTION OF THE ABYSS TO FORCE IT OPEN.
......
NO...
I...
JACK ...!
...MASTER.
MAY I HAVE A WORD WITH YOU?

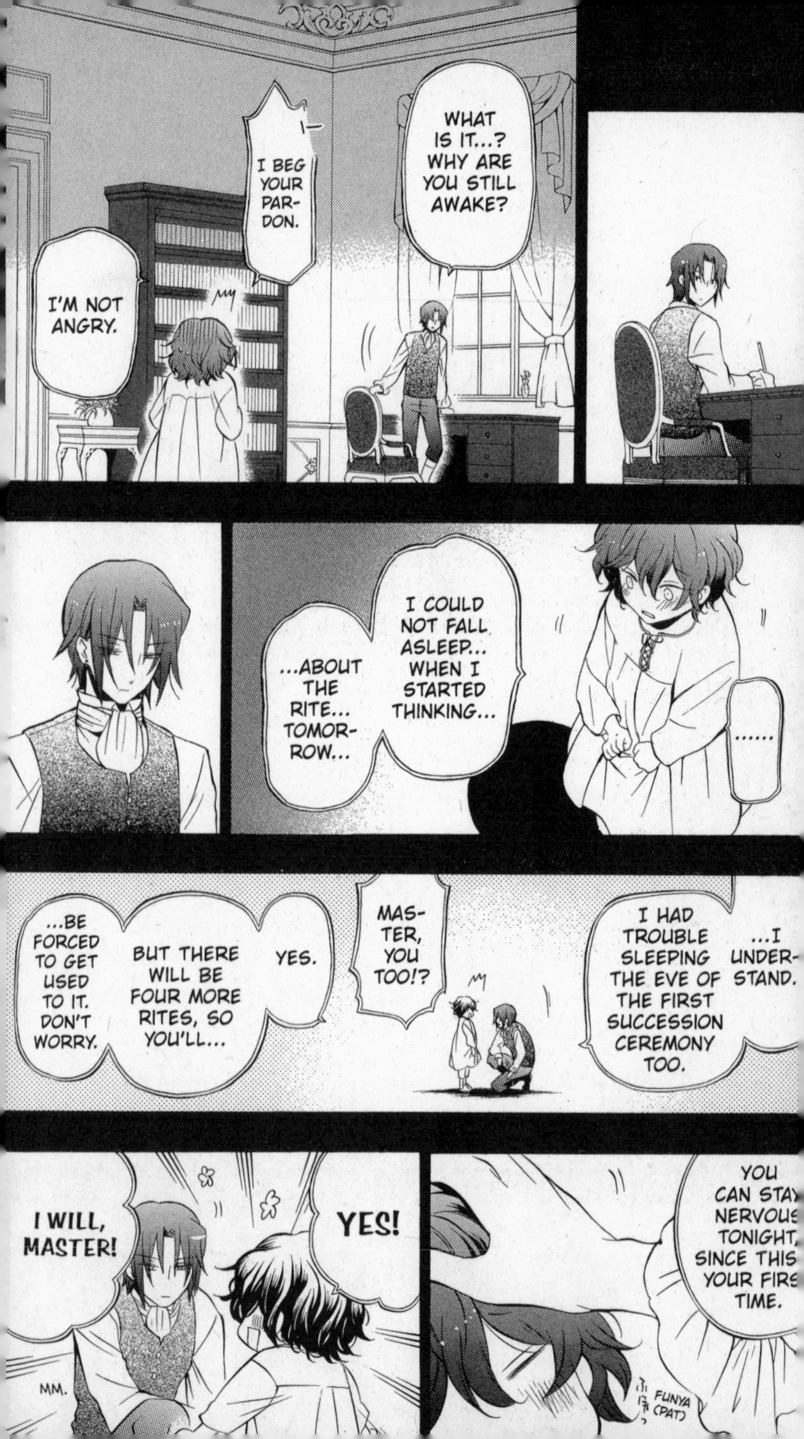
WHAT IS IT...? WHY ARE YOU STILL AWAKE?
I— I BEG YOUR PARDON.
MY
I'M NOT ANGRY.
......
I COULD NOT FALL ASLEEP... WHEN I STARTED THINKING...
...ABOUT THE RITE... TOMORROW...
...I UNDERSTAND.
I HAD TROUBLE SLEEPING THE EVE OF THE FIRST SUCCESSION CEREMONY TOO.
MY
MASTER, YOU TOO!?
YES.
BUT THERE WILL BE FOUR MORE RITES, SO YOU'LL...
...BE FORCED TO GET USED TO IT. DON'T WORRY.
YOU CAN STAY NERVOUS TONIGHT, SINCE THIS YOUR FIRS TIME.
FUNYA (PAT)
YES!
I WILL, MASTER!
MM.

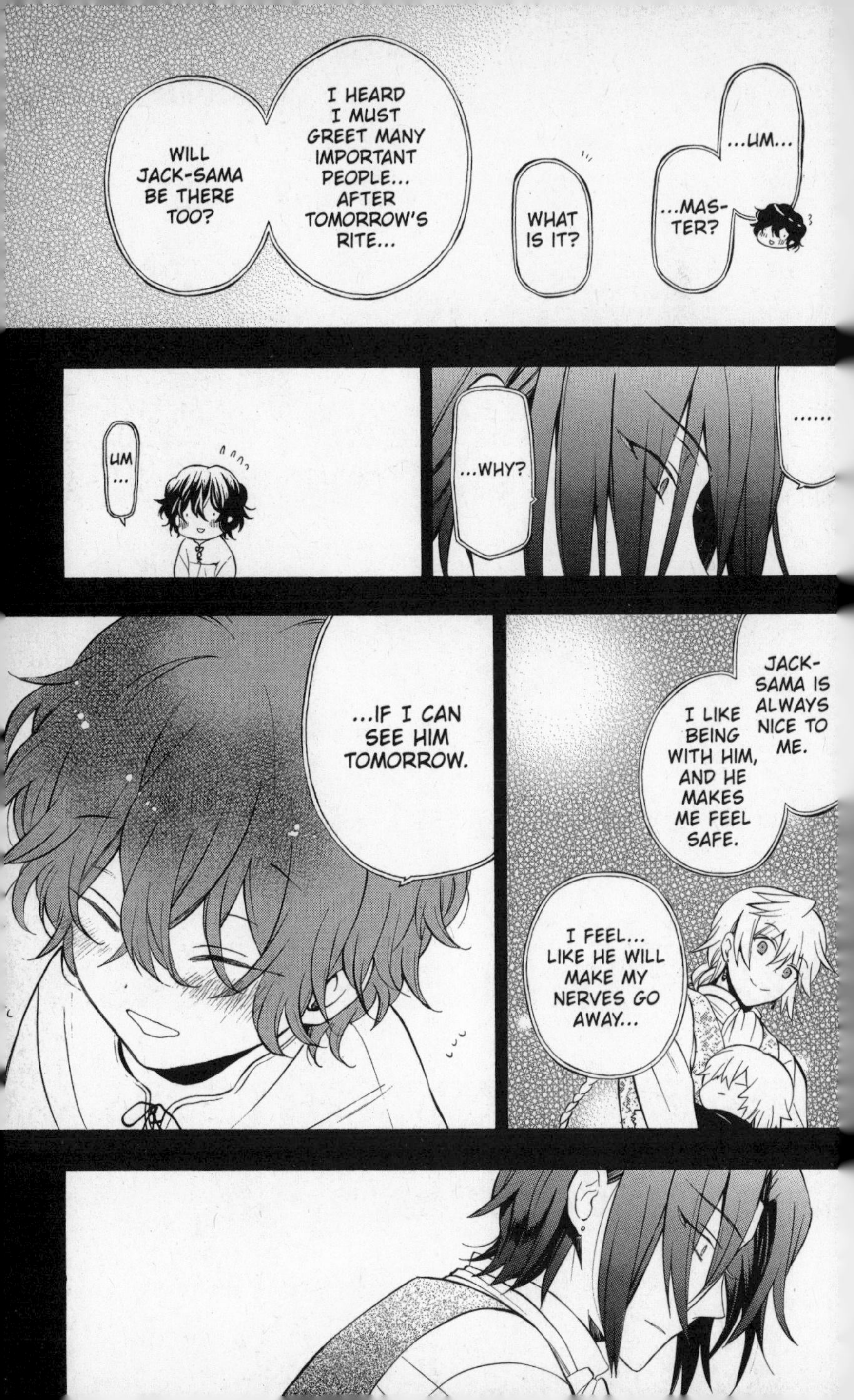
...UM...
...MAS-TER?
WHAT IS IT?
I HEARD I MUST GREET MANY IMPORTANT PEOPLE... AFTER TOMORROW'S RITE...
WILL JACK-SAMA BE THERE TOO?
......
...WHY?
UM ...
JACK-SAMA IS ALWAYS NICE TO ME.
I LIKE BEING WITH HIM, AND HE MAKES ME FEEL SAFE.
I FEEL... LIKE HE WILL MAKE MY NERVES GO AWAY...
...IF I CAN SEE HIM TOMORROW.

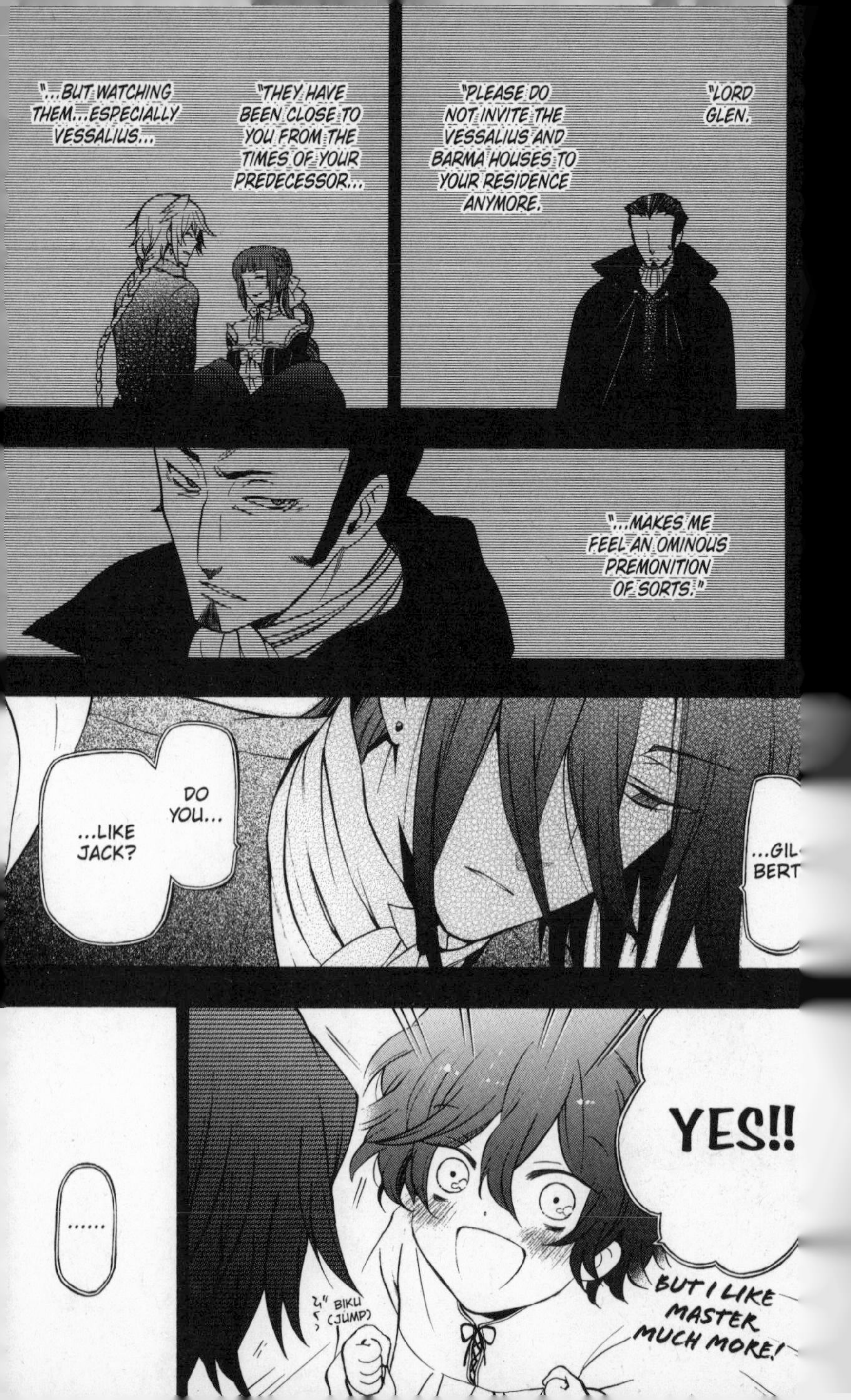
"LORD GLEN.
"PLEASE DO NOT INVITE THE VESSALIUS AND BARMA HOUSES TO YOUR RESIDENCE ANYMORE.
"THEY HAVE BEEN CLOSE TO YOU FROM THE TIMES OF YOUR PREDECESSOR...
"...BUT WATCHING THEM...ESPECIALLY VESSALIUS...
"...MAKES ME FEEL AN OMINOUS PREMONITION OF SORTS."
...GIL-BERT
DO YOU...
...LIKE JACK?
YES!!
BUT I LIKE MASTER MUCH MORE!
BIKU (JUMP)
......

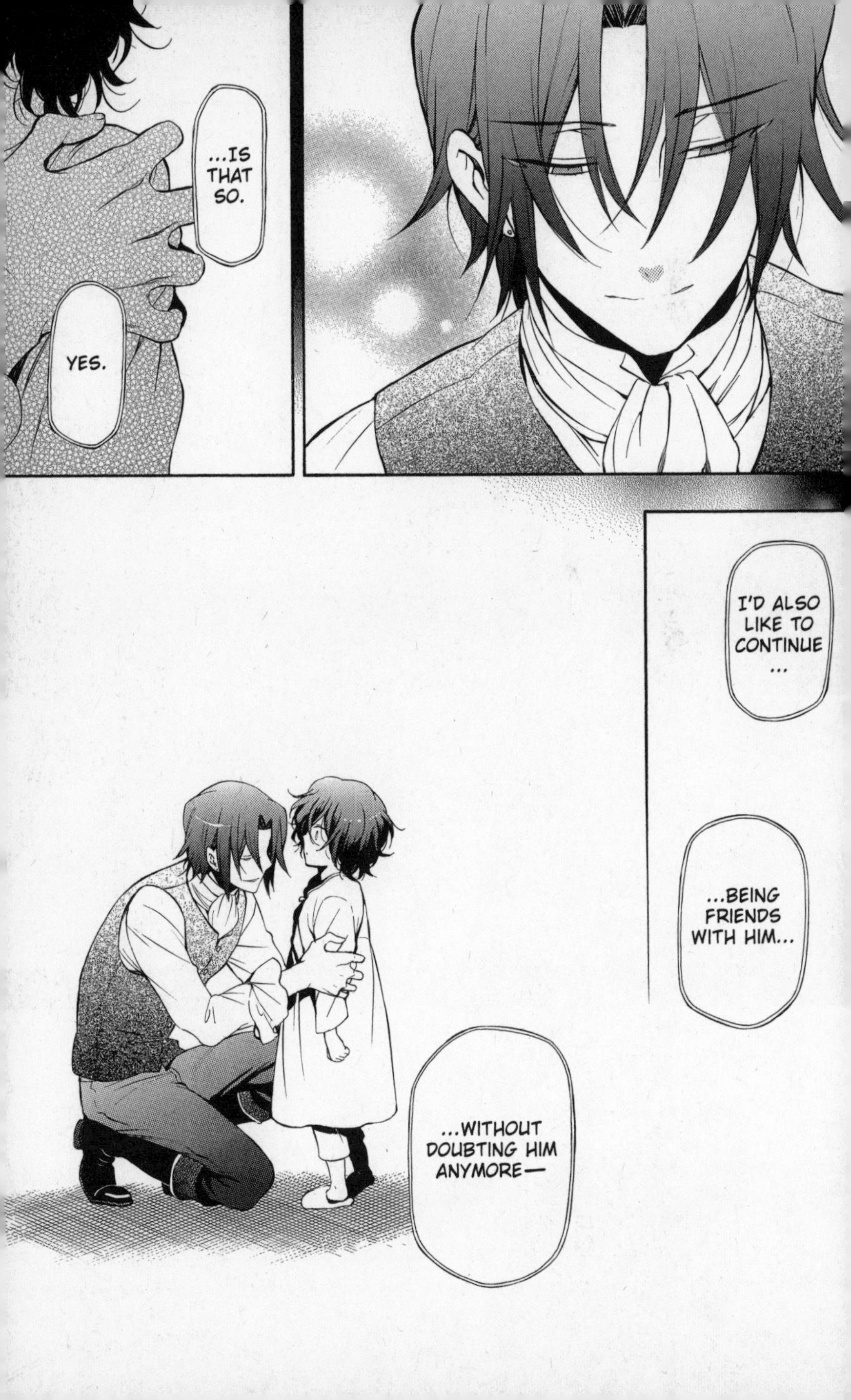
...IS THAT SO.
YES.
I'D ALSO LIKE TO CONTINUE ...
...BEING FRIENDS WITH HIM...
...WITHOUT DOUBTING HIM ANYMORE—

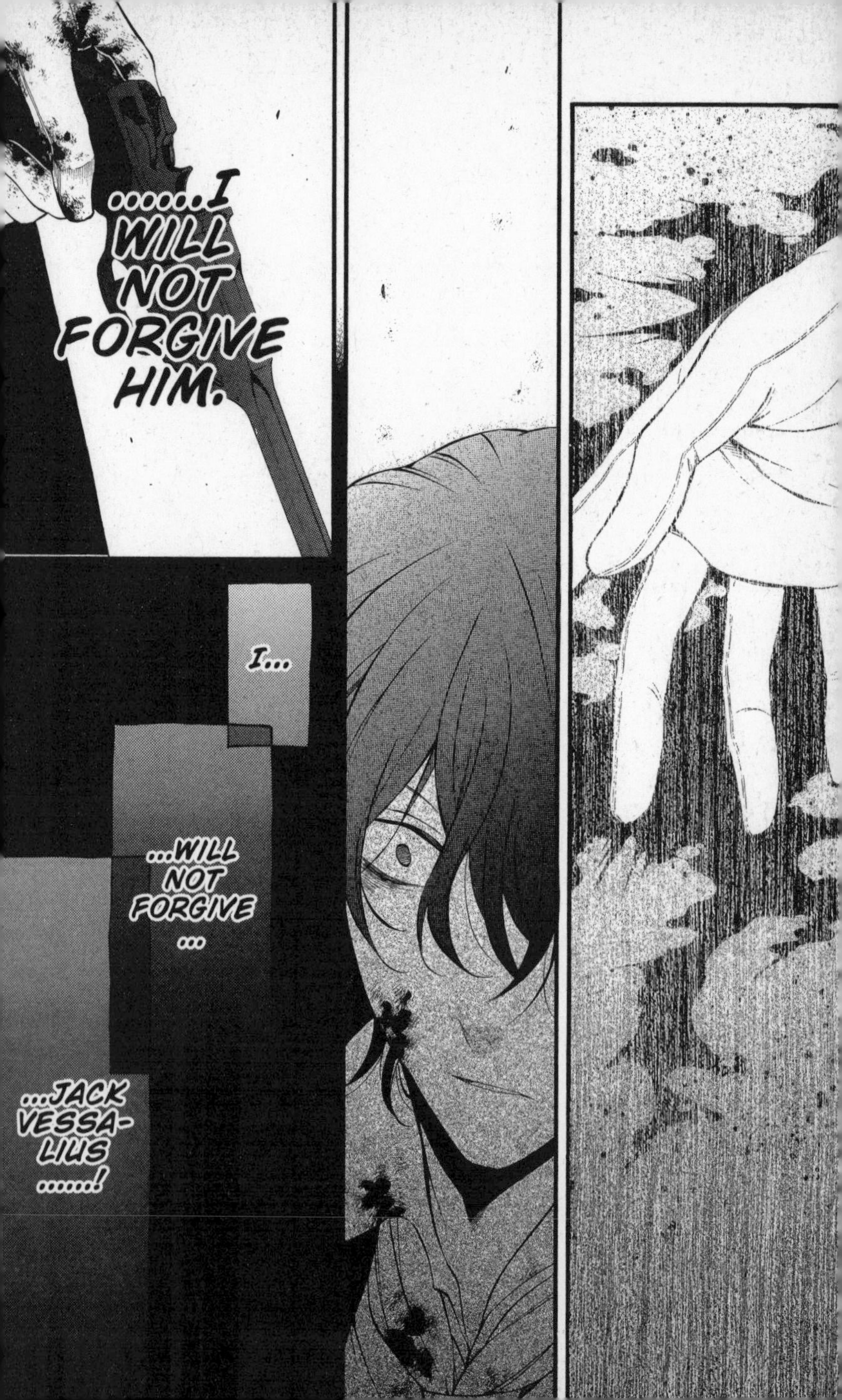
......I WILL NOT FORGIVE HIM.
I...
...WILL NOT FORGIVE ...
...JACK VESSA-LIUS ......!

Retrace:LXXIII   A note

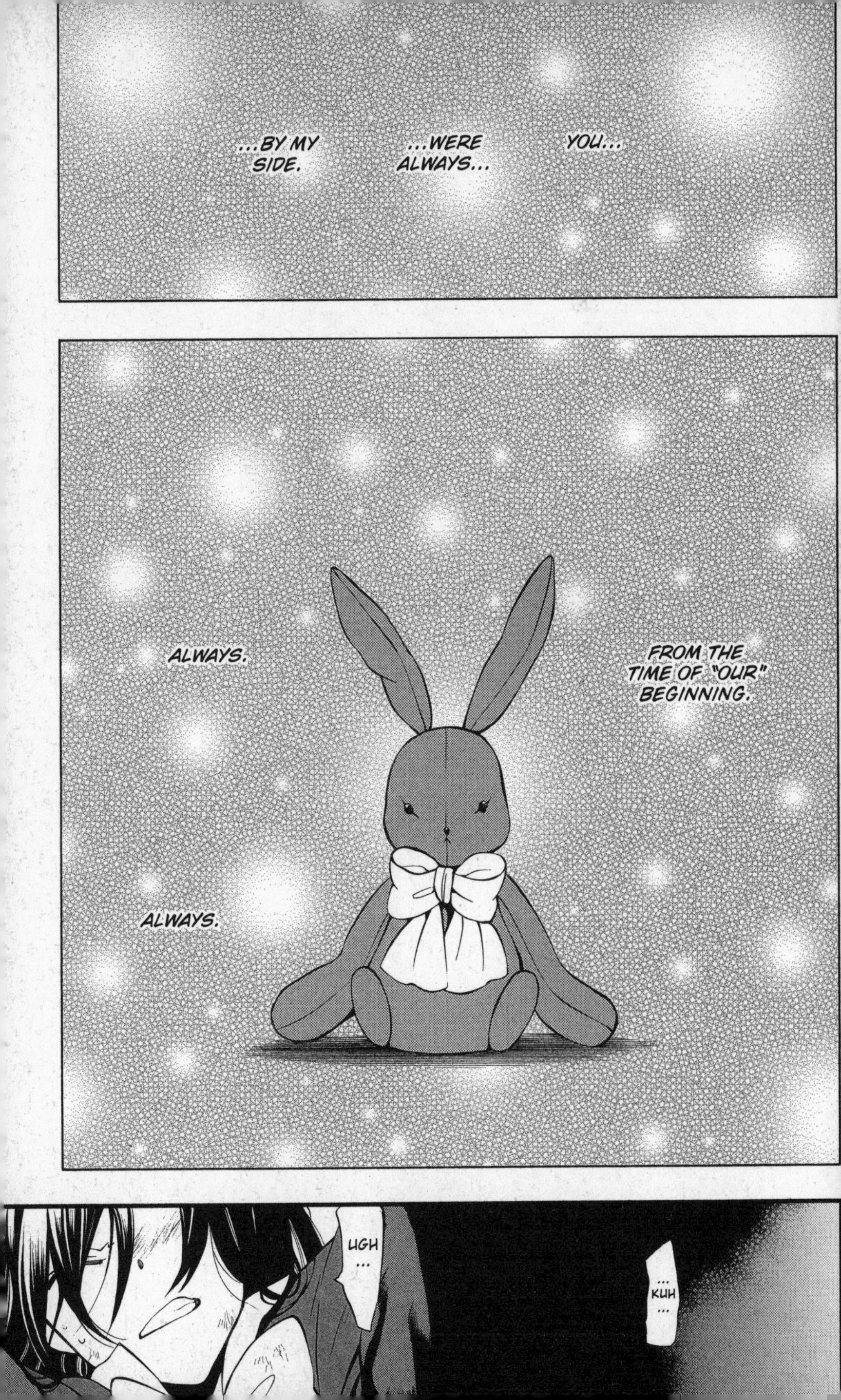
YOU...
...WERE ALWAYS...
...BY MY SIDE.
FROM THE TIME OF "OUR" BEGINNING.
ALWAYS.
ALWAYS.
...KUH...
UGH...

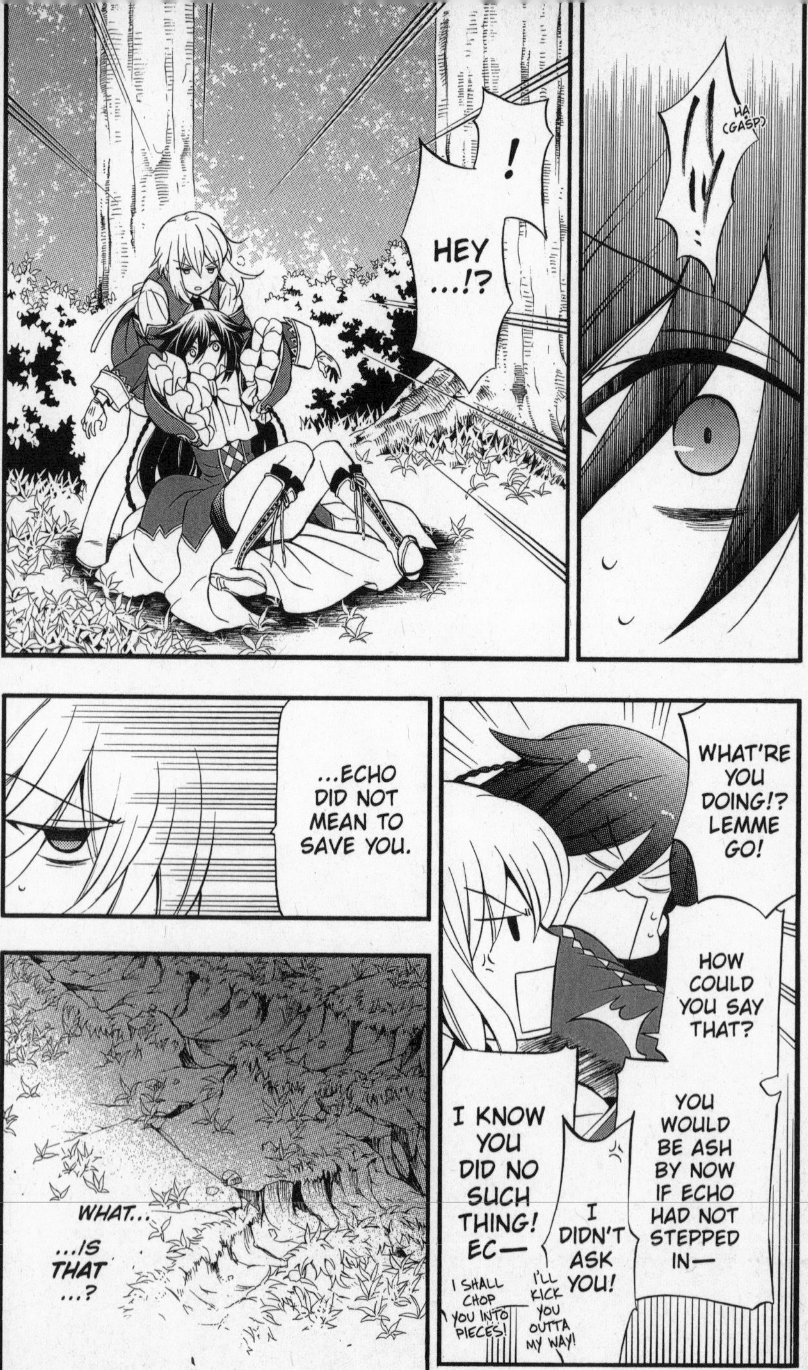
HA (GASP)
!
HEY ...!?
WHAT'RE YOU DOING!? LEMME GO!
HOW COULD YOU SAY THAT?
YOU WOULD BE ASH BY NOW IF ECHO HAD NOT STEPPED IN—
I DIDN'T ASK YOU!
I KNOW YOU DID NO SUCH THING! EC—
I'LL KICK YOU OUTTA MY WAY!
I SHALL CHOP YOU INTO PIECES!
...ECHO DID NOT MEAN TO SAVE YOU.
WHAT...
...IS THAT ...?

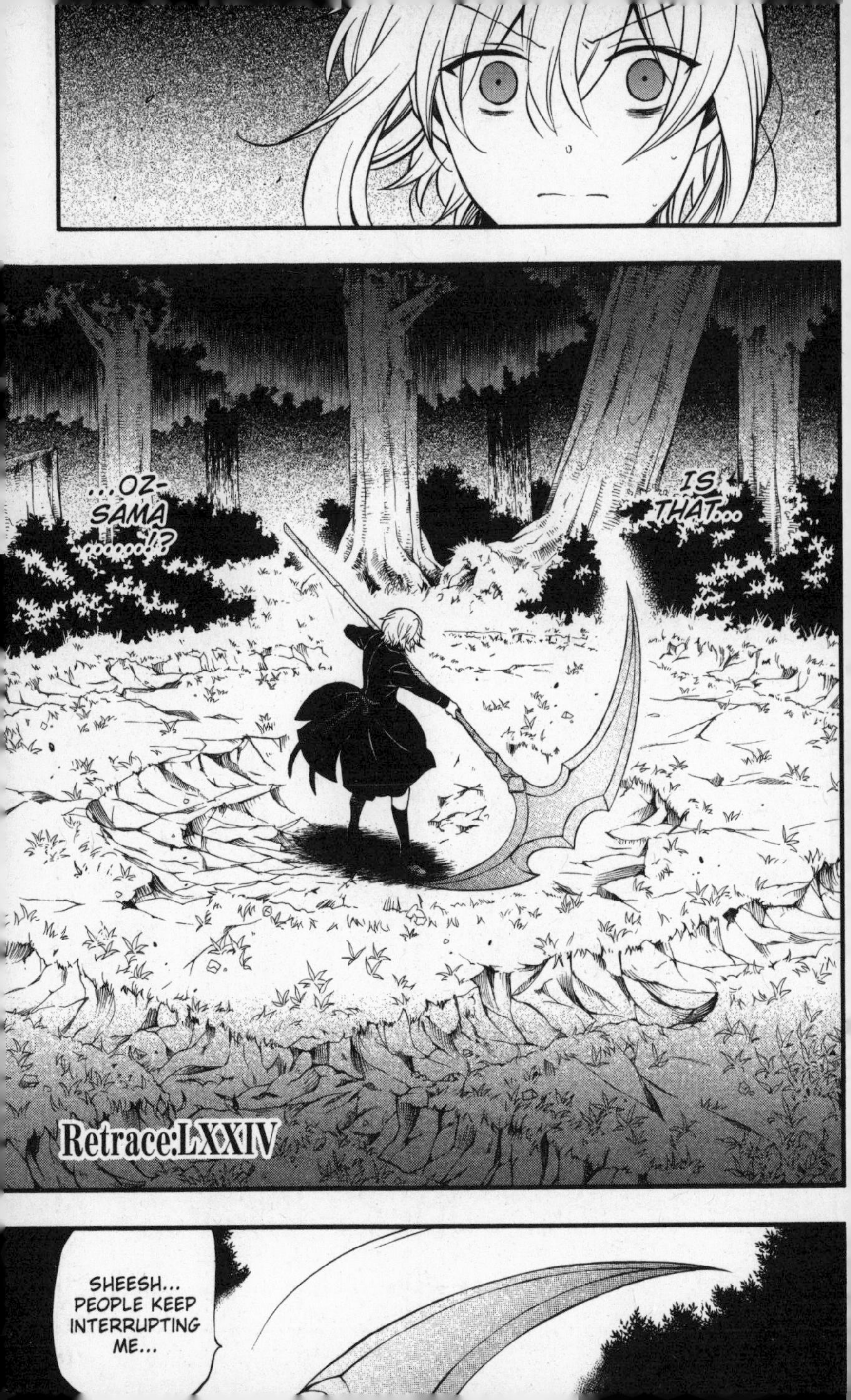
IS THAT...
...OZ-SAMA......!?
Retrace:LXXIV
SHEESH... PEOPLE KEEP INTERRUPTING ME...

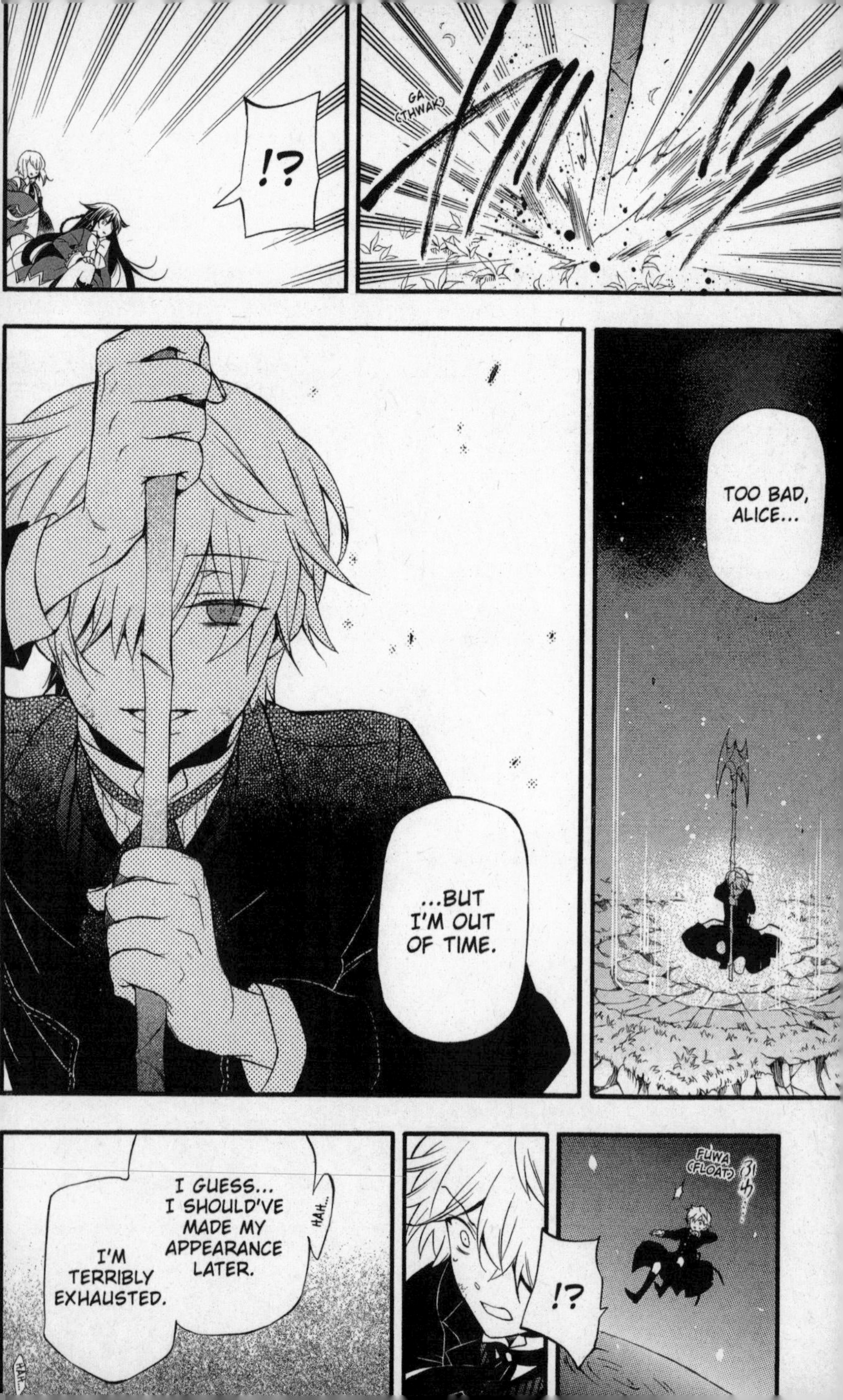
GA (THWAK)
!?
TOO BAD, ALICE...
...BUT I'M OUT OF TIME.
FUWA (FLOAT)
!?
HAH...
I GUESS... I SHOULD'VE MADE MY APPEARANCE LATER.
I'M TERRIBLY EXHAUSTED.
HAH...

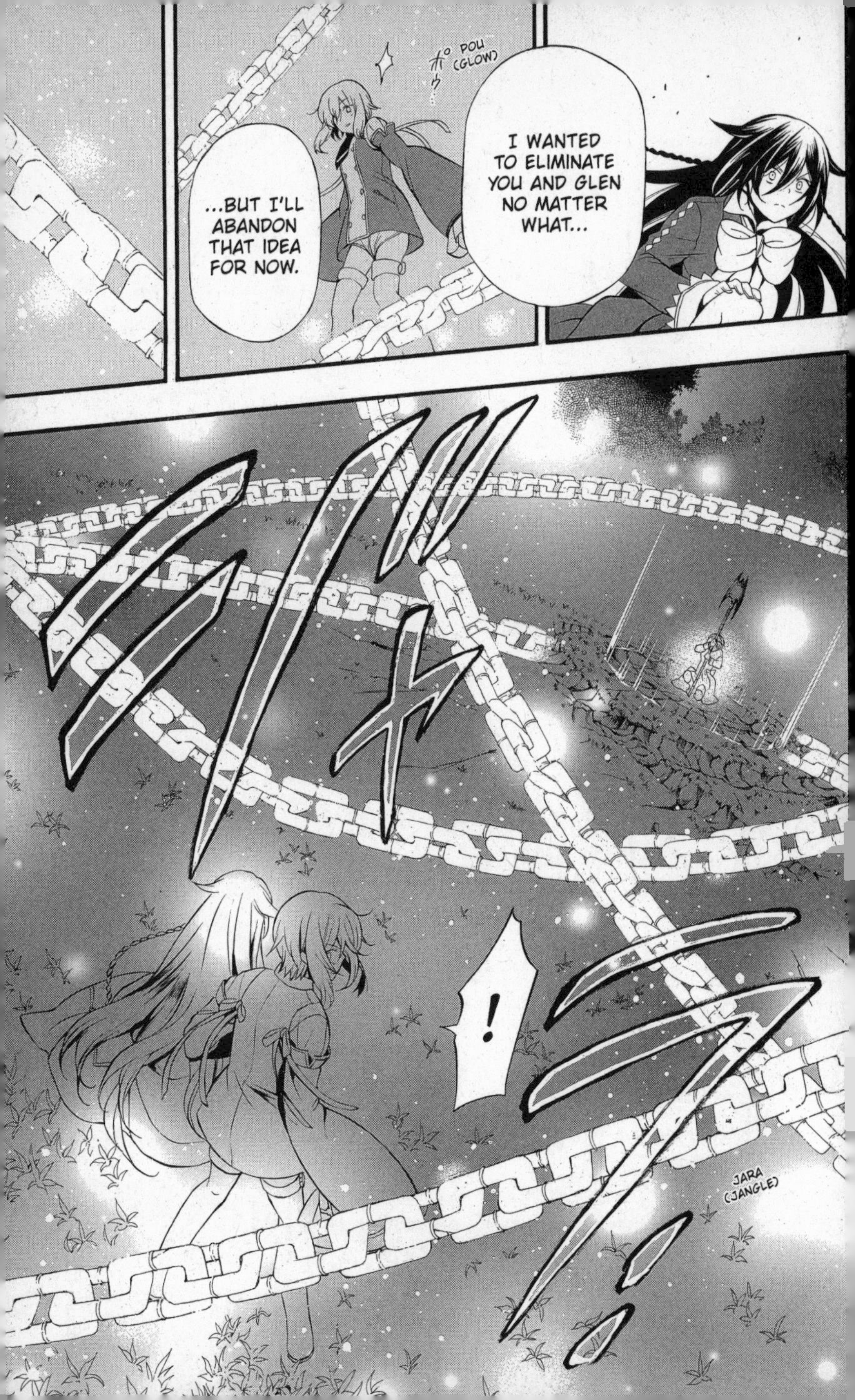
POU (GLOW)
I WANTED TO ELIMINATE YOU AND GLEN NO MATTER WHAT...
...BUT I'LL ABANDON THAT IDEA FOR NOW.
!
JARA (JANGLE)

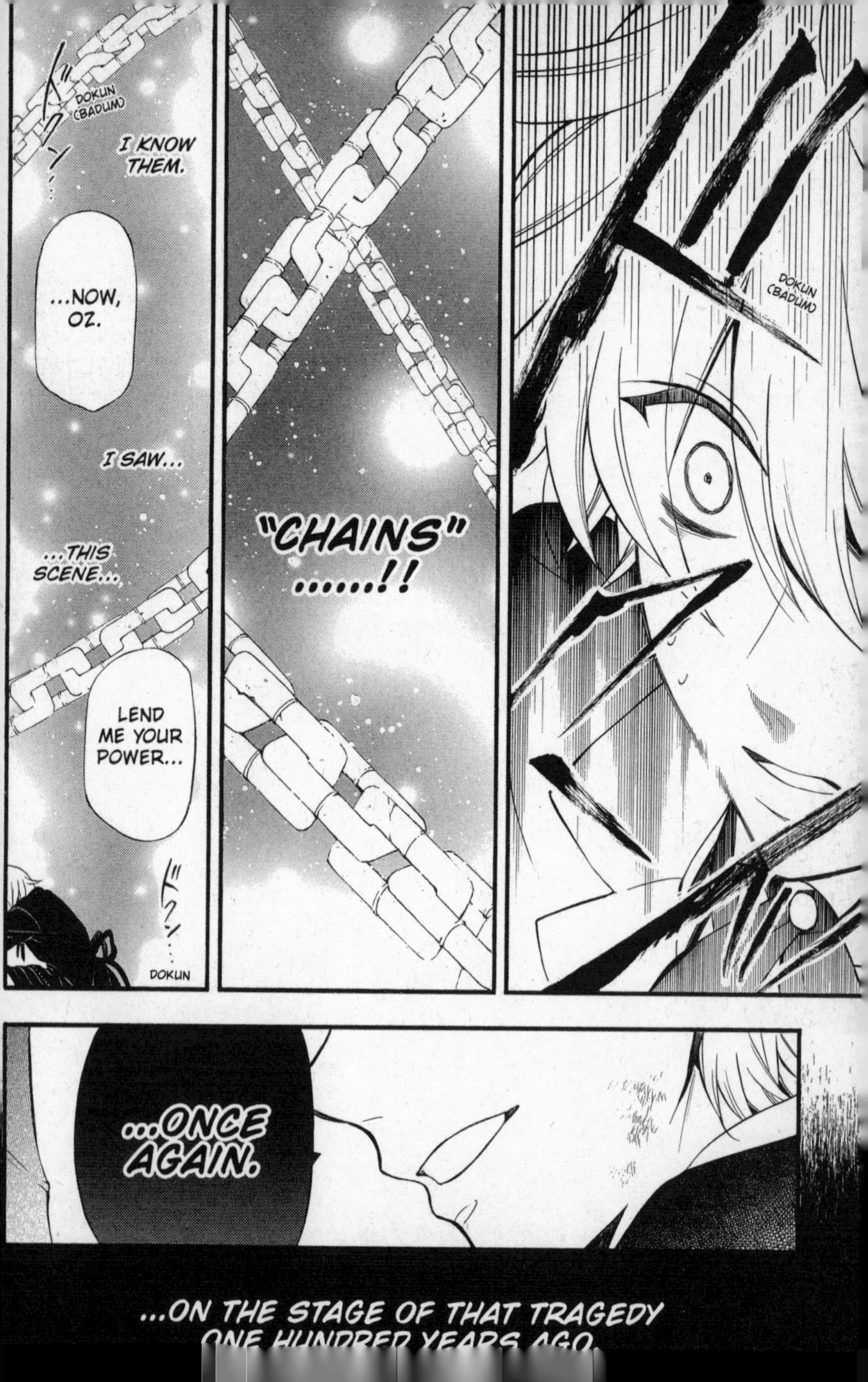
DOKUN (BADUM)
"CHAINS" ......!!
DOKUN (BADUM)
I KNOW THEM.
...NOW, OZ.
I SAW...
...THIS SCENE...
LEND ME YOUR POWER...
DOKUN
...ONCE AGAIN.
...ON THE STAGE OF THAT TRAGEDY ONE HUNDRED YEARS AGO.

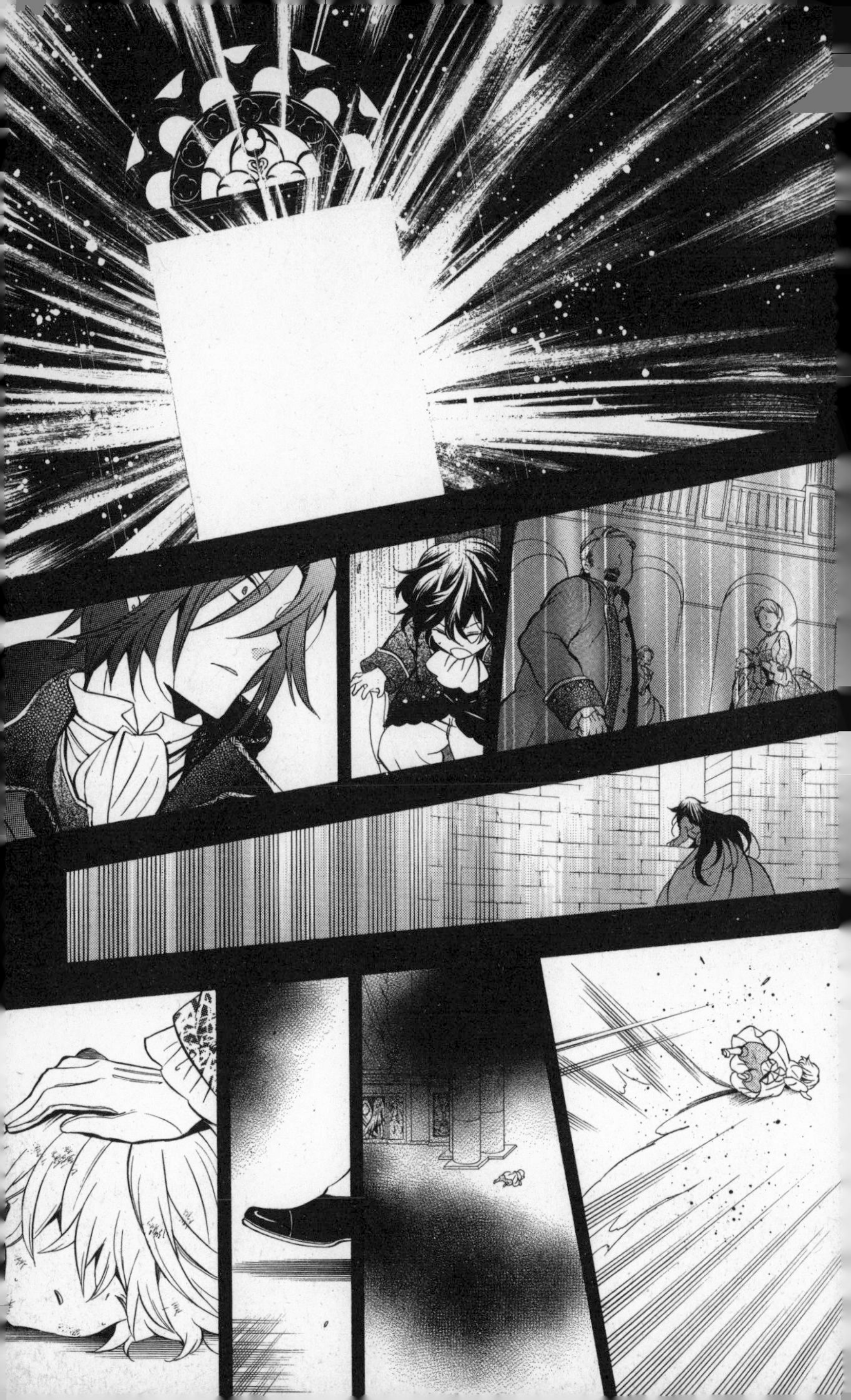

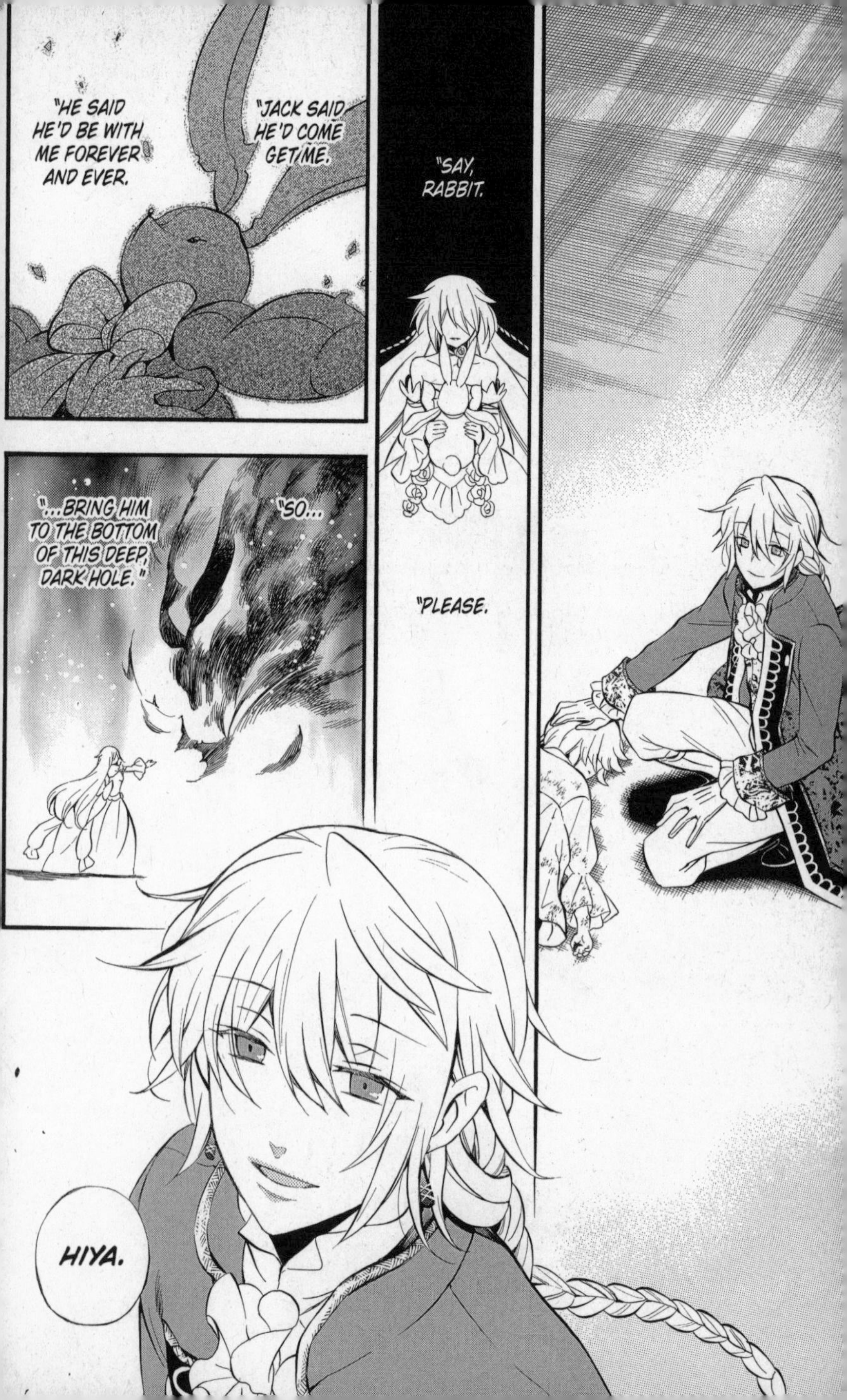
"SAY, RABBIT.
"PLEASE.
"JACK SAID HE'D COME GET ME.
"HE SAID HE'D BE WITH ME FOREVER AND EVER.
"SO...
"...BRING HIM TO THE BOTTOM OF THIS DEEP, DARK HOLE."
HIYA.

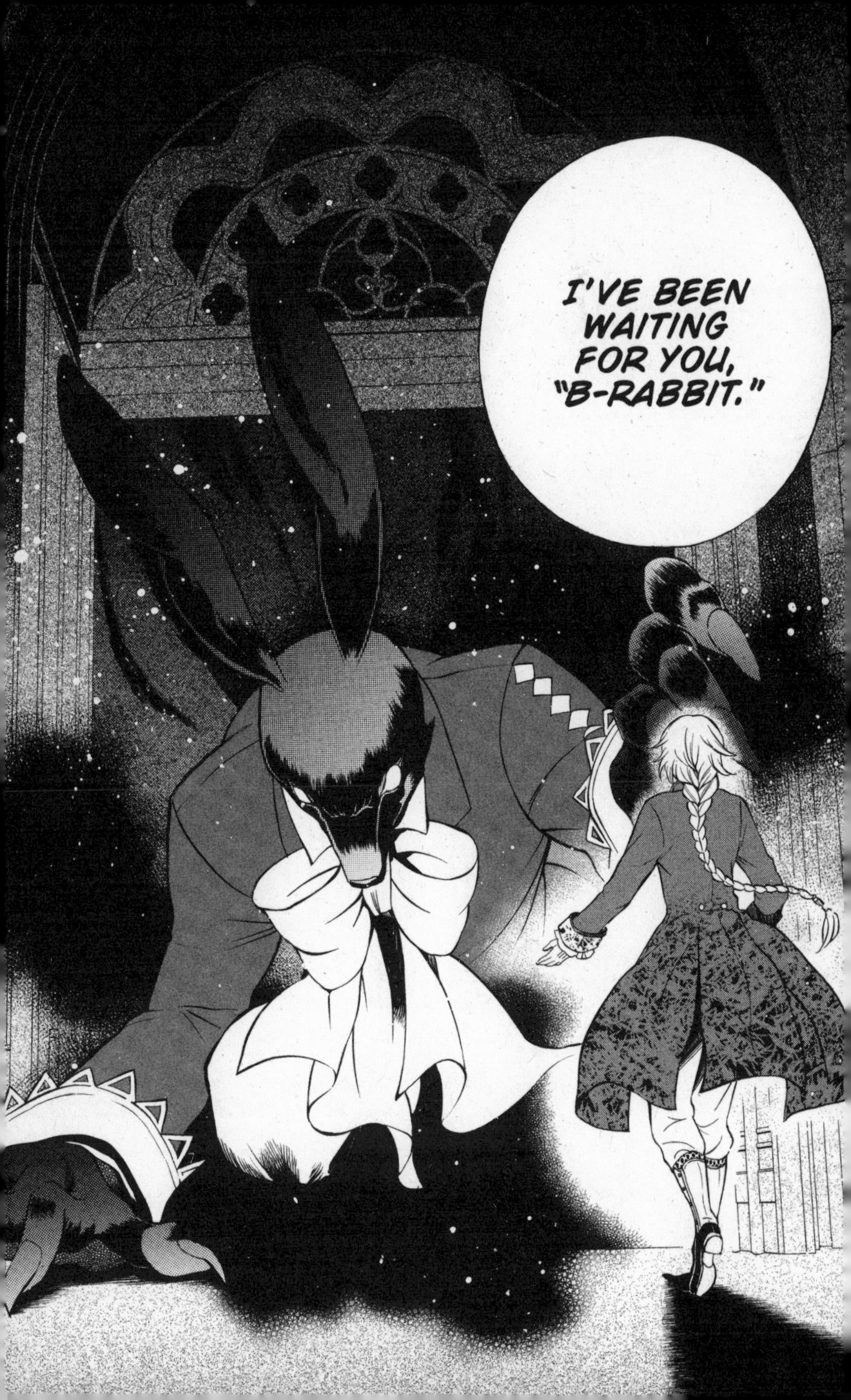
I'VE BEEN WAITING FOR YOU, "B-RABBIT."

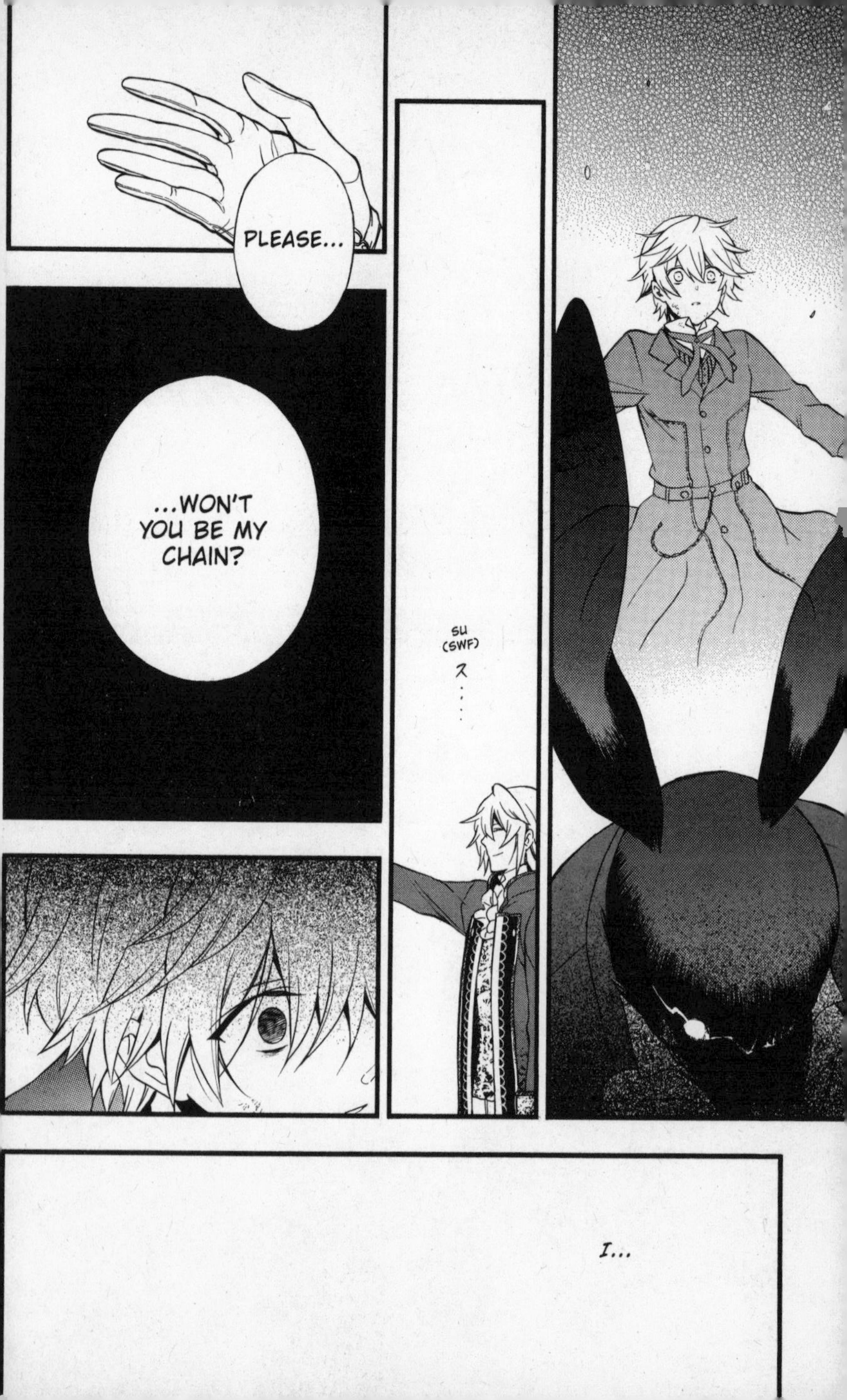
SU (SWF)
ス....
PLEASE...
...WON'T YOU BE MY CHAIN?
I...

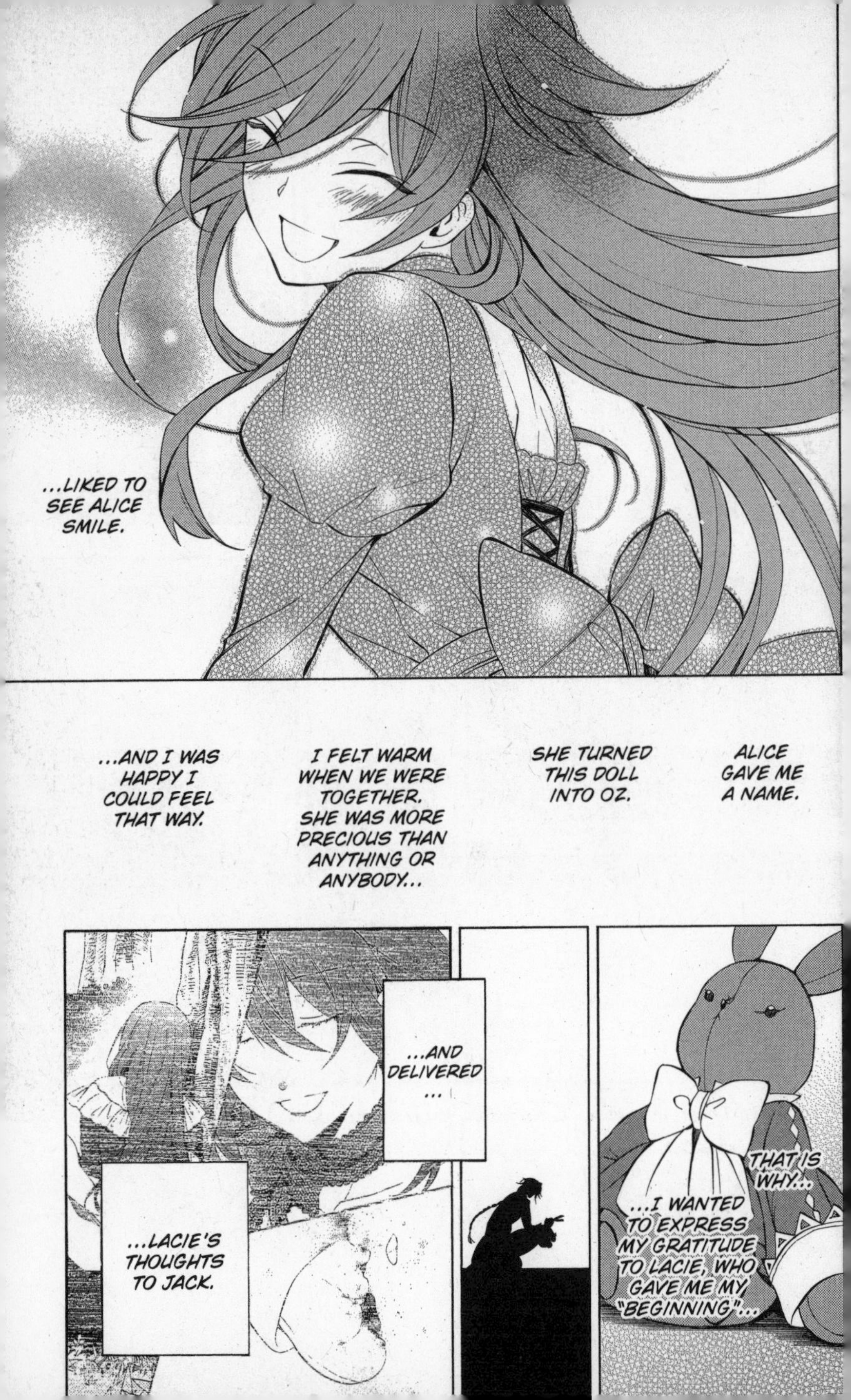
...LIKED TO SEE ALICE SMILE.
ALICE GAVE ME A NAME.
SHE TURNED THIS DOLL INTO OZ.
I FELT WARM WHEN WE WERE TOGETHER. SHE WAS MORE PRECIOUS THAN ANYTHING OR ANYBODY...
...AND I WAS HAPPY I COULD FEEL THAT WAY.
THAT IS WHY...
...I WANTED TO EXPRESS MY GRATITUDE TO LACIE, WHO GAVE ME MY "BEGINNING"...
...AND DELIVERED...
...LACIE'S THOUGHTS TO JACK.

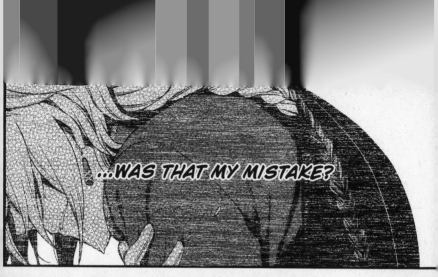

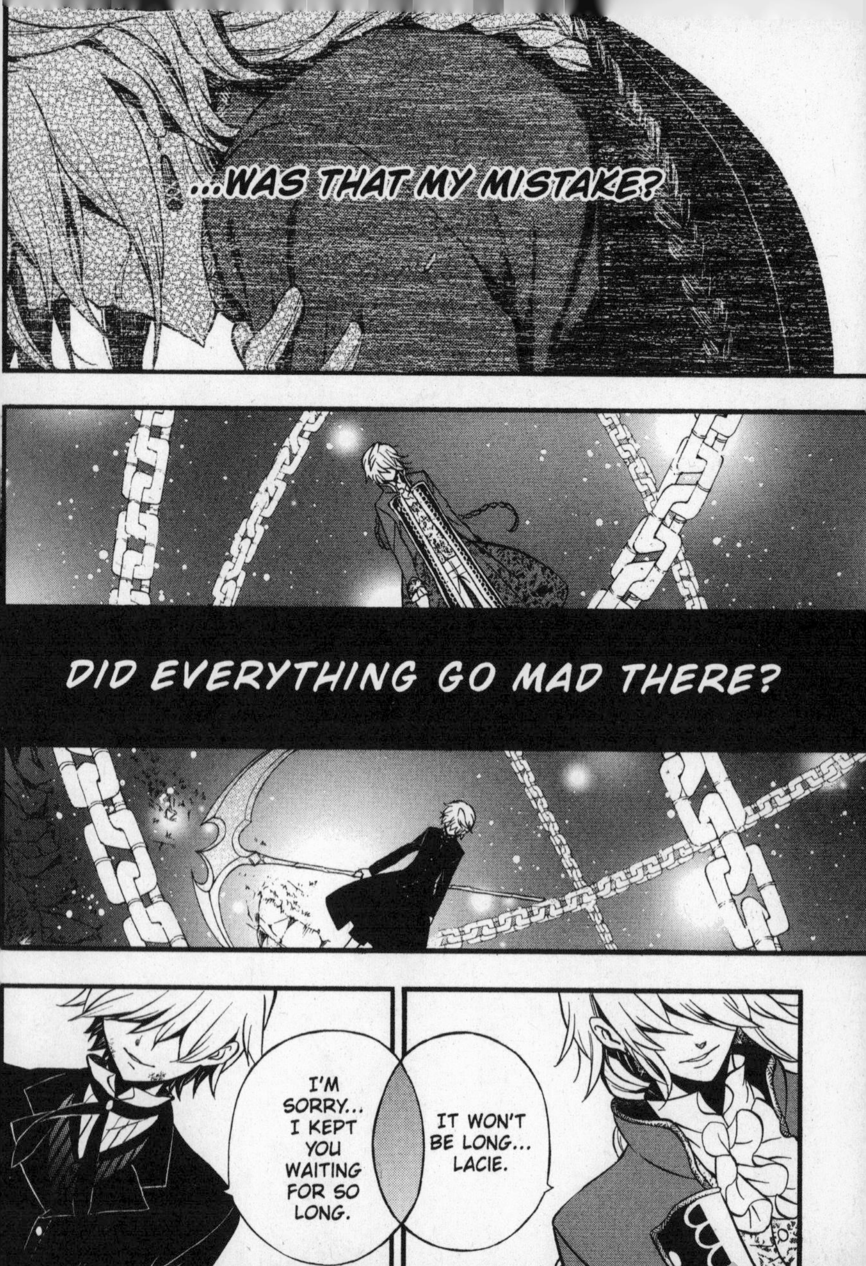
...WAS THAT MY MISTAKE?
DID EVERYTHING GO MAD THERE?
IT WON'T BE LONG... LACIE.
I'M SORRY... I KEPT YOU WAITING FOR SO LONG.

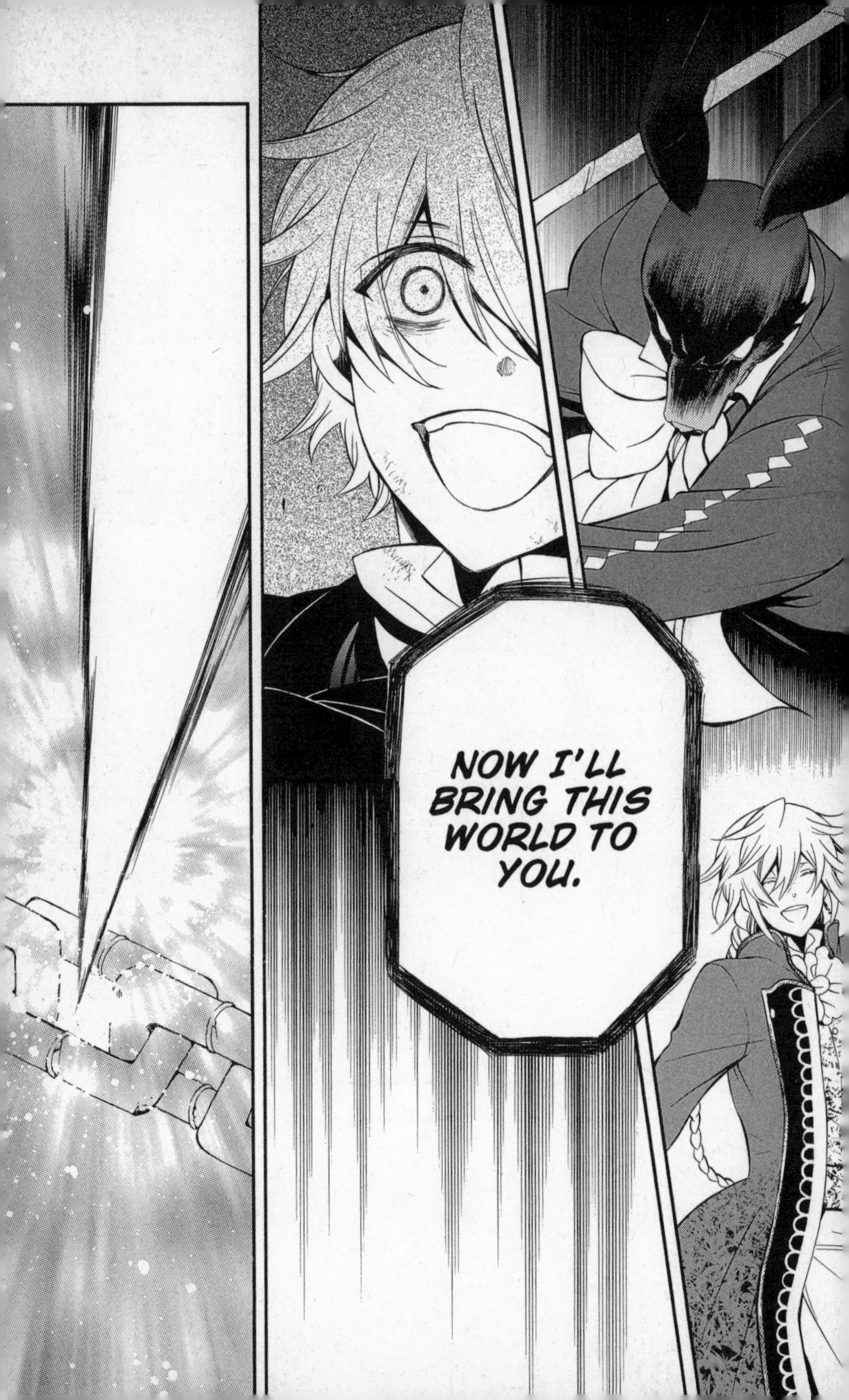
NOW I'LL BRING THIS WORLD TO YOU.

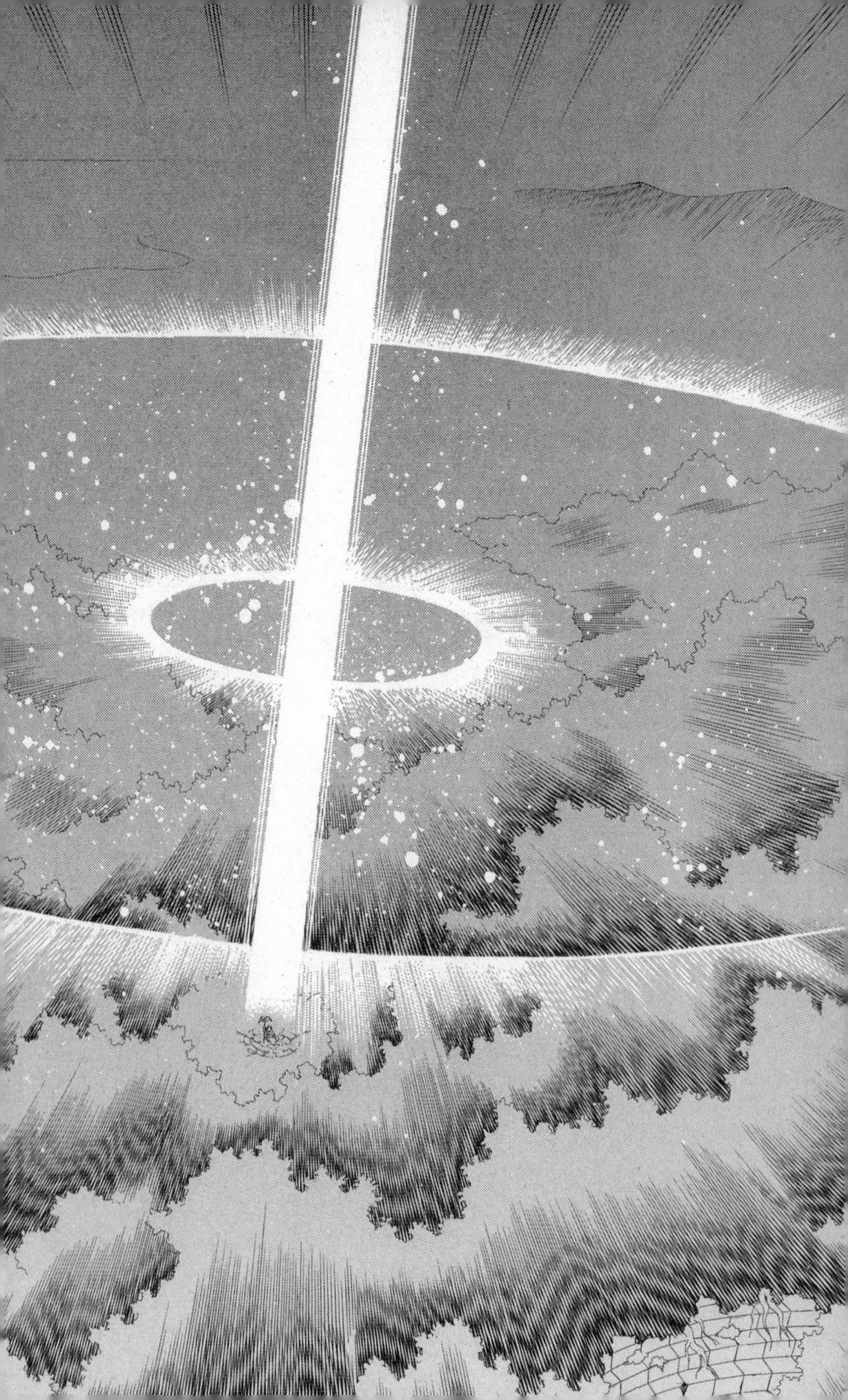

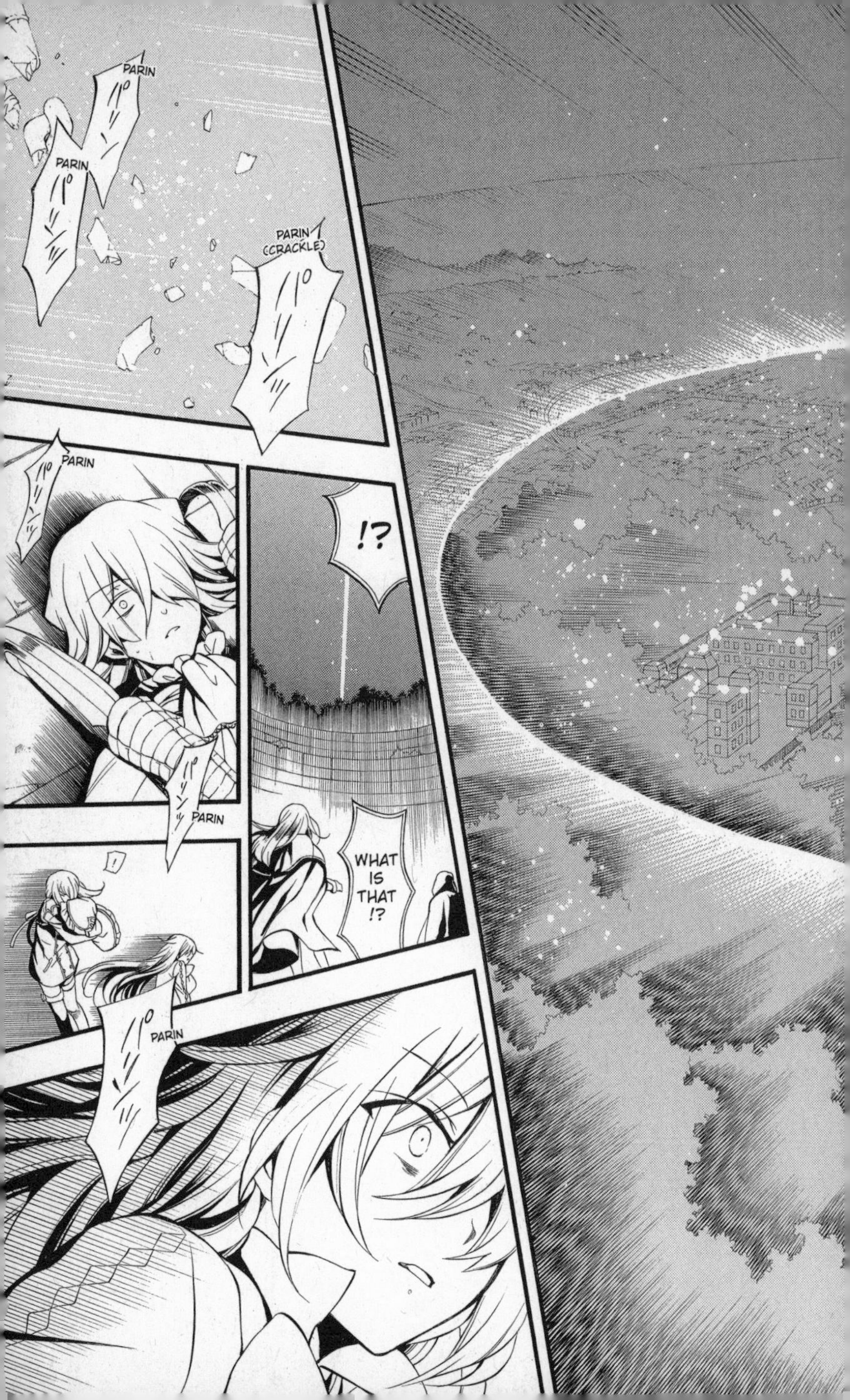
PARIN
PARIN
PARIN (CRACKLE)
!?
WHAT IS THAT !?
PARIN
PARIN
!
PARIN

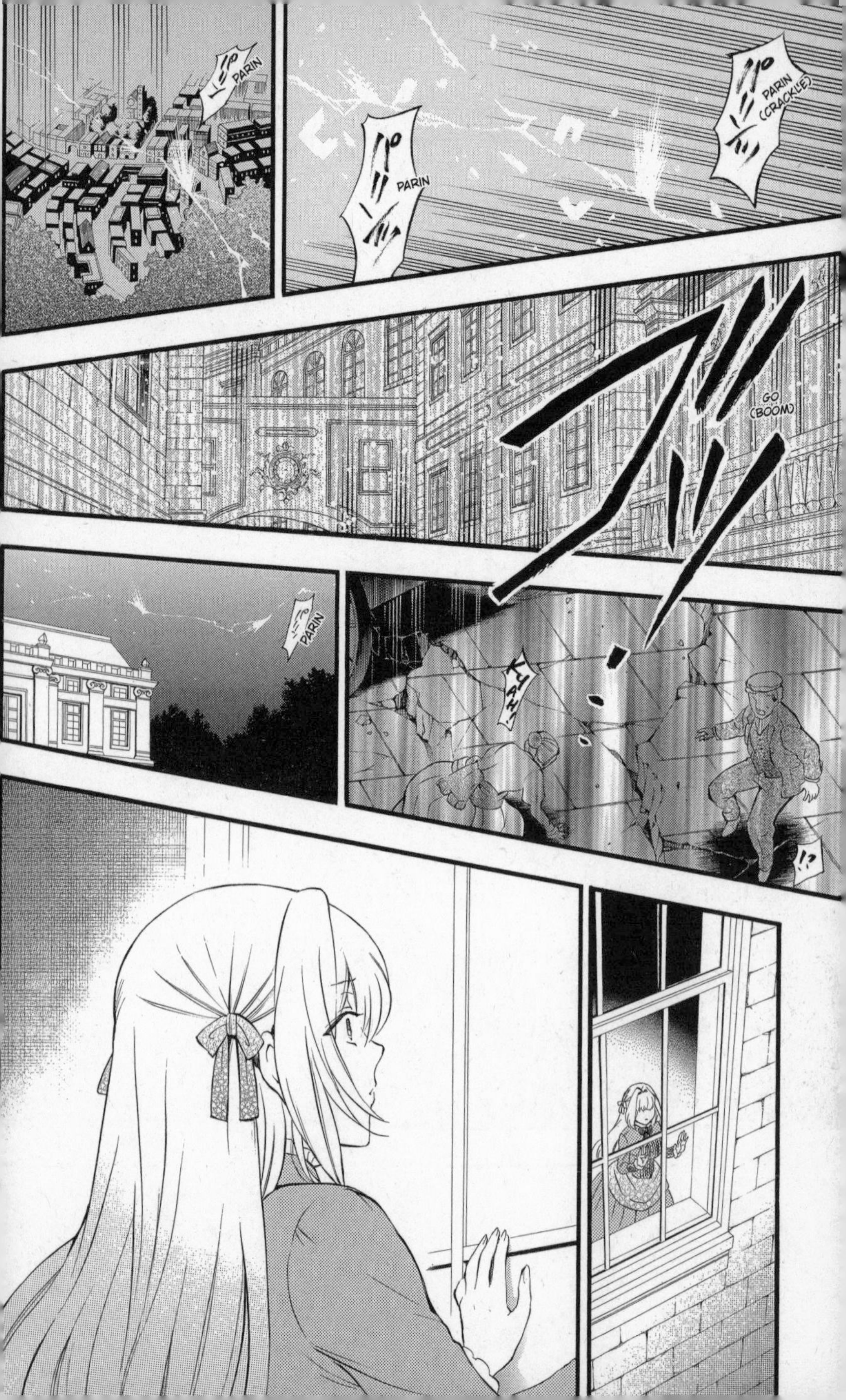
PARIN (CRACKLE)
PARIN
PARIN
GO (BOOM)
KYAH!
!?
PARIN

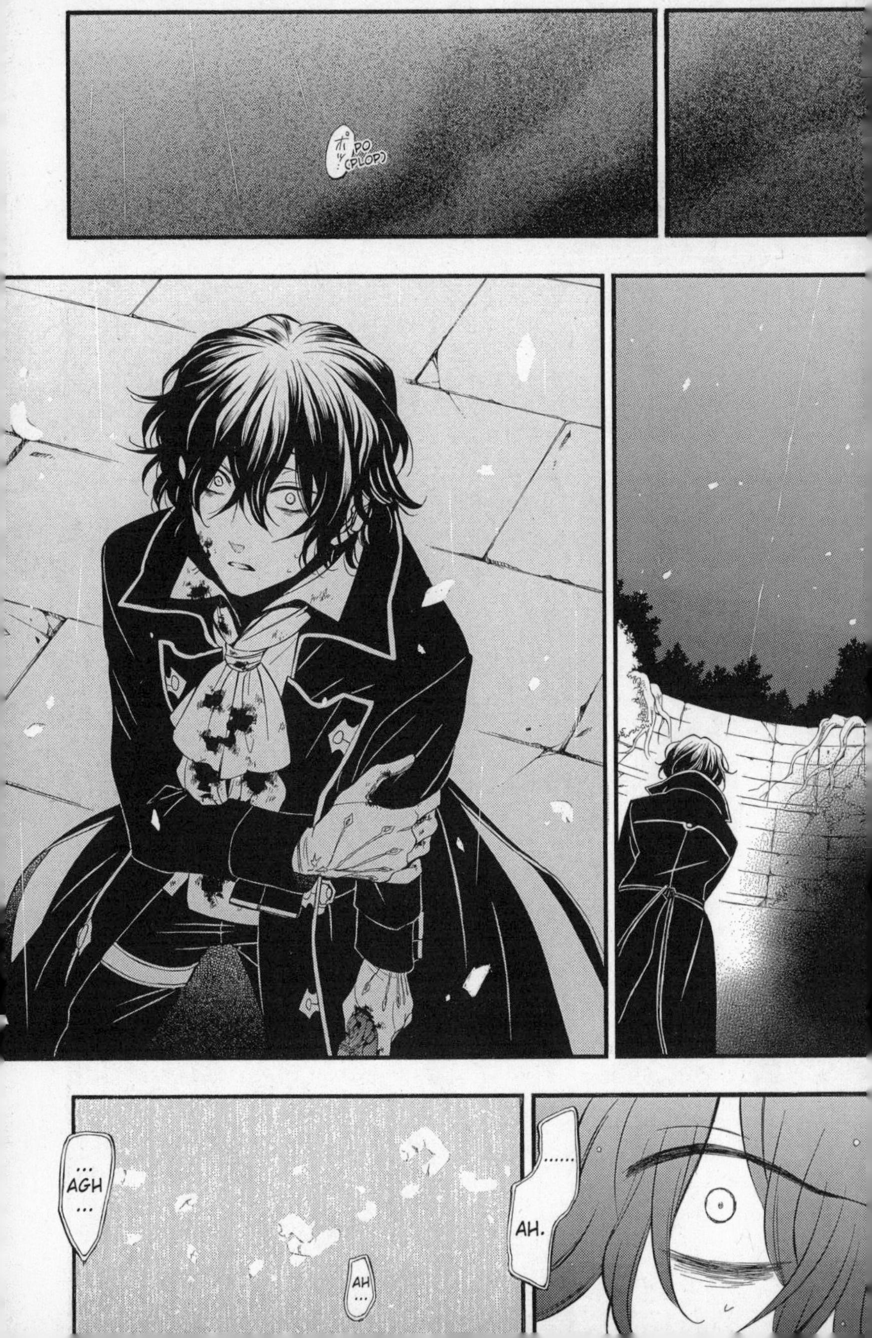
ポッ
PO (PLOP)
......
AH.
...AGH...
AH...

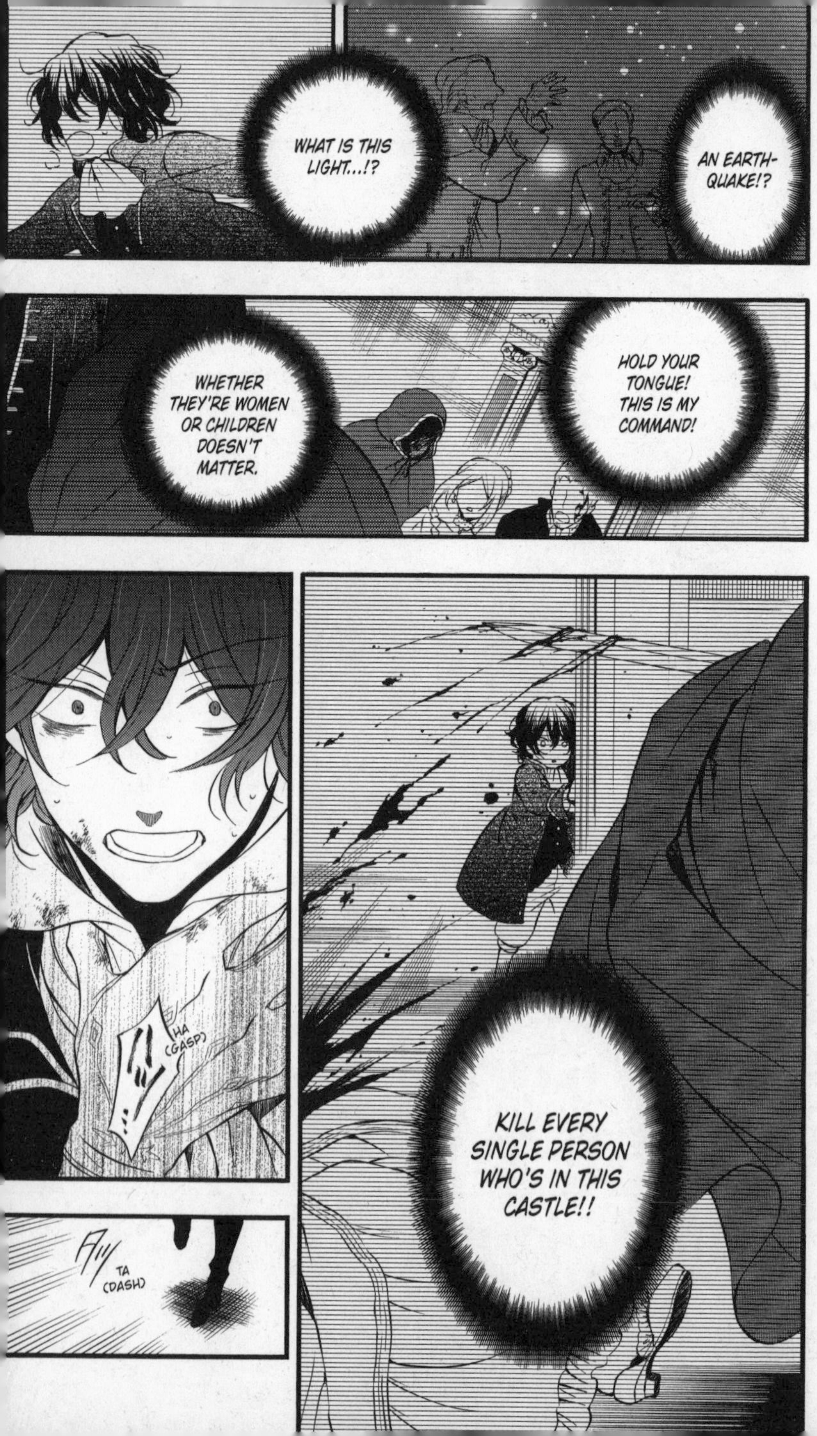
AN EARTH-QUAKE!?
WHAT IS THIS LIGHT...!?
HOLD YOUR TONGUE! THIS IS MY COMMAND!
WHETHER THEY'RE WOMEN OR CHILDREN DOESN'T MATTER.
KILL EVERY SINGLE PERSON WHO'S IN THIS CASTLE!!
HA (GASP)
TA (DASH)

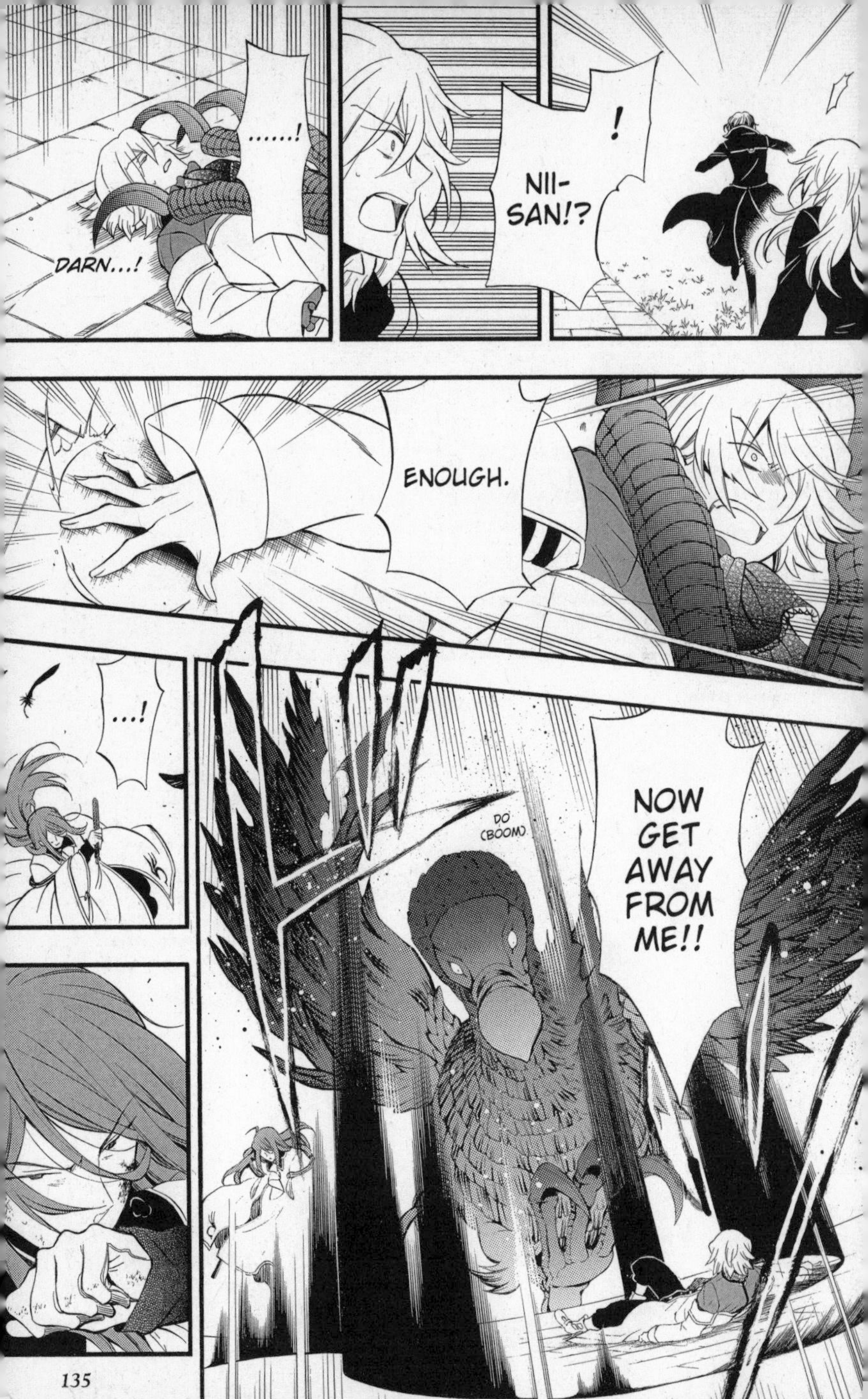
!
NII-SAN!?
......!
DARN...!
ENOUGH.
NOW GET AWAY FROM ME!!
DO (BOOM)
...!

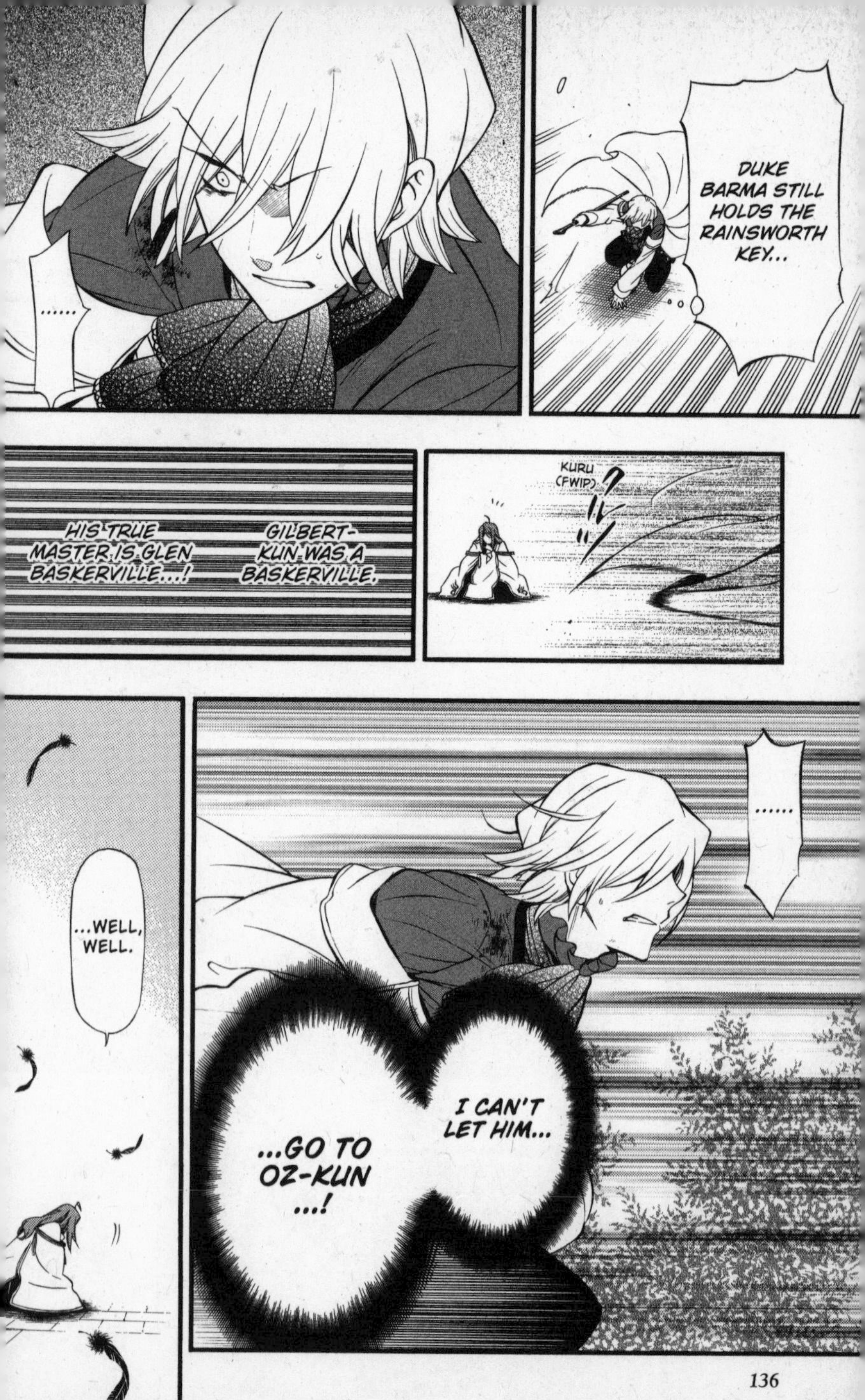
DUKE BARMA STILL HOLDS THE RAINSWORTH KEY...
......
KURU (FWIP)
GILBERT-KUN WAS A BASKERVILLE.
HIS TRUE MASTER IS GLEN BASKERVILLE...!
......
I CAN'T LET HIM...
...GO TO OZ-KUN ...!
...WELL, WELL.

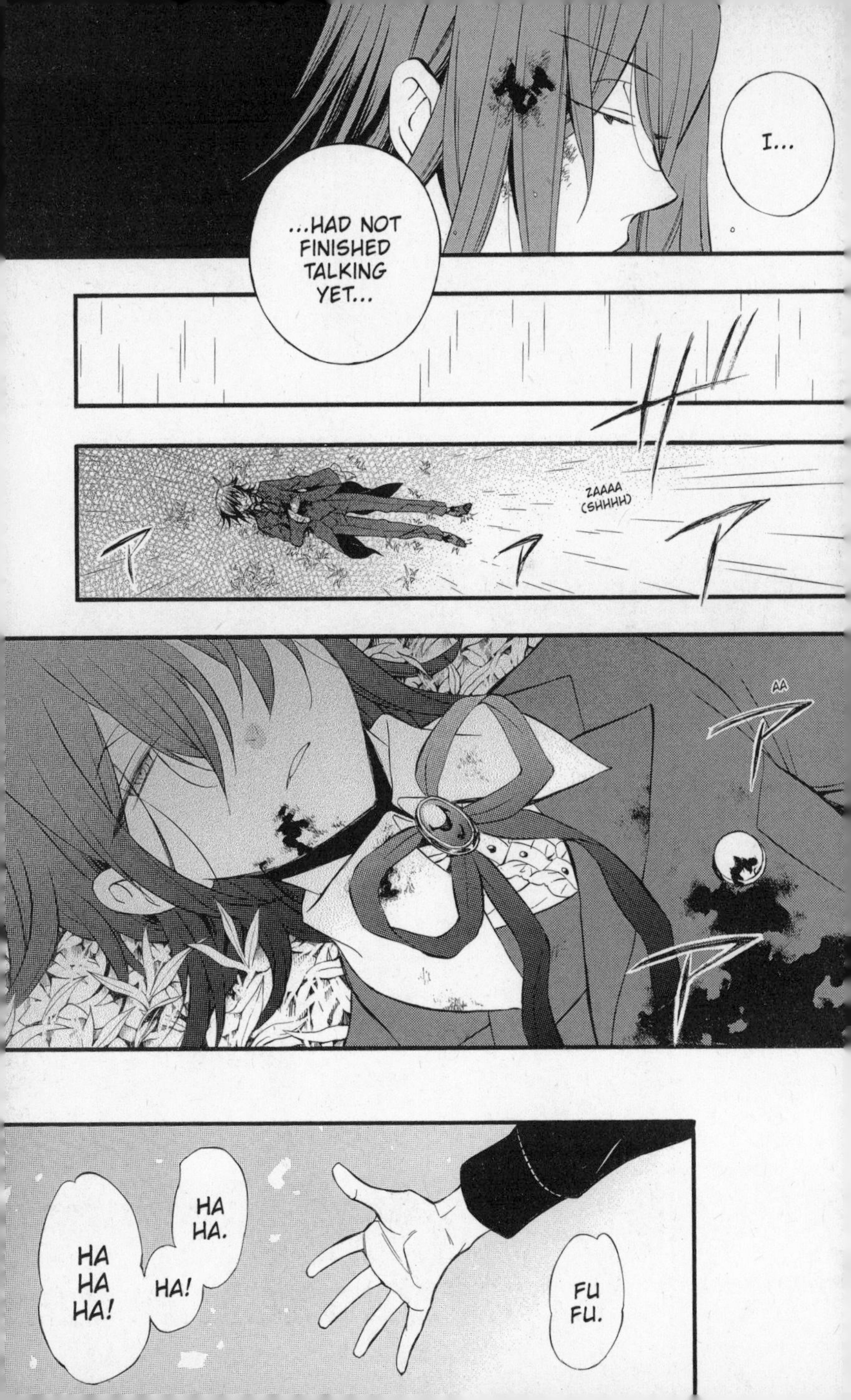
I...
...HAD NOT FINISHED TALKING YET...
ZAAAA (SHHHH)
AA
FU FU.
HA HA.
HA!
HA HA HA!

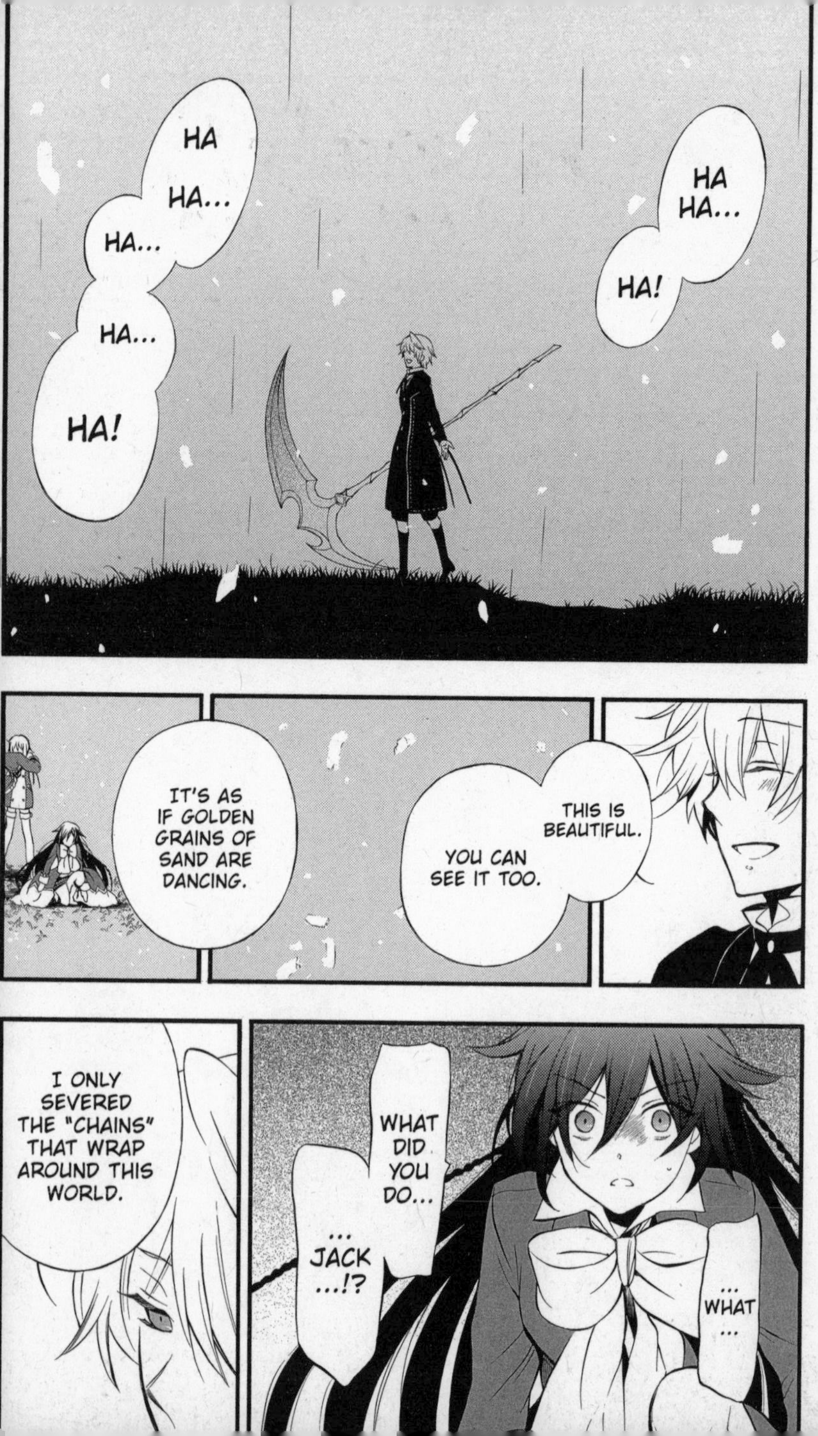
HA HA... HA!
HA HA... HA... HA... HA!
THIS IS BEAUTIFUL. YOU CAN SEE IT TOO.
IT'S AS IF GOLDEN GRAINS OF SAND ARE DANCING.
... WHAT ...
WHAT DID YOU DO...
... JACK ...!?
I ONLY SEVERED THE "CHAINS" THAT WRAP AROUND THIS WORLD.

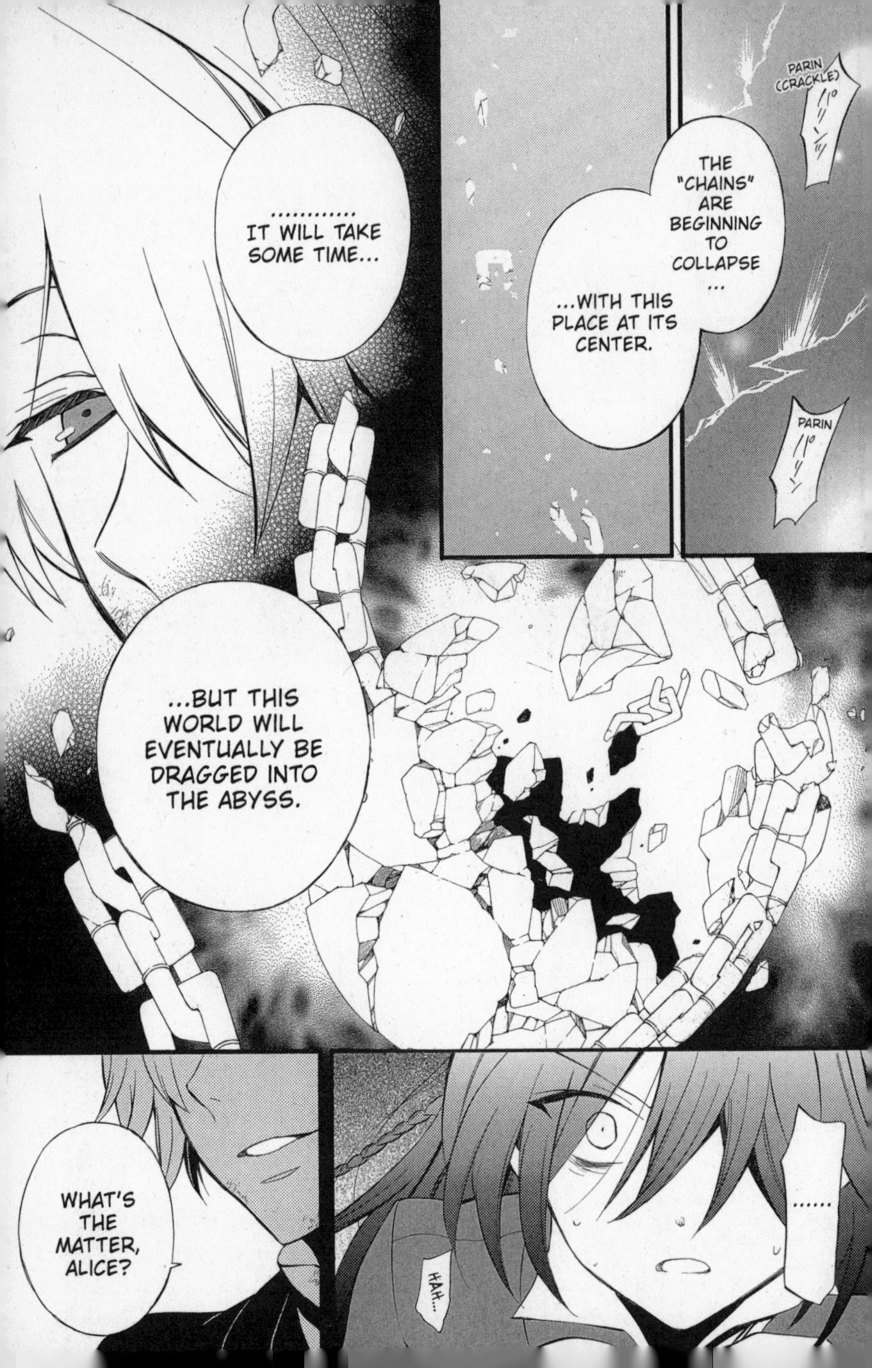
PARIN (CRACKLE)
PARIN
THE "CHAINS" ARE BEGINNING TO COLLAPSE...
...WITH THIS PLACE AT ITS CENTER.
.... IT WILL TAKE SOME TIME...
...BUT THIS WORLD WILL EVENTUALLY BE DRAGGED INTO THE ABYSS.
......
HAH...
WHAT'S THE MATTER, ALICE?

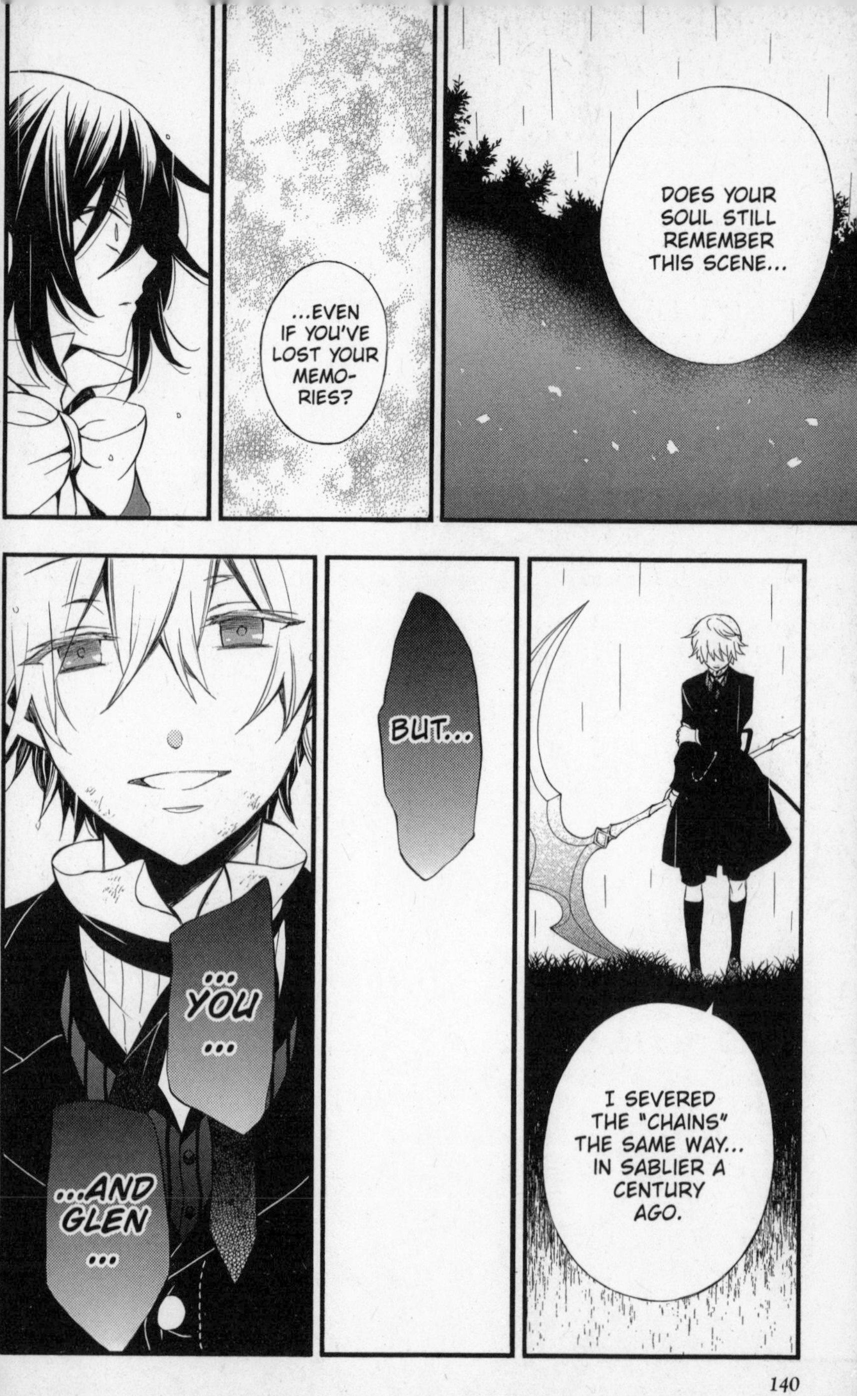
DOES YOUR SOUL STILL REMEMBER THIS SCENE...
...EVEN IF YOU'VE LOST YOUR MEMORIES?
I SEVERED THE "CHAINS" THE SAME WAY... IN SABLIER A CENTURY AGO.
BUT...
...YOU...
...AND GLEN...

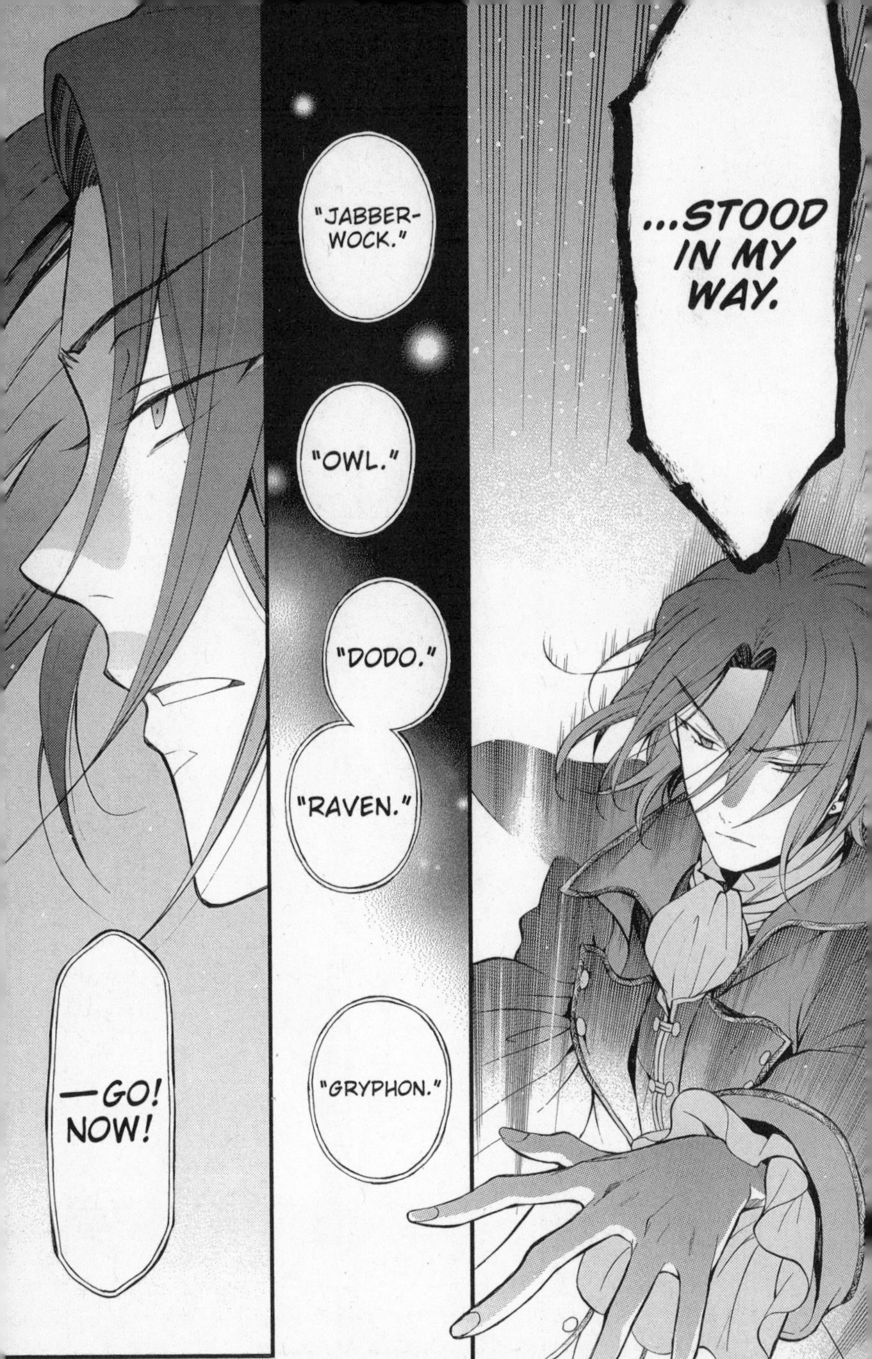
...STOOD IN MY WAY.
"JABBER-WOCK."
"OWL."
"DODO."
"RAVEN."
"GRYPHON."
—GO! NOW!

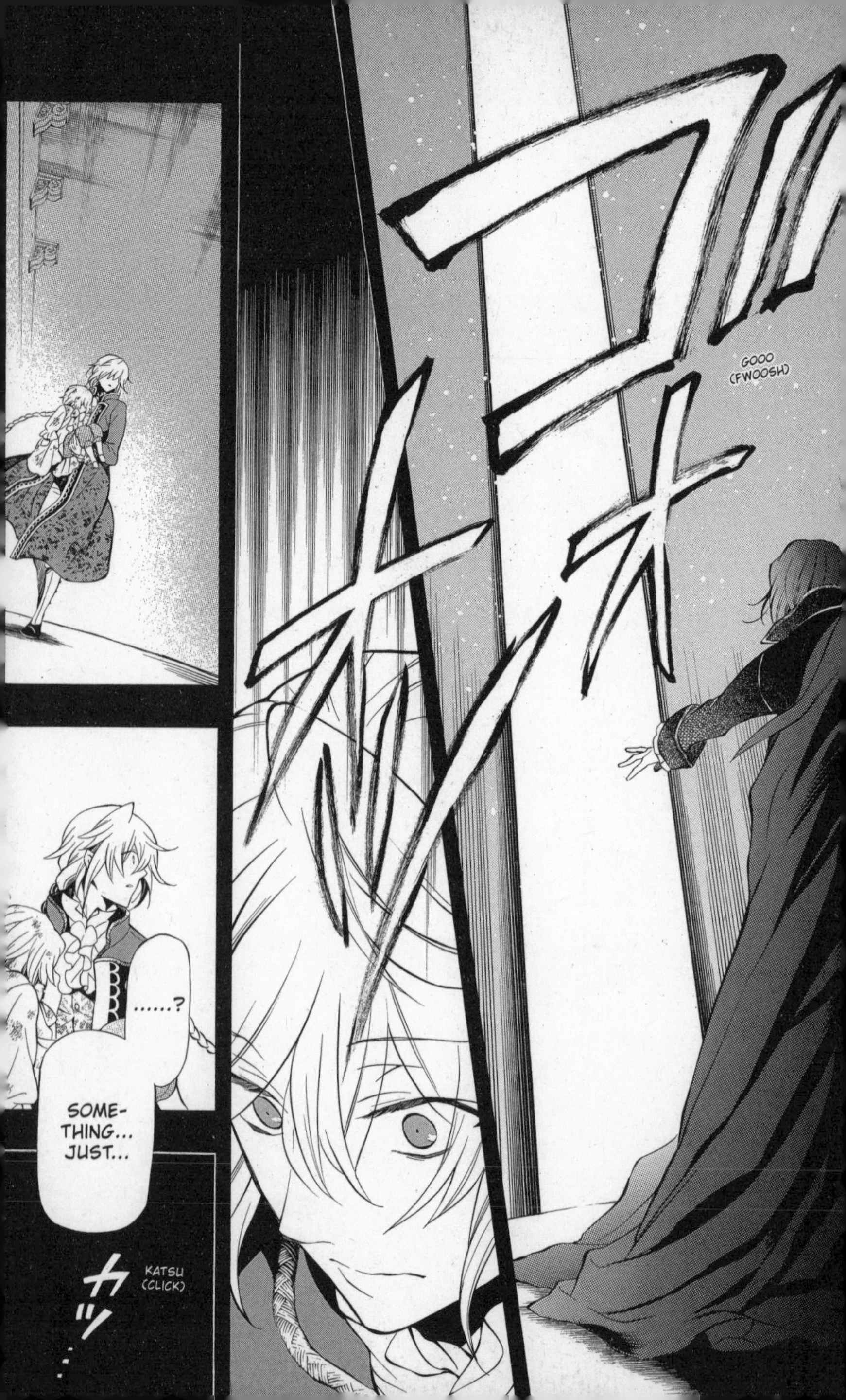
GOOO (FWOOSH)
......?
SOME-THING... JUST...
KATSU (CLICK)

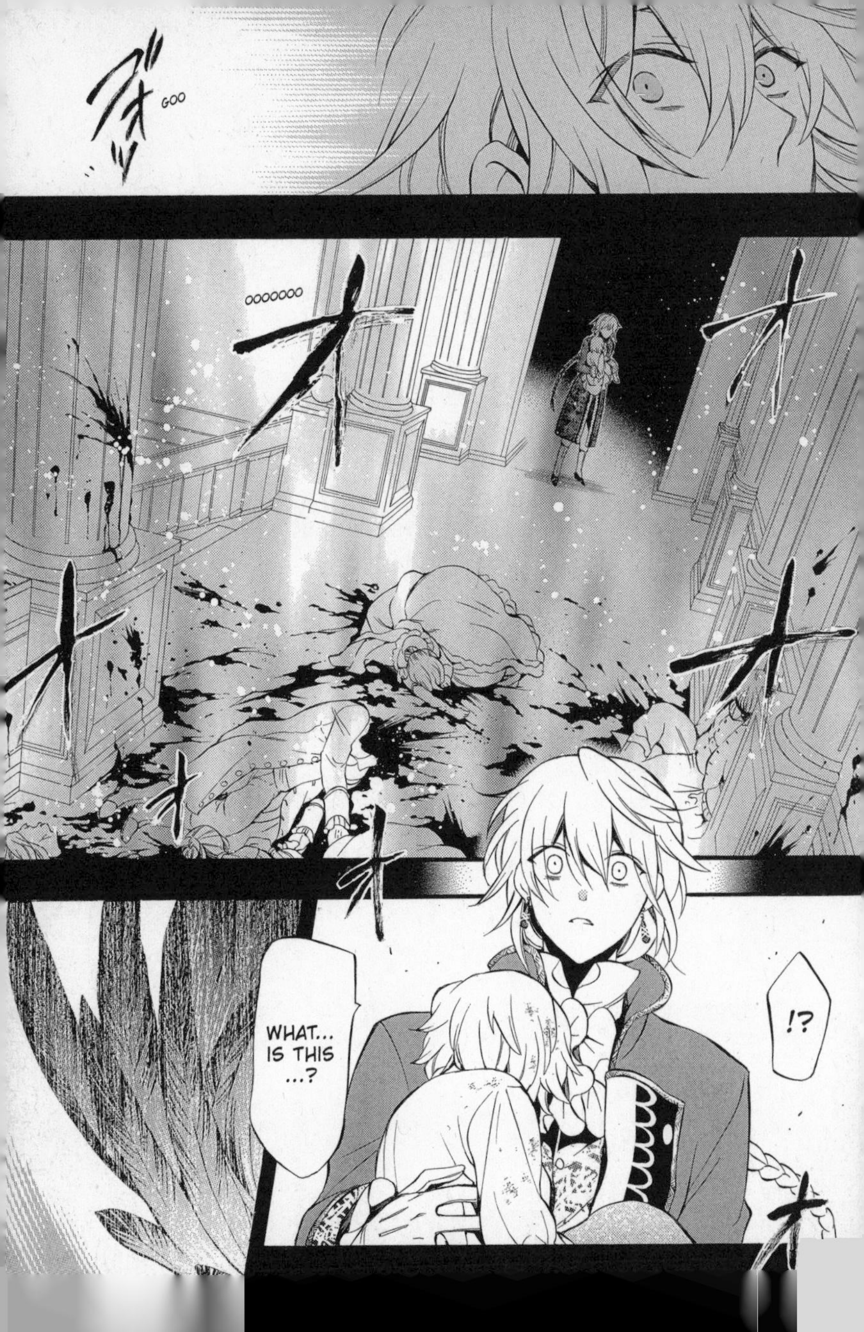
ゴオッ
GOO
オオオオオオ
OOOOOOO
!?
WHAT... IS THIS ...?

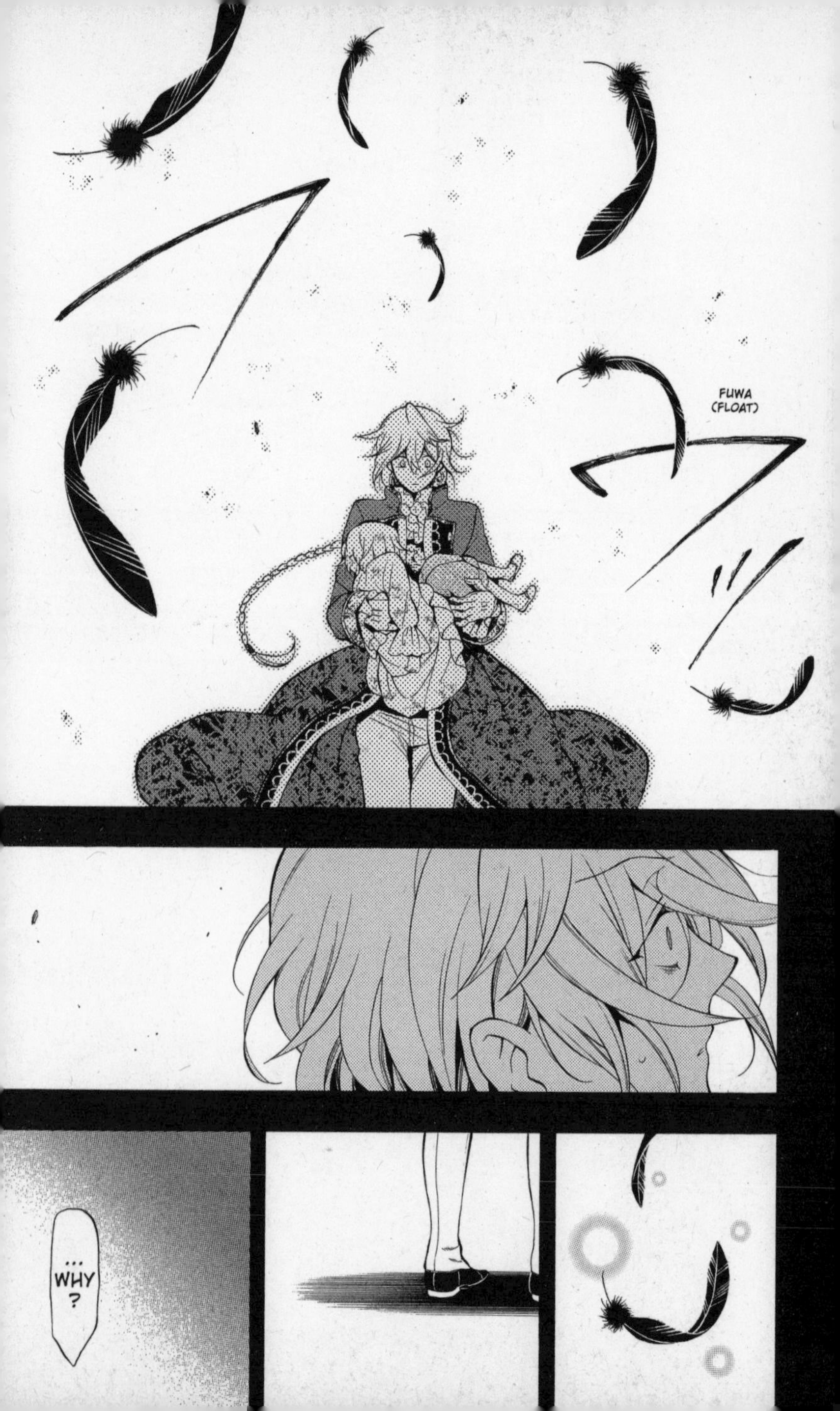
FUWA (FLOAT)
...WHY?

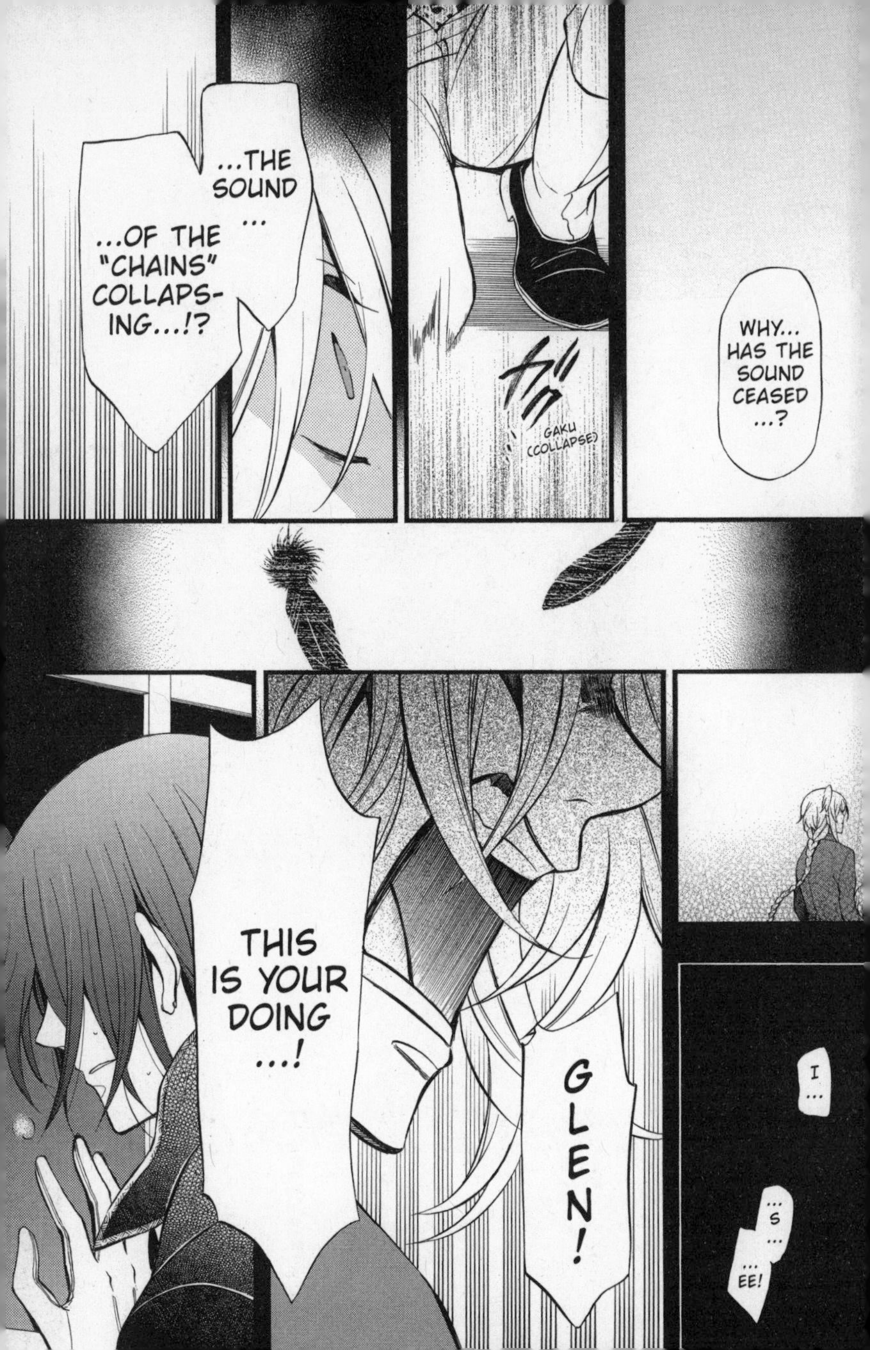
WHY... HAS THE SOUND CEASED ...?
GAKU (COLLAPSE)
...THE SOUND ... ...OF THE "CHAINS" COLLAPSING...!?
I...
...S...
...EE!
THIS IS YOUR DOING ...!
GLEN!

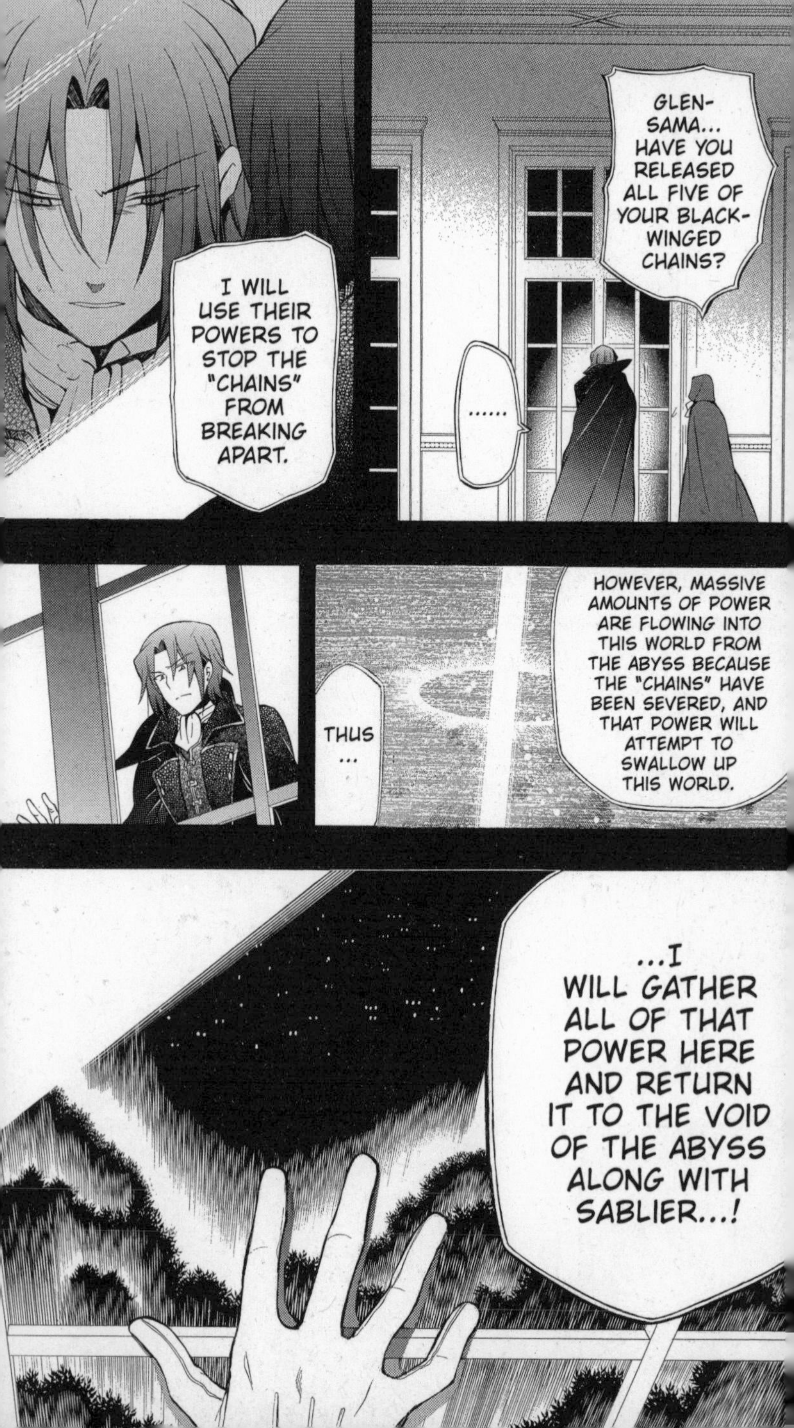
GLEN-SAMA... HAVE YOU RELEASED ALL FIVE OF YOUR BLACK-WINGED CHAINS?
......
I WILL USE THEIR POWERS TO STOP THE "CHAINS" FROM BREAKING APART.
HOWEVER, MASSIVE AMOUNTS OF POWER ARE FLOWING INTO THIS WORLD FROM THE ABYSS BECAUSE THE "CHAINS" HAVE BEEN SEVERED, AND THAT POWER WILL ATTEMPT TO SWALLOW UP THIS WORLD.
THUS ...
...I WILL GATHER ALL OF THAT POWER HERE AND RETURN IT TO THE VOID OF THE ABYSS ALONG WITH SABLIER...!

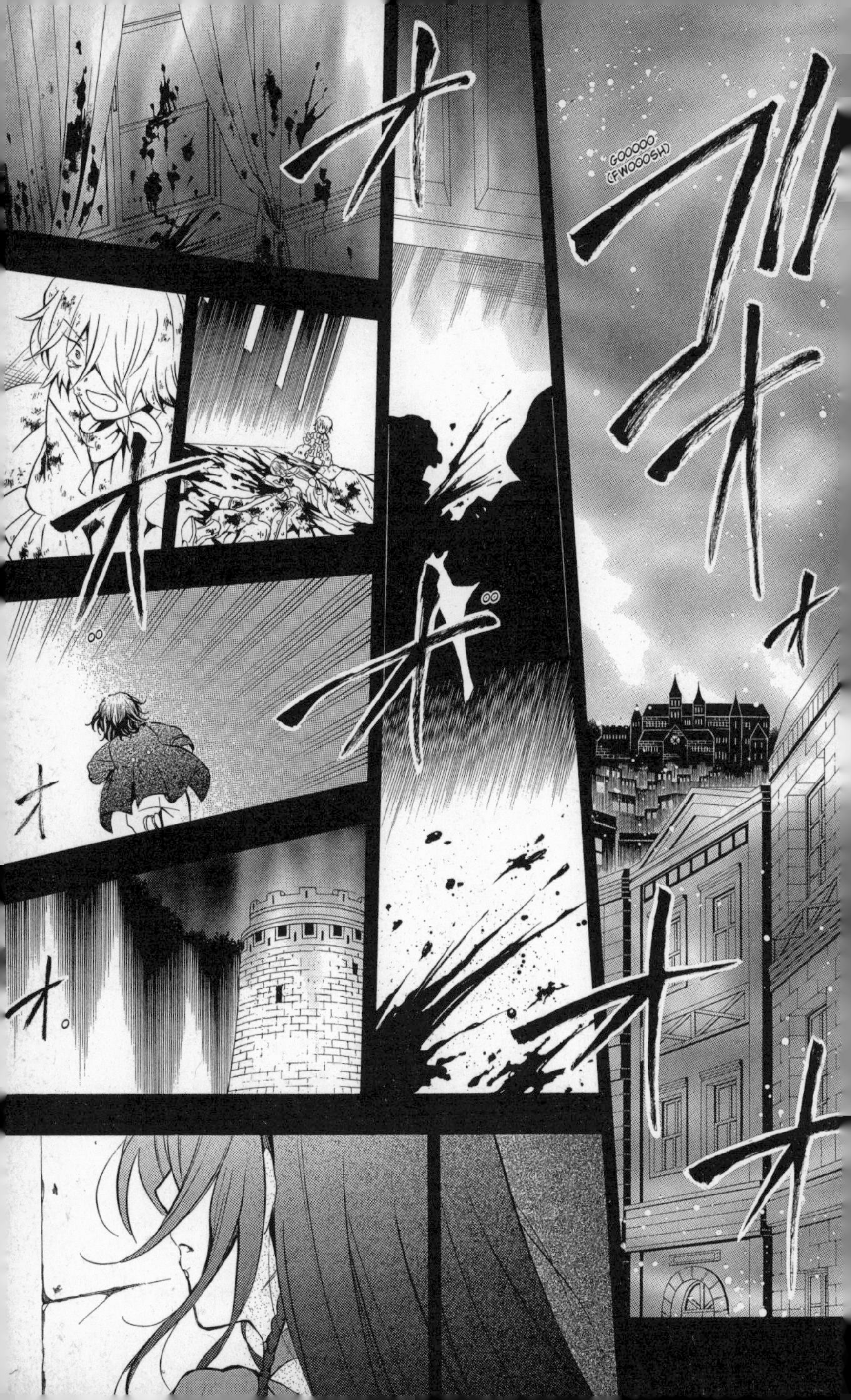
GOOOOO
(FWOOOSH)

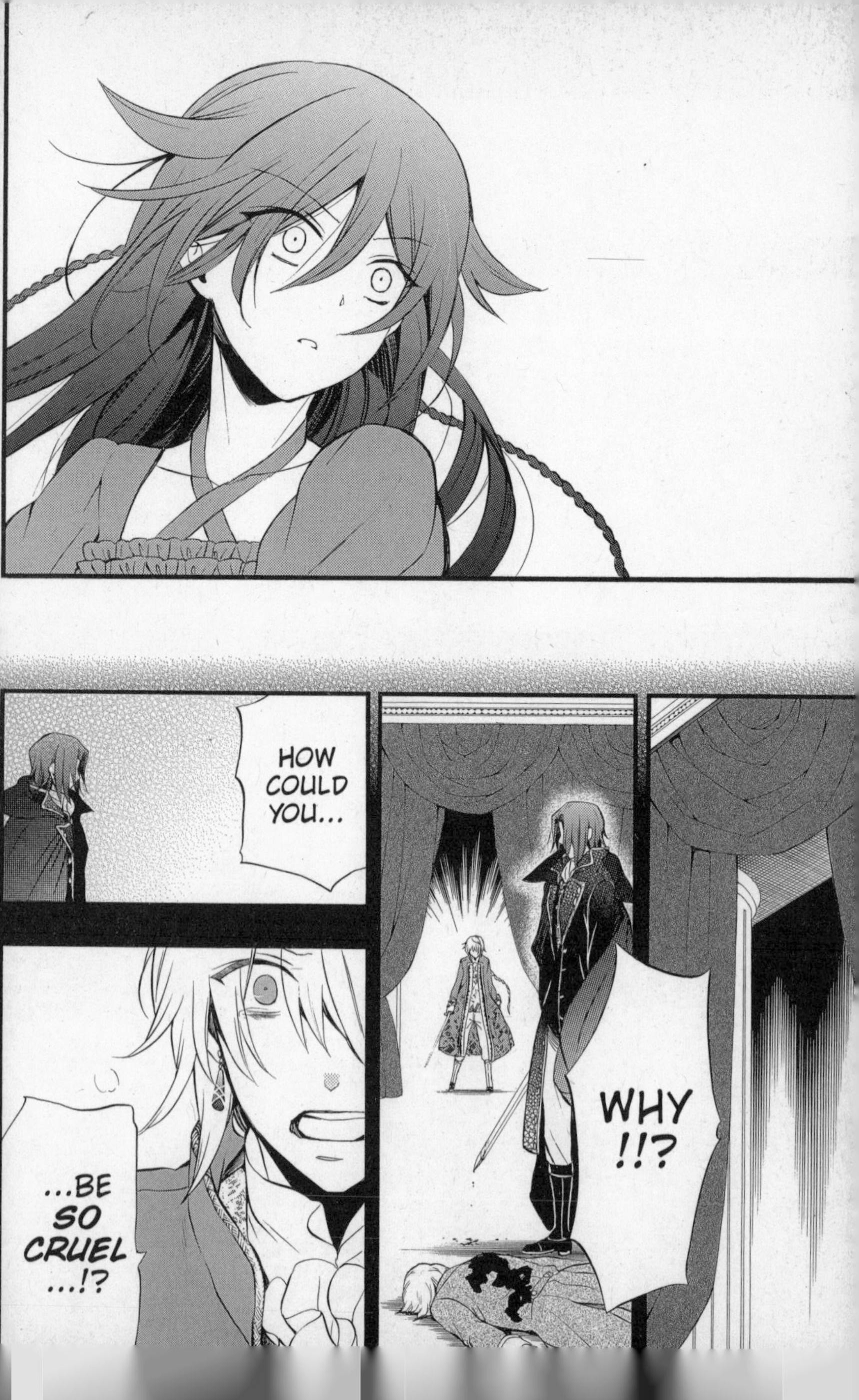
WHY !!?
HOW COULD YOU...
...BE SO CRUEL ...!?

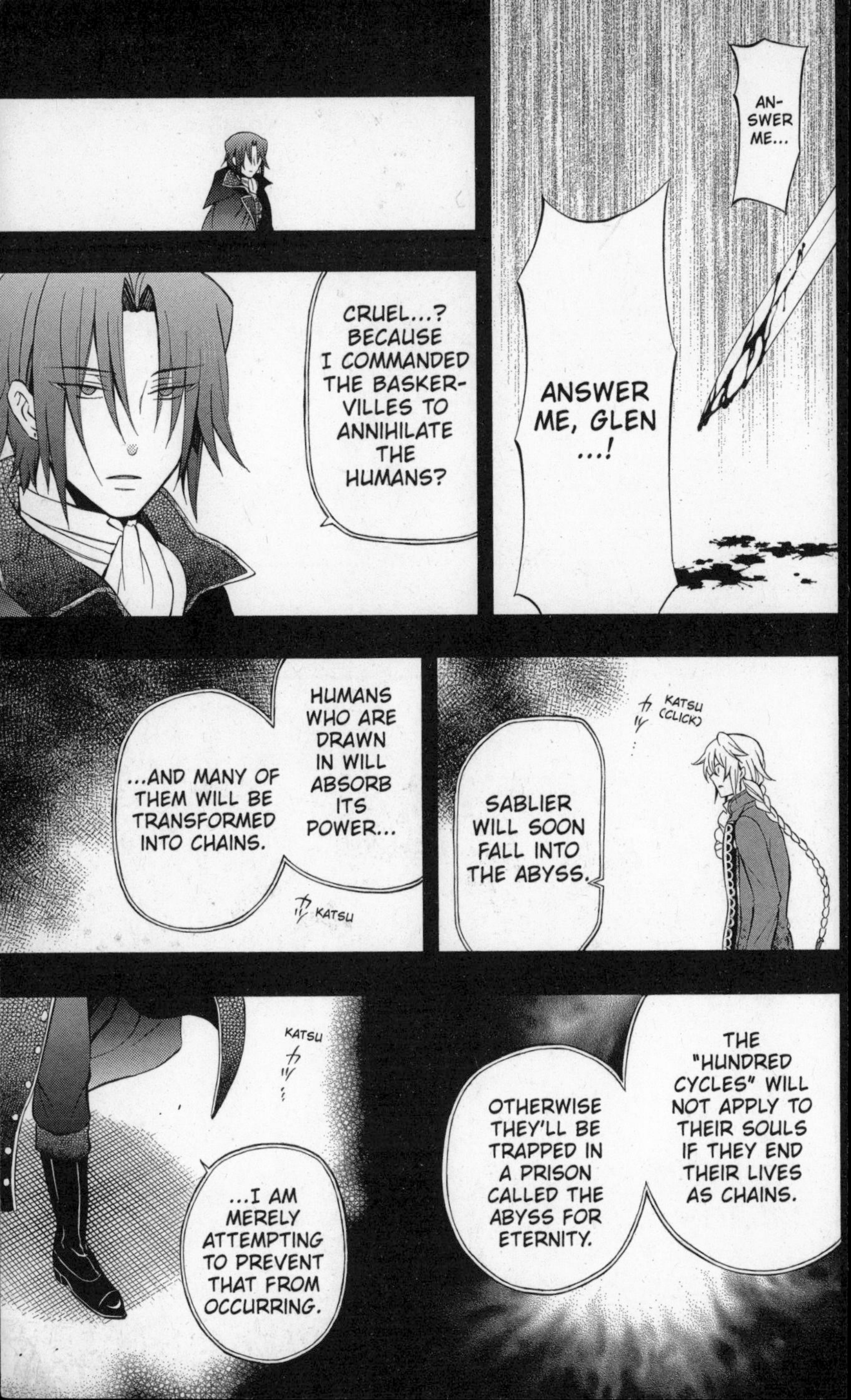
ANSWER ME...
ANSWER ME, GLEN ...!
CRUEL...? BECAUSE I COMMANDED THE BASKERVILLES TO ANNIHILATE THE HUMANS?
KATSU (CLICK)
SABLIER WILL SOON FALL INTO THE ABYSS.
HUMANS WHO ARE DRAWN IN WILL ABSORB ITS POWER...
...AND MANY OF THEM WILL BE TRANSFORMED INTO CHAINS.
KATSU
THE "HUNDRED CYCLES" WILL NOT APPLY TO THEIR SOULS IF THEY END THEIR LIVES AS CHAINS.
OTHERWISE THEY'LL BE TRAPPED IN A PRISON CALLED THE ABYSS FOR ETERNITY.
KATSU
...I AM MERELY ATTEMPTING TO PREVENT THAT FROM OCCURRING.

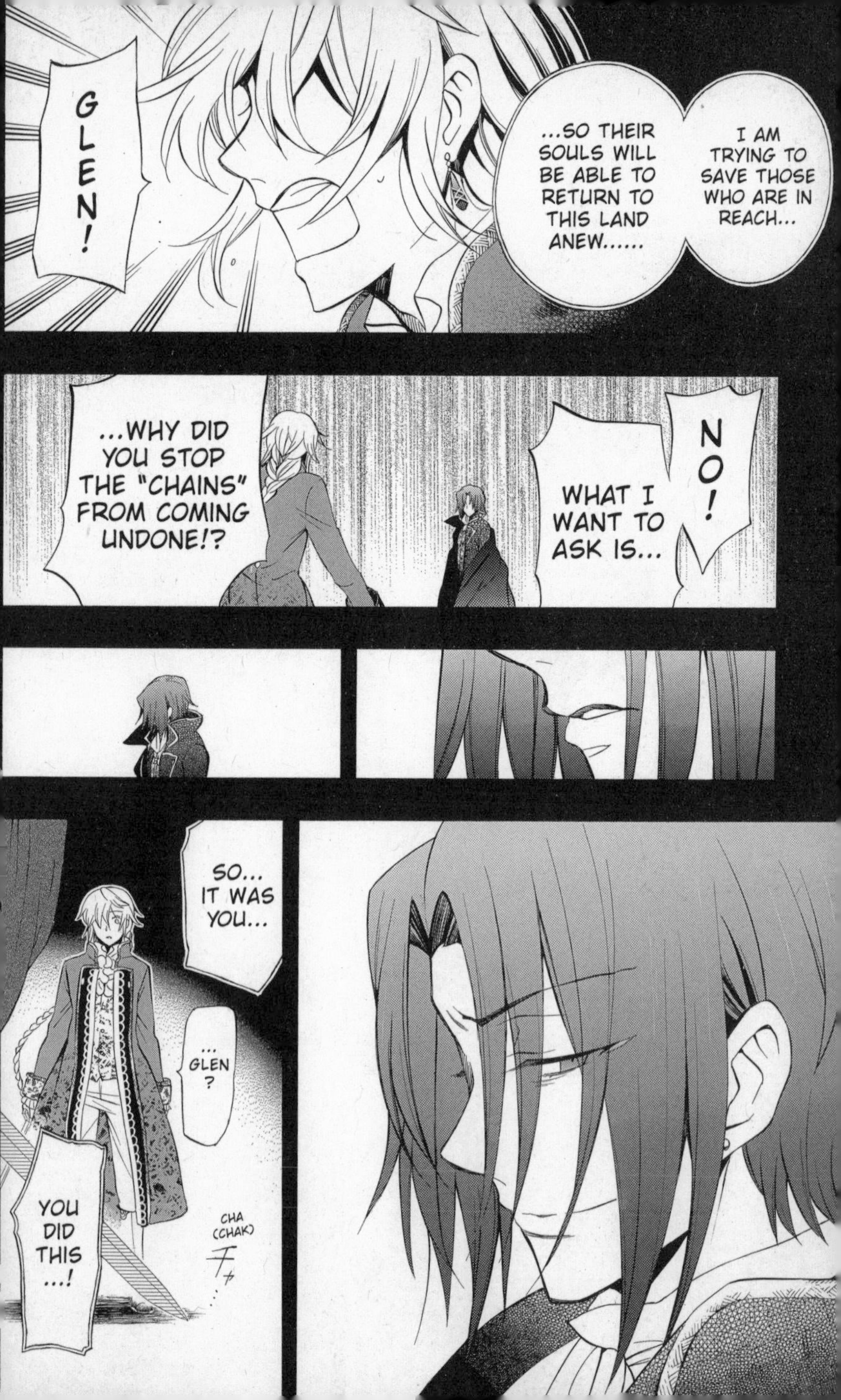
I AM TRYING TO SAVE THOSE WHO ARE IN REACH...
...SO THEIR SOULS WILL BE ABLE TO RETURN TO THIS LAND ANEW......
GLEN!
NO!
WHAT I WANT TO ASK IS...
...WHY DID YOU STOP THE "CHAINS" FROM COMING UNDONE!?
SO... IT WAS YOU...
...GLEN?
CHA (CHAK)
YOU DID THIS ...!

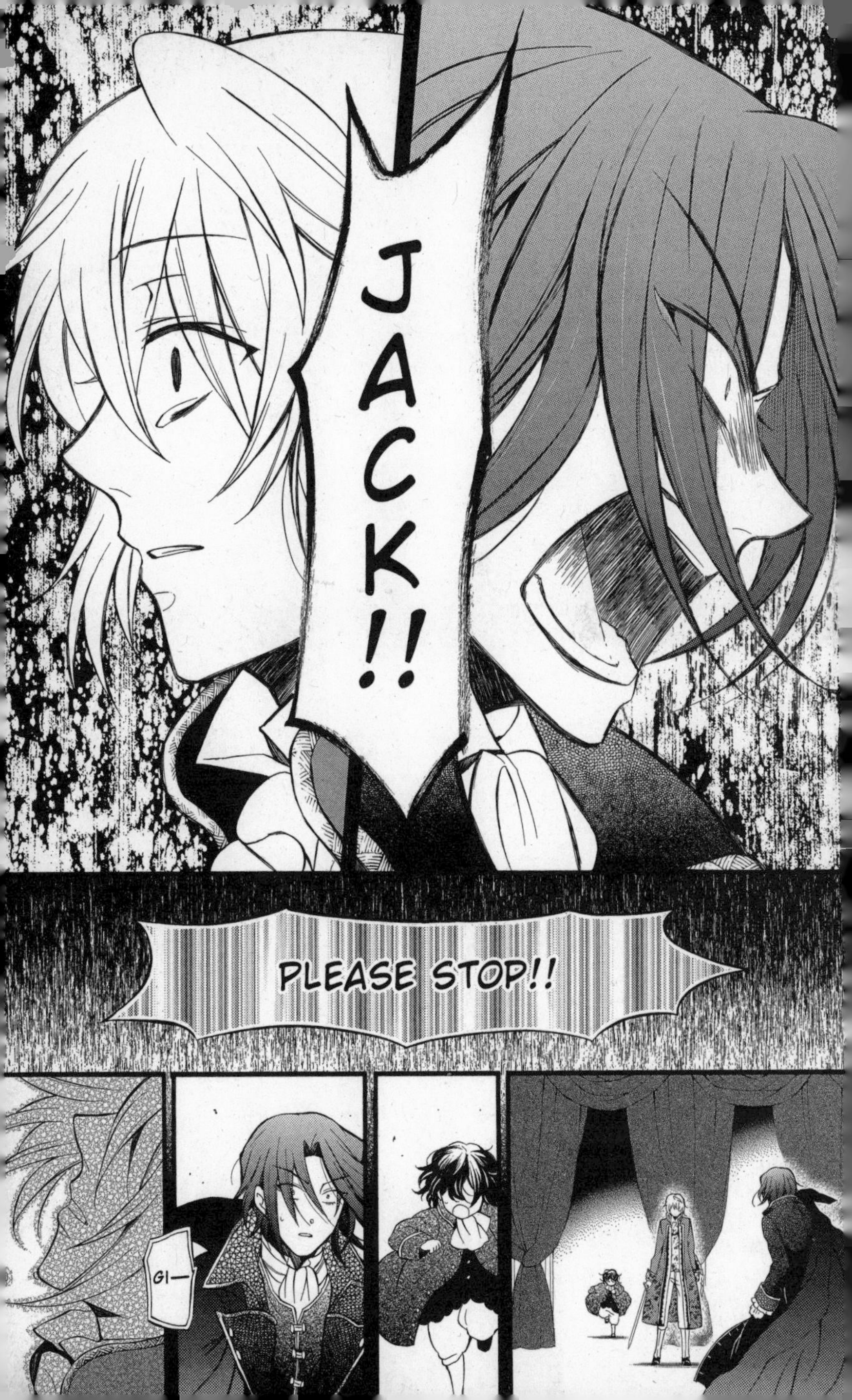
JACK!!
PLEASE STOP!!
GI—

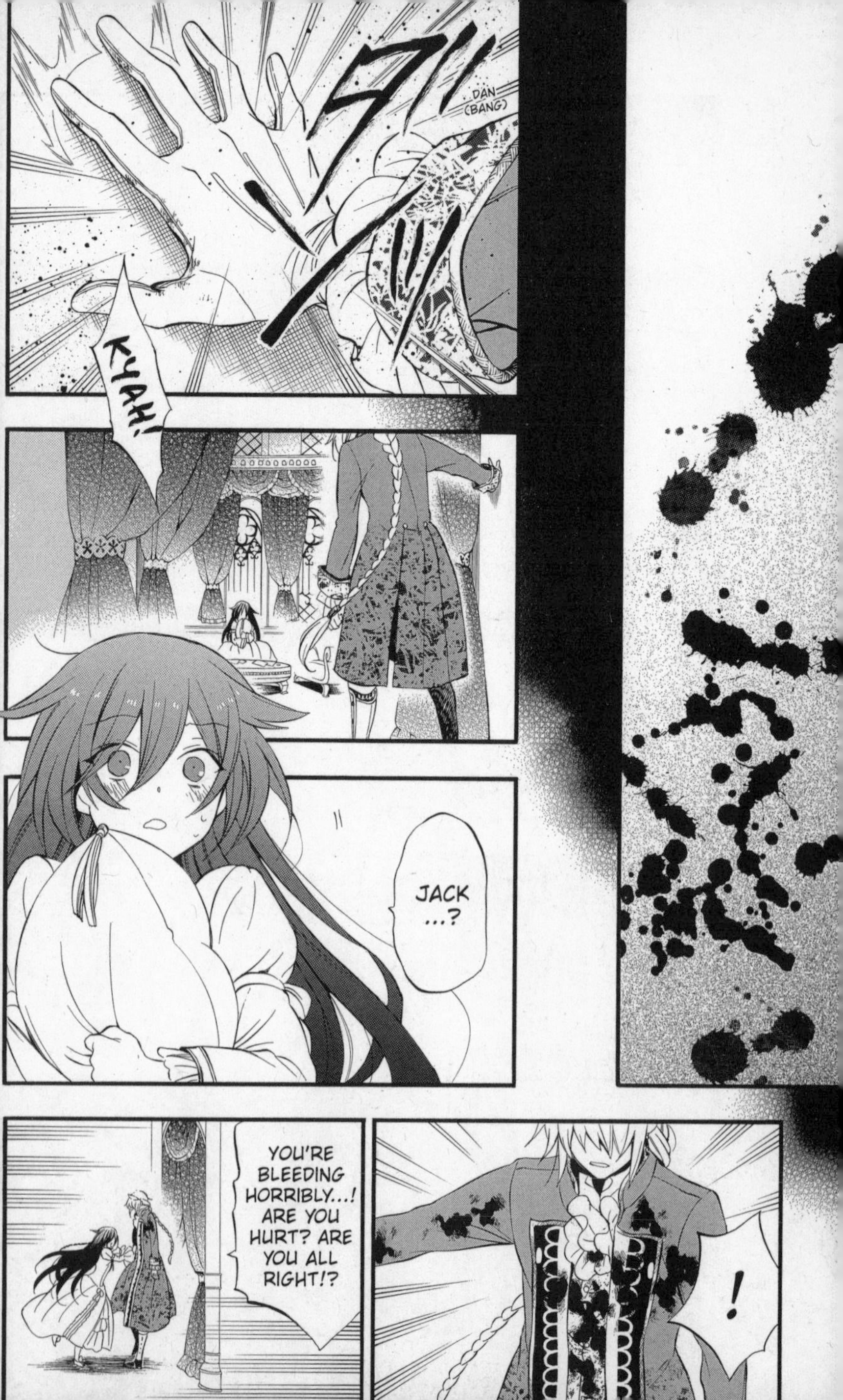
DAN (BANG)
KYAH!
JACK ...?
!
YOU'RE BLEEDING HORRIBLY...! ARE YOU HURT? ARE YOU ALL RIGHT!?

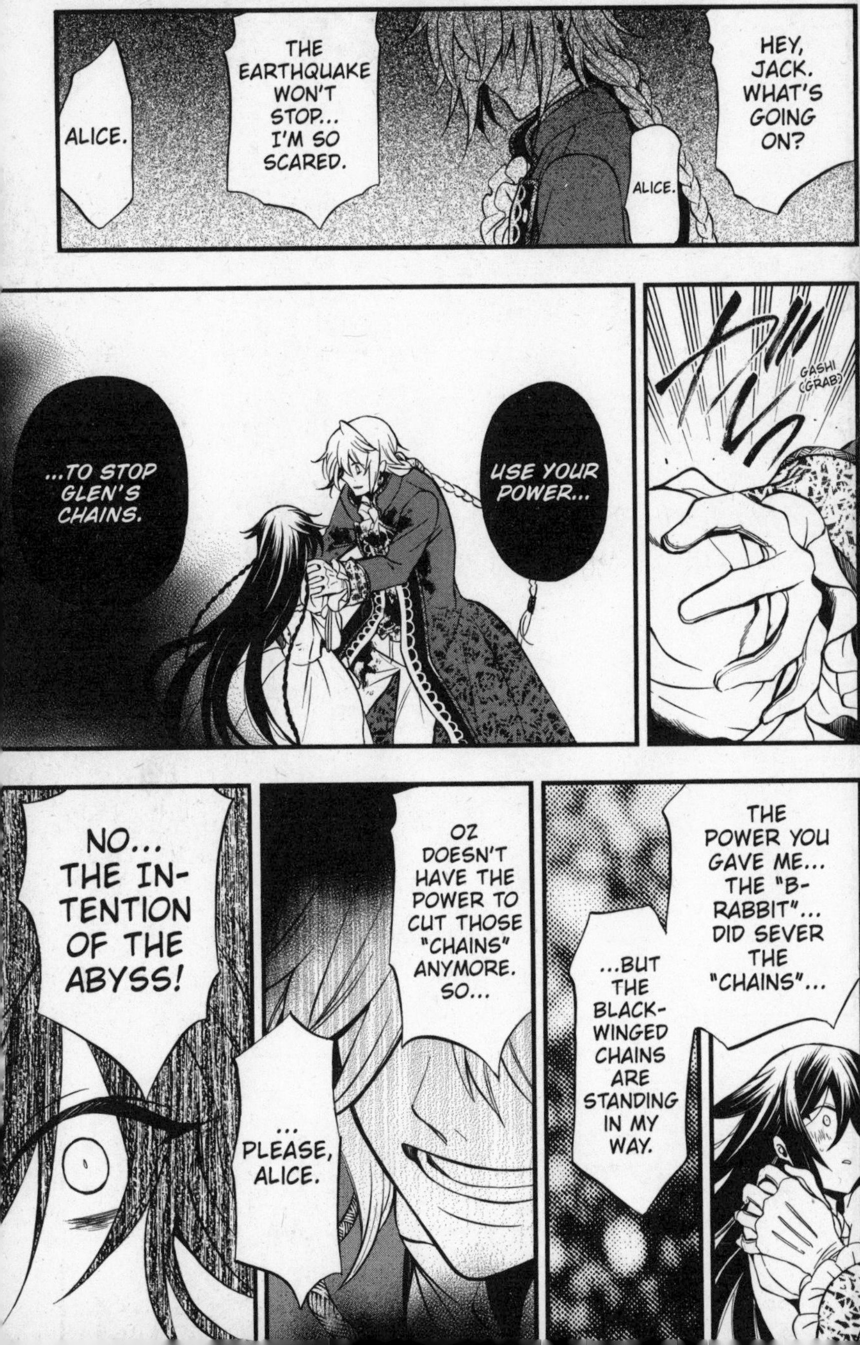
HEY, JACK. WHAT'S GOING ON?
ALICE.
THE EARTHQUAKE WON'T STOP... I'M SO SCARED.
ALICE.
GASHI (GRAB)
USE YOUR POWER...
...TO STOP GLEN'S CHAINS.
THE POWER YOU GAVE ME... THE "B-RABBIT"... DID SEVER THE "CHAINS"...
...BUT THE BLACK-WINGED CHAINS ARE STANDING IN MY WAY.
OZ DOESN'T HAVE THE POWER TO CUT THOSE "CHAINS" ANYMORE. SO...
... PLEASE, ALICE.
NO... THE IN-TENTION OF THE ABYSS!

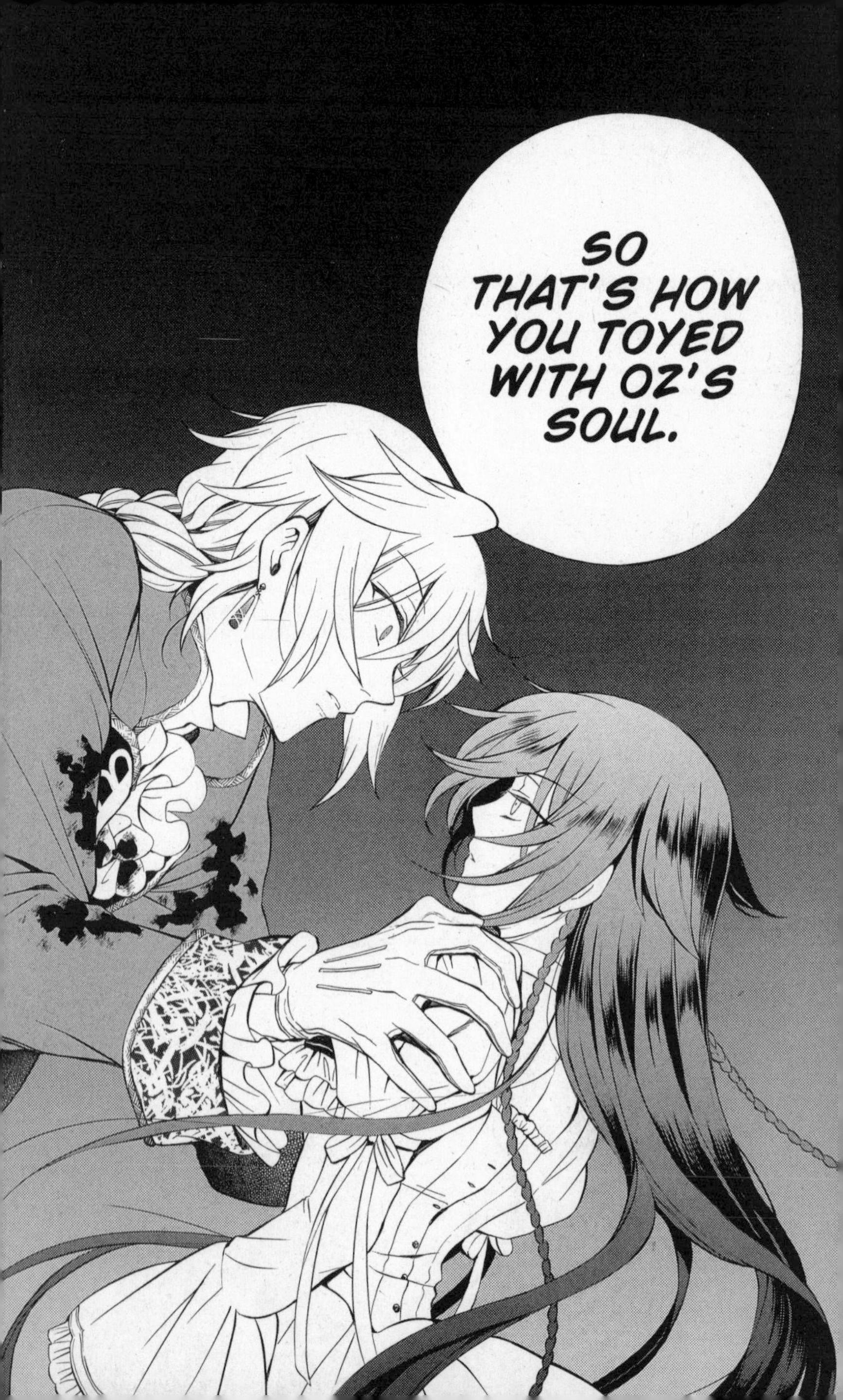
SO THAT'S HOW YOU TOYED WITH OZ'S SOUL.

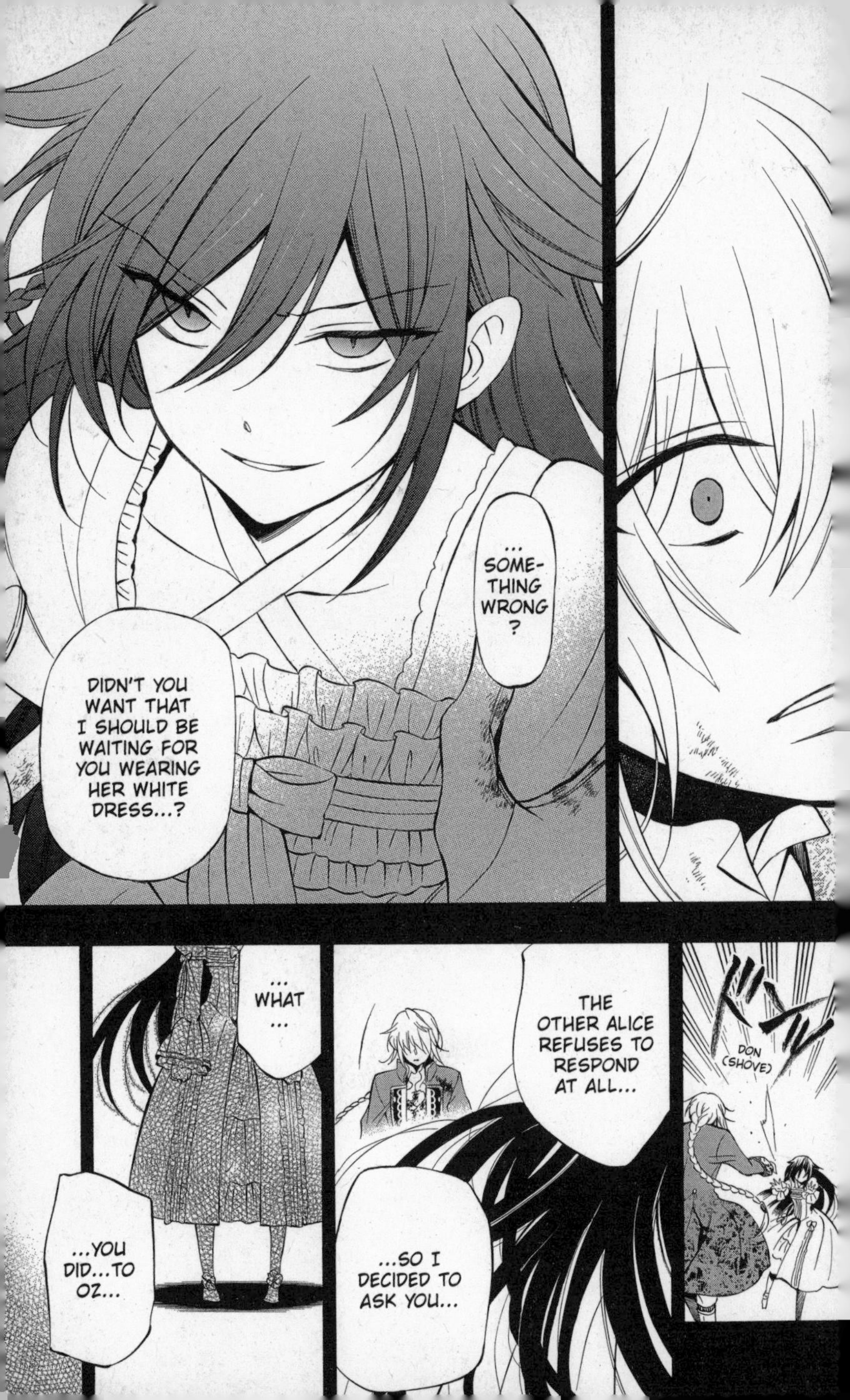
...SOME-THING WRONG?
DIDN'T YOU WANT THAT I SHOULD BE WAITING FOR YOU WEARING HER WHITE DRESS...?
ドンッ
DON (SHOVE)
THE OTHER ALICE REFUSES TO RESPOND AT ALL...
...SO I DECIDED TO ASK YOU...
...WHAT...
...YOU DID...TO OZ...

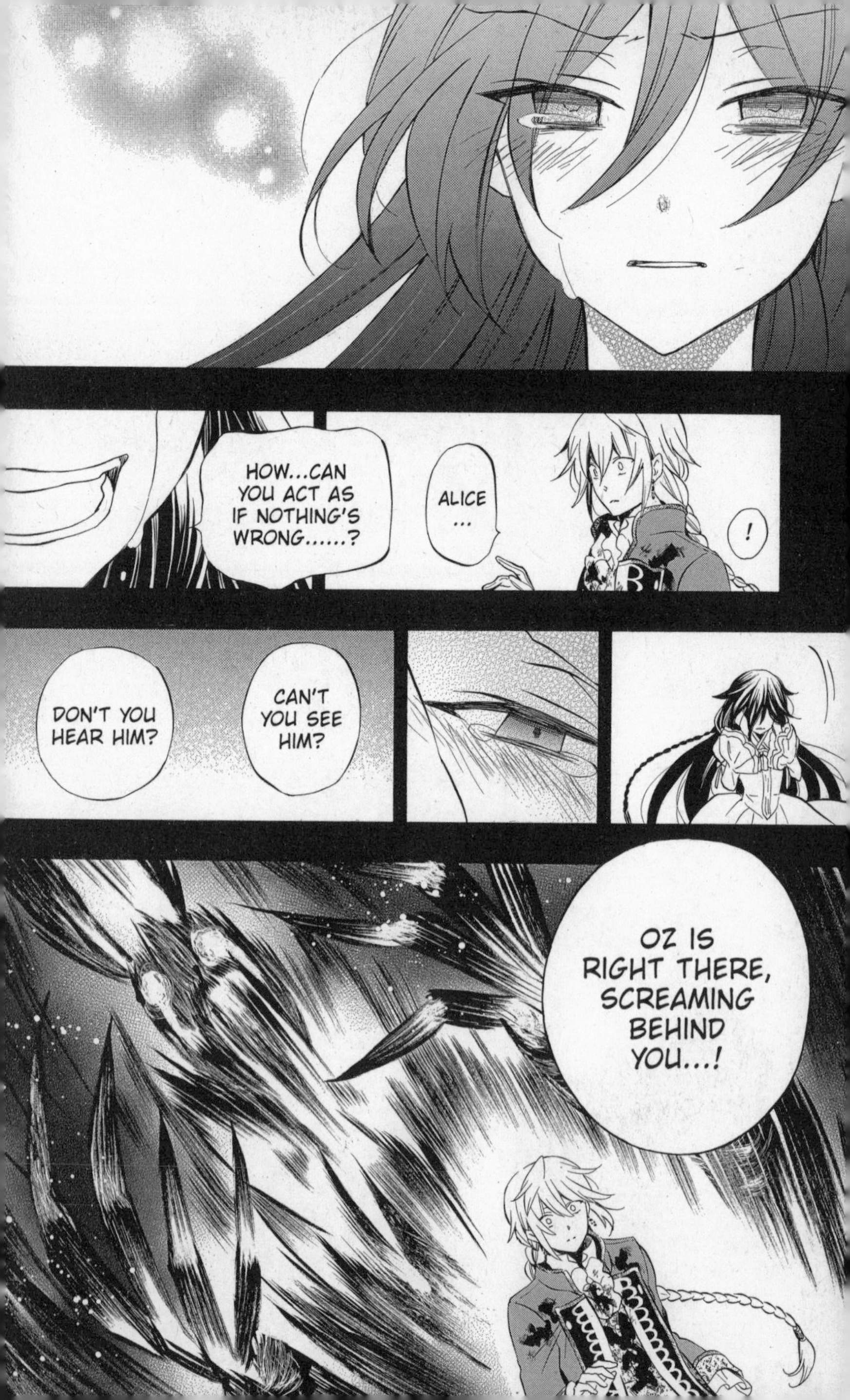
!
ALICE ...
HOW...CAN YOU ACT AS IF NOTHING'S WRONG......?
CAN'T YOU SEE HIM?
DON'T YOU HEAR HIM?
OZ IS RIGHT THERE, SCREAMING BEHIND YOU...!

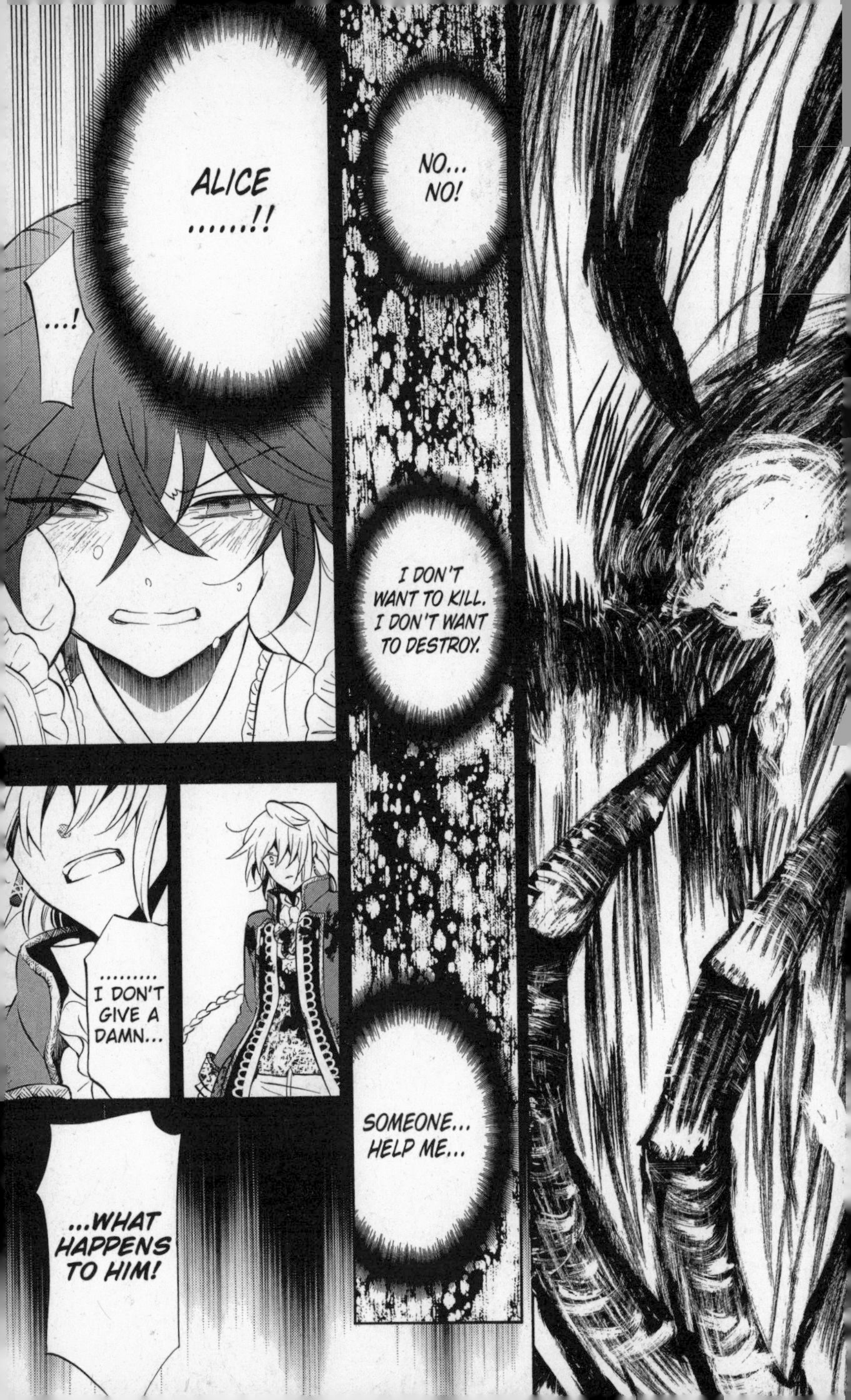
NO... NO!
I DON'T WANT TO KILL. I DON'T WANT TO DESTROY.
SOMEONE... HELP ME...
ALICE ......!!
...!
.... I DON'T GIVE A DAMN...
...WHAT HAPPENS TO HIM!

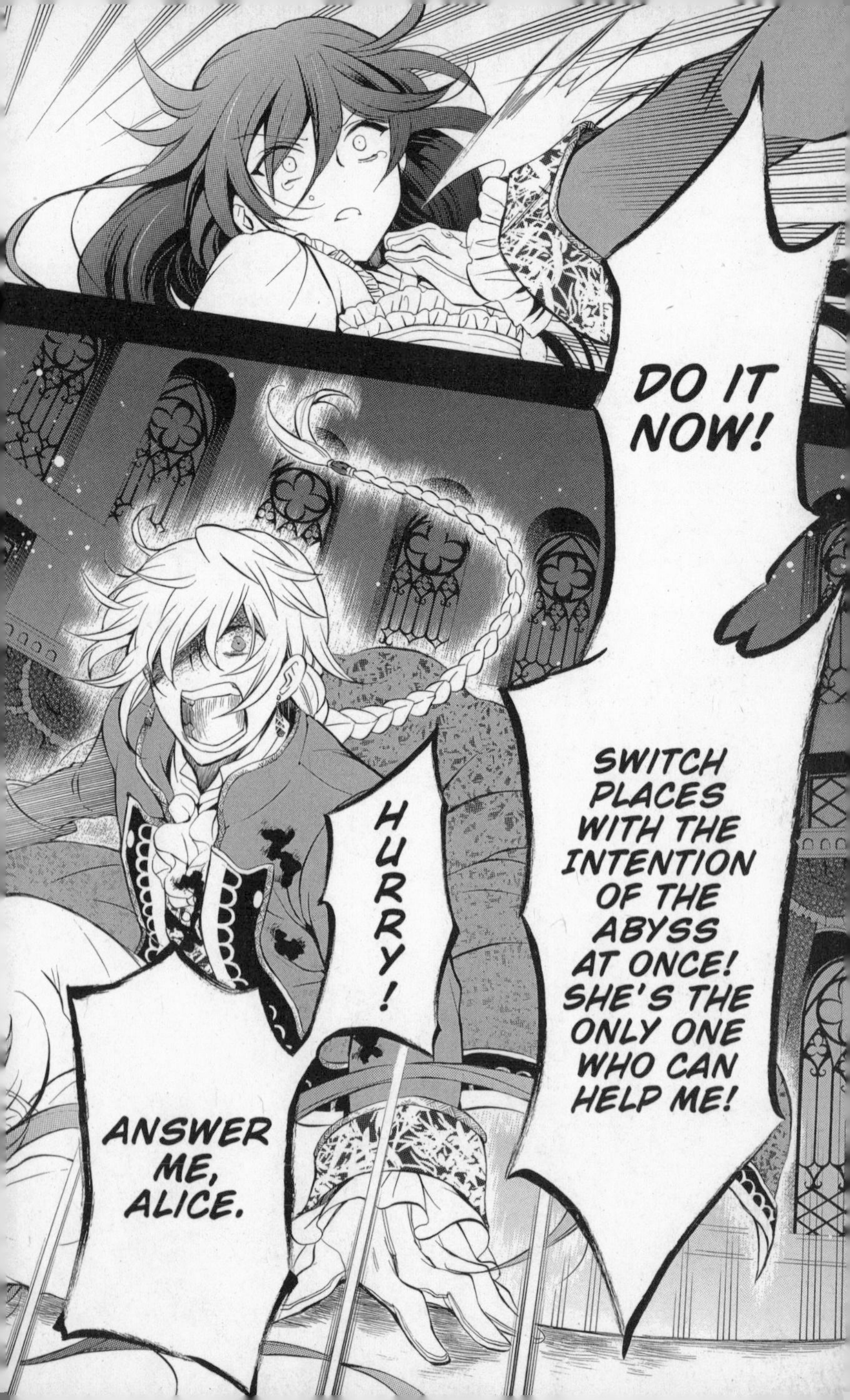
DO IT NOW!
SWITCH PLACES WITH THE INTENTION OF THE ABYSS AT ONCE! SHE'S THE ONLY ONE WHO CAN HELP ME!
HURRY!
ANSWER ME, ALICE.

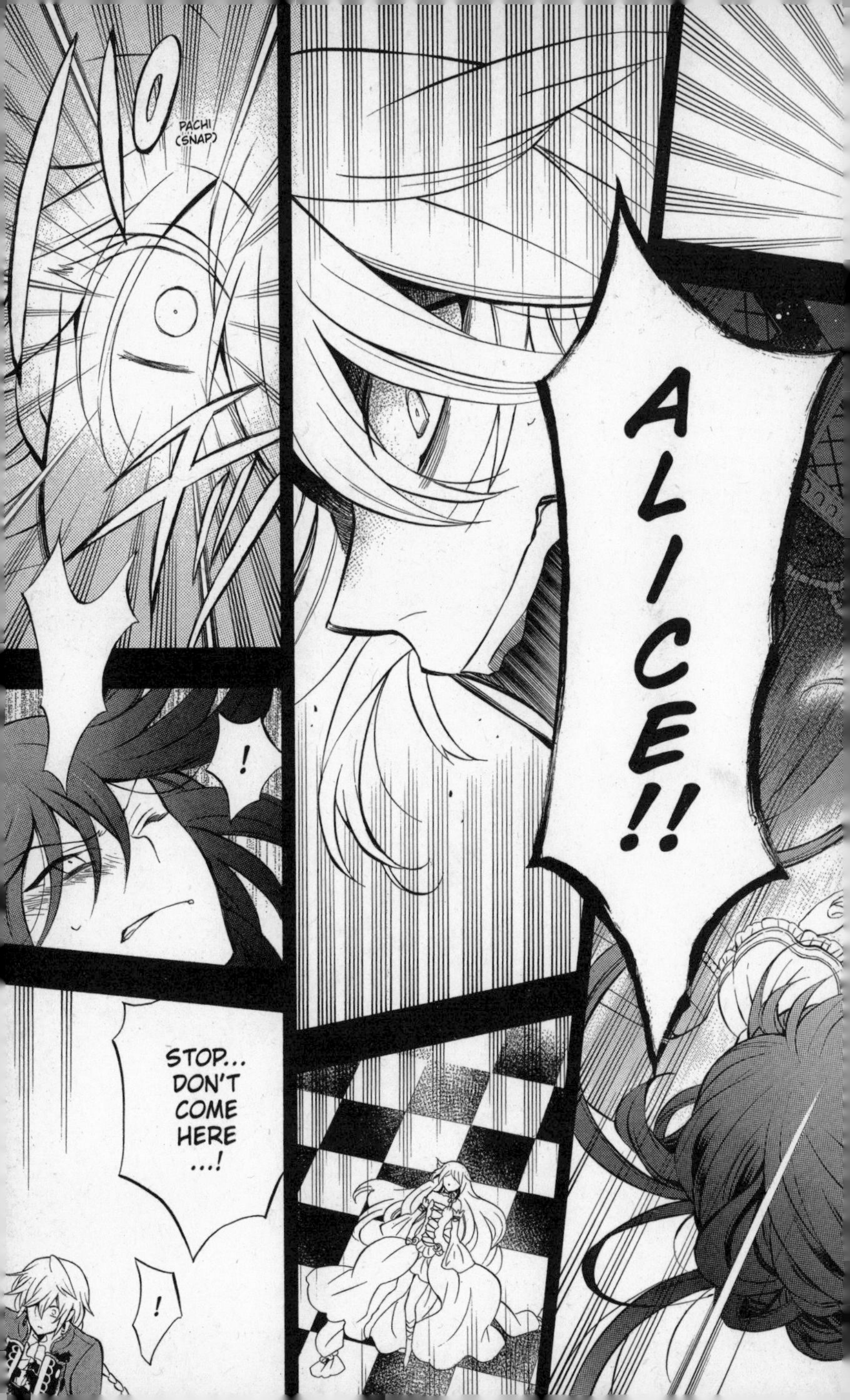
ALICE!!
PACHI (SNAP)
!
STOP... DON'T COME HERE ...!
!

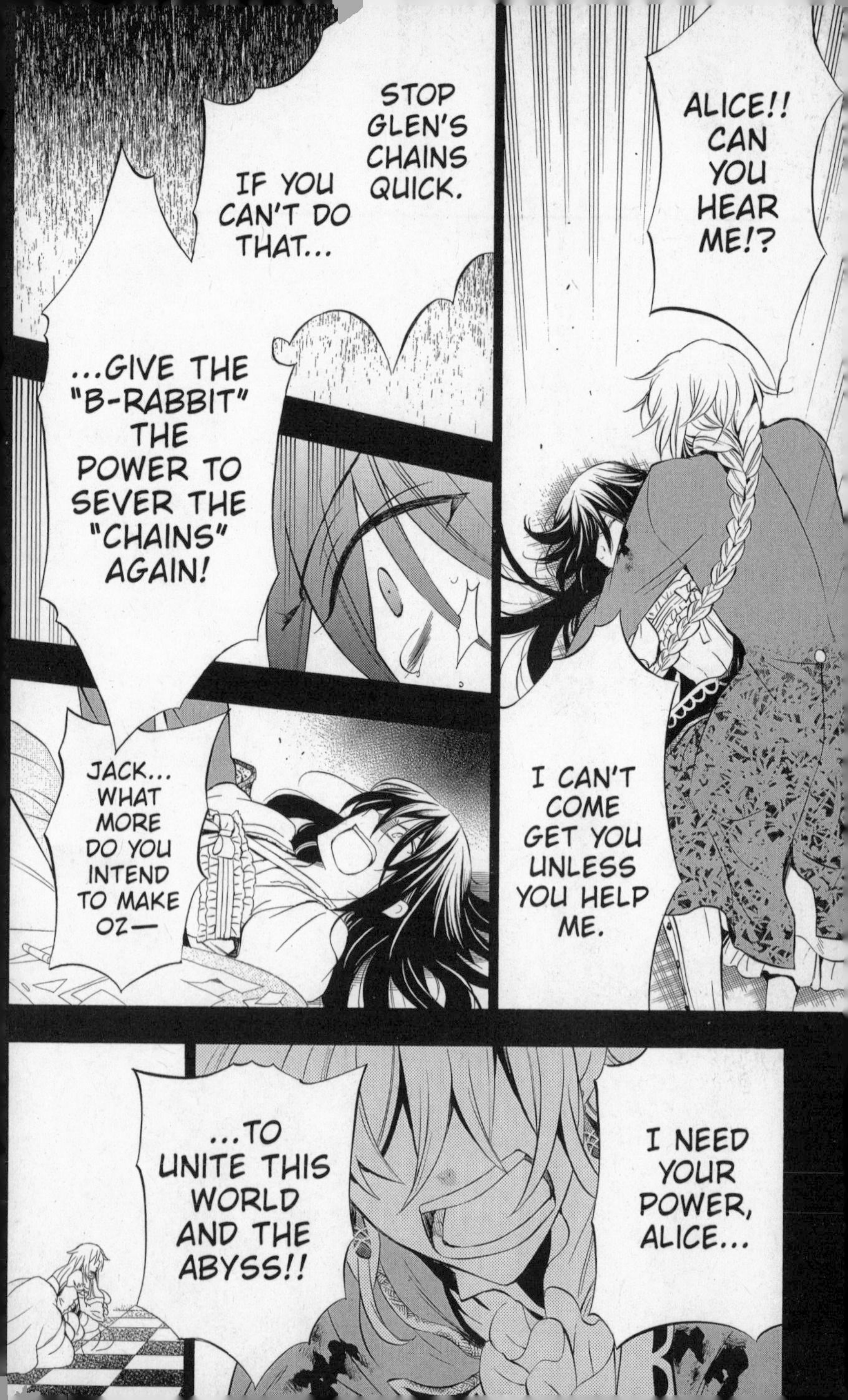
ALICE!! CAN YOU HEAR ME!?
I CAN'T COME GET YOU UNLESS YOU HELP ME.
STOP GLEN'S CHAINS QUICK.
IF YOU CAN'T DO THAT...
...GIVE THE "B-RABBIT" THE POWER TO SEVER THE "CHAINS" AGAIN!
JACK... WHAT MORE DO YOU INTEND TO MAKE OZ—
I NEED YOUR POWER, ALICE...
...TO UNITE THIS WORLD AND THE ABYSS!!

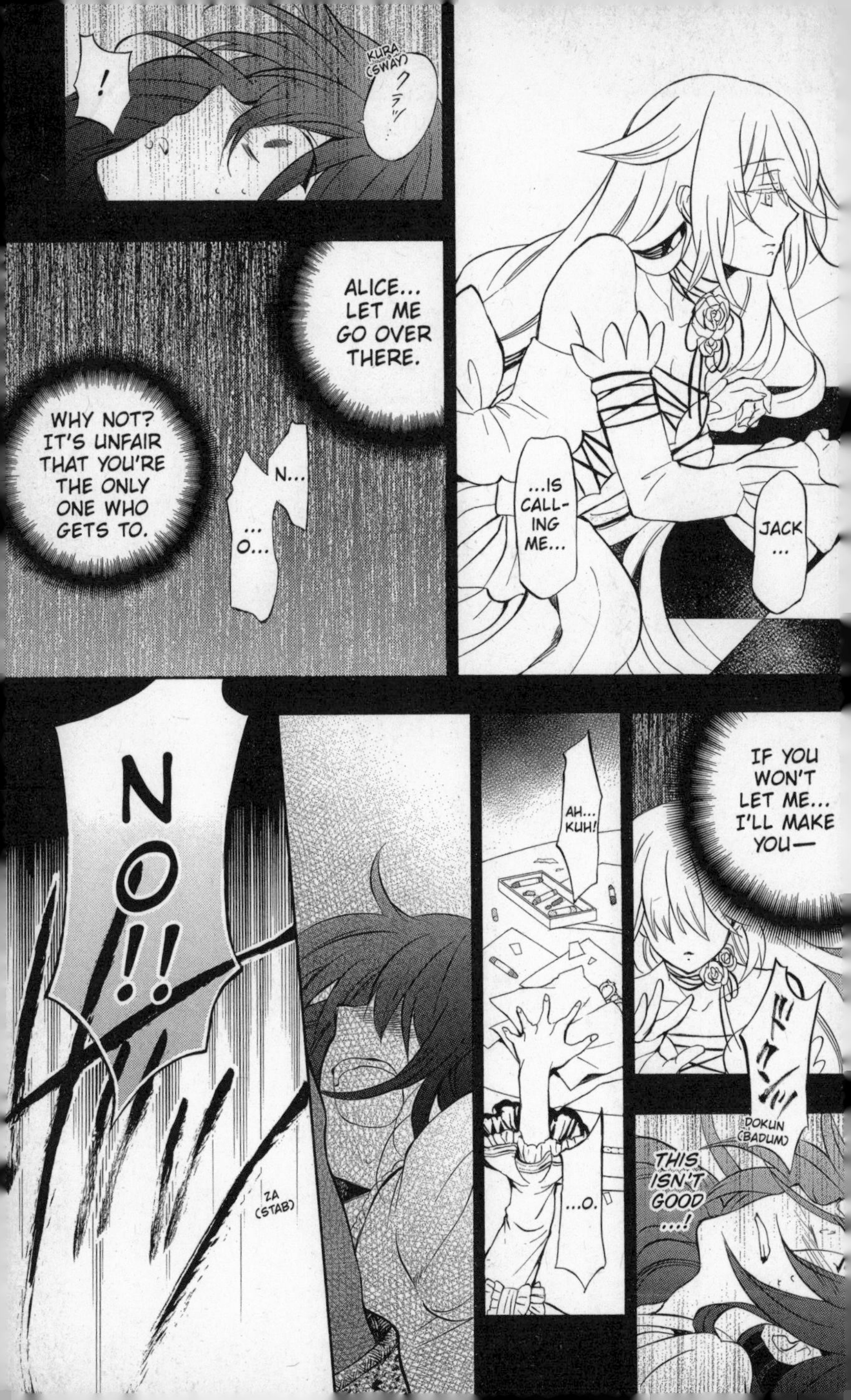
JACK...
...IS CALLING ME...
KURA (SWAY)
クラッ…
!
ALICE... LET ME GO OVER THERE.
N...
...O...
WHY NOT? IT'S UNFAIR THAT YOU'RE THE ONLY ONE WHO GETS TO.
IF YOU WON'T LET ME... I'LL MAKE YOU—
DOKUN (BADUM)
THIS ISN'T GOOD ...!
AH... KUH!
...O.
NO!!
ZA (STAB)

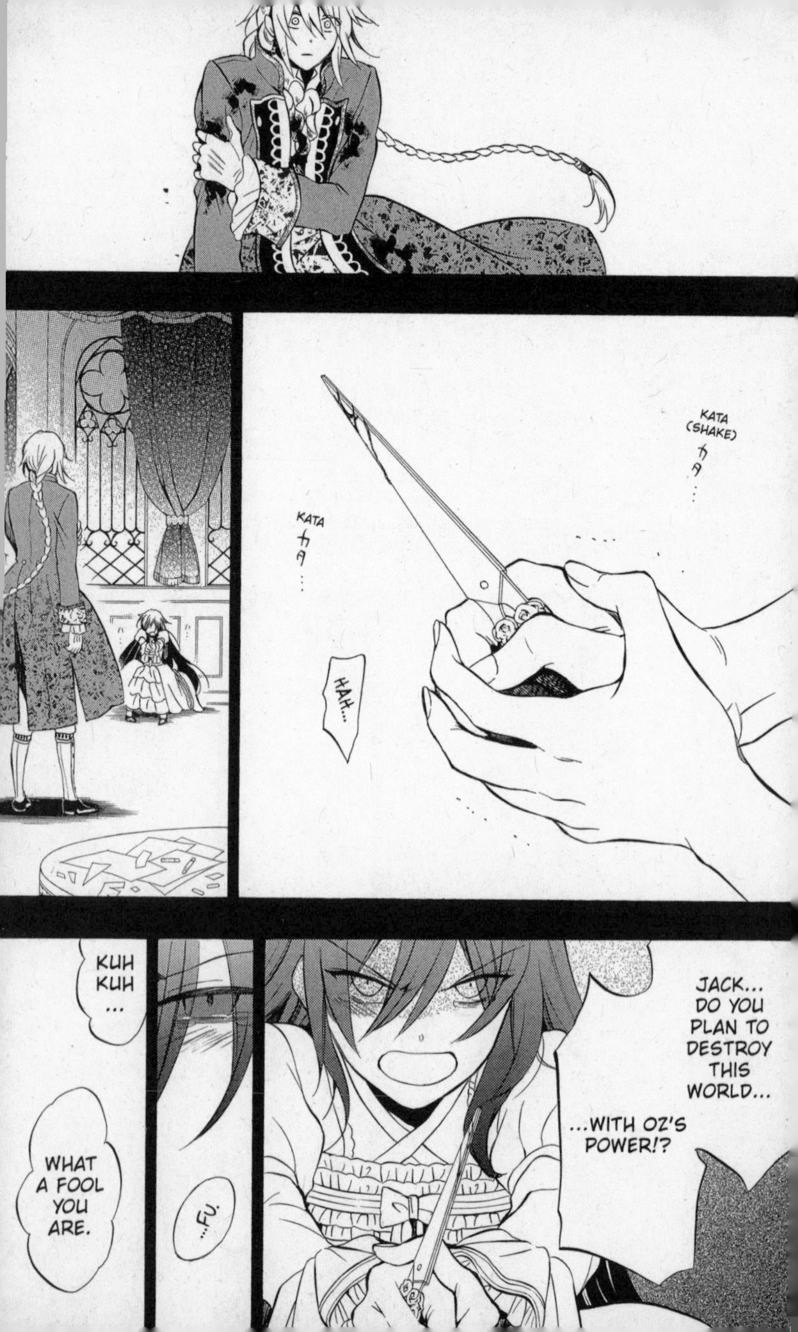
KATA (SHAKE) カタ…
…
KATA カタ…
HAH…
JACK… DO YOU PLAN TO DESTROY THIS WORLD…
…WITH OZ'S POWER!?
…FU.
KUH KUH …
WHAT A FOOL YOU ARE.

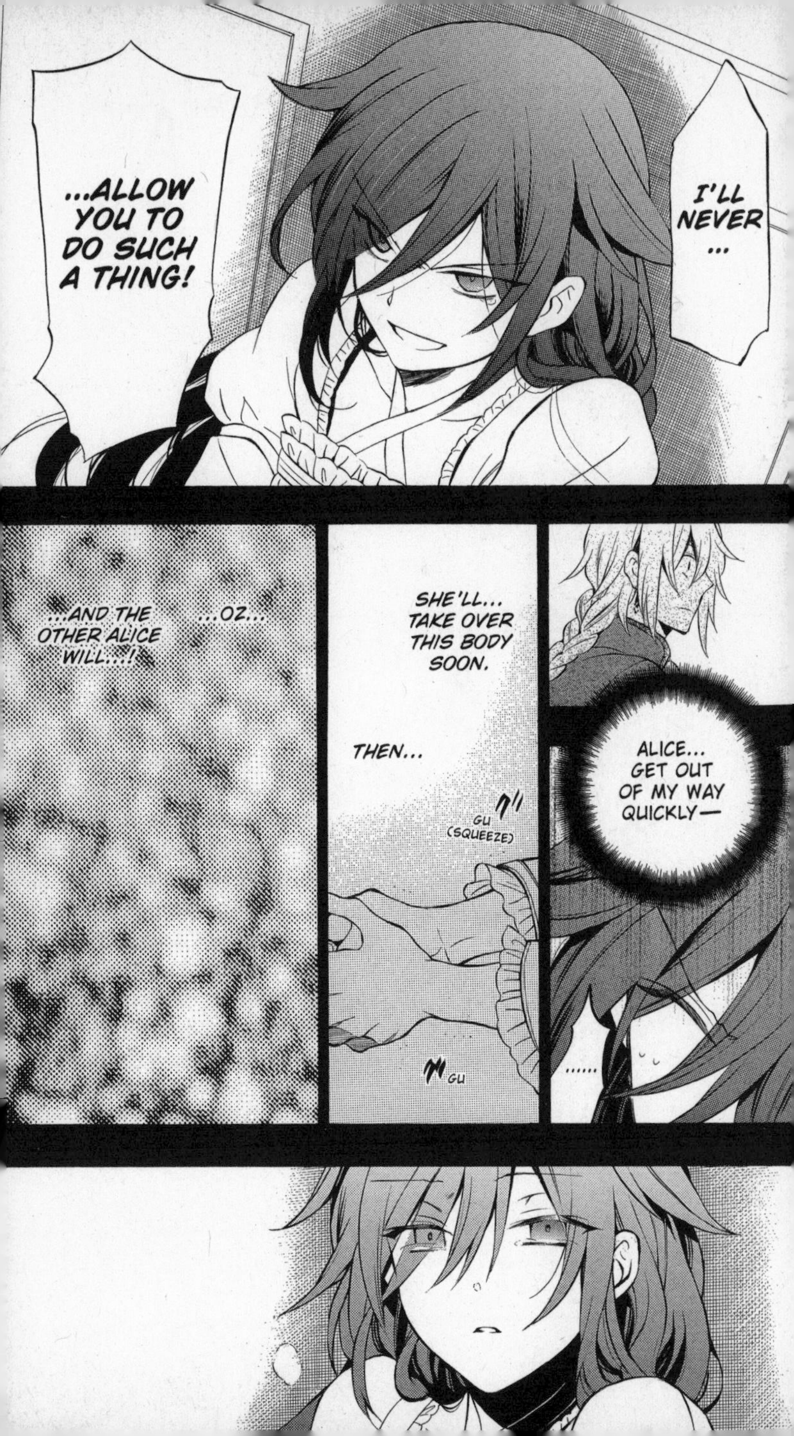
I'LL NEVER ...
...ALLOW YOU TO DO SUCH A THING!
ALICE... GET OUT OF MY WAY QUICKLY—
......
SHE'LL... TAKE OVER THIS BODY SOON.
THEN...
GU (SQUEEZE)
GU
...OZ...
...AND THE OTHER ALICE WILL...!

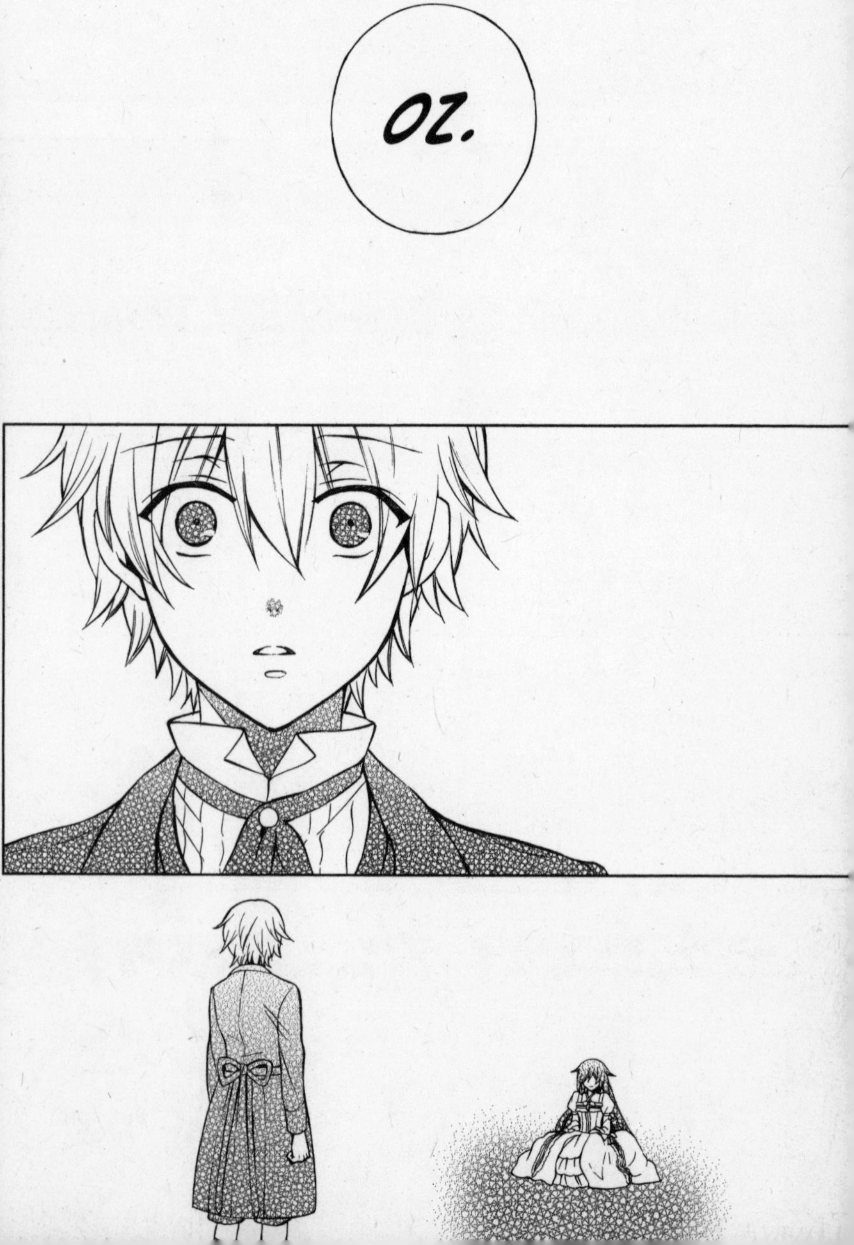
OZ.

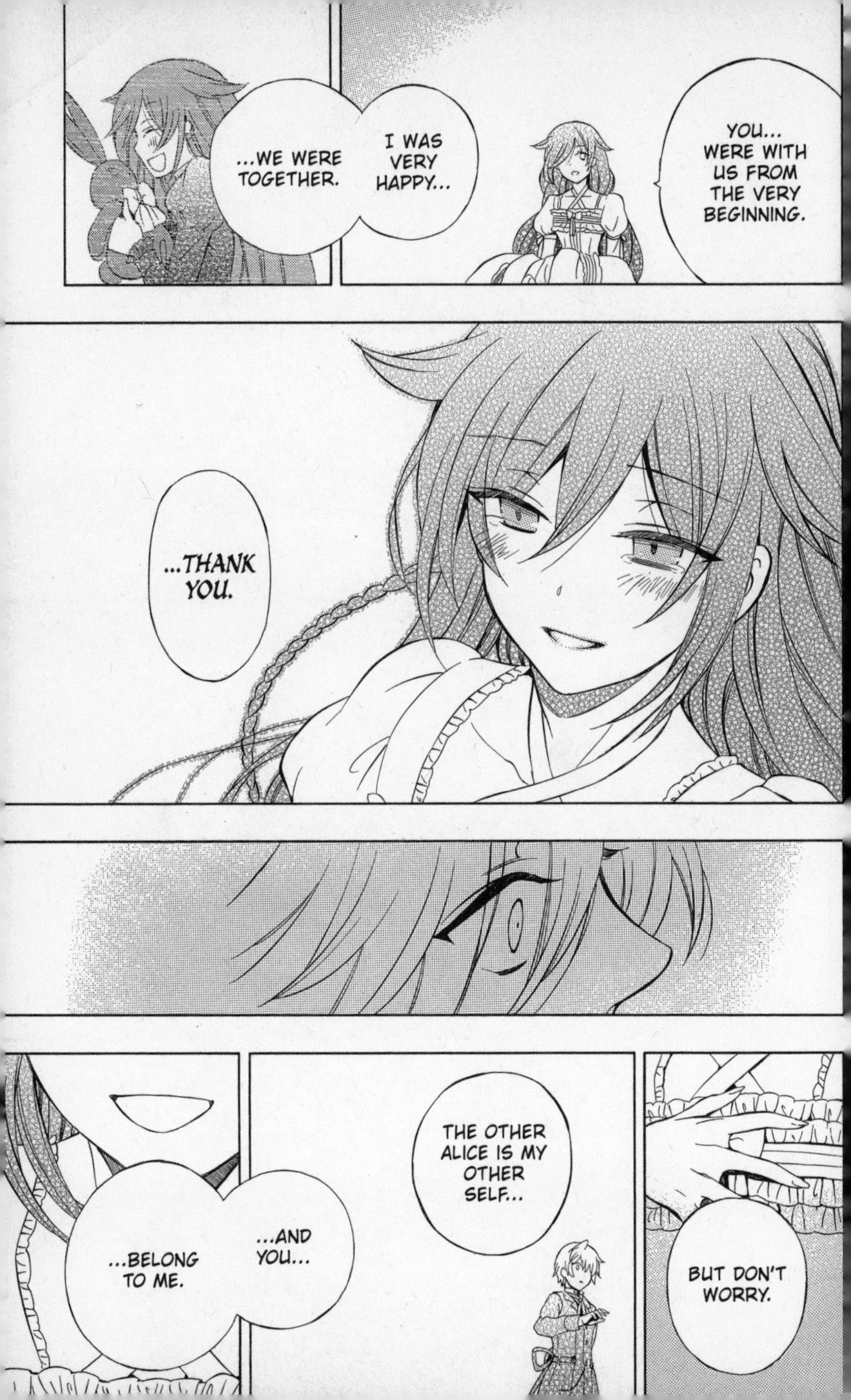
YOU... WERE WITH US FROM THE VERY BEGINNING.
I WAS VERY HAPPY...
...WE WERE TOGETHER.
...THANK YOU.
BUT DON'T WORRY.
THE OTHER ALICE IS MY OTHER SELF...
...AND YOU...
...BELONG TO ME.

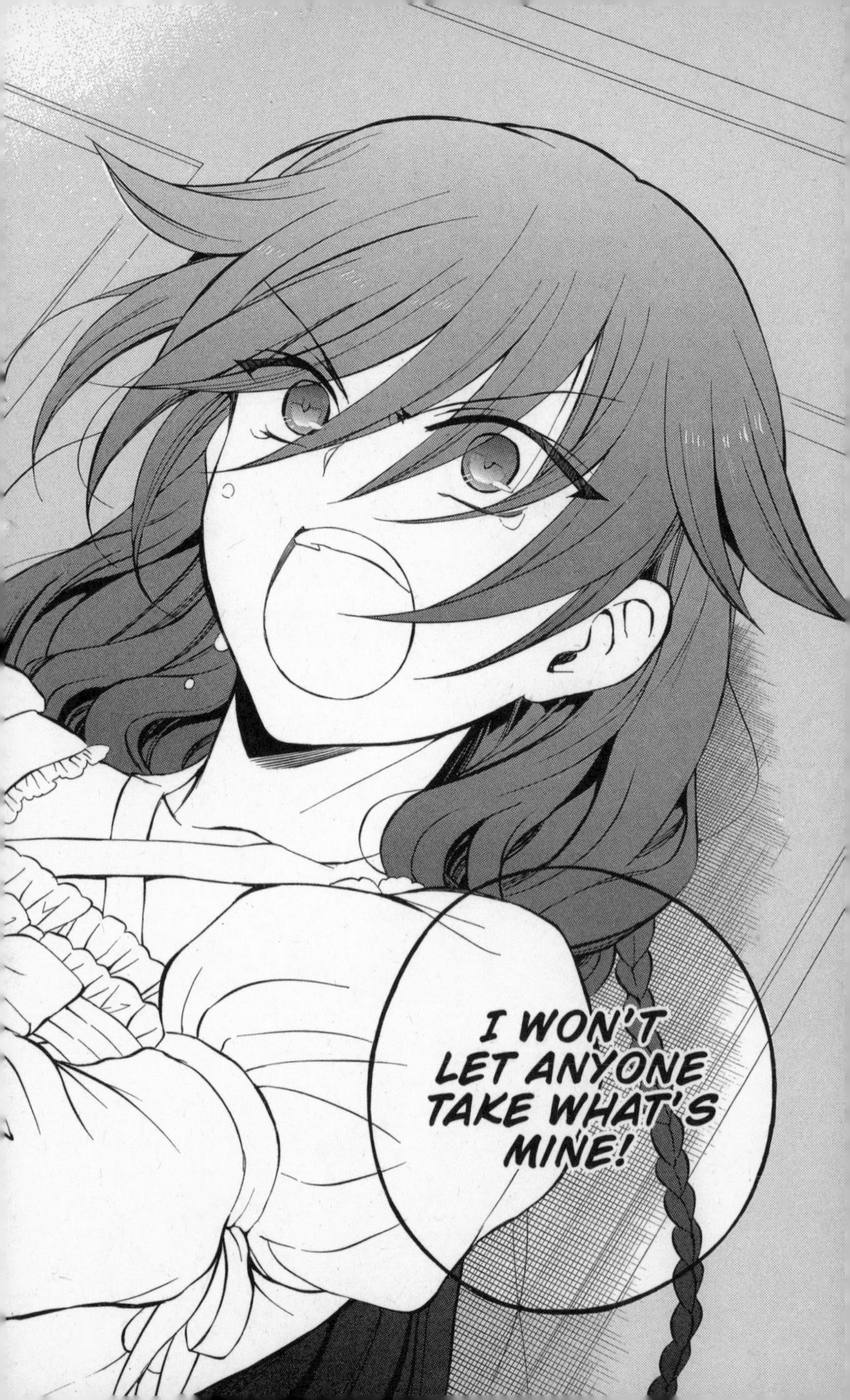
I WON'T LET ANYONE TAKE WHAT'S MINE!

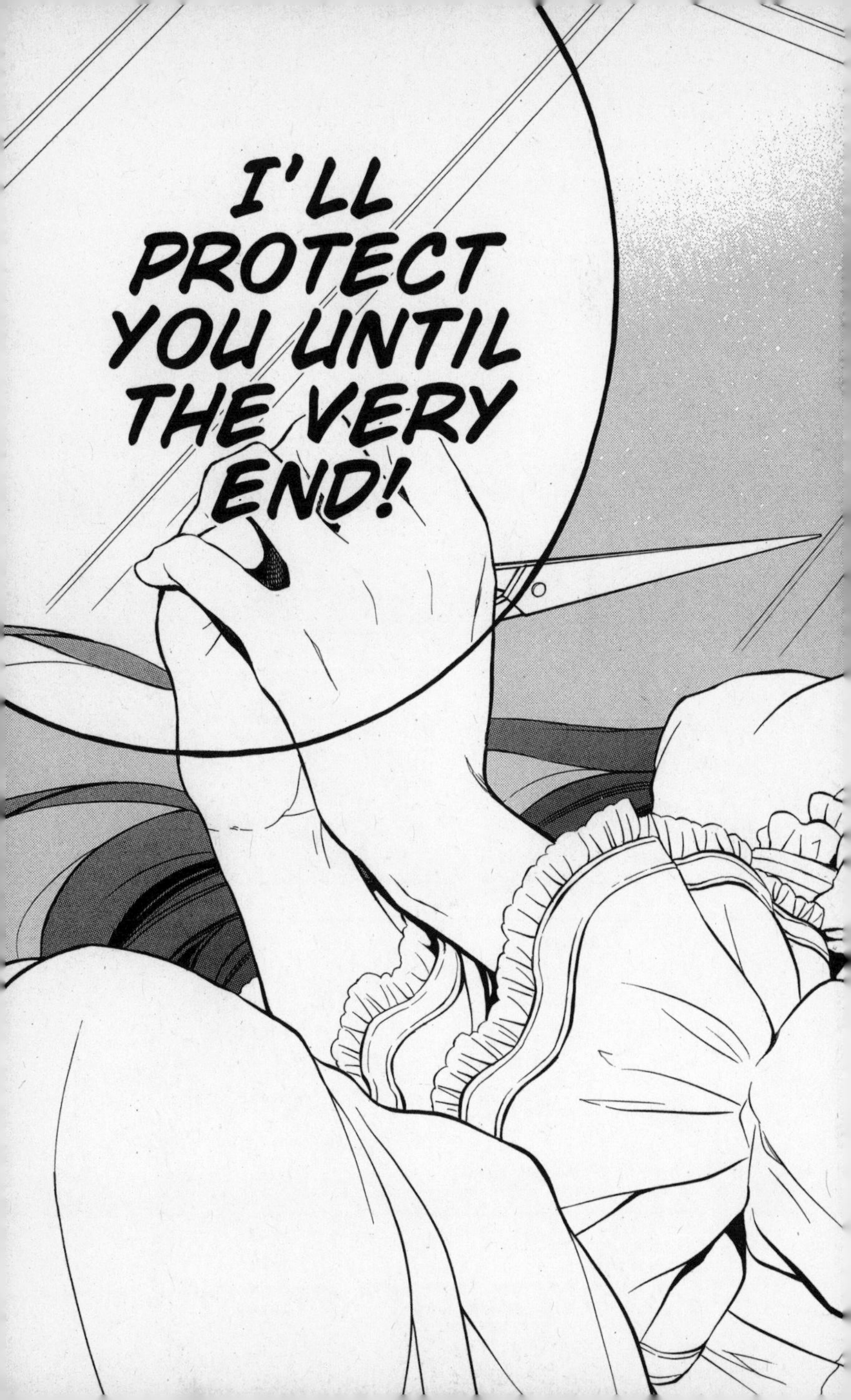
I'LL PROTECT YOU UNTIL THE VERY END!

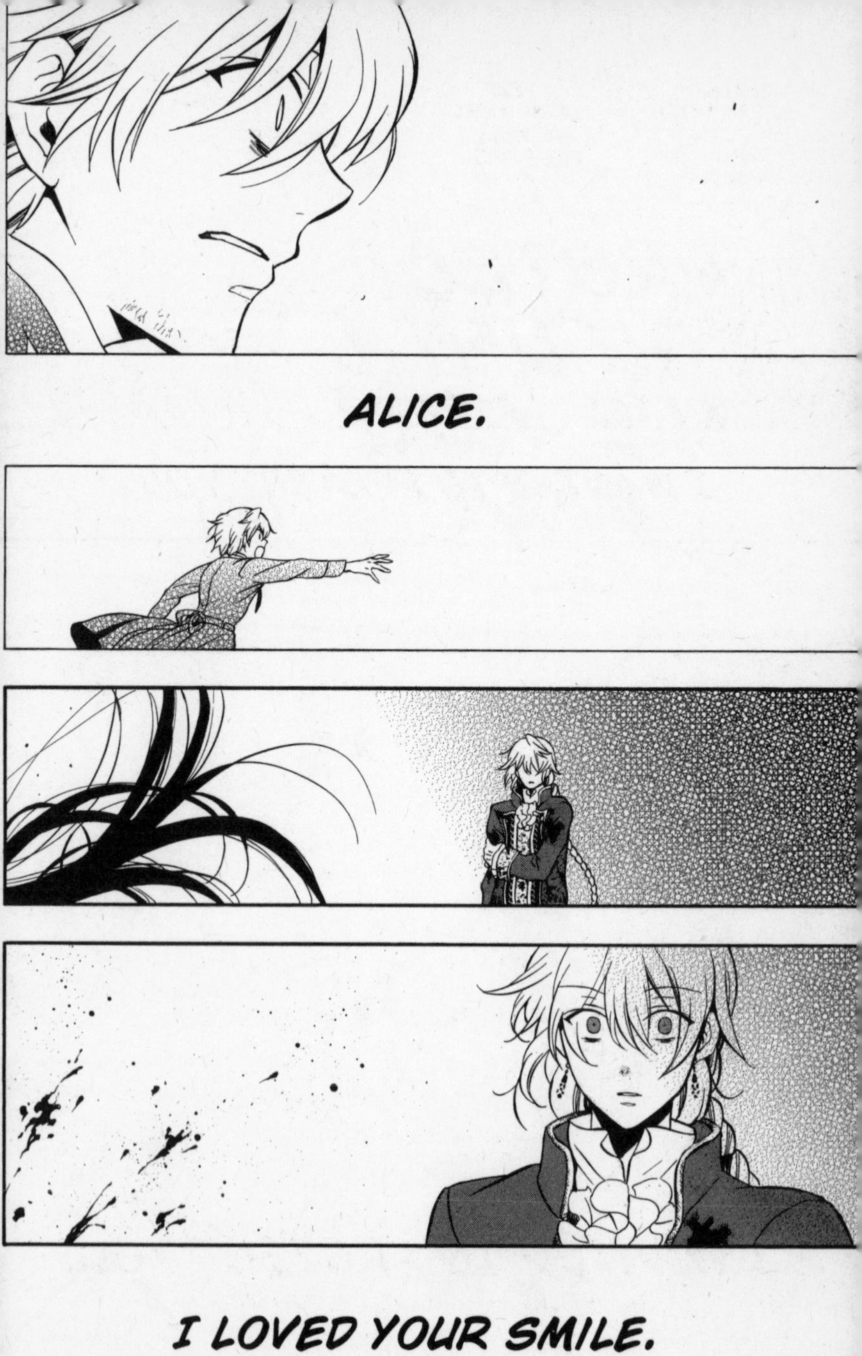
ALICE.
I LOVED YOUR SMILE.

I FELT WARM WHEN WE WERE TOGETHER.
YOU WERE MORE PRECIOUS TO ME THAN ANYTHING OR ANYBODY...
I WANTED TO PROTECT YOU.
I WANTED TO PROTECT YOU.

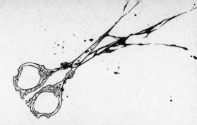

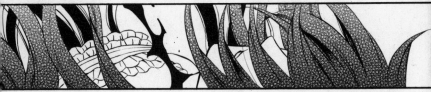

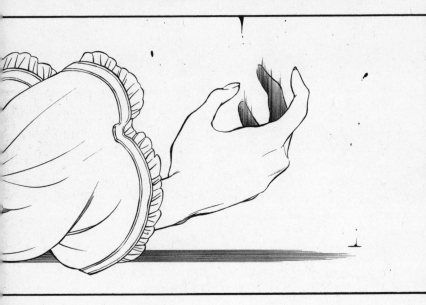

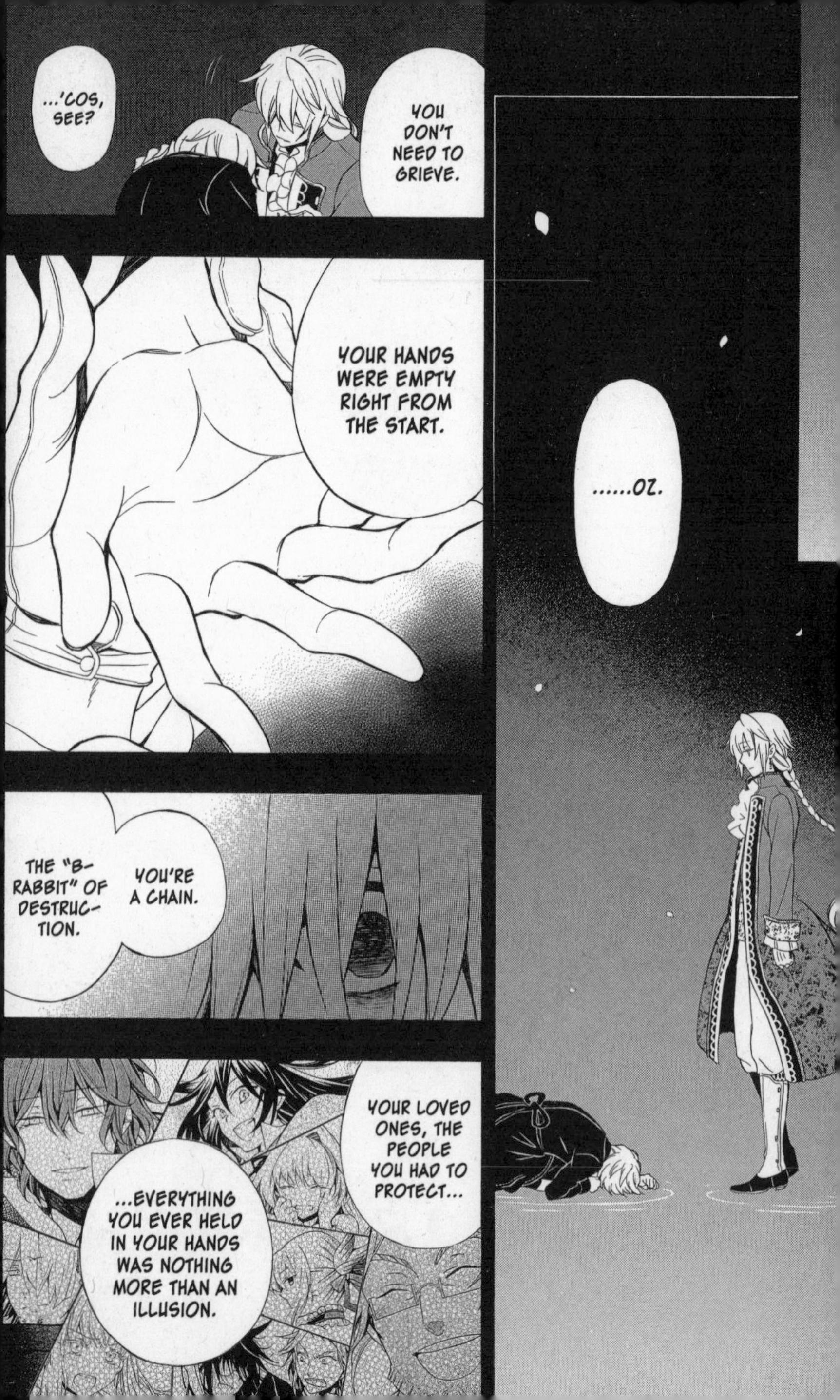

......OZ.
YOU DON'T NEED TO GRIEVE.
...'COS, SEE?
YOUR HANDS WERE EMPTY RIGHT FROM THE START.
YOU'RE A CHAIN.
THE "B-RABBIT" OF DESTRUCTION.
YOUR LOVED ONES, THE PEOPLE YOU HAD TO PROTECT...
...EVERYTHING YOU EVER HELD IN YOUR HANDS WAS NOTHING MORE THAN AN ILLUSION.

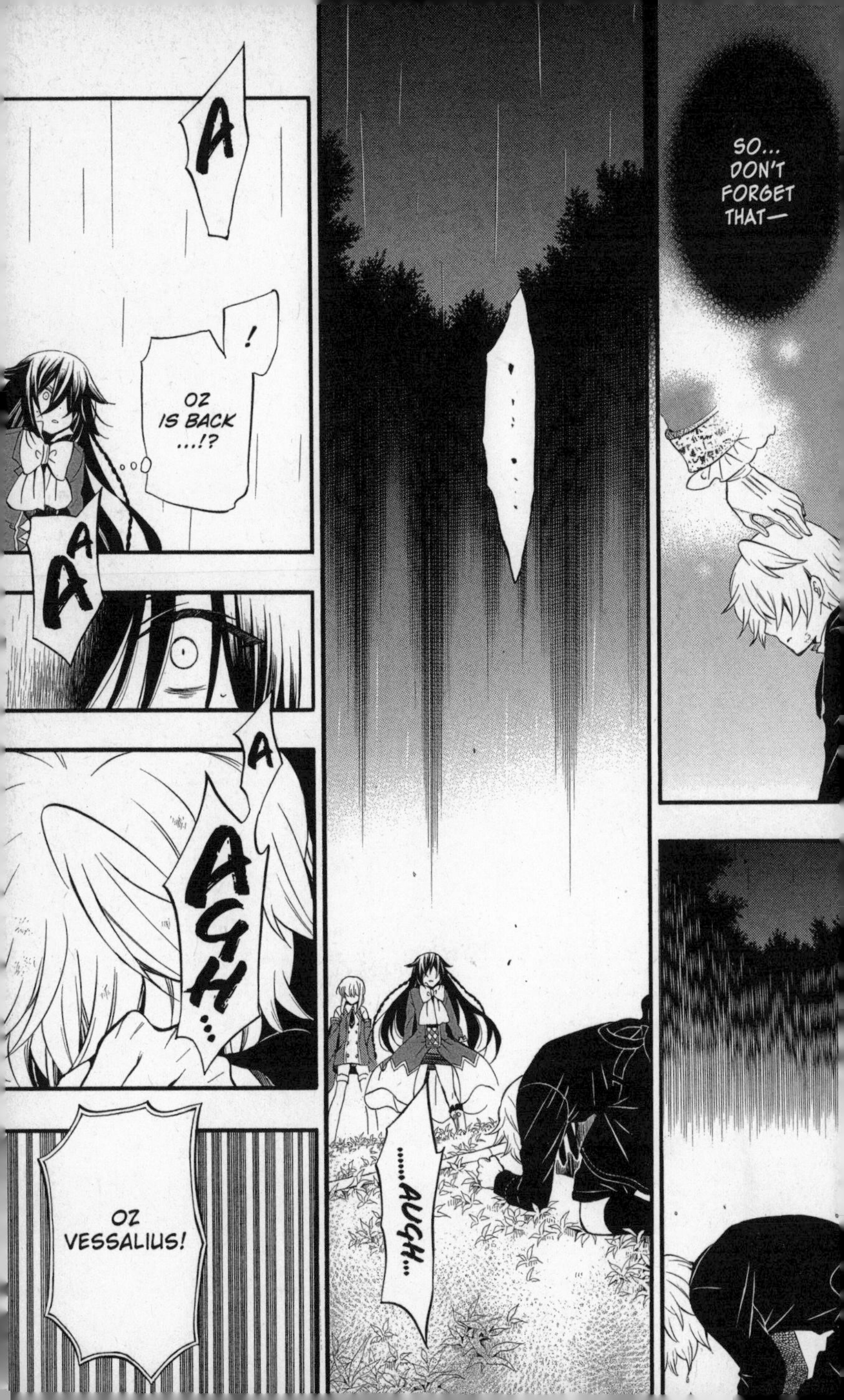
SO... DON'T FORGET THAT—
...
......AUGH...
A
!
OZ IS BACK ...!?
A A
A
AGH...
OZ VESSALIUS!

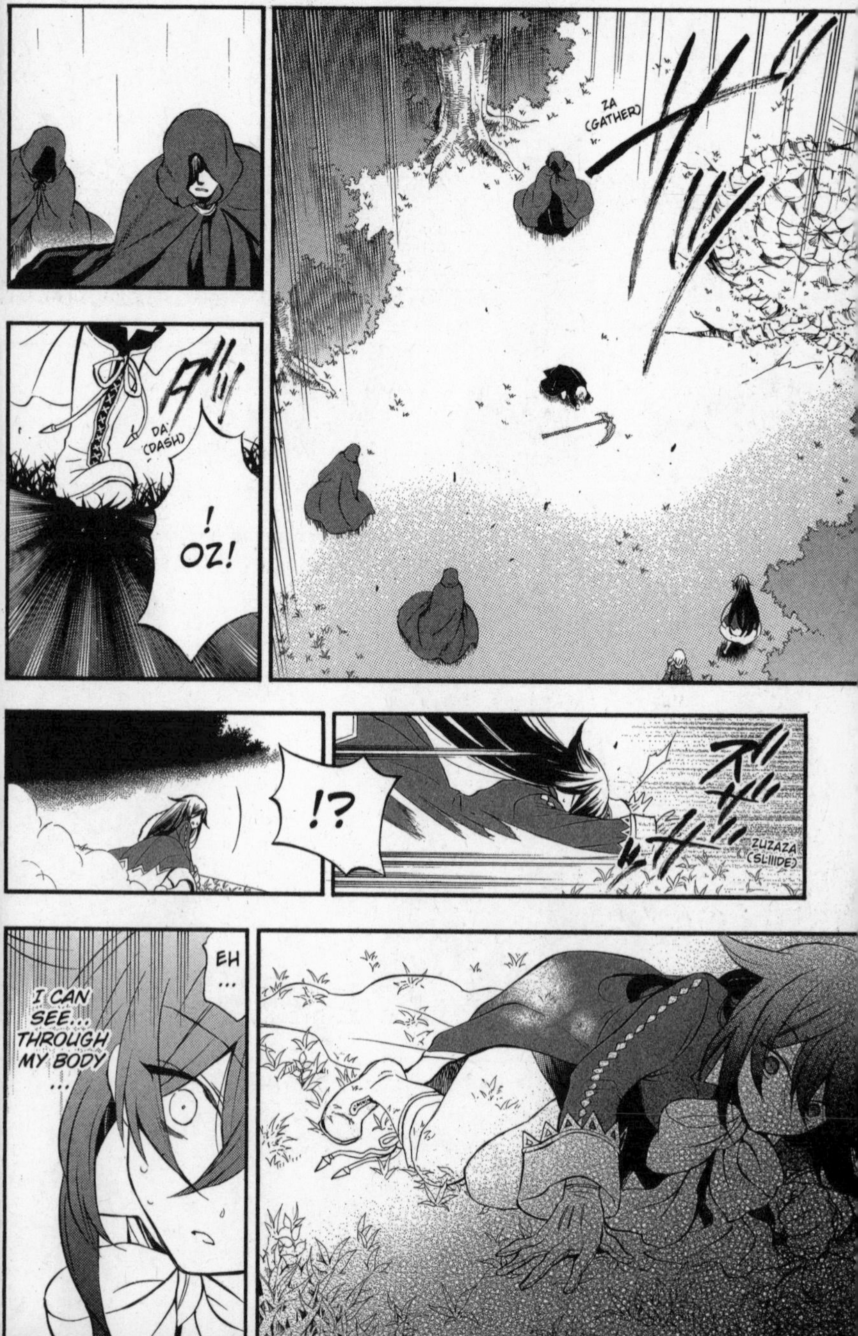
ZA (GATHER)
DA (DASH)
! OZ!
ZUZAZA (SLIIIDE)
!?
EH ...
I CAN SEE... THROUGH MY BODY ...

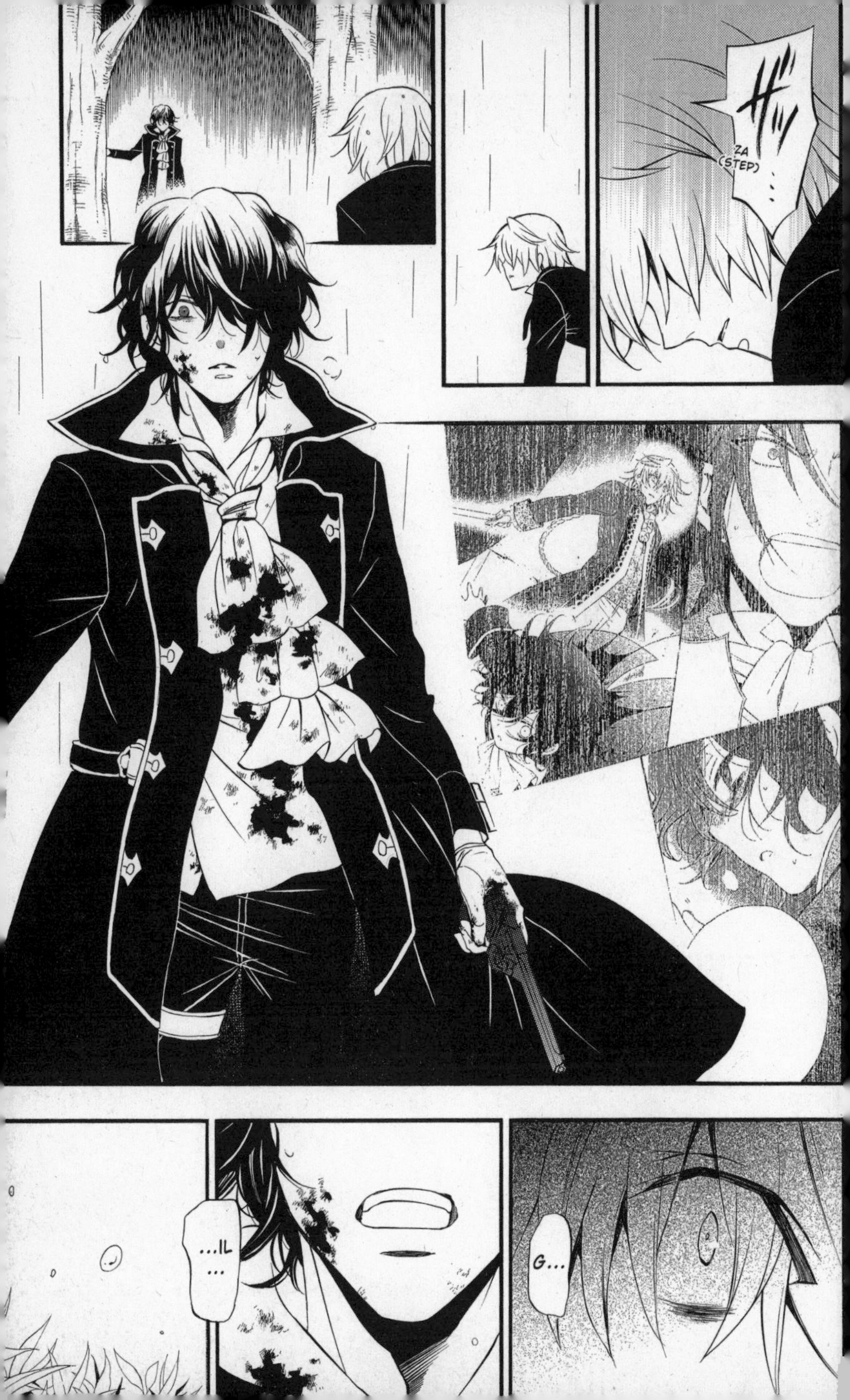
ZA (STEP)
...
...!!
...
G...

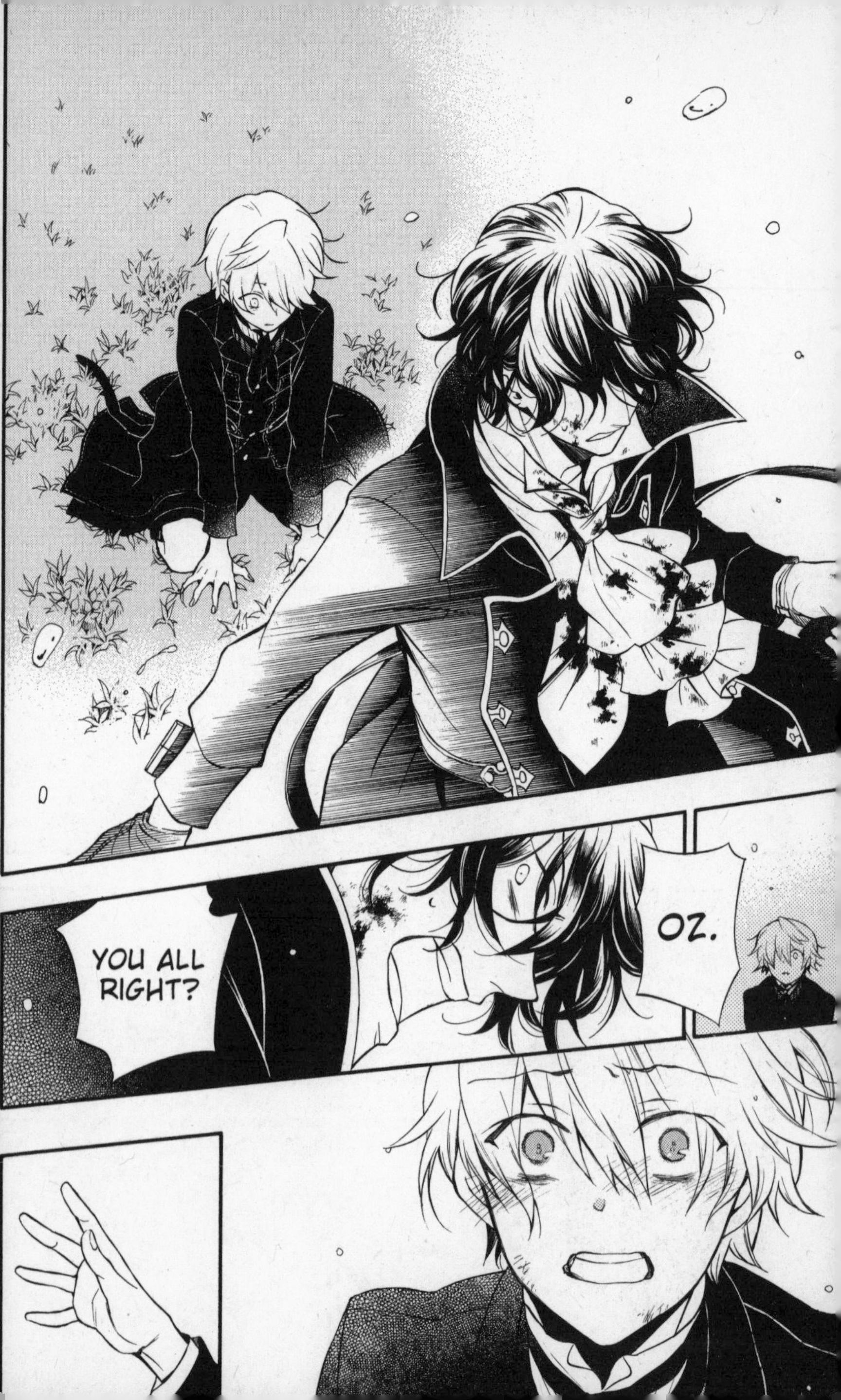
OZ.
YOU ALL RIGHT?

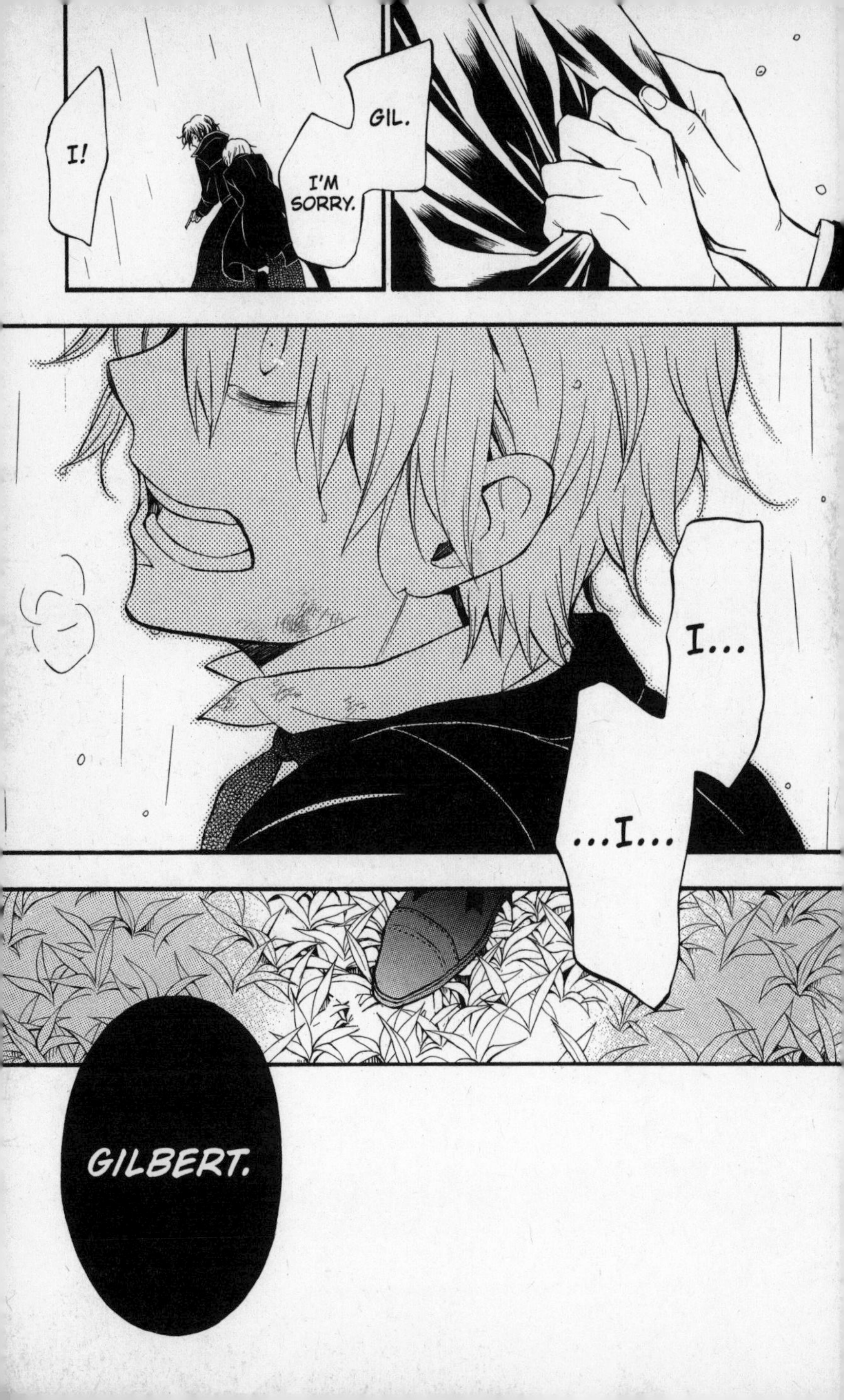
GIL.
I'M SORRY.
I!
I...
...I...
GILBERT.

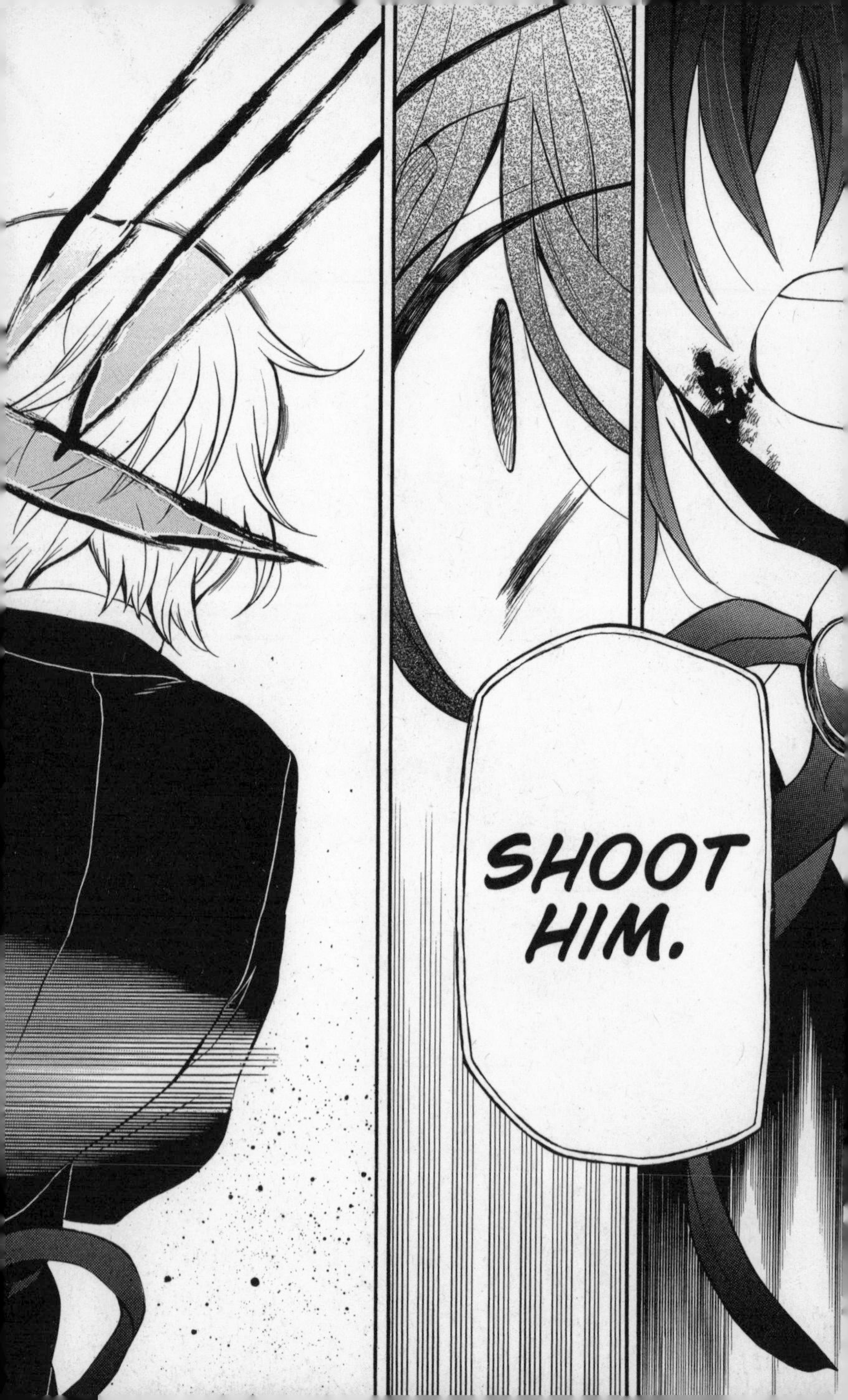
SHOOT HIM.

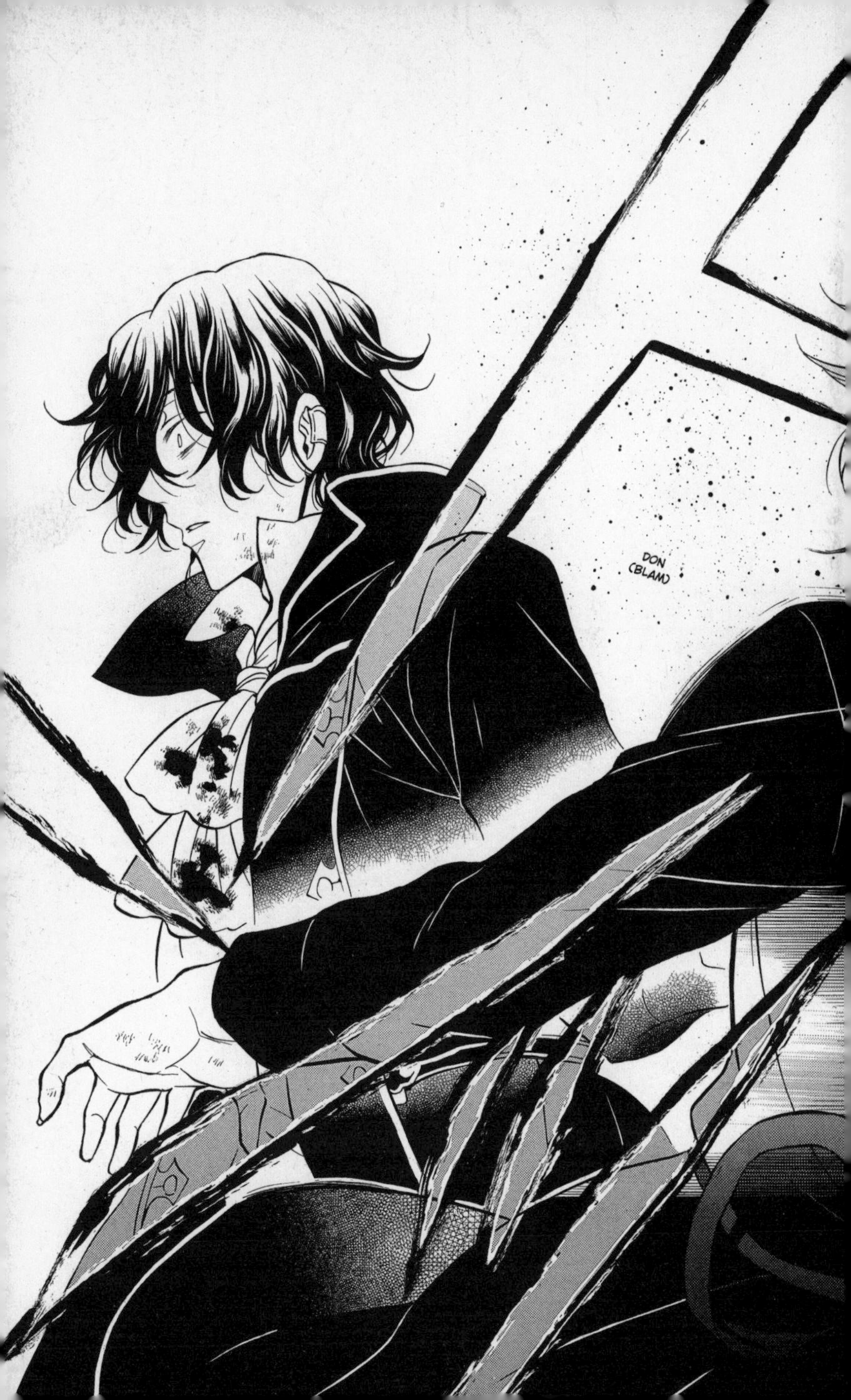
DON
(BLAM)

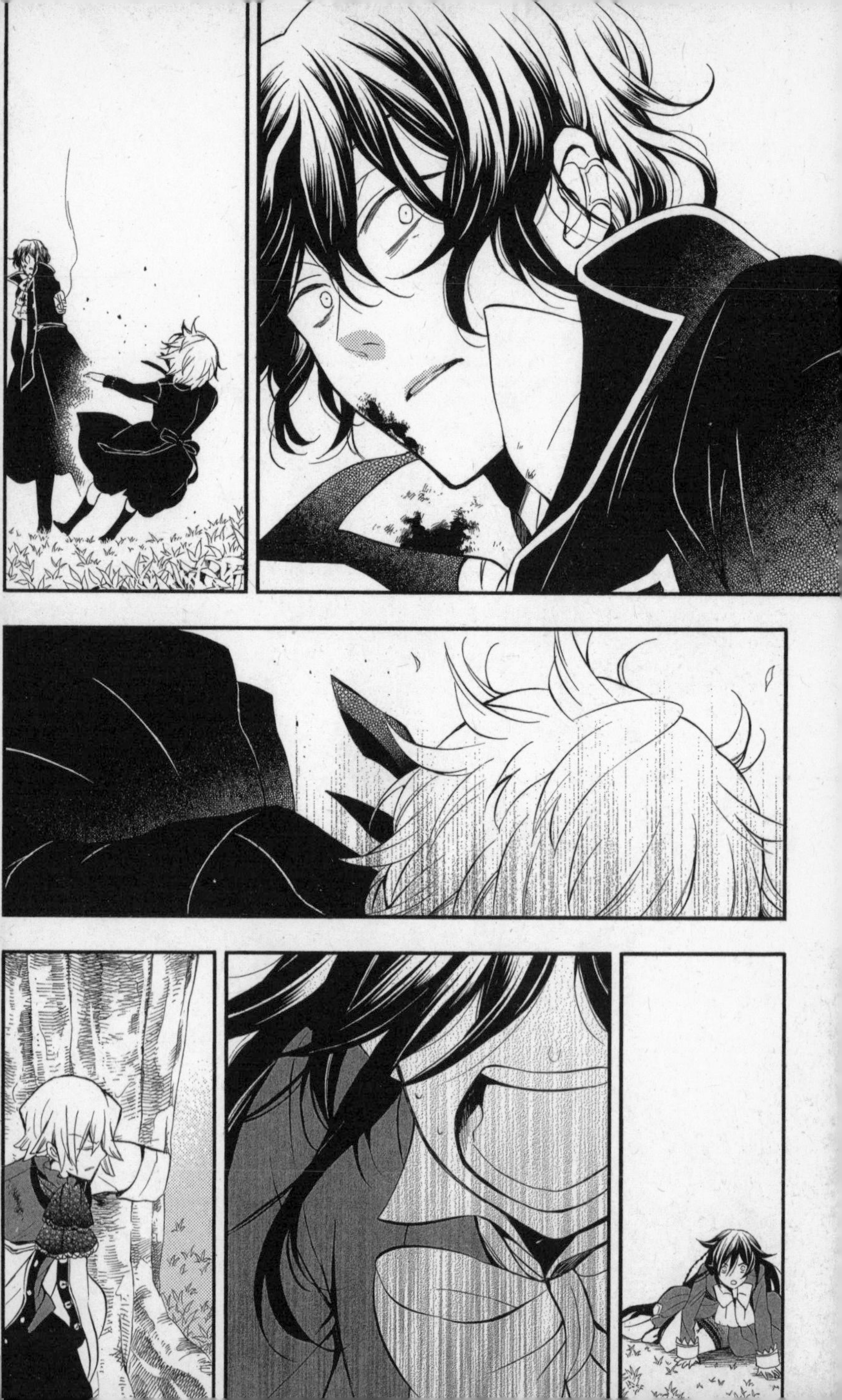

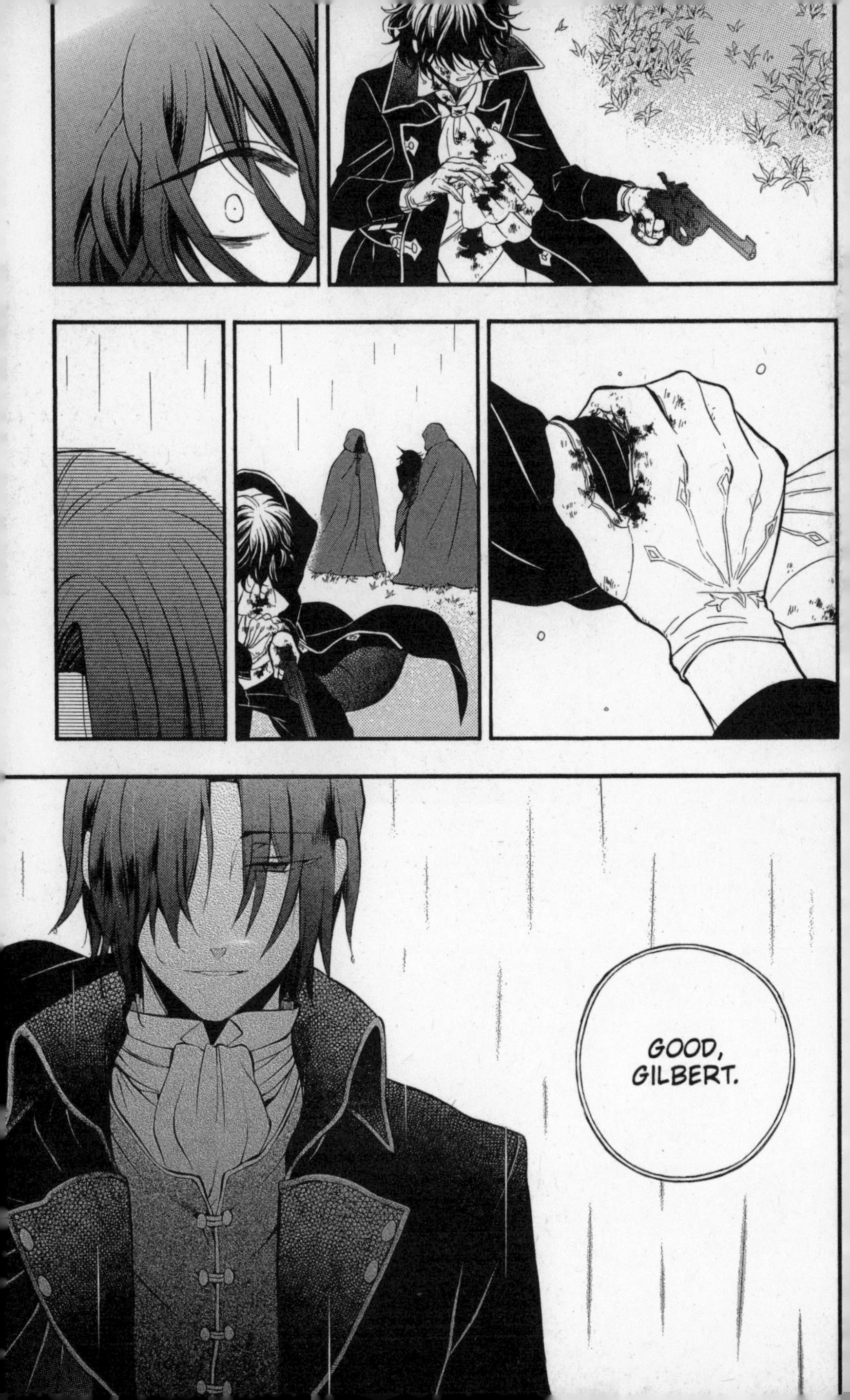
GOOD, GILBERT.

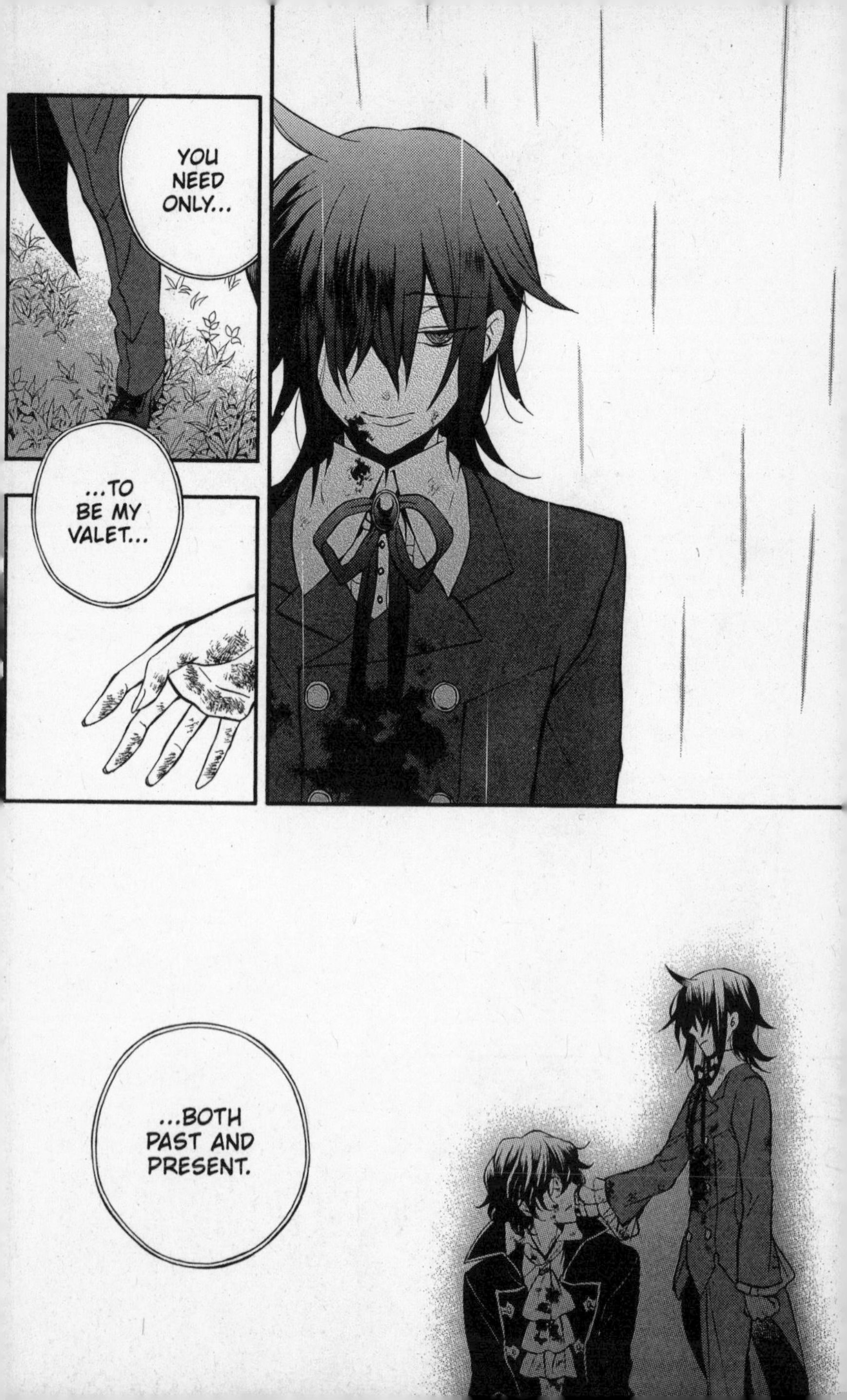
YOU NEED ONLY...
...TO BE MY VALET...
...BOTH PAST AND PRESENT.

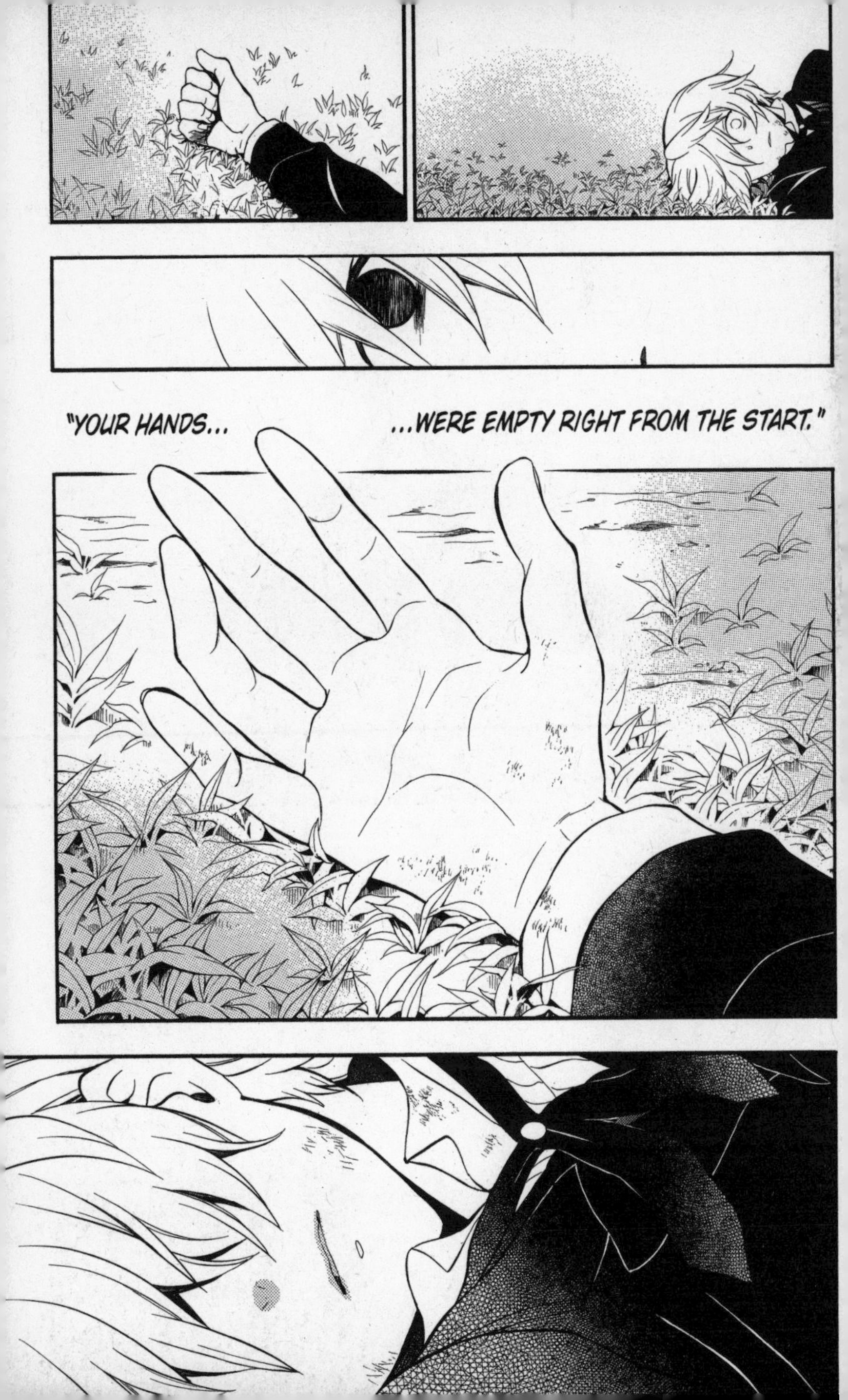
"YOUR HANDS...
...WERE EMPTY RIGHT FROM THE START."

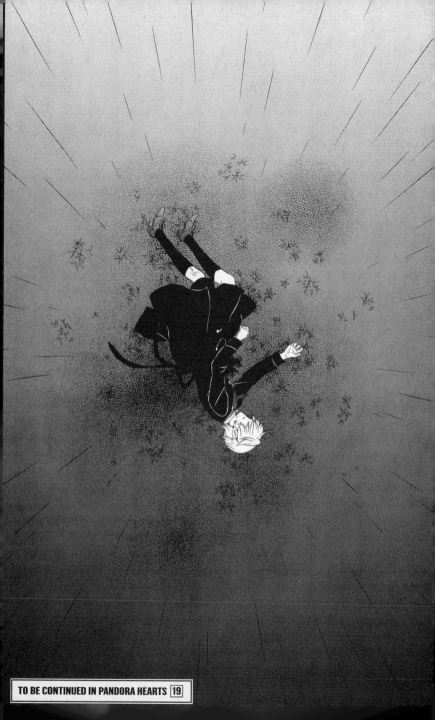

TO BE CONTINUED IN PANDORA HEARTS 19

Retrace:LXXIV Broken Rabbit

Special Thanks

FUMITO YAMAZAKI
NOVEMBER IS RIGHT AROUND THE CORNER! WHAT ABOUT THE BLACK DRESS?

KANATA MINAZUKI-SAN
TURN INTO YAMA-SAN QUICK, 'KAY!? ✧

RYO-CHAN
WHEN ARE YOU GONNA COME WORK FOR US??

TADOU-SAN
BROWN HAIR = DELINQUENT

YAJI
WELCOME BACK! NEXT UP: GERMANY!

BIG BROTHER (2) & YUKKO-SAN
I WANT TO EAT OKONOMIYAKI.

SAEKO TAKIGAWA-SAN
MY EDITOR IS WONDERING WHAT YOUR HUSBAND IS LIKE.

YUKINO-SAN
I WONDER WHAT YOU'RE TALKING ABOUT IN THE TATAMI ROOM.

MIZU KING-SAN
NICE IGNORE!! GAIA MIZU.

AYANA SASAKI-SAN
C'MOOOOON, FRANK, ANYA!!

FATHER, MOTHER, BIG SISTER, BIG BROTHER (1)
THANKS FOR ALWAYS TAKING CARE OF ME.

MY EDITOR TAKEGASA-SAN
HELLO, HELLOOOOOO. CHERRY BLOSSOMS.

—and you!

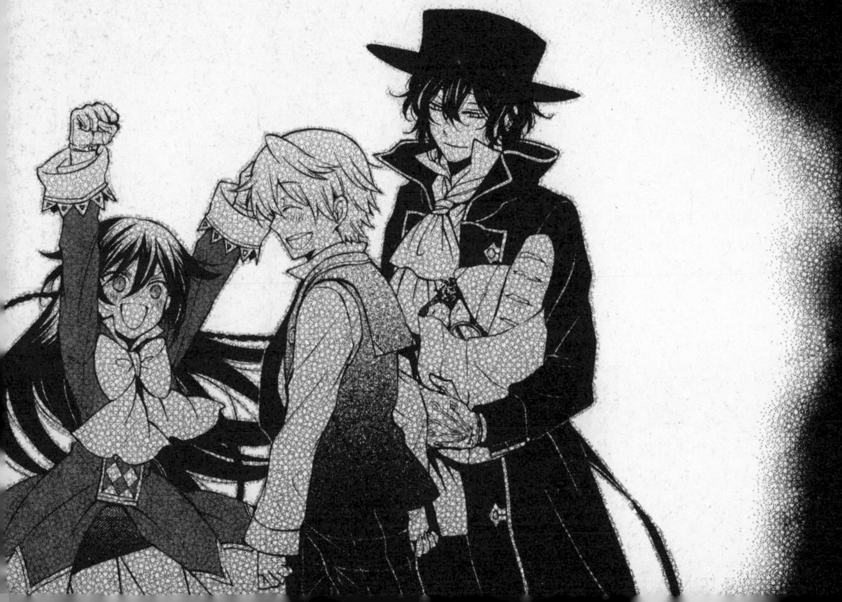

MASTER GLEN'S MAGNIFICENT DAY

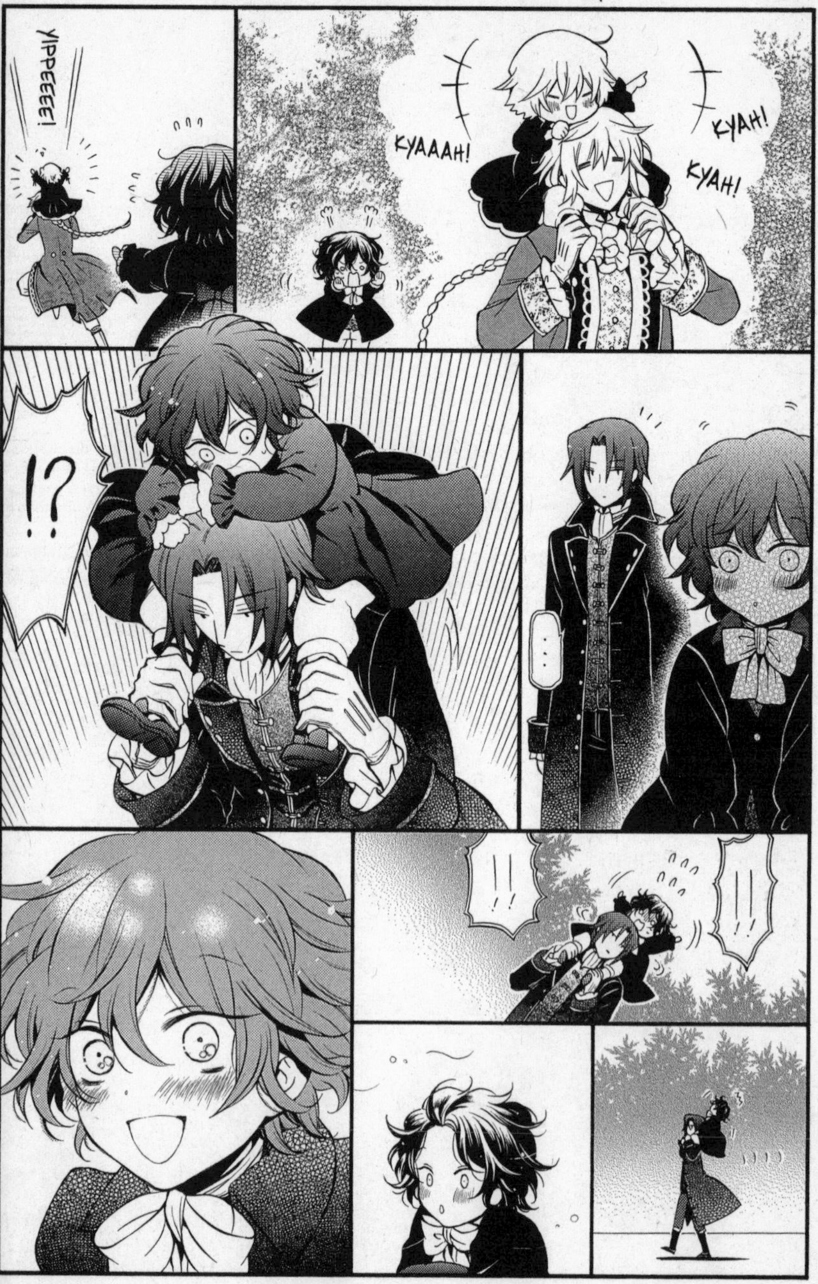
KYAH!
KYAH!
KYAAAH!
YIPPEEEE!
...
!?
!!
!!

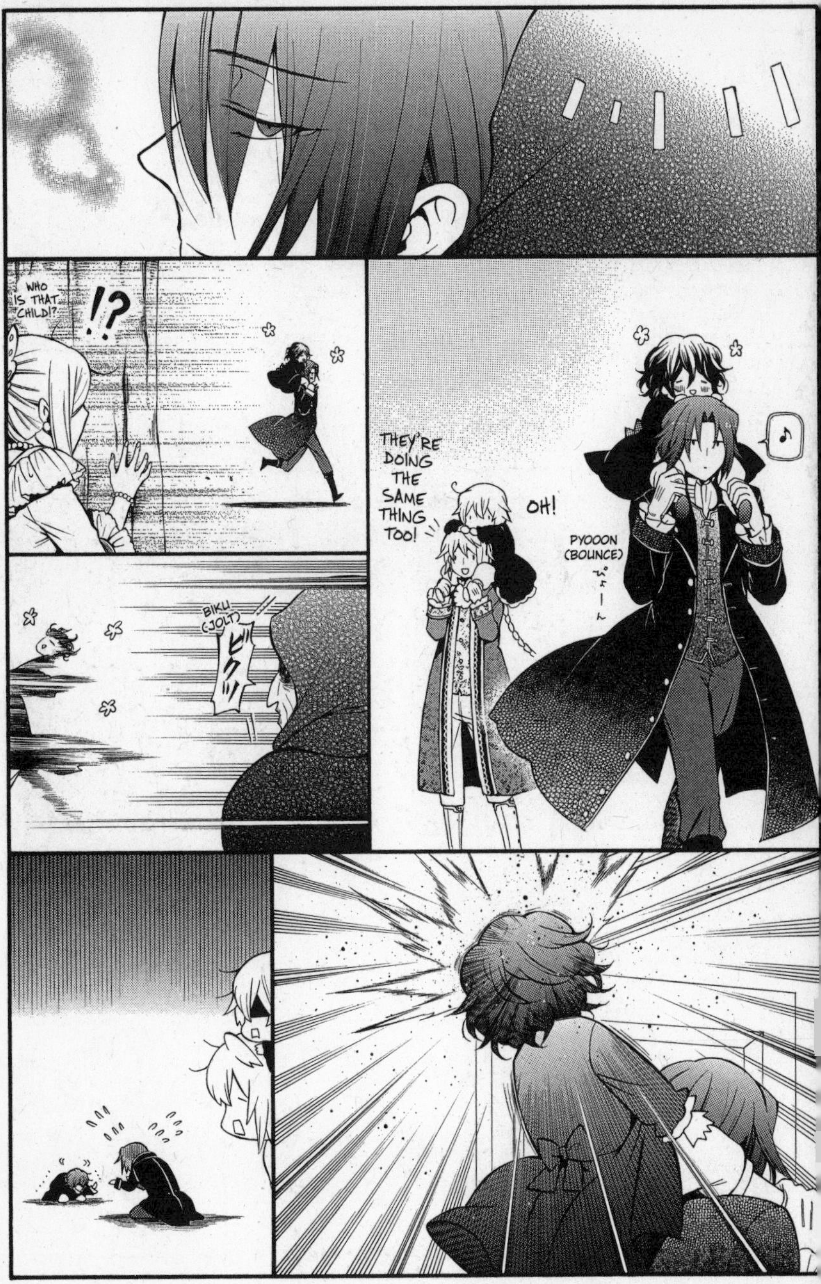
♪
PYOOON (BOUNCE)
ぴょーん
OH!
THEY'RE DOING THE SAME THING TOO!
WHO IS THAT CHILD!?
!?
BIKU (JOLT)
ビクッ

COMMON HONORIFICS

no honorific: Indicates familiarity or closeness; if used without permission or reason, addressing someone in this manner would constitute an insult.

-san: The Japanese equivalent of Mr./Mrs./Miss. If a situation calls for politeness, this is the fail-safe honorific.

-sama: Conveys great respect; may also indicate that the social status of the speaker is lower than that of the addressee.

-kun: Used most often when referring to boys (though it can be applied to girls as well), this indicates affection or familiarity. Occasionally used by older men among their peers, but it may also be used by anyone referring to a person of lower standing.

-chan: An affectionate honorific indicating familiarity used mostly in reference to girls; also used in reference to cute persons or animals of either gender.

okonomiyaki   page 185

A pan-fried, savory Japanese pancake made with a batter usually containing cabbage that can have any number of additional ingredients and toppings. *Okonomi* means "to your liking."

PandoraHearts

Volume 18 falls as deep into the depths as possible. I hope you enjoy it.

MOCHIZUKI'S MUSINGS

VOLUME 18

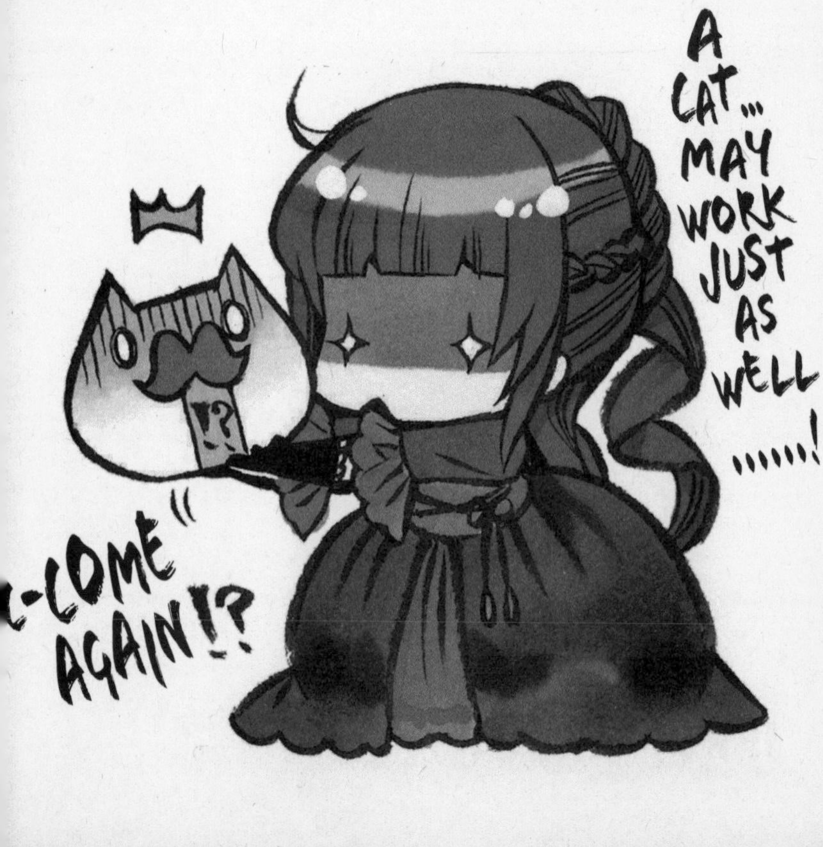
A CAT... MAY WORK JUST AS WELL ......!
C-COME AGAIN!?

PandoraHearts

JUN MOCHIZUKI

Crimson-Shell

クリムゾン-シェル

LOVE *PANDORA HEARTS*? WANT TO CHECK OUT SOME MORE OF JUN MOCHIZUKI-SENSEI'S WORK? WELL, LOOK NO FURTHER! *CRIMSON-SHELL*, MOCHIZUKI-SENSEI'S DEBUT, IS NOW AVAILABLE FROM YEN PRESS!

PandoraHearts

PANDORA HEARTS ⑱

JUN MOCHIZUKI

Translation: Tomo Kimura • Lettering: Alexis Eckerman

PANDORA HEARTS Vol. 18 © 2012 Jun Mochizuki / SQUARE ENIX CO., LTD. All rights reserved. First published in Japan in 2012 by SQUARE ENIX CO., LTD. English translation rights arranged with SQUARE ENIX CO., LTD. and Hachette Book Group through Tuttle-Mori Agency, Inc.

Translation © 2013 by SQUARE ENIX CO., LTD.

Yen Press
Hachette Book Group
237 Park Avenue, New York, NY 10017

www.HachetteBookGroup.com
www.YenPress.com

Yen Press is an imprint of Hachette Book Group, Inc. The Yen Press name and logo are trademarks of Hachette Book Group, Inc.

First Yen Press Edition: October 2013

ISBN: 978-0-316-23975-2

10 9 8 7 6 5 4 3 2 1

BVG

Printed in the United States of America